PEOPLE OF THE STONE AGE

Hunter-gatherers and Early Farmers

AMERICAN MUSEUM OF NATURAL HISTORY
The Illustrated History of Humankind

PEOPLE OF THE STONE AGE

Hunter-gatherers and Early Farmers

General Editor
GÖRAN BURENHULT

Foreword by PROFESSOR LORD COLIN RENFREW

HarperSanFrancisco
A Division of HarperCollinsPublishers

FIRST EDITION

Conceived and produced by
Weldon Owen Pty Limited
43 Victoria Street, McMahons Point NSW 2060, Australia
Fax 61 2 929 8352

and

Bra Böcker AB
S–263 80 Höganäs
Sweden
Fax 46 42 330504

The Illustrated History of Humankind
Publisher: Sheena Coupe
Series Coordinator: Annette Carter
Copy Editors: Jo Avigdor, Glenda Downing,
Gillian Hewitt, Margaret McPhee
Editorial Assistant: Vesna Radojcic
Picture Editors: Anne Burke, Jenny Mills, Ann Nicol
Art Director: Sue Burk
Design: Sylvie Abecassis and Janet Marando
Computer systems: Paul Geros
Production Director: Mick Bagnato
Production Coordinator: Simone Perryman

Weldon Owen Pty Limited
Chairman: Kevin Weldon
President: John Owen
General Manager: Stuart Laurence
Coeditions Director: Derek Barton

Bra Böcker AB
Publisher and Vice-President: Kari Marklund
Editorial Director: Claes Göran Green
Editor: Christina Christoffersson

Library of Congress Cataloging-in-Publication Data

People of the Stone Age / Göran Burenhult, general editor.
    p. cm. -- (The Illustrated history of humankind : v. 2)
    Includes bibliographical references and index.
    ISBN 0-06-250264-6
    1. Stone age. 2. Agriculture, Prehistoric. I. Burenhult, Göran.
    II. Series.
    GN281. I365 1993 vol. 2
    930.1'2 -- dc20   92-56109
                                                      CIP

93 94 95 96 97 WOHK 10 9 8 7 6 5 4 3 2 1

Manufactured by Mandarin Offset
Printed in Hong Kong

A WELDON OWEN PRODUCTION

Endpapers
Detail from the rock art site of Fossum,
in Bohuslän, western Sweden, showing a
hunting scene, a ship, and several other
figures. It dates from the Late Bronze Age,
about 800 BC.
GÖRAN BURENHULT

Page 1
A marble figurine of a style known as a "stiff
white lady" from the Cycladic islands, dating
from about 2800 BC to 2500 BC.
NICHOLAS P. GOULANDRIS FOUNDATION/MUSEUM OF
CYCLADIC & ANCIENT GREEK ART, ATHENS

Pages 2–3
A Bushman on the lookout for springhares
in the Kalahari Desert.
PETER JOHNSON/NHPA

C O N T E N T S

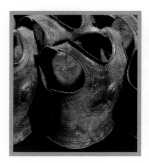

8

WE HUMANS ARE A WONDERFULLY diverse species. All over the globe, there are habitats of widely different character, with human communities adapted to their fruitful exploitation. This diversity has its roots deep in the past, well before the emergence of our own species, *Homo sapiens sapiens*, 100,000 years ago. But as little as 12,000 years ago, the extent of that diversity was still limited. At that time, all humans were hunter-gatherers. And although all the major continents had by then been peopled, there were, with very few exceptions, no permanent settlements, no villages.

Then, for reasons that we still do not understand very well, there came what was undoubtedly one of the most important episodes in the entire sweep of human diversity, aptly called here the Great Transition—the development of food production, based upon the exploitation of domesticated animals and especially of cultivated plants. The consequences of the transition were fundamental—village settlement, new beliefs, different social structures, the invention of new technologies (such as pottery, and later, in some places, metalworking), and all the foundations for the future developments of our species.

But was it only *one* transition? Or were there several? It is now increasingly clear that the transition to farming did indeed take place independently in several parts of the world—in western Asia, in China, in New Guinea, in the Americas, in West Africa, and perhaps in other places, too. And in each area, the consequences as well as the circumstances were different. Sometimes, the trajectory of development led on to the development of urban life and the formation of literate civilization. Elsewhere, as in Australia, the pattern of hunting and gathering continued with few changes, although there it was accompanied by the creation of rock art, which today is becoming much more widely known and admired as one of the most attractive and intriguing products of our species, as well as our earliest artistic endeavor.

Yet through all this striking and increasing diversity, the basic human "hardware" seems to have stayed much the same. We are all one species, and the genetic differences between us are relatively minor. Throughout this process, as reviewed here from about 10,000 BC, the genetic make-up (the hardware) of the individual has changed very little. Indeed, we are physically very much the same as our ancestors were some 40,000 years ago. For it is the *software* that has changed: the culture we learn from our parents and neighbors, the language and beliefs we have inherited through education rather than by birth.

As an archaeologist, I am fascinated by this diversity. It is to me remarkable, for instance, that already in the Neolithic period in China, about 2500 BC, there developed that fascination with jade that we see in more recent times, so that this hard stone was already considered valuable and attractive, and buried with the dead, carrying with it associations of immortality. It is to me remarkable that before 4000 BC in western Europe, great stone monuments were constructed, such as Newgrange, in Ireland. These are among the earliest surviving structures anywhere in the world.

Prehistoric archaeology has, over the last 50 years or so, succeeded in recovering remains of early human societies from almost every part of the world. New research techniques, such as the development of radiocarbon dating, have allowed sites in every continent to be dated and better understood. It is now possible to reconstruct a true world prehistory, and in doing so, to appreciate more fully the full extent of that diversity in culture and achievement, and to understand more adequately what it is to be human.

◄◙ A portal tomb in the Ox Mountains, in County Sligo, northwestern Ireland. Portal tombs are one of several types of stone-built monuments characteristic of Ireland.

Colin Renfrew
Disney Professor of Archaeology
University of Cambridge

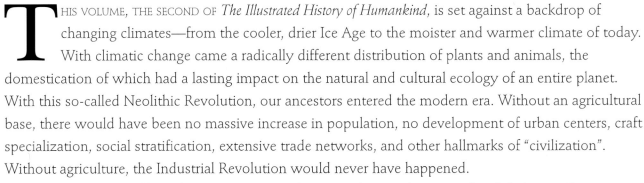

THIS VOLUME, THE SECOND OF *The Illustrated History of Humankind*, is set against a backdrop of changing climates—from the cooler, drier Ice Age to the moister and warmer climate of today. With climatic change came a radically different distribution of plants and animals, the domestication of which had a lasting impact on the natural and cultural ecology of an entire planet. With this so-called Neolithic Revolution, our ancestors entered the modern era. Without an agricultural base, there would have been no massive increase in population, no development of urban centers, craft specialization, social stratification, extensive trade networks, and other hallmarks of "civilization". Without agriculture, the Industrial Revolution would never have happened.

In these pages, we learn that Eurasian agriculture is only one chapter in the global story. Recent excavations in highland New Guinea have disclosed massive water-control projects dating from 7000 BC. We must now recognize the possibility that New Guinea highlanders have been cultivating food plants for tens of thousands of years—far longer than their Eurasian counterparts. We read, too, of the equally impressive drained field technologies used by lowland Maya farmers 3,000 years ago. In Peru, there is evidence of superbly engineered reclamation projects in the marshlands surrounding Lake Titicaca, capable of supporting perhaps 40,000 people in the nearby pre-Columbian city of Tiahuanaco.

These extraordinary cultural changes to the landscape have exacted some heavy costs. Today, as in the period covered in this volume, the sea-ice is disappearing—but for a different reason. The so-called greenhouse effect is trapping the Earth's heat in much the same way the glass panes of a greenhouse roof make it possible to grow tomatoes in a New England winter. Once set in motion, can we alter the course of global climatic change? Perhaps not.

But rather than thinking of global warming in strictly negative terms, we should look to our human past, when vast climatic changes opened up all manner of new possibilities. Beginning about 10,000 BC, global sea levels rose dramatically, ultimately submerging nearly half of western Europe. Although available land was drastically reduced, countless new bays, inlets, and lagoons were created—some of the Earth's richest ecosystems. Humans cashed in on the change. The Mesolithic shell middens that today blanket the Atlantic coast bear witness to the importance of sea resources during this period.

In this volume, you will also come face to face with some of our ancestors. You will meet the victims of a 7,000-year-old tragedy: a teenage Danish mother from Vedbæk who died in childbirth, but was united in death with her newborn son, curled up on the outstretched wing of a swan. You will gaze into the face of the Ice Man of the Tyrol, who electrified the world when discovered in 1991. As he cached his quiver and axe, his bow and backpack, did he notice the storm clouds gathering overhead? The Ice Man—the oldest preserved human body ever found—has much to teach us about life in the Late Neolithic. Once thoroughly studied, his DNA may also tell us more about ourselves.

This, and the other volumes of *The Illustrated History of Humankind*, provide a staggering amount of new knowledge about our shared human past. Many of the tales are told by the very scientists who are making the discoveries. Still, I'm willing to wager that there's not an archaeologist alive who won't learn something new from these pages.

◄● Ruins of cliff dwellings overlooking the Virgin River, Zion Canyon, Utah, in the United States.

David Hurst Thomas

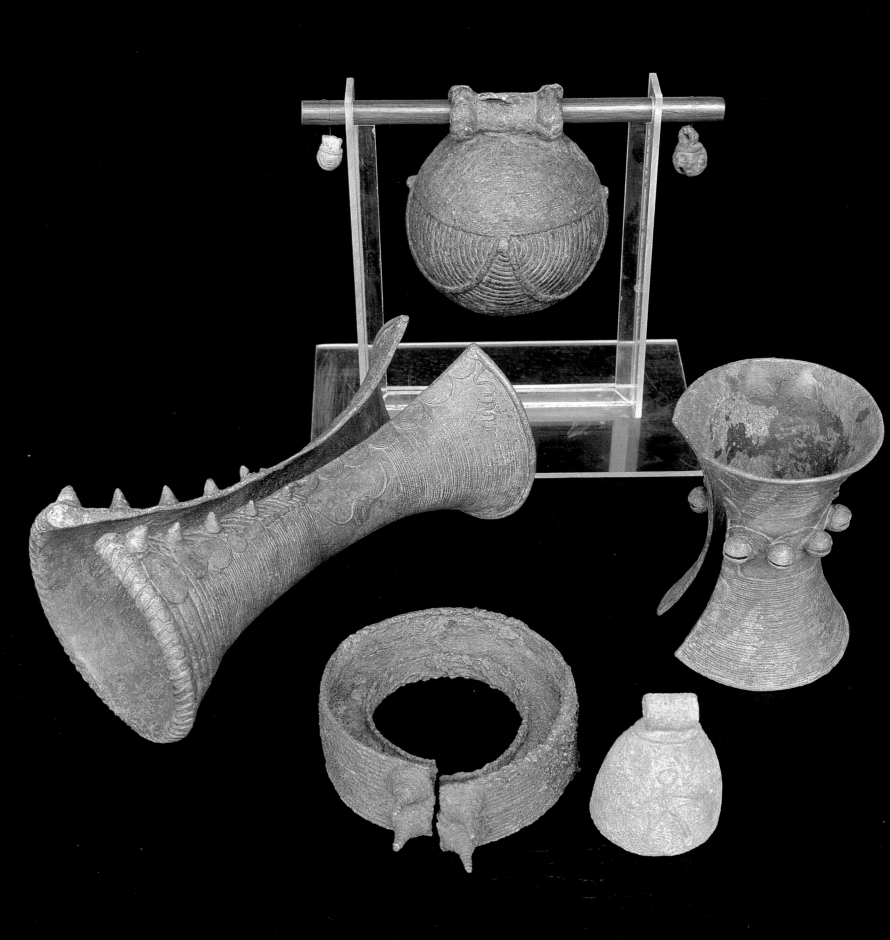

PEOPLE OF THE STONE AGE, the second volume of *The Illustrated History of Humankind,* deals with one of the most radical and fascinating changes in the history of humankind: the transition from mobile hunting-gathering to settled herding and farming, generally referred to as the Neolithic process.

The agricultural revolution involved sweeping changes in settlement patterns, social organization, and religious systems, and at the same time, population growth increased markedly. In many places, competition with neighboring communities and the need for territorial control involved increased aggression. Most experts today believe that farming developed out of need, rather than desire.

It was once thought that agriculture arose in one single area in the Near East, from where it spread to the rest of the world. We now know that agriculture developed locally and independently in many parts of the world. A major reason for these developments was the far-reaching global change in climate that occurred after the end of the last Ice Age, some 12,000 years ago, when many previously rich and fertile areas dried up and even turned into deserts.

The ways in which people adapted to the local conditions of their region are clearly visible in the archaeological record. In Southwest Asia and Egypt, the Neolithic process involved specialization in wheat and barley agriculture, as well as the domestication of sheep, goats, and cattle. In Africa, millet was the first cultivated crop. In the Yangtze River valley of China, rice formed the staple, and in Mesoamerica, maize was the main crop. Root crops of different kinds were domesticated in many tropical areas, such as the New Guinea highlands, and these developments may

prove to be the earliest Neolithic events to have taken place anywhere in the world. In some areas, it is sometimes very difficult to determine whether a particular plant or animal was domesticated without external influence, or whether the technique was adopted from other regions and then applied to local species.

In many places, there was a direct transition from the earlier, Paleolithic ways of life. This transitional phase is sometimes called the Epipaleolithic. In other areas, however, extremely rich environments fostered a totally new style of subsistence, based on fishing, beachcombing, hunting, and plant gathering. This "Middle Stone Age", or Mesolithic era, is particularly characteristic of the temperate parts of Europe, where a number of hunter-gatherer communities developed complex societies without agriculture, which lasted for thousands of years.

Not all human societies were to adopt the Neolithic way of life. In some areas, groups of people continued to live as hunter-gatherers, even until recent times. These cultures are often found in extreme environments, such as the Arctic, deserts, and tropical rainforests, where conditions are not favorable for agriculture or herding, and where people can only survive by adapting their way of life completely to the surroundings. Other hunter-gatherers are found in rich coastal areas or fertile, temperate forest regions.

"The Great Transition" deals with the development of agriculture in Southwest Asia between 10,000 BC and 4000 BC, from the beginnings of specialization in hunting and plant gathering to the formative cultural stages that would later develop into the Mesopotamian civilizations of the Euphrates and Tigris valleys. "Hunter-gatherers and Farmers in Africa" embraces

the introduction of farming and herding in the various climatic zones of Africa, between 10,000 BC and AD 200. "Stone Age Hunter-gatherers and Farmers in Europe" looks at the rich and very special Mesolithic communities in Europe, as well as the introduction of farming economies, between 10,000 BC and 3000 BC. "The Megalith Builders of Western Europe" describes one of the most enigmatic phenomena of the prehistoric world—the tradition of erecting stone-built tombs over the dead, which flourished between 4800 BC and 2800 BC. "Bronze Age Chiefdoms and the End of Stone Age Europe" deals with the period when metals first came into use in Europe and the sweeping social changes between 4500 BC and 750 BC that followed this development.

In "Stone Age Farmers in Southern and Eastern Asia", we study the rich farming cultures, based mainly on rice, that formed the basis for a number of powerful civilizations between 6000 BC and AD 1000. "Pacific Explorers" embraces the development of early farming, based on root crops, in New Guinea and the islands of Melanesia. "Farmers of the New World" describes the growth of farming cultures in the Americas between 10,000 BC and the arrival of Europeans in AD 1492. "Why Only Some Became Farmers" presents the reasons why some cultures did not adopt farming or herding as part of their subsistence strategy. It also contains two detailed descriptions of nonfarming cultures: arctic hunters and fishers of Eurasia, and the Thule culture of the Arctic. Finally, "Australia: The Different Continent" follows the fascinating history and cultural development of the Australian Aborigines, from 10,000 BC to the first contact with Europeans, at the end of the eighteenth century AD.

Göran Burenhult

◄● Bronze objects from the site of Ban Chiang, in the Songkhram Valley, northeastern Thailand.

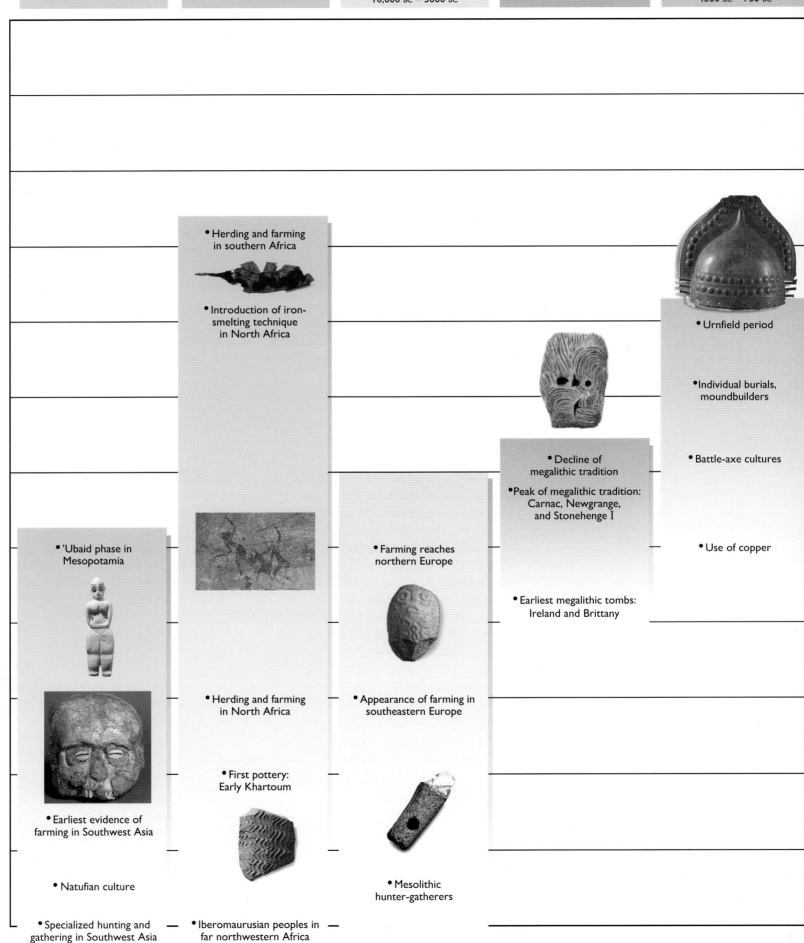

THE GREAT TRANSITION 10,000 BC – 4,000 BC	HUNTER-GATHERERS AND FARMERS IN AFRICA 10,000 BC – AD 200	STONE AGE HUNTER-GATHERERS AND FARMERS IN EUROPE 10,000 BC – 3000 BC	THE MEGALITH BUILDERS OF WESTERN EUROPE 4800 BC – 2800 BC	BRONZE AGE CHIEFDOMS AND THE END OF STONE AGE EUROPE 4500 BC – 750 BC
	• Herding and farming in southern Africa			
	• Introduction of iron-smelting technique in North Africa			• Urnfield period
				• Individual burials, moundbuilders
			• Decline of megalithic tradition	• Battle-axe cultures
• 'Ubaid phase in Mesopotamia		• Farming reaches northern Europe	• Peak of megalithic tradition: Carnac, Newgrange, and Stonehenge I	• Use of copper
			• Earliest megalithic tombs: Ireland and Brittany	
	• Herding and farming in North Africa	• Appearance of farming in southeastern Europe		
	• First pottery: Early Khartoum			
• Earliest evidence of farming in Southwest Asia				
• Natufian culture		• Mesolithic hunter-gatherers		
• Specialized hunting and gathering in Southwest Asia	• Iberomaurusian peoples in far northwestern Africa			

14

STONE AGE FARMERS IN SOUTHERN AND EASTERN ASIA 6000 BC – AD 1000	PACIFIC EXPLORERS 10,000 BC – 0 BC	FARMERS OF THE NEW WORLD 10,000 BC – AD 1492	WHY ONLY SOME BECAME FARMERS 11,000 BC – AD 1500	AUSTRALIA: THE DIFFERENT CONTINENT 10,000 BC – AD 1800	
			• Qilakitsoq mummies		AD 1500
		• Peak of Chaco culture		• First contacts with outside world?	AD 1000
		• Mogollon, Hohokam, and Anasazi cultures	• Thule culture in the Arctic		AD 500
					0
		• Hopewell culture: first farmers in eastern North America		• Appearance of X-ray paintings	
• Wet-rice agriculture reaches Korea and Japan	• Stone quarries for axeheads in the Wahgi Valley	• Establishment of agriculture in the North American southwest; drained field agriculture in Mexico			1000 BC
	• Earliest Lapita pottery			• Development of backed blades	2000 BC
• Rice cultivation reaches Southeast Asia from southern China	• First pottery		• Pitted-ware culture	• Appearance of finely shaped spear points and hatchets with ground stone heads	3000 BC
• Yangshao period in northern China		• Earliest known remains of corn		• Seas rise to present-day level: shell middens common	4000 BC
• Arrival of agriculture on the Indian subcontinent					
			• Earliest burials in Scandinavia		5000 BC
• Early millet and rice farming in China					6000 BC
	• Gardens and drainage systems at Kuk				7000 BC
		• Early domesticated plants in the Andes			8000 BC
			• Komsa and Fosna hunters in Scandinavia		
			• Jomon fishermen and potters in Japan		10,000 BC

THE GREAT TRANSITION

1 0 , 0 0 0   B C   –   4 0 0 0   B C

First Farmers of the Western World

LENNART PALMQVIST

THE PERIOD FROM 10,000 BC to 4000 BC witnessed the most important single innovation in the history of humanity before the Industrial Revolution: the seemingly simple change from acquiring food entirely by hunting and gathering to producing it through cultivation and stockbreeding. The beginnings of this momentous change can be traced to what is known as the Neolithic period—and it was the food-producing cultures that evolved in Southwest Asia during this time that eventually gave rise to Western civilization.

The area referred to as Southwest Asia comprises the modern-day states of Turkey, Iran, Iraq, Syria, Lebanon, Jordan, and Israel. The territory along the eastern coast of the Mediterranean Sea is sometimes called the Levant, and the region that now includes Israel and the western portion of Jordan is often referred to as Palestine.

An Iranian farmer tills the land with a simple wooden plow of a type known since ancient times, from as early as the fifth millennium BC.

Dating from the seventh millennium BC, this mask made of hard limestone from Kh Duma, near Hebron, in Israel, is 22 centimeters (about 9 inches) long.
ISRAEL MUSEUM, JERUSALEM

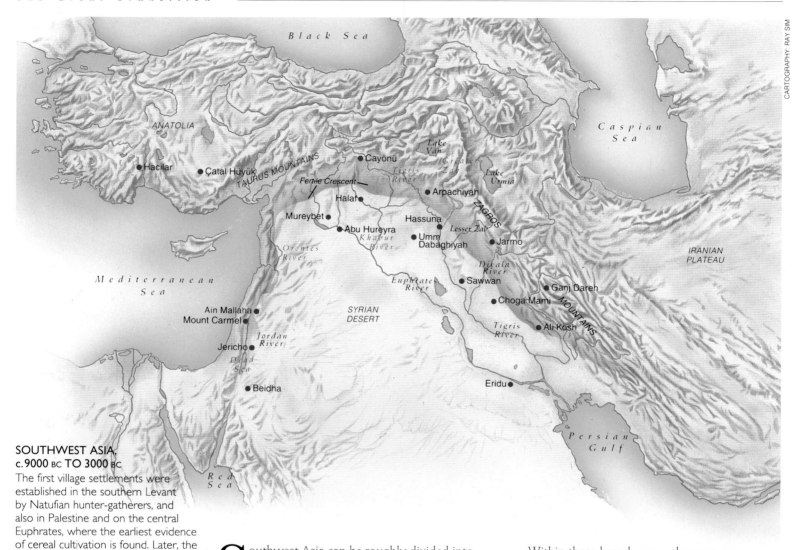

SOUTHWEST ASIA, c. 9000 BC TO 3000 BC

The first village settlements were established in the southern Levant by Natufian hunter-gatherers, and also in Palestine and on the central Euphrates, where the earliest evidence of cereal cultivation is found. Later, the first pottery appeared simultaneously in several places in the Zagros Mountains and Anatolia, and on the central Euphrates.

☝ Tools from the Zawi Chemi settlement and Shanidar Cave, in the Zagros Mountains. On the right is a curved bone sickle handle, and beside it, a bone reaping knife with a flint blade.

Southwest Asia can be roughly divided into three major vegetation zones. The first is known as the Mediterranean zone, extending in a narrow band along the eastern shore of the Mediterranean Sea and the southern and western coasts of Turkey. The vegetation here consists largely of evergreen trees, plants, and shrubs—species that are not adapted to withstand cold temperatures.

The second is the desert and desert–steppe zone, consisting of the deserts of Syria, Jordan, and Iraq and the bordering steppe region, including Mesopotamia—the area around the lower reaches of the Tigris-Euphrates river system. Rainfall is low, plant cover is sparse, and the contrast between summer barrenness and early spring vegetation is striking.

The third is the highland zone, which partly lies between the other two zones and partly surrounds them. This zone includes the Lebanon Mountains of the Levant, the mountains of eastern Turkey, and the Zagros Mountains, which extend the length of Iran's western border and into northern Iraq. To the west of this arc of mountains lies the Anatolian plateau, with an average altitude of 1,370 meters (4,500 feet). The characteristic vegetation of this highland zone is temperate forest of oak, cedar, pine or fir, pistachio, and juniper. Edible fruits, nuts, and wild cereals abound, and sheep, goats, cattle, and pigs are found in large numbers.

Within these broad zones, there are considerable local variations in natural resources. In most areas, the rainfall is insufficient to support perennials, but rain is more plentiful in the uplands that sweep from the Levant to the Zagros Mountains, which form the backbone of the so-called Fertile Crescent: the broad arc of territory curving from the head of the Persian Gulf, around the northern edge of the Syrian Desert, to Palestine and the Egyptian border.

The proximity of these zones to one another and the localized nature of certain resources encouraged the movement of people and the exchange of goods, and it is likely that farming became established in several places at more or less the same time. Archaeological evidence suggests that farming began on the hills and grasslands that flank the arid Syrian steppe and on the southern Mesopotamian floodplains. Just as they did thousands of years ago, these slopes still harbor the wild ancestors of the cereals and animals that became the basis of the region's agricultural economy—wild barley, two forms of wild wheat, plant foods such as legumes, and wild cattle, sheep, goats, and pigs.

The Beginnings of Settled Life

The warmer and wetter climate that developed in Southwest Asia at the end of the Pleistocene era, about 12,000 years ago, brought about great environmental changes. Open woodlands flourished, with nuts that could be harvested and grasses that had the potential to be domesticated, and the warmer winters enabled communities to move from caves in mountainous areas to regions where wild cereal grasses, such as barley and emmer, grew, and could be gathered. The harvesting of grain, in turn, stimulated the development of such tools as sickle blades and grinding stones, and the building of storage facilities—developments that paved the way for the emergence of agriculture.

Probably the single most important factor in the transition from a hunter-gatherer economy to a food-producing economy was the establishment of settled communities. Plants and animals were originally domesticated as a minor part of a general subsistence strategy, but they soon became so important that farming became an almost universal way of life.

The earliest Neolithic settlements were confined to the Levant and the western foothills of the Zagros Mountains. In these regions, and on the uplands of Anatolia, there was sufficient rainfall for wild wheat and barley to grow. As long ago as 9000 BC, people in these areas ate a wide variety of plants, and with time, cereal grains, pulses, and nuts made up an increasing proportion of their diet.

The current method of investigation used by paleoethnobotanists and archaeologists to establish where each plant species was first domesticated is to determine the genetic ancestors of early domestic plants and then to chart the present-day distribution of these wild species. The distribution of these plants, adjusted for changes in climate over time, together with details obtained from plant remains recovered from archaeological sites, provides the necessary information.

Similarly, by analyzing the remains of bones in such sites, archaeologists can determine whether animals that were eaten were hunted in the wild or kept in domestic herds. The archaeological record suggests that each of the five species characteristic of Neolithic animal husbandry (sheep, goats, cattle, pigs, and dogs) was initially domesticated in a different region.

By the end of the Neolithic period, after cereals had been domesticated and cultivated, and stock-breeding was established, people in Southwest Asia had developed farming methods geared to open landscapes. This, in turn, gave rise to urban settlements in the floodplains of the Tigris and Euphrates rivers, in ancient Mesopotamia.

♂ A large pottery storage jar from the Jordan Valley, dating from the fourth millennium BC.

♀ The landscape near Diyarbakir, in southeastern Turkey, not far from the remarkable Neolithic site of Çayönü.

☞ A human skull from Jericho, dating from the eighth millennium BC, with molded plaster features and cowrie shells set into the eyes.

☞ *Opposite:* Plaster head of a human figurine, carved in bas-relief and painted, found in Jericho. It dates from the seventh millennium BC.

⚲ This massive circular stone tower, about 9 meters (30 feet) high, is built against the inside of the town wall of Jericho. It dates from the Pre-Pottery Neolithic period, during the eighth millennium BC. The entrance is at the bottom.

The Natufian Culture

The transitional phase, during which people lived a settled existence based on the intensive collection of wild cereals, is best documented in Palestine. One of the most ancient settlements known to date was built in Jordan at Tell es-Sultan, Jericho, near the Dead Sea. Today, the site of ancient Jericho is marked by a great settlement mound—*tell* being the Arabian name for a mound formed from the accumulated remains of human occupation.

Jericho is one of a series of archaeological sites in the Levant and southern Turkey that are connected to the Natufian culture, named after a cave site in the Wadi en-Natuf, in the Judean hills, in Israel. Other well-known sites are El Wad, in the Mount Carmel area, and Ain Mallaha, in the Jordan Valley. Some of these sites date back to 12,500 years ago.

The Natufian culture is characterized by small villages of circular, stone-walled huts and relatively large populations. Artifacts include numerous mortars and grinding stones, apparently used for grinding grains and seeds, and many-toothed sickle blades of flint, which often still bear what is known as a sickle sheen along their cutting edges, indicating that they were used for harvesting wild

cereals. No domestic plants or animals have been identified at Natufian sites, although the bones of many hunted animals have been found, and wild emmer wheat was once native to the area. The largest Natufian sites and cemeteries contain considerable evidence to suggest that Natufian society was hierarchical and that such commodities as seashells, obsidian, and stone bowls were widely exchanged between communities.

Situated beside a perennial spring, the ancient site of Jericho is today marked by a settlement mound. Jericho began as a camp of Natufian hunters and food gatherers about 9000 BC. Archaeologist Kathleen M. Kenyon re-excavated the site in the 1950s, with remarkable results. By 8000 BC, a massive stone wall enclosed the settlement. On the bedrock that lies below the accumulated debris of Neolithic settlements and later civilizations, Natufian implements have been found, along with traces of a stone structure dating from about 7800 BC. This structure had sockets for massive poles—possibly totem poles—which suggests that it was a sanctuary or shrine. It would appear that Natufian hunters were accustomed to visiting the spring, and recognizing its importance, established a holy place beside it.

Muddy land watered by the spring provided excellent conditions for cereal farming in an otherwise arid environment, and by 7500 BC, Jericho had grown to a size of 1.6 hectares (4 acres). The people of early Jericho lived in mudbrick huts clustered within the stone wall, but they did not make clay vessels. The huts were circular, with floors of beaten mud, and their walls inclined inwards, suggesting that they were once domed. They may have been roofed with plastered branches, as there are many traces of wattle and daub in the walls.

It is unlikely that early Jericho's economy was based solely on agriculture. Imports found in the area include obsidian from Anatolia, turquoise from Sinai, and cowrie shells from the Red Sea.

THE NATUFIAN PERIOD: THE BEGINNINGS OF SETTLED LIFE

KATE DA COSTA

THE NATUFIAN CULTURE, one of several Levantine cultures that appeared towards the end of the Paleolithic period, dates from 12,500 to 10,300 years ago. This was roughly the end of the last Ice Age, a time when the climate in the Levant became warmer and moister. Natufian material has been found from southern Turkey to the Sinai, although to date the overwhelming amount of evidence has come from the southern Levant—modern-day Israel and Jordan.

The Natufian culture has been recognized since Dorothy Garrod defined it in 1932 and proposed naming it after the Wadi en-Natuf, in Israel—a wadi being the channel of a watercourse that is dry except during periods of rainfall. The culture is of particular interest, because it may have been during this time that people started to settle in villages. While it is known that some groups had adopted a sedentary way of life before agriculture developed, living all year round in the same settlement, it is unclear whether this happened in the Early Neolithic or the Natufian period.

Some Natufian sites are obviously temporary camps, used by people collecting seasonally available plants or animals, or on special journeys to acquire other resources, such as basalt for grinding stones.

⚑ The walls of Natufian houses were made of rough stones, reeds, and mud. Here, the foundation stones of a circular house are being uncovered during excavations at Wadi Hammeh.

The larger sites—of more than 1,000 square meters (3,280 square feet), with deposits up to 3 meters (10 feet) thick—were not necessarily year-round settlements but may simply represent the accumulated debris of communities that used the same site for part of the year over several years. Different groups were almost certainly living in a variety of ways at this time—for instance, some may have been semisedentary, others nomadic—depending on the local environment, the resources available, and each group's preferences. Certainly, most Natufian settlements were used more intensively than sites from earlier periods, and the Natufian culture was more elaborate and varied than any before it.

Circular Houses

The few complete Natufian houses that have been excavated are circular or elliptical and up to 10 meters (30 feet) in diameter. At some sites, there is evidence of houses having been rebuilt on the same alignment as many as three

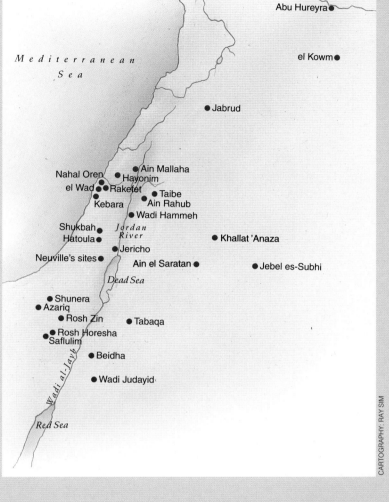

CARTOGRAPHY: RAY SIM

times. Natufian dwellings consisted of a circle of stones only one course high, with an opening in part of the wall spanned by posts. The walls must have been made of some perishable material, probably a combination of reed matting and mud. Internal postholes indicate that the houses had roofs. Most have several features within them, mainly fireplaces surrounded by stones and a raised rectangular area made of stones or tamped earth, which may have been a food preparation area. Shallow pits, roughly plastered with mud, and stone-lined basins have also been found, and have often been identified as grain storage bins or silos. None has been reported as containing grains, however, and there are many examples of these pits being used as graves.

IMPORTANT NATUFIAN SITES IN THE LEVANT

Shukbah is in the Wadi en-Natuf, after which the culture was named.

Although we have no idea what clothing was worn, we do know that, at least in death, body ornament was considered appropriate. Necklaces, headdresses, and belts made of mollusk shells or the toe bones of gazelles were found with many skeletons. Other animal bones were also found, but less frequently, and some skeletons were marked with colored ochers. There was no pattern to the burials, some being primary, others secondary; some individual, some multiple. One remarkable grave contained the skeletons of a child and a puppy. Many sites have graves of adults and children within the

J. CARTER/J. HALFHIDE

⊕ These bone sickle hafts and lunate blades, together with a handful of smooth agate pebbles, were found lying on the floor of a house in Wadi Hammeh, exactly as they had been left more than 10,000 years ago.

boundaries of the site, and often within houses. We have no way of knowing whether houses were abandoned after they had been used for burials.

The Natufian Toolkit

The characteristic stone tools of the Natufians are blades and bladelets, microlithic tools being the most common. Some microliths were mounted in wood or bone handles, and it seems likely that some were used for hunting, although no weapons specifically designed for hunting have been found. The most remarkable of the composite tools are sickles, which have been discovered lying on floors, some with their tiny bladelets still in grooves in the handles. The sheen on the cutting edges shows that they were used to gather plants, but whether cereals, vegetables, or reeds is not known. Artifacts were clearly produced on a large scale: more ground stone tools—in the

form of mortars, pestles, hand mills, shaft straighteners, and shallow bowls—are found on a typical large Natufian site than have been recovered from all the sites known from the immediately preceding periods put together. In contrast with earlier periods, most stone tools have been found within houses or other structures. It has been commonly assumed that the mortars and pestles were used for processing plant foods, but the only recorded residues on the pestles are of ocher.

Some of the mortars have linear decoration incised around the outer rim, and this practice of decorating utilitarian objects marks a dramatic change from earlier periods. While art is known from quite early times,

portable art and the decoration of tools such as mortars and sickle handles became much more common in the Natufian period. Sculptured objects that are not tools have also been found, but perhaps what speak most eloquently from the past are the collections of what appear to be souvenirs—river-smoothed agate pebbles, fossils, odd-shaped or pretty colored stones—found within Natufian dwellings. These are the kinds of souvenirs we ourselves might collect when wandering about the countryside.

Food Sources

These ancient people had a varied diet, but probably relied mainly on plant foods. The numerous finds of sickles, mortars, and hand mills imply that either the types of plants they ate or the way food was processed had changed from earlier periods. Their favored prey were the larger animals, such as gazelles, cattle, pigs, deer, and members of the horse family, but they also ate migratory birds; small animals, such as hares; and aquatic animals, such as turtles, fish, and shellfish.

⊕ A fine example of Natufian decorative work, this bone sickle haft from Kebara Cave has a deer or gazelle head carved on the handle.
ISRAEL ANTIQUITIES AUTHORITY

⊕ These mortars and pestles were ground from basalt at a time long before metal tools were in use.
R. WORKMAN

J. CARTER/ J.HALFHIDE

⚘ This animal carved from limestone was found in a Natufian cave dwelling at Umm es-Zuitina, in the Judean desert.

⚘ A field of maturing wheat. The use of wheat in Southwest Asia goes back to the eighth millennium BC. Emmer is one of the oldest varieties of domesticated wheat and is thought to have been the principal species grown in prehistoric and early historic times.

Being an oasis, strategically situated on the trade routes between the Red Sea and Anatolia, its early prosperity probably resulted from extensive trading activities.

Farming in Northern Syria

The next phase in the development of agriculture in Southwest Asia occurred when, instead of just collecting wild cereals, people began to sow the seeds of these plants outside their natural habitat. Two recently explored sites in northern Syria—Mureybet and Tell Abu Hureyra, on the banks of the Euphrates River, near the modern-day town of Aleppo—have yielded materials dated to the earliest period of farming, between 7600 BC and 6000 BC. Mureybet is of particular interest, being the earliest village site from which remains of a domesticated plant have been recovered, in the form of einkorn. Since in its wild state this variety of wheat grows far away, in the foothills of the Taurus and Zagros mountains, it must have been cultivated here.

Abu Hureyra lies outside the area where wild cereals grow today, but between 9500 BC and 8000 BC, when the site was first occupied, the climate here was somewhat warmer and moister, and the village lay in a well-wooded steppe area, where animals and wild cereals were abundant.

The Hureyra people initially built a semi-permanent settlement here and harvested wild cereals as part of their subsistence strategy. They also had access to a reliable source of meat in the form of the Persian gazelles that arrived from the south each spring. About 7600 BC, a new village rose on the site of the earlier settlement, extending over nearly 12 hectares (30 acres). At first, the inhabitants hunted gazelles intensively, but about 6500 BC, they switched to herding domestic sheep and goats and to growing pulses, einkorn, and

other cereals. Their rectangular, single-storied, multi-roomed mudbrick houses were linked by narrow lanes and courtyards and had black, burnished plaster floors, sometimes decorated with red designs. Each house was probably occupied by a single family.

The Switch to Farming

Why did the hunter-gatherers of Southwest Asia give up a way of life that had been successful for tens of thousands of years? What caused them to become reliant on domesticated animals and plants for their food? With the emergence of the village-based farming life these developments made possible, great cultural changes must have been set in train.

The eminent Australian archaeologist V. Gordon Childe saw the change to agriculture and an assured food supply as analogous to the change that attended the Industrial Revolution. In his epoch-making synthesis of prehistory, *Man Makes Himself*, published in 1936, he accordingly labeled it the Neolithic Revolution. Some years later, Childe advocated the so-called Oasis Theory to explain this phenomenon, a theory based on the climatic change that took place at the end of the last glacial period. He proposed that increasing aridity throughout Southwest Asia forced people and animals to gather at a few, dwindling oases, where close association led to the domestication of animals and plants.

This explanation was challenged by Robert Braidwood, of the Oriental Institute of Chicago, who advocated the so-called Hilly Flanks Theory. According to this theory, humans "settled in" to their environment—that is to say, people developed increasingly efficient means of exploiting plants and animals as their culture evolved. To test this theory, Braidwood initiated a series of excavations at Jarmo, in the foothills of the Zagros Mountains. By focusing on the threshold of cultural change, he hoped to find traces of the beginnings of this early agricultural revolution.

Early Farming Villages in the Zagros Mountains

The earliest evidence of settlement in the Zagros Mountains is less substantial than that found in northern Syria, although there were semipermanent encampments in northern Iraq, such as those at Karim Shahir, Zawi Chemi, and Shanidar Cave, about 10,000 BC to 9000 BC. In the upper excavation levels of Zawi Chemi and Shanidar Cave, domesticated sheep account for 80 percent of the remains of the animals that were eaten, making this site the earliest known example of human control of food production in Southwest Asia. But many startling discoveries are sure to be made in years to come.

The first of the early village-based farming communities to be discovered, and probably the best known, is Jarmo, situated in the Chemchemal Valley, east of Kirkut, in northeastern Iraq. It dates from the seventh millennium BC, but more precise dates are difficult to establish, because radiocarbon datings at this site are uncertain. Braidwood is convinced that Jarmo flourished for about 300 years in the mid-seventh millennium BC.

Lying at an elevation of 800 meters (2,600 feet), and covering an area of some 4 hectares (10 acres), Jarmo has archaeological deposits 7 meters (23 feet) deep. In the upper third of these, pottery is found in quantity for the first time. The economy was based on village-style agriculture, along with hunting and gathering. Two-row barley, wheat (einkorn and emmer), and several large-seeded annual legumes were cultivated, and sheep and goats were herded. The first certain evidence of domesticated pigs has also been found in these upper levels. This is of particular interest, because pigs, like dogs, eat the same range of foods as humans and are not adapted to the nomadic herding way of life.

The site apparently never had more than 25 houses at any one time, and had a population of 150 or so. The rectangular houses, each consisting of several small rooms and a courtyard, were built of molded mud. The clay walls were often built on a stone base, and clay floors were laid over beds of reeds. Storage bins and domed clay ovens were found, and it is thought that the latter may have been used for drying grains. Tools of chipped stone were found in huge quantities, a high proportion of them of obsidian and flint. There was also a great number of ground stone objects, including marble bracelets and a variety of attractive stone bowls.

The most remarkable artifacts from Jarmo are a striking quantity of lightly fired clay figurines, representing both animals and humans, plus a variety of other clay objects, such as stamps.

WERNER BRAUN

☝ Iranian farmers winnowing grain with wooden forks—a technique for separating the chaff that has been in use since ancient times.

JENNIFER FRY/BRUCE COLEMAN LTD

◄◙ The Zagros Mountains, between Hamadan and Bisitun. Many human settlements dating from the beginning of the Neolithic period have been found in the mountainous regions of Southwest Asia, possibly reflecting an environment that offered an abundant and varied supply of food.

➔ This terracotta "goddess" excavated from the upper levels of Munhata, in the Jordan Valley, dates from the sixth millennium BC. Several of its features are common to figurines found throughout the Levant from the early seventh millennium BC: the exaggerated buttocks, the elongated back of the head, and the emphasis on the eyes. The frightening appearance is a particular characteristic of Munhatan figurines.

ISRAEL MUSEUM, JERUSALEM/ERICH LESSING/MAGNUM

⚲ Part of the prehistoric village excavated at Jarmo, in modern-day Iraq, showing the walls of two adjoining houses. The walls found in all excavation levels were built of pressed mud, packed into courses. Traces of reed matting can be seen on several of the floors.

The pottery, buff to orange in color, is mostly plain and handmade, although often burnished.

Archaeologists find pottery very useful as a means of dating sites relative to each other, particularly when the sites are fairly similar. In prehistoric periods, pottery was often elaborately decorated, and styles of decoration had a relatively short life. Although pots are easily broken, their sherds are virtually indestructible.

ORIENTAL INSTITUTE, THE UNIVERSITY OF CHICAGO

Braidwood and his team of natural scientists believed that the climate had been essentially stable during the period when animals and plants were domesticated, which would mean that Childe's Oasis Theory could be rejected. Through his work at Jarmo and other sites in the Zagros, Braidwood concluded that agriculture had arisen in Southwest Asia as a "logical outcome" of specialization and the elaboration of culture. The hunter-gatherers simply "settled in" during the Holocene period, becoming intimately familiar with their plant and animal neighbors. As their culture evolved, people developed more efficient means of exploiting their environment, and agriculture thus formed a natural link in the long evolutionary chain.

While Braidwood's work made a number of worthwhile contributions to solving the problem of when, where, and why hunter-gatherers adopted a settled way of life, subsequent information accumulated from similar investigations throughout Southwest Asia has complicated as well as enriched our picture of the Neolithic period.

Ali Kosh

The mound of Ali Kosh, in Khuzistan, on the Deh Luran plain, provides the first evidence outside Palestine and northern Syria of a farming community in a lowland area. The major food crop from the earliest period of Ali Kosh was emmer, which was not native to the area. Wild two-row hulled barley was also present, and presumably cultivated. The earliest people known here also herded goats and sheep, and supplemented their diet by hunting, fishing, and collecting wild food. No acceptable radiocarbon datings exist for this stage of occupation, but the succeeding Ali Kosh phase appears to date from some time between 7200 BC and 6400 BC, which would make it roughly contemporary with the early Jarmo and early Palestinian sites.

In the second Ali Kosh phase, there is increasing evidence that winter-grown cereals were cultivated. The villagers here harvested their cereals with flint sickles, which were set into wooden handles by means of asphalt. Grains were probably collected in the simple twined baskets found at this site. Wheat, barley, and seeds from wild herbs were ground on stone slabs in the shape of a saddle or a shallow basin, using simple disk-shaped handstones or pitted limestone. This use of a stone mortar for grinding was a notable innovation.

At this time, about 100 people are thought to have lived at Ali Kosh. External contacts seem to have increased in this phase, for obsidian had been brought from Anatolia and seashells possibly from the Arabian Gulf, while copper probably came from somewhere in Iran. Pottery appears in the next phase, about 6000 BC to 5500 BC, together with several types of artifacts similar to those found in Mesopotamia later in the sixth millennium BC, particularly at the site of Tell es-Sawwan.

ABU HUREYRA: THE WORLD'S FIRST FARMERS

PETER ROWLEY-CONWY

Abu Hureyra lies on the Euphrates River in Syria, 120 kilometers (75 miles) east of Aleppo. It is a huge "tell" mound, made up of the superimposed remains of mudbrick houses mixed with household rubbish. Most of the site dates from the earliest period of farming, between about 9000 BC and 7000 BC. At the bottom, however, is a much smaller settlement that dates from the final prefarming phase, perhaps 11,000 BC to 9500 BC.

The excavation of Abu Hureyra is a story of success against the odds. The discovery of the site, in 1971, caused consternation: not only is it enormous, covering about 12 hectares (30 acres), but it was about to be flooded by the construction of a dam. Only a tiny proportion of the site could be excavated in the two seasons available. The excavator, Andrew Moore, chose to use modern but time-consuming methods of data recovery, and his decision has been fully vindicated by the spectacular results. The second excavation season coincided with the October War of 1973, but despite the difficulties, Moore excavated seven trenches at different places on the site. This work has provided a rare glimpse of what life was like among both the last hunter-gatherers and the first farmers.

Gazelle Hunters

Animal bones were found in profusion. The hunter-gatherers of the first settlement hunted mainly gazelles, as well as a few wild cattle, sheep, and onagers (a type of wild ass). Young gazelles can be aged very accurately by their teeth, and a curious pattern emerged at Abu Hureyra: many jaws of newborn animals were present, as were many from animals aged 12 months, but there were none in between. As gazelles are born in May, this indicated a very short hunting season, confined to that month. Probably, entire herds were killed by being driven into a trap, and most of the surplus meat was stored by salting or drying for use through the year.

TELL ABU HUREYRA EXCAVATION

Why was the hunting season so short? Possibly, the hunters camped at Abu Hureyra only in May, but other data argue against this. Plant remains were recovered in bulk by modern flotation methods, showing that no fewer than 157 species of plants were eaten—more than is known to be eaten by any modern hunter-gatherer group, and far more than have been found in any other archaeological site. No plants were cultivated; seeds were collected from wild grasses and other plants available at various times of the year from early spring to late autumn. Clearly, Abu Hureyra was occupied for longer than just the period when the gazelle hunt took place. The gazelles must, therefore, have been migratory, moving into this area only in May.

Early Plant Foods

But were plant seeds or was gazelle meat more important in the diet? Another modern analytical method provides the answer. Many human burials were found at Abu Hureyra, and the skeletons often have peculiar pathological conditions. The state of the toe, ankle, and knee joints reveals that people spent many hours kneeling down with their toes curled under; strong development of the shoulders and upper arms indicates

labor using the arm muscles; and pathologies of the lower back show that the movement involved was one of continuously rocking the trunk backwards and forwards. The only activity that can account for all these at once is using grindstones to make flour. This must have been done on a very large scale, suggesting that plant foods were more important than meat in the diet.

After 9500 BC, there was a gap of a few centuries in the use of the site. From about 9000 BC, the story resumes with a large farming township, and the plant remains from this period are quite different. Far fewer species are present, but they include cultivated plants: barley, rye, lentils, chickpeas, two species of wheat, and several other plants. The pathologies of human bones continue to show that people spent much time grinding seeds into flour, but the seeds now came from cultivated plants. Interestingly, both male and female skeletons show these pathologies, indicating that both sexes prepared plant foods—a remarkable challenge

to our (usually unconscious) assumption that only women would have done this kind of work, even in the distant past.

Despite the fact that these farmers cultivated crops as the mainstay of their diet, they continued to depend largely on wild animals for meat. Gazelles still account for two-thirds of the bones at the site and, again, were killed exclusively in the month of May. From about 7500 BC, however, gazelle bones suddenly become less numerous, being replaced by those of sheep and goats. Female goats were kept into adulthood for breeding, while most males were killed at two years of age for their meat. This pattern could not have resulted from hunting, so these animals must have been domesticated. Clearly, not all species were domesticated at the same time; throughout Southwest Asia, plants were domesticated before animals.

The results achieved at Abu Hureyra show what can be achieved by modern scientific methods. Only a very small part of the site was excavated before it was flooded in 1974; but the methods have been tried and tested, and can now be used at other sites to increase our knowledge of the most important economic change the world has ever seen—the emergence of agriculture.

⚭ At Abu Hureyra, the early farming village lay above a settlement used by the last hunter-gatherers. Here, a rectangular house built by the farmers has been cut through to reveal the circular dwellings of the hunter-gatherers.

⚲ Grindstones such as this were essential for preparing plant foods. The farmers at Abu Hureyra used them to process cultivated crops such as wheat and barley, while the earlier hunter-gatherers used them to grind wild plant seeds.
THE BRITISH MUSEUM

⚱ The grill-plan buildings at Çayönü have a series of parallel foundation walls running the length of each building. This form of construction, incorporating passages to allow the circulation of air beneath the floor, may have been a means of keeping the building dry during the damp winter months.

☞ A view of Çayönü taken in 1972. The rolling plains that surround the site are intensively cultivated today, but when the site was occupied about 7000 BC, they were covered in forest. The mountains in the distance are part of the Tauros range.

Early Neolithic Sites in Anatolia

Anatolia provided a diverse and favorable environment for human settlement from early in the Holocene period, about 8000 BC. The settlement of Çayönü, near Diyarbakir, in southeastern Turkey, is situated on the high bank of a tributary of the Tigris, and the river terrace runs for only a few kilometers before meeting the foothills of the Taurus Mountains.

The site was occupied from about 7250 BC to 6700 BC by people who grew domesticated plants

⚱ A reconstruction of the north and east walls of the so-called Second Vulture Shrine at Çatal Hüyük. The vultures have human legs and are thought to represent priests in disguise. A headless corpse lies between them. In other shrines, there are scenes of more bird-like vultures picking at corpses, possibly reflecting the practice of exposing dead bodies for defleshing.
ARLETTE MELLAART

☞ Excavations at Çatal Hüyük, showing several houses. The structure in the center is one of those thought to have been shrines, because of the unusual painted or plaster decorations on their walls.

such as wheat, peas, and lentils. It is especially interesting in that the animal bones found in the different levels of this settlement show a clear shift from the hunting of wild animals to the keeping of domesticated ones.

Extensive areas of the site have been investigated since 1964 by a joint team from the University of Istanbul and the Oriental Institute of Chicago. Çayönü covers an area of about 100 meters by 200 meters (330 feet by 660 feet). Its architectural remains are fascinating, consisting mainly of residential buildings, although at least three are monumental in size, suggesting that they had a communal function and possibly indicating that there was some kind of chieftainship system. The domestic buildings include strange, so-called grill-plan buildings and more regular cell-plan buildings. The nondomestic structures have floors paved with flagstones. The substantial proportions of its buildings and the relative sophistication of their construction are what sets Çayönü apart from other early sites with fully domesticated cereals.

Almost all the excavated levels can be attributed to a cultural phase known as the Pre-Pottery Neolithic. While the people here had not yet begun to use pottery, they produced tools made of flint and obsidian, or fashioned from stone by grinding; ornaments made of polished stone; and clay figurines. Most surprising was their use of copper, presumably obtained from the nearby source at Ergani-Maden. The metal was shaped by heating and then pounded to make pins, hooks, reamers (a finishing tool for shaping holes), and beads. This is so far the earliest evidence of people intentionally using metal.

JAMES MELLAART

Çatal Hüyük

In 1958, James Mellaart discovered another Anatolian settlement at Çatal Hüyük, situated on a small river 48 kilometers (30 miles) southeast of modern-day Konya. Çatal Hüyük covers an area of 13 hectares (32 acres) and is three times the size of Pre-pottery Jericho. A flourishing township by 6000 BC, it consisted of brick houses arranged side-by-side like a honeycomb. The most unusual feature of these houses is their highly standardized plan, each occupying some 25 square meters (30 square yards) of floor space. Access must have been by means of a wooden ladder from the courtyard onto a flat roof, and from there through a shaft and, finally, a low doorway. The living rooms had built-in benches and platforms, as well as hearths and ovens, all made of earth and plaster.

The extraordinary standardization of the estimated 1,000 houses, accommodating a population of 5,000 to 6,000, suggests deliberate planning and a high level of cohesion and cooperation within the community. Of particular interest are groups of rooms, each with a storeroom, that were apparently used as shrines. The elaborate murals and other contents of these rooms strongly indicate that organized ritual activities took place here.

⚕ A scene depicting a red-deer hunt, painted on the antechamber wall of a hunting shrine found in level III of Çatal Hüyük, dating from about 5800 BC.

◄◙ This baked clay figure of an enthroned female, from Çatal Hüyük, may represent a goddess giving birth. She is supported on either side by cat-like animals, which are probably leopards. The statue was found in a grain bin.
C.M. DIXON

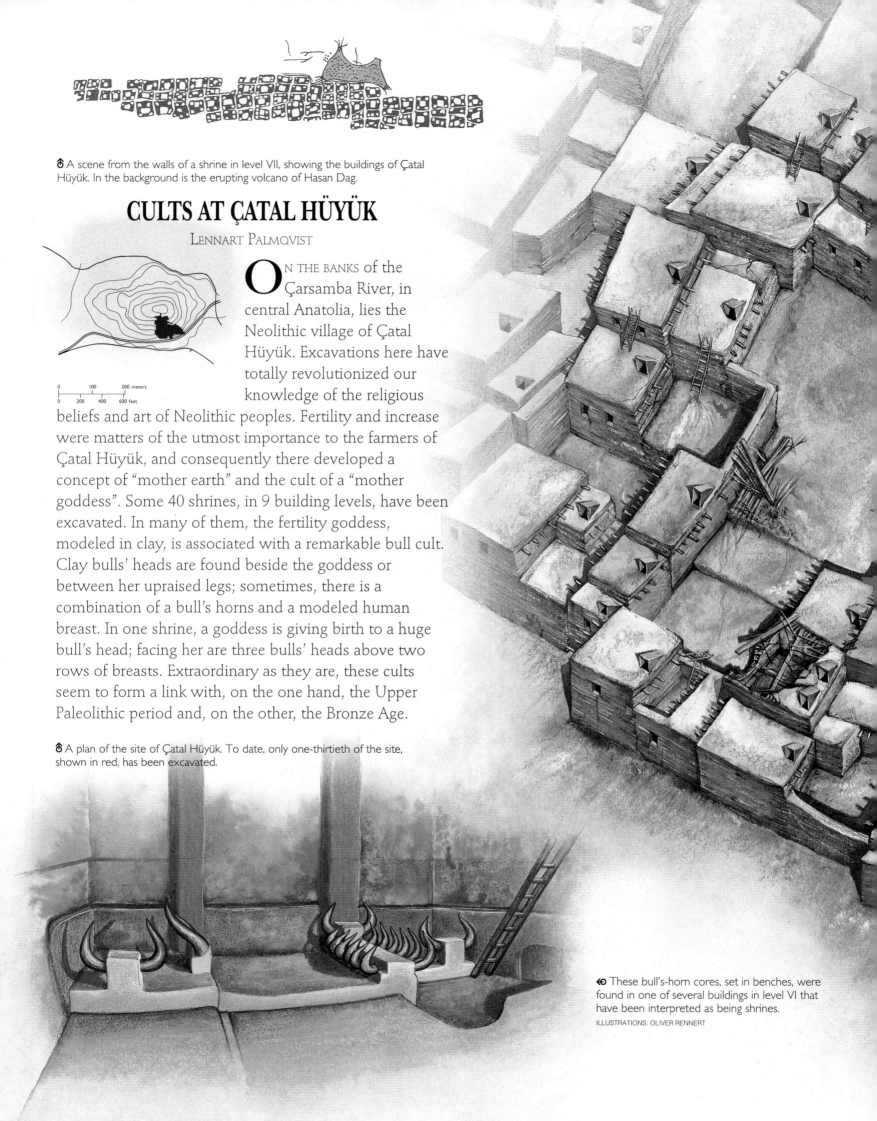

⚲ A scene from the walls of a shrine in level VII, showing the buildings of Çatal Hüyük. In the background is the erupting volcano of Hasan Dag.

CULTS AT ÇATAL HÜYÜK

LENNART PALMQVIST

O N THE BANKS of the Çarsamba River, in central Anatolia, lies the Neolithic village of Çatal Hüyük. Excavations here have totally revolutionized our knowledge of the religious beliefs and art of Neolithic peoples. Fertility and increase were matters of the utmost importance to the farmers of Çatal Hüyük, and consequently there developed a concept of "mother earth" and the cult of a "mother goddess". Some 40 shrines, in 9 building levels, have been excavated. In many of them, the fertility goddess, modeled in clay, is associated with a remarkable bull cult. Clay bulls' heads are found beside the goddess or between her upraised legs; sometimes, there is a combination of a bull's horns and a modeled human breast. In one shrine, a goddess is giving birth to a huge bull's head; facing her are three bulls' heads above two rows of breasts. Extraordinary as they are, these cults seem to form a link with, on the one hand, the Upper Paleolithic period and, on the other, the Bronze Age.

⚲ A plan of the site of Çatal Hüyük. To date, only one-thirtieth of the site, shown in red, has been excavated.

◄ These bull's-horn cores, set in benches, were found in one of several buildings in level VI that have been interpreted as being shrines.

ILLUSTRATIONS: OLIVER RENNERT

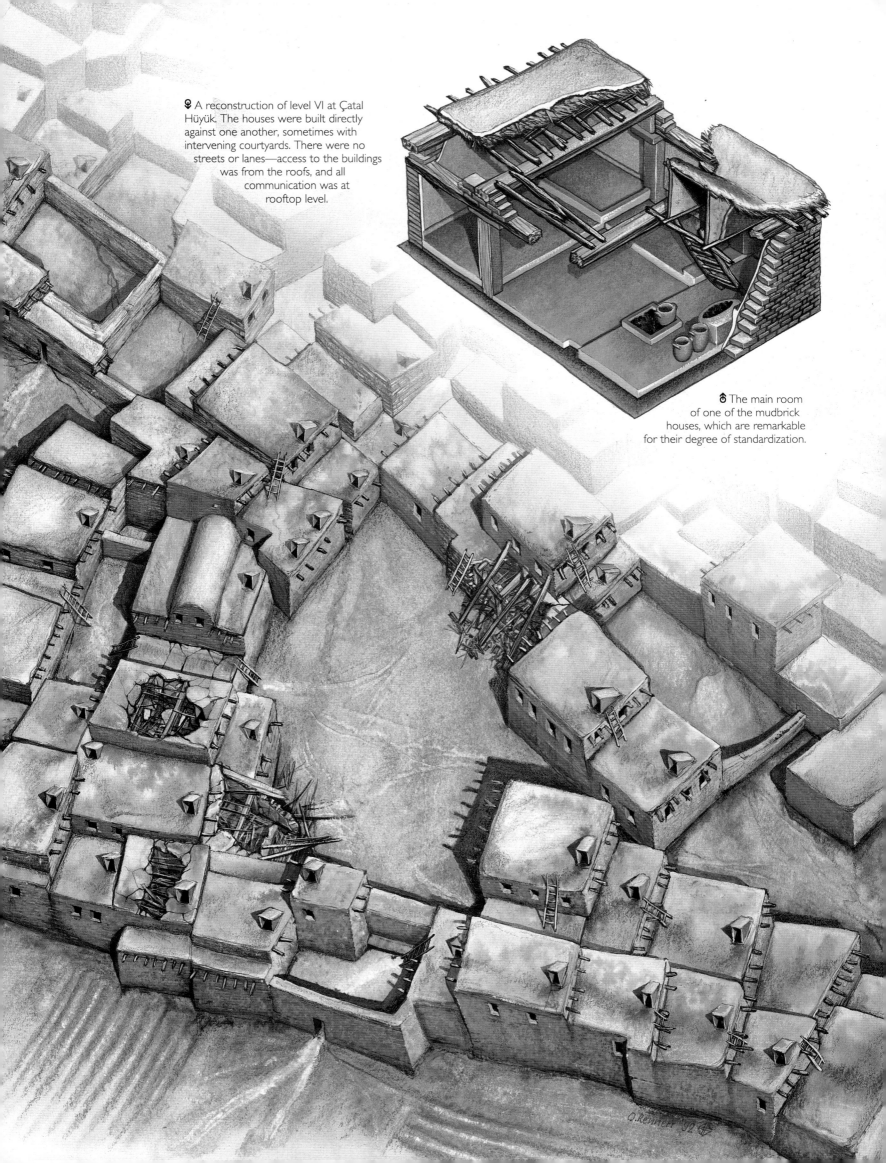

⚲ A reconstruction of level VI at Çatal Hüyük. The houses were built directly against one another, sometimes with intervening courtyards. There were no streets or lanes—access to the buildings was from the roofs, and all communication was at rooftop level.

♁ The main room of one of the mudbrick houses, which are remarkable for their degree of standardization.

O.Reshert '92

☞ This female skull excavated from one of the shrines at Çatal Hüyük is encrusted with cinnabar (mercury sulfide): an example of a so-called ocher burial.

ARLETTE MELLAART

⚀ A valley in the central Zagros Mountains near the modern-day town of Isfahan, in Iran. The interior slopes of the Zagros are dotted with trading centers that formed part of a wide-spread trading network dating back to Neolithic times. This network skirted the central desert to the east and west across the Zagros Mountains and extended down onto the Mesopotamian plain.

THE MACQUITY COLLECTION

The paintings on the carefully plastered walls depict hunting scenes or women giving birth, or consist of numerous geometric patterns. The shrines also contain groups of human and animal figures chipped from stone or modeled in clay. There are groups or rows of bull's-horn cores set in benches or in stylized bull's heads. The rites performed in the shrines, undoubtedly concerned with fertility, seem to form a link with the Upper Paleolithic period, on the one hand, and with the Bronze Age (for example, Early Minoan Crete) on the other.

Çatal Hüyük's wealth was founded on agriculture and trade. Evidence of cattle breeding is found in the earliest excavation levels—the first evidence of unquestionably domesticated cattle

known in western Asia—and the inhabitants obtained obsidian for trade from the nearby volcano of Hasan Dag.

The archaeological evidence from Çatal Hüyük is fascinating in many respects. Neolithic villages in Southwest Asia do not appear to have had cemeteries or elaborate tombs comparable with those of the same period in western Europe. In early Jericho, for instance, the dead were buried under house floors, with their heads buried separately. At Çatal Hüyük, the corpses were placed beneath sleeping platforms. Wall-paintings in three of the shrines show vultures together with headless human figures, the figures often lying curled on their left side. Mellaart has interpreted these scenes as depicting part of the burial process, and a considerable amount of evidence supports this view. For instance, many of the bodies buried beneath the house floors were lying on their left side; human skulls were found on house floors separated from bodies; flesh was removed from bodies before burial—perhaps by vultures.

Undecorated pottery vessels were in general use, and well-preserved prototypes in wood or basketwork have survived, along with equally well-preserved fragments of woven fabrics. The wooden vessels show a variety of form, a mastery of technique, and a sophistication in taste that is unparalleled in the Neolithic period elsewhere in this area.

Among the specialized crafts of Çatal, the chipped stone items, exemplified by a number of ceremonial weapons and ground and polished obsidian mirrors, are by far the most elegant in Southwest Asia. High-quality woolen textiles, in a variety of weaves, were also produced.

Clearly, the crafting of specialized and even luxury items from certain materials was an important feature of Çatal's economy. The fact that many essential raw materials had to be brought from elsewhere points to a commercial basis for much of the community's wealth. The unusual size of Çatal itself strongly suggests that its people exercised some form of political control over the surrounding region.

The site appears to have been occupied from some time late in the seventh millennium BC until the latter part of the sixth millennium BC, when, for unknown reasons, it was abandoned.

Late Neolithic Mesopotamia

The reasons why an advanced, though isolated, settlement such as Çatal Hüyük came to nothing in terms of further social and economic development remain obscure. In Mesopotamia, early farming villages were established in an area that was far less viable economically than Anatolia, yet it was in this arid zone, virtually devoid of natural resources, that urban civilization first developed. From the sixth millennium BC, Mesopotamia was to be the center of the social, technological, and political progress that led to the world's first truly urban society.

Development throughout Southwest Asia had been more or less constant until about 6000 BC, and methods of producing and storing food were well developed. As there was no longer a pressing need to obtain food by hunting, fishing, or gathering, the need to settle in places that offered wild food resources gradually diminished. For the first time, it became possible to establish settlements outside previously favored areas.

During this period, increasing experience in plant cultivation made it possible to raise the yield per unit of land, and with the aid of irrigation, two or three harvests could be produced a year. Less land was needed to feed the inhabitants of a settlement, which meant that settlements could be established closer together. This was important, because the geographical proximity of settlements was a prerequisite both for the creation of settlement systems and for the division of labor within communities. The finely painted pottery of the Halaf period, named after Tell Halaf, in northern Syria, is an example of craftwork produced by specialists—clear evidence of division of labor.

Most of what we know about Southwest Asia from about 6000 BC to 3500 BC is based on styles of pottery. Little is known about other evolving technologies that changed settlement patterns or about new forms of economic organization.

The first phase of Late Neolithic culture in Mesopotamia (6000 BC to 5500 BC) is commonly

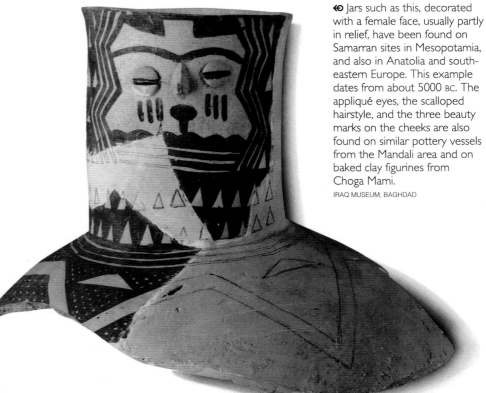

◄● Jars such as this, decorated with a female face, usually partly in relief, have been found on Samarran sites in Mesopotamia, and also in Anatolia and southeastern Europe. This example dates from about 5000 BC. The appliqué eyes, the scalloped hairstyle, and the three beauty marks on the cheeks are also found on similar pottery vessels from the Mandali area and on baked clay figurines from Choga Mami.
IRAQ MUSEUM, BAGHDAD

considered to be the Hassunan, named after the site of Tell Hassuna, which lies west of the middle Tigris River, about 30 kilometers (20 miles) south of modern-day Mosul. While the country is undulating and merges imperceptibly with the uplands, it is low-lying in comparison with the hilly region where nearby Jarmo is located. Other sites of the Hassuna culture are restricted to a limited region of similar terrain in northern Iraq.

In content and style, the early Hassunan artifacts—stone tools and simple pottery—were clearly a continuation of what had been produced in Jarmo, as though the Jarmo culture had spread downhill. Although construction methods improved during Hassunan times, dwellings remained simple. Settlements were, in fact, nothing more than villages of farmers.

The next phase of Late Neolithic culture in Mesopotamia (about 5600 BC to 5000 BC) is often called the Samarran, after the Islamic city of Samarra, beneath which a particularly attractive and elaborately painted style of pottery was first found. Similar pottery was found at Hassuna in levels III to VIII, and was long thought to have been imported luxury ware. Recent excavations at Tell es-Sawwan and Choga Mami, however, have confirmed that Samarra must be considered a separate culture and that its people flourished north of Baghdad, on the fringes of the floodplain, some time in the sixth millennium BC.

Perhaps the most important single discovery from these excavations relates to the Samarran economy. In contrast with Hassunan sites, Samarran sites are well to the south of the zone

IRAQ MUSEUM, BAGHDAD

⚱ This male figurine made of clay, excavated from the Samarran site of Tell es-Sawwan, dates from the sixth millennium BC. In the later excavation levels of this site, upright alabaster figures of a quite different type have been found in large numbers.

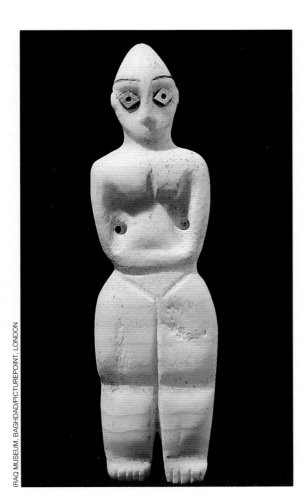

IRAQ MUSEUM, BAGHDAD/PICTUREPOINT, LONDON

◄● An alabaster statuette from a grave at the Samarran site of Tell es-Sawwan, dating from the sixth millennium BC. The eyes have been emphasized by means of bitumen inlays.

⚱ A Samarran bowl from Hassuna, with a centrifugal design of stylized ibexes. Pottery of this kind was first found in graves dating from the sixth millennium BC, below the Abbasid capital of Samarra.
IRAQ MUSEUM, BAGHDAD/HIRMER FOTOARCHIV

↪ A polychrome Halaf plate from a potter's workshop excavated at Arpachiyah, dating from early in the fifth millennium BC. It has a diameter of 32 centimeters (about 12 inches).
IRAQ MUSEUM, BAGHDAD

where rain-fed agriculture is now possible. Paleobotanical evidence from both Sawwan and Choga Mami suggests that irrigation was practiced in both areas in the sixth millennium BC. It has even been suggested that agriculture at Sawwan was probably based on seasonal flooding. At both Sawwan and Choga Mami, emmer, bread wheat, naked six-row barley, and hulled two-row barley have been identified, as have considerable quantities of linseed. The villages at both sites are large in comparison with those from earlier periods, occupying areas of up to 5 hectares

(12 acres). Stamp seals have been found, suggesting that private ownership was recognized, and a more conscious professionalism among Samarran craftspeople is indicated by the widespread use of potter's marks. Surplus wealth had become available for nonproductive purposes.

This is especially evident at Tell es-Sawwan. Here, beneath several unusually large buildings, numerous graves have been found, many containing the remains of infants. The graves also contained an extraordinary collection of hundreds of ground stone objects—in particular, female statuettes and a variety of elegantly shaped bowls made of alabaster. These objects indicate that Sawwan was a settlement with some special significance.

The discovery of a distinctive pottery style at Tell Halaf, on the Syrian-Turkish border, midway between the Tigris and the Euphrates, gave a name to the third phase of Mesopotamian protohistory (5500 BC to 4300 BC). Like the Hassunan, the Halafian culture was centered on northern Iraq, but was considerably more widespread. Halafian sites are also found in northern Syria and somewhat further down the Tigris and Euphrates rivers than Hassunan sites.

Halafian settlements were still no more than villages, but construction techniques had improved, and there were cobbled streets between the houses. Although most walls were formed of packed mud, at some sites there is evidence of mudbricks—the first known in Mesopotamia. Also for the first time in Mesopotamia, structures or chambers are found that differ from dwellings or other utilitarian buildings. These consist of vaulted, circular rooms shaped like beehives, ranging from about 5 to 10 meters (15 to 30 feet) in diameter, and built of packed mud. Sometimes, rectangular antechambers are attached to them, but these buildings were seldom, if ever, lived in. They may represent the first step towards temple architecture.

Halafian pottery was the finest ever produced in prehistoric Mesopotamia. (The historic period begins with the first written sources, about 3200 BC.) Handmade from very fine clay, it had thin walls and was decorated with skillfully applied paintings of geometric motifs and, occasionally, figures of animals, birds, and flowers. Flat stamp seals of steatite or other stone, engraved with simple geometric figures and used to impress ownership marks on lumps of clay attached to goods, were abundant in the Halafian period.

The dating of Halafian sites is controversial, but various authorities place the end of the Halafian culture well into the fifth millennium BC, as late as 4300 BC. From about 6000 BC to 4500 BC, the middle reaches of the Tigris and Euphrates river valleys in northern Mesopotamia were settled by farming peoples who had probably moved in from one or more regions of the central Zagros Mountains area to the east, north, and west. Farming techniques were established but not elaborate, and permitted

only a moderate increase in the number, size, and quality of settlements during the period. Some developments are especially notable: native copper was occasionally worked, although not for the first time in Southwest Asia; pottery was greatly improved, aesthetically and technologically; and the plow came into use as an aid to agriculture.

Early Settlement in Sumer

It is only from a relatively late stage that there is archaeological evidence of settlement in the arid southern plains of Mesopotamia. The 'Ubaid culture, which extended from 5000 BC to 3750 BC, is generally thought to be the earliest manifestation of settled farming in the southern floodplains. The earliest phase, known as 'Ubaid 1, or Eridu, was very limited geographically, but these settlers from the south soon moved up the Tigris and Euphrates rivers in search of new land. At this point, Mesopotamia became the center of civilized Southwest Asia—the place where the foundations of the Sumerian civilization were laid.

At Eridu, slightly west of the present-day course of the Euphrates, a series of small square rooms fitted with altars has been found in very early excavation levels in association with distinctive monochrome-painted pottery. These buildings represent the beginnings in the south of the long and much elaborated tradition of Mesopotamian temple architecture.

Little is known about the early 'Ubaid economy, but it seems almost certain that the 'Ubaid peoples were irrigation farmers who harnessed the destructive spring floods of the Euphrates River to improve their crop yields.

Certainly, there is evidence that settlements were becoming bigger. Eridu may have covered an area of 10 hectares (24 acres) in the later 'Ubaid periods, with as many as 4,000 inhabitants. Populations of this size must have increased the need for some form of centralized control, but evidence of social stratification, such as differences in grave goods or in houses, is extremely limited.

A number of technological innovations took place in 'Ubaid times: copper casting; the use of fired bricks for building; and the use of simple sailboats for river transport. The fine-quality decorated pottery of the Halafian and Samarran cultures gave way to technologically improved but mass-produced wares, often crudely decorated. Some pottery was manufactured on the tournette, a forerunner of the fast-spinning potter's wheel. Engraved stamp seals depicted animals and humans together, whereas in the Halafian period they had borne only simple geometric figures.

While agriculture in southern Mesopotamia must have been extremely productive, it seems likely that wealth was increasingly based on mercantile trade during this period, and that command over the organization of commerce and the exaction of tributes would have been centered in the temples. Never before had a single culture been able to spread its influence over such a vast area. So widespread was this influence that the prosperous 'Ubaid culture, on the plains of Mesopotamia, provided the basis for the cultural explosion represented by the emergence of the later historic—and first literate—civilizations.

☝ The Euphrates River flows almost due south after leaving the Turkish mountains. Downstream, after passing through agricultural lands, it cuts its way through a dry plain on either side. At intervals along its course, villages have sprung up, with orchards and crops that flourish on the alluvial soil left behind by the river. The ancient island of Ana is seen here from the river's northern bank.

☝ Beyond the hilly flanks of the Fertile Crescent—the foothills of the Zagros Mountains proper—only limited agriculture is possible, and the area is consequently given over to the herding of sheep and goats. Farming here follows traditional ways, as shown in this scene of wheat threshing.

'AIN GHAZAL: THE LARGEST KNOWN NEOLITHIC SITE

GARY O. ROLLEFSON

IN THE COURSE OF ITS 2,000-YEAR HISTORY, 'Ain Ghazal, in Jordan, witnessed a remarkable period of human cultural development. The settlement was founded as a small permanent hamlet in 7250 BC, and its residents combined farming, hunting, and herding to provide an abundant and stable food supply that allowed sustained population growth on a scale never before possible. While it grew constantly over some 750 years, 'Ain Ghazal experienced a sudden population explosion in the centuries immediately before and after 6500 BC—probably as a result of people abandoning settlements in the region as the land was exhausted. By 6000 BC, the village extended over 12 hectares (almost 30 acres) and housed about 2,000 people.

The period between 7250 BC and 6000 BC is the "classic" phase of Neolithic development—known to archaeologists as the Pre-Pottery Neolithic B (PPNB) period—which extended south from eastern Turkey to the fringes of the southern deserts of Palestine and Jordan. In the previous period, from 8500 BC to 7600 BC (known as the PPNA), a few communities in the Levant had begun to grow crops, but there is no evidence of animal domestication.

PPNB people produced long flint blades of exceptionally fine quality, using them as arrowheads and sickles as well as for a range of other purposes. They built spacious and sturdy houses, with durable plaster floors that reflect a sophisticated technology. Their agricultural crops included several species of cereals and legumes, and by 6000 BC they had domesticated sheep, goats, cattle, and pigs. But of all their accomplishments, perhaps the most impressive are the rich expressions of religious belief that have come down to us in the form of their ritual objects and burial remains.

Toys, Cults, and Amulets

Many tiny clay animal figurines, which may have served various purposes for the people of 'Ain Ghazal, have been found. A unique sitting dog, for example, may have been simply a child's toy, since nothing comparable has been found at 'Ain Ghazal or anywhere else in Southwest Asia. The vast majority of animal figurines depict cattle, which were not domesticated until near the end of the PPNB period, and it has been suggested that they may have been related to a "cattle cult".

Human figurines are less numerous, and may have been personal amulets. With one exception, all were found "decapitated", either as heads or headless bodies. Some figurines have grossly extended abdomens and pendulous breasts, and probably represented fertility spirits that were thought to ensure women's good health during pregnancy.

⚱ Plaster was used to recreate the faces of some individuals, presumed to have been family members. As time passed and the plaster cracked, the "portraits" were buried and replaced with those of people who had died more recently.
HISAHIKO WADA

Burial Customs

The dead were usually buried beneath the floors of houses. After a waiting period long enough for the flesh and ligaments to decay, the burial pit was reopened and the skull removed. Many skulls appear to have been simply reburied elsewhere, some under the same floor.

◄◙ Most children and adults were buried beneath the plaster floors of houses. After a time, the burial pits were reopened to extract the skulls, and a new floor was then built.

CURT BLAIR

5Cm

But others received unusual treatment: plaster was used to recreate facial features, producing what archaeologist Kathleen M. Kenyon called "portraits" of the dead. Such people may have been family or lineage members.

Infants under the age of about 15 months were disposed of with considerably less regard. Although the remains of some very young children have been found under doorways, possibly implying that they served as "foundation deposits", or in a ceremonial context, such as in a pit of plastered human skulls, most appear to have been discarded in rubbish heaps. About a third of the adult burials have similarly been found in rubbish heaps, the bodies not decapitated, suggesting that these people did not enjoy the degree of respect accorded to most other members of the community.

Ancestor Worship

The human and animal figurines represent a link with the spiritual world on an individual level, and the human burials demonstrate this link on the level of the family. Communal expressions of religion took a more overt form. So far, more than 30 plaster statues and busts have been

☝ Projectile points made with exemplary skill show how important hunting was to the people of 'Ain Ghazal. Half of their meat supply came from wild animals during the PPNB period; in later periods, this had declined to less than 10 percent. Large points like these were characteristic of the PPNB.

☝ Statues and busts, made from bundles of reeds coated with plaster and decorated with red paint and bitumen, were focal points of communal activities. They were probably displayed (at least occasionally) in a special building. This statuette may have been a village's "mother goddess".

☝ One of two clay figurines of wild cattle, ritually "killed" with flint bladelets, that were found buried beneath the plaster floor of a house. This isolated find may represent an act of magic, believed to bring luck during the hunt.

recovered from huge "burial pits". The busts, standing about 45 centimeters (18 inches) high, are clearly an elaboration of the plastered skulls, and may represent mythical ancestors of family groups. The taller statues (about 90 centimeters, or 3 feet, high) depict both men and women—the latter including fertility statuettes—and probably portray mythical ancestors believed to have founded the settlement.

More than a thousand years of intensive farming and grazing took their toll on the soils and plant life around 'Ain Ghazal and the other settlements of the southern Levant. By 6000 BC, most of the villages had been deserted. Only a few, such as 'Ain Ghazal, situated near the edge of the steppes, where goats could be herded, survived, if in somewhat reduced circumstances.

Between 6000 BC and 5500 BC (known as the PPNC period), 'Ain Ghazal continued to grow, extending over about 14 hectares (35 acres), but judging by the less dense housing in this period, the population had probably declined. Some people may have lived at the site for only a few months of the year, spending the rest of their time tending their flocks of goats in the steppes and desert.

By 5500 BC, local residents were making pottery for storage and cooking purposes, ushering in what is known as the Pottery Neolithic period. But this technical innovation could not compensate for the damage suffered by the surrounding farmland. Within a few centuries, 'Ain Ghazal had been all but abandoned, serving as nothing more than a temporary camp for nomadic pastoralists visiting the spring that lay at the heart of the original and once thriving settlement.

HUNTER-GATHERERS AND FARMERS IN AFRICA

1 0 , 0 0 0   B C   –   A D   2 0 0

The Transformation of a Continent

RICHARD G. KLEIN

ABOUT 12,000 YEARS AGO, there was little difference between the cultures and economies of Africa and Eurasia, and both continents remained largely unchanged from the way they had been thousands, or even tens of thousands, of years earlier. People everywhere still used Stone Age technologies, and they relied entirely on hunting and gathering wild resources for their subsistence. What marks this period out as one of the most significant in prehistory is that it was a time of profound, global climatic change—from the cooler and generally drier conditions of the last Ice Age to the warmer and generally moister conditions of the present interglacial period, known as the Holocene.

Almost everywhere, changed climatic conditions led to a radical redistribution of plants and animals, to which people had to adapt. This they did in many ways, one of the most significant being that they undertook the first serious experiments in plant and animal domestication. To begin with, hunting and gathering probably continued to be more important, but in most societies that adopted them, cultivation and herding rapidly took over as the main mode of subsistence. In some places, the larger populations and economic surpluses made possible by cultivation and herding eventually led to the development of urban centers with monumental architecture, craft specialization, social stratification, wide trade networks, and other markers of "civilization".

◄◙ A herd of cattle at an agricultural village in Niger, West Africa. At the end of the last Ice Age, many of the continent's hunter-gatherers took up farming and herding.

◙ This barbed bone harpoon head comes from a fishing settlement dating to about the fifth millennium BC at Lowasera, on the ancient shoreline of Lake Turkana, in northern Kenya.
DAVID PHILLIPSON

DAVID PHILLIPSON

☝ These microlithic tools were made by the Iberomaurusians (sometimes called the Oranians), who inhabited northwestern Africa between 16,000 and 10,000 years ago.

☟ A galloping herd of Cape, or African, buffaloes (*Syncerus caffer*) in Kruger National Park, Transvaal, South Africa.

It may be that Africa played a smaller role in the domestication of plants and animals and in the evolution of civilization than did other regions, especially nearby Southwest Asia, but its role was far from peripheral. Cattle may have been domesticated in the deserts of North Africa as early as anywhere else, and many important crops—including yams, sorghum, peanuts, and bulrush and finger millet—were native to Africa and must first have been cultivated there. On a broader scale, in the millennia following the end of the Ice Age, Africa, like most other parts of the world, was progressively transformed from a continent of hunter-gatherers to one of mainly pastoralists and mixed farmers, some of whom built civilizations of lasting renown.

Of these, the civilization that sprang up along the Nile Valley, in Egypt, about 5,100 years ago, is by far the best known, but the indigenous civilizations that appeared much later in the savannas and forests of West Africa and in the woodlands of south central Africa were also extraordinary. This chapter summarizes what is known of the hunter-gatherers of these regions, and traces their progressive replacement by pastoralists and mixed farmers.

This process began in the northeast between 7000 BC and 5000 BC, and culminated in the extreme south of the continent between the beginning of the first century AD and AD 200— and in some places even later, perhaps only after contact with Europeans.

Africa in 10,000 BC

In a strictly archaeological sense, Africa in 10,000 BC differed little from the Africa of many thousands of years before. People everywhere still lived by hunting various large mammals, by gathering wild plants, tortoises, and other ground game, and, wherever practical, by fishing and gathering food from the beaches. They did not make pottery or work metal, and their most conspicuous stone artifacts tended to be tiny (microlithic) pieces, often trimmed or backed (dulled) along one end or edge, mainly to facilitate hafting on wooden or bone handles or shafts. These small stone tools vary significantly from region to region, reflecting the existence of numerous local cultures or ethnic groups, each with its own distinct subsistence strategy, manufacturing or hafting technology, and style. At sites where bone is preserved, the stone artifacts are usually accompanied by points, awls, and other well-made bone implements, and by bone or shell beads and pendants. The bone and shell artifacts are broadly similar to much earlier ones, and their specific forms likewise vary from place to place, reflecting regional differences in culture.

Among the people who inhabited Africa at that time, none are better known or more typical than the Iberomaurusians (sometimes called the Oranians), who occupied the Northwest African coastal plain and its hinterland between north-western Morocco and northeastern Tunisia. They appeared in this region about 16,000 years ago, or slightly before, after a long interval when Northwest Africa had been largely abandoned because of extreme aridity. The return of moister conditions is signaled by the pollens and animal remains recovered from Iberomaurusian sites, as well as by the Iberomaurusians themselves. Somewhat ironically, their successful adaptation to these conditions is most conspicuously reflected in their prolonged use of numerous cemeteries, some of which contain more than 100 skeletons.

Like most of their contemporaries in Africa (and elsewhere), the Iberomaurusians made a wide

ANTHONY BANNISTER/NHPA

PETER JOHNSON/NHPA

The Bushmen of the Kalahari Desert, in southern Africa, are one of the few populations of hunter-gatherers found on the continent today. Here, a group of Bushmen are collecting wild berries.

ANTHONY BANNISTER/NHPA

A woman of the !Kung Bushman group of the Kalahari empties her apron of the mongongo nuts she has gathered.

variety of stone and bone artifacts. Their stone tools comprised numerous small, elongated backed blades or bladelets, including pointed ones that may have been used to tip arrows or other projectiles; larger retouched pieces, including many that were probably used to scrape skins; grindstones that may have been used to crush grass seeds; and perforated stone balls like those that some Africans in historic times attached as weights to pointed wooden digging sticks. Their bone tools include a range of carefully shaped pieces that probably served as punches, projectile points, hide burnishers, and knives. Among their personal ornaments were seashells and small stones, with carefully drilled holes.

Iberomaurusian sites often contain the bones of Barbary sheep, hartebeest, wild cattle, gazelles, zebra, and other large mammals that were hunted, together with the shells of land or marine gastropods (a class of mollusks, which includes snails) that were eaten. Although no plant remains other than charcoal and pollen have been found, the grindstones and what appear to be digging-stick weights suggest that these people also ate wild plants, as most hunter-gatherers living in comparable conditions in historic times are known to have done.

From about 8000 BC, the Iberomaurusians were succeeded locally by various "cultures", of which by far the best documented is the Capsian. Capsian people appear to have been physically different from the Iberomaurusians, and this may indicate that the Capsians migrated into the area, most probably from the east, bringing their culture with them. Their stone artifacts tend to be larger than those of the Iberomaurusians, endscrapers

and backed blades being particularly abundant. At least some Capsians also manufactured large numbers of geometric microliths—small chips of stone trimmed into triangles, crescent shapes, trapezoids, and other regular forms. They produced a remarkable range of bone artifacts, and are famous for their art, which includes stone figurines and engraved ostrich eggshells, as well as more commonplace bone or shell pendants, and beads. As evidenced by the large number of shells excavated from their sites, terrestrial snails formed a major part of their diet. Like the Iberomaurusians, they also hunted Barbary sheep and other large mammals, and ate wild plant foods. As well as grindstones and digging-stick weights, Capsian sites have yielded microliths that would have been mounted in bone or wooden handles and were used to cut wild grasses, as indicated by the distinctive "sickle sheen", or polish, on the surface of the stone that can still be seen today.

About 5000 BC, the range of Capsian artifacts was augmented by pottery and ground stone tools, and at about the same time the Capsians began to herd sheep and goats, while continuing to hunt wild animals. Neither sheep nor goats are indigenous to Africa, and their appearance at this time clearly points to pastoralism. It may be that domesticated grains were introduced at the same time, but even if these arrived a little later, 5000 BC marks an important turning point in Northwest African prehistory. From this time onwards, farming and herding progressively replaced hunting and gathering as the principal means of livelihood, and by Roman times the region was better known for its granaries than for its wildlife.

DAVID PHILLIPSON

Traces of vegetable mastic (or resin) remain on this backed microlith from the rock shelter of Makwe, in eastern Zambia, close to the Mozambique border, showing how such tools were hafted.

41

⚱ An Early Khartoum potsherd with the characteristic decoration of wavy lines. Ceramic remains such as this are the oldest known pottery in Africa and are contemporary with the earliest pottery found in neighboring Southwest Asia.
ASHMOLEAN MUSEUM, OXFORD

☞ A Kalahari Bushman digs a springhare (*Pedetes capensis*) from its burrow with a stick. Springhares are fairly large, nocturnal rodents, which inhabit open, sandy country in eastern and southern Africa.

⚱ Bored stones, like these from Kalemba, in eastern Zambia, are frequently found at hunter-gatherer sites in southern Africa. Rock art confirms that the larger stones were used as digging-stick weights.
DAVID PHILLIPSON

☞ Barbed points from Early Holocene deposits at Lowasera, on the eastern shore of Lake Turkana, in Kenya. The people here lived mainly by fishing. Wavy-line pottery found at Lowasera is very similar to that found at Early Khartoum sites.

The Earliest African Herders and Farmers

Despite what historical and environmental considerations might suggest, the oldest known farming sites in Africa have been found not in the Nile Valley, or in some equally lush environment, but in the Sahara. The explanation for this is partly that the Sahara was not always as arid as it is now: between 10,000 BC and 4500 BC—or even later in some places—it was commonly much moister. While never truly wet, it was moist enough to support seasonal stands of grass and ephemeral lakes or ponds. Some time between 10,000 BC and 8000 BC, it was extensively, if sparsely, occupied by groups that resembled their Iberomaurusian contemporaries in Northwest Africa, both in the kinds of artifacts they made and in their hunting-gathering way of life.

PETER JOHNSON/NHPA

The southern Sahara seems to have been particularly attractive, and about 7000 BC it was settled by groups who lived by hunting antelopes and other large mammals, by gathering wild grasses and other plants, and, most notably, by fishing in the widely scattered lakes and streams. The sites occupied by these groups contain a rich range of artifacts, including large flaked "scrapers" or "adzes", backed microliths, upper and lower grindstones (known as manos and metates to New World archaeologists), perforated or drilled stone digging-stick weights, grooved stones that may have been net sinkers, barbed bone points that were surely harpoon heads, and, perhaps most striking, pottery decorated with a distinctive wavy line or dotted wavy line.

Broadly similar stone, bone, and pottery artifacts have been found at sites of a similar age in parts of East Africa, which also enjoyed a far higher rainfall at that time than they have in recent times. The pottery, which has been dubbed "Early Khartoum", after a site at Khartoum, on the Sudanese Nile, where it is found in abundance, is the oldest known pottery in Africa and, it would appear, as old as any in neighboring Southwest Asia. This may even mean that ceramic technology was independently developed in the Sahara or East Africa.

In Southwest Asia, pottery seems to have been invented and adopted by farming people who lived a settled, village-based existence. But even the richest Early Khartoum sites, including Early Khartoum itself, have provided no evidence of cultivated plants or herded animals. Until recently, it could have been argued that the appearance (or development) of pottery in Africa was not connected with the emergence of food production, but discoveries in the Western Desert of Egypt now suggest otherwise.

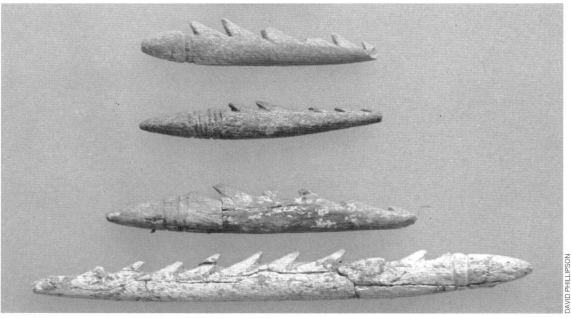

DAVID PHILLIPSON

In the Western Desert, people who were making Early Khartoum-like pottery about 7000 BC lived in a harsher environment than most Early Khartoum people to the south and west, and they supplemented hunting, gathering, and fishing with cattle herding. (See the feature *The Use of Plants in the Sahara*.) By 6000 BC, these people were also cultivating barley, and may have added sheep or goats to their herds. The sheep and goats (these species cannot always be distinguished from their bones) surely originated in Southwest Asia, where their wild progenitors were domesticated some time between 9000 BC and 6000 BC. The cattle, however, may have been domesticated in North Africa, since wild cattle were widely distributed in the north in prehistoric times, and the earliest firm evidence of domesticated cattle elsewhere (in western Asia and southeastern Europe) dates from only about 6000 BC. The barley may also have been domesticated in North Africa, but is more likely to have come from Southwest Asia, where it was being cultivated by 7300 BC.

By 5000 BC, the herding of cattle, sheep, and goats, perhaps accompanied by cereal cultivation, appears to have been widespread throughout the Sahara, and it would probably have continued in the region for much longer if the climate had not started to become drier at about this time. This probably encouraged pastoralists to congregate around the relatively well-watered mountain massifs that dot the Sahara, and it may also have forced some to retreat progressively southwards into the savannas just south of the Sahara.

Possibly, the drying up of the Sahara or related climatic changes may also explain the rather sudden appearance of farming villages in the Egyptian Nile Valley between 5000 BC and 4500 BC. At this time, mixed farming based on wheat, barley, flax, sheep, goats, cattle, and pigs seems rapidly to have replaced pure hunting and gathering as the means of subsistence, and on the rich soils of the Nile floodplain, cultivation and animal husbandry allowed far larger populations to develop.

Initially, the farming villages were small and relatively simple, but as the population increased, some villages grew into towns, some of which in turn became the capitals of kingdoms vying for control of the Nile Valley. About 3150 BC, the rulers of one kingdom succeeded in unifying the entire valley north of Aswan—and Egyptian dynastic civilization was born.

⬆ Tall stands of nerium grow along the shores of the partly water-filled Wadi Iherir, in Tassili n'Ajjer, southeastern Algeria. After about 5000 BC, the increasingly dry climate forced pastoral peoples of the Sahara to congregate in these relatively well-watered mountain massifs.

⚲ A herd of Baggara goats at Musawwarat es-Sofra. The Arabic-speaking Baggara people are nomadic cattle owners who inhabit the dry savannas between the Nile and the Chad border, in Sudan. Goats and sheep are kept for their meat.

Sub-Saharan Africa

Although herding, sometimes accompanied by cultivation, flourished in the Sahara and other parts of northern Africa before 5000 BC, neither herding nor cultivation seems to have spread southwards at any speed. In West Africa, the appearance of pottery and of ground stone axes or hoes between 5000 BC and 4000 BC may indicate that pastoralists or farmers were present, but so far, domestic animals are well documented only from 2500 BC onwards, and domestic plants only from about 1200 BC. Herding apparently became established in East Africa about 4000 BC, when the inhabitants of the central Sudan started to herd cattle, sheep, and goats while continuing to hunt wild mammals and fish on a large scale.

⚲ These edge-ground stone axes are from the Neolithic site of Esh Shaheinab, on the eastern bank of the Nile, some 50 kilometers (30 miles) north of Khartoum, in Sudan. They date from about 4000 BC.
DAVID PHILLIPSON

The early Sudanese herders possessed pottery, backed microliths, barbed harpoon heads of bone, and other objects that could well have been derived from local, Early Khartoum prototypes, together with ground stone axes, amulets of foreign stone, and types of pottery that indicate influences from far to the north or northwest. These herders relied heavily on sorghum and millet, possibly gathered wild rather than cultivated. Further east and south, in present-day Ethiopia, Kenya, and northern Tanzania, pastoralism—again, it would appear, without domesticated plants—seems not to have become well established until about 2500 BC. Even further south, there is no evidence of pastoralists or farmers before the beginning of the first century AD.

Among the early sub-Saharan pastoralists, none are better studied than the so-called Pastoral Neolithic peoples who appeared in the highlands of southern Kenya and northern Tanzania about 2500 BC, or perhaps a little earlier. Bones of cattle, along with those of sheep and/or goats, are found at most Pastoral Neolithic sites, but they are sometimes significantly outnumbered by the remains of wildebeest, zebra, gazelles, and other wild species. This is often the case at earlier Pastoral Neolithic sites in particular—those dated as earlier than 1000 BC—suggesting that herding may initially have supplemented hunting and gathering in a fairly minor way and that it only later took over as the main means of subsistence.

There is no unequivocal evidence that any Pastoral Neolithic people ever cultivated plants, but like herder-gatherers throughout sub-Saharan Africa in historic times, they almost certainly relied heavily on wild plant foods. Some later Pastoral Neolithic sites contain traces of comparatively substantial structures, which may mean that the people had settled in these localities or, what seems more likely, that they were extremely regular in their movements and often returned to the same place year after year. The predominance of bones of animals of breeding age at some later sites may indicate that herds were kept mainly to provide milk and blood products, like those consumed by many East African pastoralists in historic times. The latter rarely slaughtered immature animals, since the milk and blood these would provide when they were fully grown more than offset their own needs for milk and pasture.

The artifacts made by Pastoral Neolithic peoples include skillfully shaped obsidian flakes and blades, a remarkable range of pottery, and carefully crafted ground stone bowls and platters that are especially associated with grave sites. These stone bowls are so conspicuous and distinctive that the Pastoral Neolithic was originally called the Stone Bowl culture. About AD 700, or perhaps a little earlier, Pastoral Neolithic populations were replaced or absorbed by pastoralists who knew how to work iron. These people may have been ancestors of the Masai and other similar East African herding peoples known in historic times.

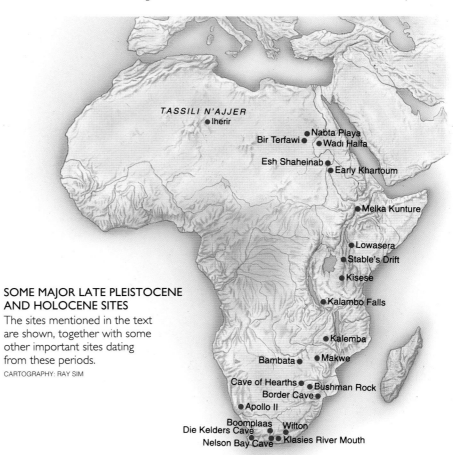

SOME MAJOR LATE PLEISTOCENE AND HOLOCENE SITES
The sites mentioned in the text are shown, together with some other important sites dating from these periods.
CARTOGRAPHY: RAY SIM

DAVID PHILLIPSON

☝ A sherd of Bambata ware from southwestern Zimbabwe, dated to about 200 BC. Pottery of this type may be associated with the earliest evidence of herding in southern Africa.
DAVID PHILLIPSON

◄◙ An example of Nderit ware from Stable's Drift, southern Kenya. Nderit ware is probably the oldest pottery made by East African Pastoral Neolithic people. As well as being decorated on the outside, the vessel is deeply scored on the inside.

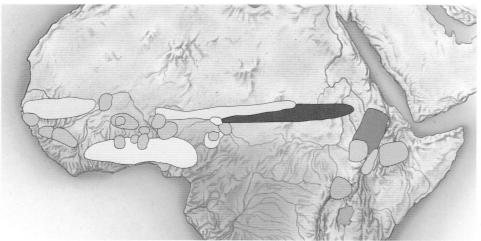

CARTOGRAPHY: RAY SIM, AFTER D.W. PHILLIPSON (1985): *AFRICAN ARCHAEOLOGY*, CAMBRIDGE UNIVERSITY PRESS, CAMBRIDGE, P. 114.

PROBABLE AREAS OF DOMESTICATION OF INDIGENOUS AFRICAN CROPS

Most crops were grown near the areas where they were first domesticated, but sorghum and millet became staples throughout much of the continent.

- Yams
- African rice
- Sorghum
- Bulrush millet
- Teff
- Finger millet
- Fonio
- Peanuts
- Ensete and noog
- Bulrush millet, teff, ensete, and noog

☞ This iron blade from Muteshti, in Zambia, dates from shortly after the beginning of the Christian era, when iron-working became common over wide areas of south central Africa.
DAVID PHILLIPSON

Speculation continues as to the reasons for the late and relatively slow southward spread of pastoralism in Africa, but they may include both natural and cultural factors. Although the Ancient Egyptians and, perhaps, other groups attempted to domesticate gazelles, oryxes, and other hoofed animals found in Africa, only one—the donkey or ass—ever became important economically, and it was used mainly for draft in or near the drier parts of Northeast Africa, where its wild ancestor lived. Otherwise, pastoralism in Africa, as in most other parts of the world, centered on cattle, sheep, and goats, which were not indigenous to sub-Saharan Africa and which may at first have been poorly suited to tropical African environments.

Perhaps it was only after an interval during which new breeds were developed that economies based on the herding of cattle, sheep, and goats could compete effectively with entrenched hunter-gatherer traditions in equatorial East and West Africa. Competition may have been especially difficult under the relatively moist conditions that prevailed before 5000 BC, when it seems likely that the tsetse fly—which devastated African herds into the present century—may have ranged much further to the north and west.

Cultivation appears to have spread southwards even more slowly than pastoralism, probably at least in part because it required the domestication of indigenous plants. The principal crops on which early North African farmers depended— barley and wheat—could not be grown in tropical Africa, except in some relatively isolated highland areas. African cultivators solved this problem by domesticating a wide variety of sub-Saharan plants, of which the most important for the subcontinent as a whole

N. COHEN/COMSTOCK

are certainly sorghum and varous kinds of millet. It is difficult to document the process of plant domestication, partly because identifiable plant remains are not preserved in many archaeological sites; partly because the earliest domestic millets, sorghum, and other crops would in any case have closely resembled their wild ancestors; and partly because relatively few relevant sites have been excavated.

While the oldest date we have for a variety of millet is 1200 BC, and that for sorghum is about the beginning of the first century AD, it may be that these grains, along with other important crops, such as African rice, yams, and peanuts, were first cultivated long before this. What is clear is that

⚱ A traditional container from eastern Nigeria for storing yams. Yams were one of the most important crops in precolonial Africa, but their domestication in prehistoric times has not been documented.

⬿ A wooden spade and pitch-fork used to cultivate and process millet in Ethiopia. Millet became a staple of farming peoples throughout much of sub-Saharan Africa during the Christian era.

⚱ About 6000 BC, barley, together with wheat, was introduced to northeastern Africa from Southwest Asia. It spread along the Mediterranean coast and down the Nile Valley to Sudan and Ethiopia, but was not cultivated in the tropics, where the climate was unfavorable.

whenever various African plants were domesticated, plant cultivation was largely, if not entirely, restricted to the northwestern and northeastern parts of sub-Saharan Africa until between 500 BC and 300 BC. At about that time, some West Africans who relied on cattle and sheep, as well as on domesticated millet, sorghum, and, perhaps, other crops, acquired the technique of iron-smelting, probably from North Africa, where it had been introduced about 800 BC. Armed with iron implements for felling trees and tilling the soil, and with iron weapons for subduing enemies, these people were able to carry their mixed farming way of life to places where before it had been impractical or successfully resisted.

Iron-aided mixed farming swept rapidly through the savannas bordering the central African rainforest, reaching the Great Lakes region of East Africa by the beginning of the first century AD, and the extreme southeastern tip of Africa no more than two or three centuries later. Almost everywhere, this type of farming tended to supplant or incorporate economies and societies based simply on herding or hunting and gathering. Its spread was halted only where climatic conditions were totally unsuitable, as in the deep tropical rainforest of central Africa and at the southwestern corner of the continent, where rainfall was insufficient or fell during the winter, the wrong season for indigenous African crops.

47

THE USE OF PLANTS IN THE SAHARA

Fred Wendorf, Angela E. Close, and Romuald Schild

◈ Carbonized plant remains were recovered from ash deposits surrounding potholes in the floor of an 8,000-year-old house at Nabta Playa, in Egypt.

◄● A 5,500-year-old grinding stone at the Stone Age settlement of Iheren, on the Iherir Plateau, in Tassili n'Ajjer, provides a reminder of the Sahara's verdant past. As humus does not form in the desert, Stone Age relics are often found exposed on the surface.

The eastern Sahara was without rain from before 70,000 years ago until about 11,000 years ago. At some time between 12,000 and 11,000 years ago, there was a northward shift of the summer monsoon system, and seasonal rainfall returned. Except for brief periods of aridity lasting no more than a century or two, rainfall continued until about 3400 BC, when the modern period of aridity began. Estimates of the rainfall during this period range between 50 and 200 millimeters (2 and 8 inches) per year, so even during the "wet" periods, the eastern Sahara was still a desert.

Between about 8000 BC and 3000 BC, people lived in the eastern Sahara, the earliest sites probably being short-term camps of cattle herders, who most probably came from the Nile Valley and made forays westwards to exploit the grasslands that flourished in the Sahara after the summer rains. After about 6200 BC, organized villages became established, with rows of houses and storage pits, and several sites had large, deep, walk-in wells. Cattle were still herded, although most meat was obtained by hunting gazelles and hares, and a considerable quantity of wild plant food was collected.

The Site of Nabta Playa

Plant food remains have been recovered from several sites dating to between 7000 BC and 5400 BC, the most extensive collections coming from houses and pits at a site found partly buried under silt and clay at Nabta Playa, one of the largest erosional basins in the Sahara, about 100 kilometers (60 miles) west of Abu Simbel. With the onset of rains, temporary lakes, known as playas, would form in these basins.

At Nabta Playa, there are traces of hearths on the floors of the houses, and small hemispherical depressions, or potholes, had also been dug in the floors. Half of one house alone had at least 74 such potholes. Brown, ashy sediments had piled up around the rims of some of the potholes, and this sediment was rich in plant remains. Probably, containers of food had been placed in the potholes, and hot ash (the brown sediment) piled up around them in order to cook the food. The contents had sometimes boiled over or fallen into the ash, eventually carbonizing and thus being preserved.

A wide range of plants has been identified, the collection being dominated by *Zizyphus* stones, grass grains, legume seeds, and what appear to be seeds of the mustard and caper families. (*Zizyphus* fruits grow on a small tree or bush and are still eaten today in Egypt and elsewhere in North Africa.) Clearly, the local vegetation was varied and, in some seasons, fairly luxuriant. Sedges and some grasses that favor wet habitats grew around the lake; a more restricted range of vegetation, including *Zizyphus* trees and perennial grasses, grew where surface or ground water was available for most of the year; and annual grasses developed after the summer rains.

All the plants in the collection are members of the natural sub-desertic (also known as the Sahelian) flora. The sorghums and millets are morphologically wild, but sorghum and millet were probably first cultivated in the African Sahelian zone. Chemical comparisons with modern wild and domestic sorghums suggest that the Nabta sorghum may have been cultivated.

A Wide Variety of Plants

Certain plant varieties were found to be associated with particular potholes. Some potholes yielded predominantly legumes (sometimes one variety, sometimes several); some yielded grasses (including sorghums and millets); some crucifers, cucurbits, sedges, or varieties of borage; some *Zizyphus* fruits; and some yielded mixtures in differing proportions. Altogether, the people of Nabta were collecting and eating at least 44 different kinds of plants.

The fact that specific plant food remains were found in individual potholes, together with the large number of potholes, suggests that each hole was probably used only once or, in some instances, several times. Probably, the food remains result from a series of very short stays of a few weeks, or even a few days. These discoveries have shown, in some detail, the way in which Neolithic plant gatherers exploited the Holocene environment in the Egyptian Sahara, how they used what was seasonally available, what they chose to eat from what was available, and the ways in which they combined various plant foods.

◄● A trench cut through the Early Neolithic site at Nabta Playa exposed several house floors and large storage pits.

RICHARD G. KLEIN

⚉ The mouth of Die Kelders Cave, on the Indian Ocean, about 120 kilometers (75 miles) southeast of Cape Town. The Later Stone Age deposits at this cave show that pottery and sheep herding reached the southern tip of Africa between the first and fourth centuries AD. The herders continued to hunt and gather extensively, and they made essentially the same kinds of stone and bone artifacts as their hunter-gatherer predecessors.

DAVID PHILLIPSON

⚉ The pastoral Khoikhoi people of southwestern Africa made pots like this, the inset lugs serving as handles. The history of these people can be traced to at least AD 400, when sheep and cattle herders with characteristic Khoikhoi pottery spread widely along the western and southern coasts of the Cape Province of South Africa.

☞ A female bushbuck (*Tragelaphus scriptus*) in Hwange National Park, Zimbabwe. The appearance of bones of this and other forest-dwelling species at cave sites in southern Africa at the end of the last Ice Age reflects a considerable change in vegetation and the food supply available to humans.

Southern Africa: The Last Hunter-gatherers

People in southern Africa continued an exclusively hunting-gathering way of life for much longer than anywhere else on the continent. While herders or mixed farmers were widely established in North Africa by 5000 BC and in East (and probably West) Africa by 2500 BC, herding and mixed farming did not appear in southern Africa until between the beginning of the first century AD and AD 200. At this time, Iron Age mixed farmers swept rapidly southwards through the moister eastern third of southern Africa, replacing or absorbing Stone Age hunter-gatherers. At much the same time, Stone Age pastoralists, with their herds of sheep and cattle, spread through the western and southern coastal regions, where summer rainfall was inadequate for indigenous Iron Age crops such as sorghum and millet.

These pastoralists used pottery, but no iron or other metals, and both physically and culturally (as reflected by the types of artifacts they made) they resembled their hunter-gatherer predecessors more than they did their Iron Age contemporaries, continuing to rely heavily on hunting and gathering. While they probably spread in response to the Iron Age diaspora, they may have absorbed rather than replaced many previous hunter-gatherers, and some hunter-gatherers may simply have grafted herding onto their established way of life.

This was the situation that prevailed in southern Africa at the time of European contact, which began with Bartholomeu Diaz's epoch-making voyage around the Cape of Good Hope from AD 1487 to AD 1488. Subsequent European travelers and explorers found Stone Age pastoralists, whom they called "Hottentots" or Khoikhoi, in the south and west; Bantu-speaking, Iron Age

mixed farmers in the east; and surviving bands of hunter-gatherers, whom they called "Bushmen" or San, in the remote mountains and the very dry regions of the interior—and assumed it had always been thus.

The Stone Age of southern Africa is unique not only because it lasted so long, but also because we are able to interpret archaeological finds in the light of historical records going back to the end of the fifteenth century. The observations of early Europeans have proved useful in deducing the functions of many types of artifacts found in prehistoric sites throughout Africa. They have also provided a record of practices, such as the collection of particular plants and insects, that were probably important in prehistoric times but that would be difficult, if not impossible, to infer from the archae-ological record. In addition, a long tradition of archaeological research in southern Africa, beginning in the 1860s, combined with the presence of many rich sites, has resulted in an unusually detailed record of interrelated cultural and environmental change from 10,000 BC to the present.

Nowhere did the climatic and environmental changes that occurred at the end of the last Ice Age affect human populations more than in southern Africa, where broad expanses of coastal plain were drowned by the rising sea, and large areas that had been open grassland were transformed into bush and forest. One result of the changing coastline was that caves that had previously been up to 80 kilometers (50 miles) from the sea were now within walking distance of it. Reflecting this change in the food supply, these cave sites have yielded abundant remains of shellfish, fish, seals, and sea birds in addition to the bones of antelopes, tortoises, and other terrestrial game. Reflecting the change in the vegetation, grassland creatures such as wildebeest, bontebok, hartebeest, springbok, wart hog, and zebra were replaced by bush or forest species such as bushbuck, bushpig, and a type of small antelope known as the gray duiker.

The extent and relative speed of the change in vegetation may partly explain why some grassland species—including a huge, long-horned buffalo

ANTHONY BANNISTER/NHPA

(*Pelorovis antiquus*), a giant relative of the wildebeest and hartebeest (*Megalotragus priscus*), and a comparably large species of zebra (*Equus capensis*)— apparently disappeared from southern Africa around that time. This cannot be the sole explanation, however, since the same species survived a similar change during the transition from the previous glaciation to the last interglacial period, about 130,000 years ago. The explanation is probably to be found in the kind of hunter-gatherers who were present in 10,000 BC. These were so-called Later Stone Age people, who replaced Middle Stone Age populations between 50,000 and 40,000 years ago. It was Middle Stone

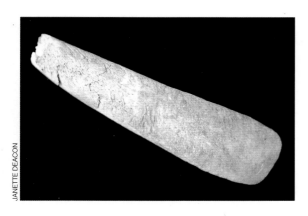

Age people who occupied southern Africa 130,000 years ago. Unlike their Later Stone Age successors, they do not seem to have used bone, ivory, or shell to make artifacts, and produced no known art or personal ornaments. They made a small range of stone artifacts, but none of the microlithic items for which Later Stone Age peoples are justly famous. What is perhaps most significant, they did not make any bone or stone objects that could be associated with the use of bows and arrows, such as are found in Later Stone Age sites from at least 10,000 BC.

Using the bow and arrow, Later Stone Age people were able to kill dangerous game, such as buffalo and wild pigs, far more often than their Middle Stone Age predecessors. With other advances in technology, such as bone gorges (double-pointed bone slivers the size of a toothpick, which could be baited and tied to a line) and net sinkers, they also became the first people to fish and hunt fowl on a large scale. This is probably why Later Stone Age populations were much larger and denser than their predecessors, as shown by the fact that Later Stone Age sites are much more numerous per unit of time, and by the small average size of the tortoises and shellfish they contain. The much larger size of these species in Middle Stone Age sites almost certainly indicates that Middle Stone Age people exploited them much less intensively, probably because there were fewer people at this time. Considering all the available information, it seems probable that Later Stone Age hunters contributed to the extinction of some prominent big-game species simply by continuing to hunt big game at a time when the game supply was rapidly being depleted by environmental changes.

☝ These fragments of ostrich eggshell decorated with incised patterns, from the Later Stone Age culture known as Robberg, in South Africa, are between 14,000 and 12,000 years old. The largest is just over a centimeter (half an inch) wide.
JANETTE DEACON

☜ A polished bone tool about 15 centimeters (6 inches) long, from the Albany culture in the southern part of Cape Province, South Africa, dating to about 8000 BC.

♀ These bone gorges made by people of the Albany culture, dating to about 8000 BC, were possibly used for fishing. Consisting of slivers of bone, polished and pointed at both ends, they are 2 to 3 centimeters (about 1 inch) long.

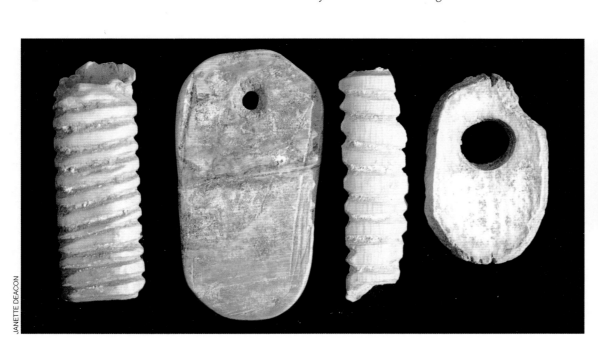

☜ Also made by the Albany people, these two hollow bone tubes with spiral grooving and the two flat bone pendants date to between 9000 BC and 7000 BC. The larger pendant is about 2.5 centimeters (1 inch) long.

⊕ These ornaments made from seashells, dating from about 3000 BC, are from the Wilton culture, which widely replaced the Albany culture between 7000 BC and 6000 BC.
JANETTE DEACON

⚲ Stone blades such as this, about 1 centimeter (half an inch) long, were blunted, or "backed", along the curved edge and sharp along the straight edge. They were made in small numbers by the Robberg people, from 18,000 to 12,000 years ago, and in larger quantities by the Wilton people, between 5000 BC and 2000 BC. They were hafted for use as arrowheads and for cutting purposes.
JANETTE DEACON

⚲ These ostrich eggshell "buttons", about 1 centimeter (half an inch) across, were made by people of the Wilton culture about the first century AD.

The Later Stone Age people who occupied much of southern Africa in 10,000 BC are known as the Robberg people, after a locality on the south central (Indian Ocean) coast where their artifacts and food debris have been especially well described. At that time, or shortly afterwards, the Robberg culture was replaced by the Albany culture (also known as the Oakhurst, or Smithfield A, culture). Unlike their Robberg predecessors, Albany people seem to have made few, if any, microlithic tools. They did, however, make an unusual range of well-crafted bone artifacts, which may have been better suited to hunting and gathering in the bushier environments that developed in the postglacial period.

Between 7000 BC and 6000 BC, the Albany culture was widely replaced by the most famous of all Later Stone Age cultures in southern Africa—the Wilton, named after a site in the eastern part of Cape Province, in South Africa. Wilton people manufactured large numbers of tiny convex stone scrapers and crescents (also called segments), the latter backed along the thick edge, together with larger, less formal, flaked stone tools; upper and lower grindstones; bored stones that appear to be digging-stick weights; points, awls, and other standardized bone artifacts; and a range of pendants, beads, and other objects that were probably ornaments.

The surviving food debris consists mainly of bones of small antelopes, hyraxes, tortoises, and other ground game, but at sites where conditions favor preservation, large numbers of plant remains have also been recovered. The most conspicuous plant species are members of the iris family, which the people of this region were noted to have been exploiting heavily at the time of European contact. Taken together with such evidence from the historical record, the plant remains at Wilton sites serve as a potent reminder that archaeologists have sometimes exaggerated the importance of hunting versus gathering in prehistoric times, simply because animal bones are more commonly preserved than plant tissues. In fact, it is likely that plants formed a major, possibly the predominant, part of the diet of all prehistoric hunter-gatherers in Africa, including people such as the Robberg, whose sites are especially rich in the bones of big-game animals.

Wilton people were living in southern Africa when Iron Age mixed farmers seized the eastern

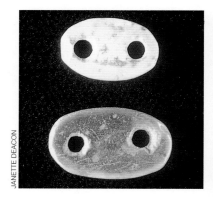

⊕ Small stone scrapers were hafted on bone or wooden handles by means of mastic and used to work skins. They are frequently found in Wilton sites, between 5000 BC and the first century AD.

JANETTE DEACON

ANTHONY BANNISTER/NHPA

third of this region and Stone Age pastoralists spread along its western and southern coasts between the beginning of the first century AD and AD 200. Iron Age mixed farming all but destroyed Wilton-style hunting and gathering, whereas the herding of cattle and sheep supplemented rather than replaced this way of life.

Pastoralism succeeded because it supported larger human populations than pure hunting and gathering, but southern African pastoralists continued to hunt and forage on a large scale, and their sites are commonly dominated by the bones of indigenous animals. In part, these people planned their movements to take advantage of the seasonal availability of different plants and animals. Their thriving culture was noted by early European visitors, and it was primarily to trade European goods for local sheep and cattle (to provision passing ships) that the Dutch East India Company established the first permanent European settlement in southern Africa, at what is now Cape Town, in 1652.

Unfortunately, this settlement rapidly changed from a trading post to a staging point for European colonists who brought crops such as wheat and barley that could grow where only

pastoralism had been practicable before, and who also introduced firearms and epidemic diseases that rapidly reduced the native population. The indigenous pastoralist culture disintegrated, and had all but ceased to exist by 1750. Individual pastoralists survived, but only as clients or servants of the Europeans, and the native pastoralist languages were largely lost. By 1850, European incursions into the southern African interior had similarly eradicated or displaced the last surviving Stone Age hunter-gatherers. People continued the hunting-gathering way of life in the Kalahari Desert and in some other marginal environments, but came increasingly to rely on introduced Iron Age or European technology for their subsistence, and they have shown a remarkable willingness to grow crops or tend animals when circumstances permit. Very likely, the people of this region have combined food production with hunting and gathering for various periods over the centuries, and it now seems unlikely that any southern African people known from recent times can be regarded as largely unaltered survivors of the hunting-gathering populations that dominated the subcontinent until 2,000 years ago.

⬧ These !Kung Bushmen are cutting up tsama melons, a wild species of gourd which is an important staple for many Kalahari hunter-gatherers.

F. JACKSON/ROBERT HARDING PICTURE LIBRARY

⬧ People of the Peuhl tribe, from the Falingé region, in Niger, herding their long-horned cattle. Cattle were an important symbol of wealth among African Iron Age people, and probably also among many of their prehistoric Stone Age predecessors.

Art of the African Stone Age

No summary of African Stone Age prehistory from 10,000 BC would be complete without some mention of the art. People were clearly creating art, both portable and mural, long before that time. Painted rock slabs from excavation levels dated between 27,500 and 19,500 years ago at Apollo II Cave, in Namibia, may be the oldest paintings so far found anywhere in the world. A few later African cave sites, all more recent than 10,000 BC, have yielded painted or engraved stones buried in the ground, but throughout Africa, the art that is most abundant and most famous is in the form of paintings and engravings on exposed rock surfaces. In general, this rock art cannot be reliably dated, but the very fact that it has survived despite the harsh climatic conditions suggests that most of it is no more than a few thousand years old. Some, however—most probably the paintings of elephants, giraffes, and other sub-Saharan species on Saharan rock surfaces—may be much older.

While the style or subject matter of some paintings implies that the artists were Iron Age people, many others would appear to have been painted by Stone Age pastoralists or hunter-gatherers. It seems reasonable to assume that paintings showing herders and cattle were produced mainly by pastoralists, while many paintings depicting wild species only were probably produced by hunter-gatherers. Paintings with pastoralist themes are relatively much more common in North Africa than in southern Africa, where pastoralism appeared far later. In some remote mountain ranges of southern Africa, there are paintings depicting domestic horses, wagons, and even a mid-seventeenth-century galleon. Stylistically, these paintings resemble the paintings that portray indigenous animals or people, but their subject matter indicates a date between the seventeenth and mid-nineteenth centuries AD. The artists must have been among the last African Stone Age people to practice their age-old craft.

What motivated people to produce rock art has been a matter of intense debate among archaeologists and cultural historians, and no agreement is in sight. At different times and places, the art may have functioned to enhance hunting or herding success, to celebrate rites of passage (births, deaths, or the transition to adulthood), or to mark the territories of particular groups. Much of it, particularly in southern Africa, may have been produced by folk-doctors, or shamans, as they attempted to reproduce their experiences when in a state of trance. Based on what is known of such communities in historic times, perhaps the only firm conclusion that can be drawn is that little of the art was produced for its own sake. Almost certainly, most of it was motivated by social, economic, or religious concerns that varied somewhat from culture to culture. But even if the purpose of the art remains poorly understood, its aesthetic appeal is enduring, and it is an especially poignant reminder of Africa's Stone Age past.

Rock engravings of animals at Twyfelfontein, in Namibia.
MARY JELLIFFE/ANCIENT ART & ARCHITECTURE COLLECTION

The Stone Age hunter-pastoralists who occupied the Sahara between 8000 BC and 3000 BC often painted or engraved on exposed rock surfaces. An archer poised on a sandstone surface in Tassili n'Ajjer, in present-day Libya, is a superb example.

Herds of animals on a rock wall in Tassili n'Ajjer, central Sahara.
JAMES WELLARD/SONIA HALLIDAY PHOTOGRAPHS

ROCK ART IN THE CENTRAL SAHARA

GÖRAN BURENHULT

GÖRAN BURENHULT

☝ The Stone Age *abri* settlement and rock art site of Iheren. The strange rock formations of the isolated Iherir Plateau, in the mountain massif of Tassili n'Ajjer, southeastern Algeria, shelter some of the Sahara's most exquisite art treasures.

♀ The Iheren frieze, on the Iherir Plateau, includes a number of vivid scenes, the most spectacular being the portrayal of a lion hunt. With their spears raised, three men with elaborate hairstyles or wigs approach a lion that has attacked a sheep.

T HE HEAT VIBRATES in the air between the black walls of rock, but everything is peaceful and silent—relentlessly silent. The sun's dazzling rays shine from a cloudless sky over the ocean of sand and the mountain formations, and the shadows become short and as black as night. Not a green shoot can be seen, and no breath of wind cools the dry landscape. It is hard to imagine that anything has ever been able to live here, least of all human beings.

Yet the rocks swarm with life. If you crawl into the shade under a rock shelter and let your eyes become accustomed to the darkness, you will encounter an amazing world made up of thousands of vivid images of human beings and animals. This treasure-trove of pictures, thousands of years old, lies in the heart of the Sahara, 10 days' journey from the Mediterranean coast, in a four-wheel drive, through an expanse of sterile desert that was once a region of streaming water and lush vegetation.

Rivers and Lakes

Traces of these very different climatic conditions are many and obvious. Innumerable wadis (dry watercourses) run from the mountain regions out towards the plains that were once dotted with lakes, on whose shores lived many varieties of plants and animals. In most valleys, the vegetation consisted mainly of cedars, cypresses, oaks, and walnut trees, and there were also tamarisks and acacias—species that still grow in the mountain regions of the central Sahara, particularly in Tassili n'Ajjer.

Between 9000 BC and 3000 BC, the Sahara was a very favorable place to live, both for food producers and hunter-gatherers, and there is hardly a place in the region that does not bear traces of their activities. Pottery and stone tools, grinding stones, hearths, graves, and rock art are found everywhere, and as humus does not form in the desert, these Stone Age relics are often exposed on the surface.

The earliest art may date to the final stage of the Upper Paleolithic period, before 9000 BC, when big-game hunters made monumental rock carvings in most mountain regions of the Sahara. Their carvings depict a great variety of plants and animals that disappeared from the area long ago: antelopes, buffalos, giraffes, elephants, lions, and hippopotamuses. This period was once named the Bubalus period, after the now-extinct giant buffalo, *Bubalus antiquus*, which is often featured in these carvings.

About 8000 BC, paintings—again, often very large—began to appear on rocks. The bearers of this art tradition were mainly negroid hunter-gatherers, but common finds of grinding stones show that they were becoming increasingly dependent on the gathering of wild seeds. About this time, pottery was first made in the central parts of the present-day desert area.

A Wealth of Detail

It seems likely that there was a food crisis during a period of drought about 6000 BC, which may have led to the domestication of indigenous

GÖRAN BURENHULT

GORAN BURENHULT

animals. The dark-skinned African herders of the region were the descendants of earlier hunter-gatherers, and their cattle were short-horned. At a later stage, long-horned cattle were introduced by light-skinned immigrants from the east, people who today are found in the Sudan and Ethiopia. At the same time, sheep and goat herders were spreading southwards from the Mediterranean coastal areas.

The rock art these herders produced, between 6000 BC and 2000 BC, represents the high point of this art form in the Sahara. The rocks are covered with scenes of remarkable liveliness that abound in humans and animals rendered in splendid colors. The humans are always depicted in action, and often in groups: hunting, fighting,

dancing, or riding cattle. The paintings are extremely elegant, and rich in such details as masks, wigs, costumes, body decorations, and tattoos.

From about 2000 BC, the increasingly dry climate of the Sahara gradually drove out these cattle herders. Today, these pastoral cultures are found mainly in the southerly border areas of the Sahara: the Sudan, Chad, Niger, Mali, and Burkina Fasso. But in the intervening period, there were two more distinct phases of rock art.

Between 1500 BC and 100 BC, horses were used for transport through the Sahara, and along the routes they followed are found paintings from this period depicting mounted riders and two-wheeled carts.

The final period of rock art, which began about 100 BC and is characterized by early Tuareg script and images of camels, shows the desert as it is today. Overgrazing, first by cattle and then by goats and sheep, accelerated the natural process of desertification, and now all that is left to bear witness to a period of teeming life are the grinding stones that lie exposed on the surface, amid the silence and the trembling heat, and the rock picture galleries with their multitude of vivid images.

⤴ A group of giraffes painted on a rock wall in the central part of the settlement of Tin Abaniora, on the Iherir Plateau, Tassili n'Ajjer.

GORAN BURENHULT

⤵ This elegant portrayal of a dancing male figure with elaborate body painting is at the site of Tadjelamin. The other two images, one of which represents a female figure dressed in a puffy robe, may be part of the same dance scene.

STONE AGE HUNTER-GATHERERS AND FARMERS IN EUROPE

1 0 , 0 0 0   B C   —   3 0 0 0   B C

From Forager to Food Producer

PETER ROWLEY-CONWY

THE LAST ICE AGE reached its peak about 18,000 years ago. At this time, ice sheets covered most of Britain and Scandinavia, the Alps, the Pyrenees, and many smaller mountain ranges throughout Europe. Much of the rest of Europe, away from the Mediterranean, was covered by treeless tundra vegetation. The most common large animal in these tundra regions was the reindeer, but red deer, aurochs (wild cattle), bison, and horses were also to be found, in smaller numbers. Humans, during this period, were largely confined to southwestern France, the Italian and Iberian peninsulas, and parts of central and eastern Europe, away from the glaciers.

Some time after about 15,000 years ago, the climate began to grow warmer, culminating in a fairly warm spell before another, and final, period of intense cold set in 13,000 years ago. The end of the last Ice Age is put at 11,500 years ago, when temperatures rapidly increased to about their present levels.

◄◙ Skara Brae is an early farming village in the Orkney Islands, off northern Scotland. Shortly before 2500 BC, it was covered by a sand dune, which preserved most of the village intact.

◙ A bone comb found in the Late Mesolithic shell midden at Meilgård, in Denmark. Archaeologists will never be able to reconstruct such things as hairstyles, but finds of this sort suggest that hunter-gatherers who lived thousands of years ago had a similar interest in personal display to modern peoples.
NATIONAL MUSEUM OF DENMARK

⚱ This stone statue, carved by hunter-gatherers at Lepenski Vir, in Serbia, is one of the earliest pieces of monumental art known in Europe.
MARIJA GIMBUTAS

The most sensitive indicators of temperature we have are insects. Different species can tolerate different temperatures, and insects are able to migrate to newly habitable lands very rapidly after climatic changes, so their preserved remains are a good guide to climatic conditions of the past. In southern England, for example, insect remains dated to 11,500 years ago show that average July temperatures increased from 9 to 17 degrees Celsius (48 to 63 degrees Fahrenheit) in little more than a century. There have been climatic changes since, but none to compare with this.

Not surprisingly, the result of this global warming was massive ecological change. Trees spread north into the tundra—some much faster than others, as we know from studies of preserved pollen grains. (Trees emit huge numbers of pollen grains. These are preserved in waterlogged areas, and the plant family or species to which they belong can be identified under a microscope. As the layers build up, changing proportions of pollen provide a history of the vegetation.) The first postglacial forests of central and northern Europe were largely of birch, a species that originated north of the Alps and is a fast colonizer. Pine followed, then hazel, and finally the main forest trees—oak, ash, lime, and elm—which slowly spread northwards from their Italian and Iberian glacial refuges. Land mammals similarly moved north, reindeer migrating as far as Scandinavia, where they are still found today. Red deer and wild cattle became more numerous, and were joined by such true forest animals as elk (known as moose in North America), roe deer, and wild boar.

At the same time, another major change was taking place. When the last Ice Age was at its coldest, so much water was landlocked in the form of glaciers that the sea level was more than 100 meters (330 feet) lower than it is today. Ireland and Britain were joined to continental Europe, and much of the area now covered by the North Sea, the Bay of Biscay, the Adriatic, and seas in other parts of the world was dry land. As the glaciers melted, the sea level rose rapidly. This continued throughout the earlier part of the postglacial period, with the result that many low-lying areas were inundated. Britain, for example, was separated from Europe about 7500 BC.

This was the rapidly changing environment to which the inhabitants of Europe had to adapt. The period between the end of the Ice Age and the first appearance of farming in Europe is usually termed the Mesolithic. During this period, groups of people spread northwards into previously unoccupied areas, learning to cope with dramatically different conditions of life in terms of climate, vegetation, and resources.

New Sources of Evidence

Archaeologists will rarely admit to having enough evidence, but the Mesolithic period does have some advantages over preceding periods in terms of the amount of evidence that has survived. Like their predecessors, Mesolithic people were hunters and gatherers and made use of caves and open-air camp sites. But thanks to the warmer climate of Mesolithic times, two new sources of archaeological evidence have come down to us in the form of bog sites and shell middens. Each of these has added immensely to our understanding of the period.

Bog sites can preserve objects spectacularly well. Since the end of the Ice Age, many lakes have gradually filled up with peat, a type of soil formed by partly decomposed vegetation. Early people living on lake shores often threw their rubbish into the water, and as the peat built up

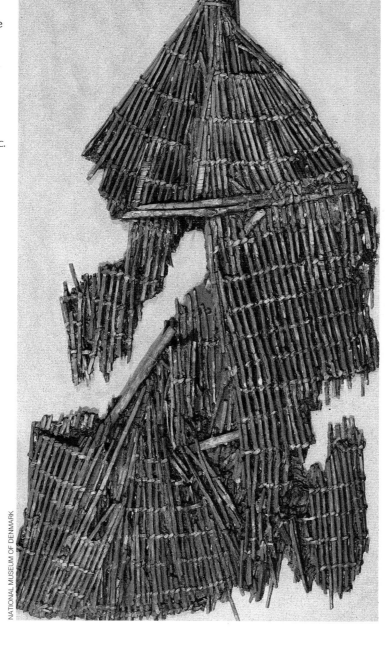

☞ Bog sites provide excellent conditions of preservation for otherwise perishable items, such as this fishtrap made of withies, which was lost by prehistoric fishers at Lille Knabstrup, in Denmark, some time between 4000 BC and 5000 BC.

NATIONAL MUSEUM OF DENMARK

and covered the rubbish, all kinds of objects were preserved in the wet, anoxic conditions. Without oxygen, the microbes that normally attack and destroy organic objects cannot survive. As a result, lake peats sometimes preserve a remarkable range of organic items that would otherwise long since have decomposed, such as bones, wooden tools, cordage of various sorts, and plant remains. Mesolithic people probably behaved in much the same way wherever they lived, but thanks to the preservative qualities of peat, we know more of the life of those who lived in these lakeside settlements than we do of those who lived elsewhere, where the only materials to survive are often flint tools.

Shell middens can tell us a great deal about early seashore settlements and how the people of these times exploited marine resources, including fish, shellfish, mammals, and birds. (See the feature *Shell Middens: The Rubbish Dumps of History*.) The first coastal settlements known in Europe date from the later Mesolithic period, about 5000 BC, by which time the sea had risen to near its present level. Any evidence of coastal occupation from earlier periods has, of course, long since been drowned by the rising seas.

The extent of coastal settlement during the earlier Mesolithic period has long been a matter of debate among archaeologists. In the middle of this century, many researchers believed that people did not occupy coastal areas to any significant extent until the Late Mesolithic period. At this time, deciduous forests, mainly of oak and lime, were widespread, and it was believed that these would have supported few game animals or edible plants, thus forcing people to make more use of coastal resources instead.

More recently, new evidence has emerged to suggest that people have always exploited coastal resources and also that game and plant foods were plentiful in the Late Mesolithic forests. First, Late Mesolithic sites are still being discovered in inland areas, some of which have yielded the bones of such game as red deer and wild boar. Secondly, seashells have been found in Early Mesolithic sites near the present-day coast in areas such as northern Spain, where the steeply sloping terrain shows that these sites would have been only a few kilometers inland during the late Ice Age and early postglacial period—not in large quantities, but enough to show that marine resources were being exploited at this time. This raises the intriguing possibility that Early Mesolithic shorelines lying many meters below the present-day sea level may still have shell middens on them. Perhaps one day it will be possible to locate and study them.

Life during the Mesolithic

Modern hunter-gatherers live in many different ways. Many, like the Bushmen of the Kalahari, are mobile, living in small groups and moving from camp to camp according to the availability of food. Such people have an intimate knowledge of their environment and monitor resources closely, showing great skill in the way they plan their movements so that food is available in all seasons of the year. Other groups, such as the Tsimshian and Tlingit people, who occupy the coast of British Columbia, live in a base camp all year, sending out hunting and fishing parties to satellite camps in appropriate seasons. This more sedentary way of life, of course, is possible only in areas where a variety of food resources is available in the immediate vicinity, and even these groups usually have to store food to get through the bad seasons. Other present-day groups of hunter-gatherers do both, staying put in the good seasons, and moving in the bad. This is perhaps the most common pattern.

⚭ Amber was used by hunter-gatherers for ornaments, such as this pendant from Holme, in Denmark.
NATIONAL MUSEUM OF DENMARK

Enough is known of the Mesolithic period in Europe to suggest a similar picture. Many of the known sites are small, indicating that they were temporary camp sites, and some are sufficiently well preserved to reveal quite a lot about the way their inhabitants lived. Finds of animal bones are particularly valuable in this respect, as they can indicate not only what people ate but, in many cases, in which season the prey was killed.

The bones of migratory species are one source of such evidence. Many European birds migrate; for example, the whooper swan (*Cygnus cygnus*)

⚭ At Ringkloster, in Denmark, Late Mesolithic people lived close to a lake shore. Little survives of their original settlement, but the rubbish they threw into the lake has been well preserved. The people hunted mainly red deer and wild boar, and trapped pine martens for their pelts. Bones of these three species are common finds, as are wooden artifacts and many other items.

SHELL MIDDENS: THE RUBBISH DUMPS OF HISTORY

PETER ROWLEY-CONWY

A midden is a rubbish dump, and a shell midden is exactly what the words imply: a mound consisting predominantly of the discarded shells of edible shellfish, along with other refuse. Accumulated over the years, these rubbish heaps mark sites of prehistoric human habitation.

There was nothing special about shell middens to the people responsible for them—rubbish would have been dumped at every camp site the group occupied, and if shellfish were eaten, their shells would have formed part of the rubbish. There is, therefore, no fundamental distinction between shell midden sites and any other type of site. The quantity of shells found in middens depends simply on how frequently shellfish were eaten.

This bulk is the result of one particular attribute of shellfish: what you throw away takes up more space than what you eat. One red deer supplies as many kilojoules (or calories) as about 50,000 oysters, but its butchered and broken remains, even if they were all preserved, would take up only a fraction of the space that the oyster shells would occupy. At camp sites where shellfish were an important part of the diet, middens can accordingly be very large. Some found in Europe are as much as 100 meters by 40 meters (330 feet by 130 feet) in area, and between 2 and 3 meters (6 and 10 feet) deep. Not surprisingly, these are by far the largest Mesolithic sites known, but shellfish probably formed a smaller part of Mesolithic people's diet than the huge bulk of shells might imply.

To archaeologists, shell middens are a virtual treasure trove of information. In the first place, they are relatively easy to find, both by virtue of their bulk and because they tend to be predictably strung out along the prehistoric shorelines from which the shellfish were collected. Secondly, the calcium

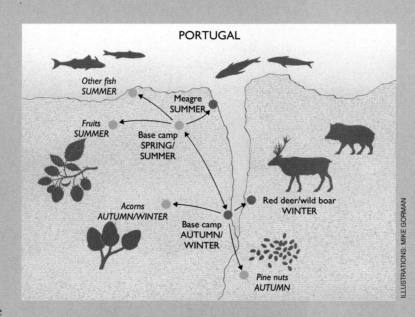

Generalized settlement patterns in Late Mesolithic Denmark and Portugal, based on the combined evidence from a number of separate areas. The foods obtained at each site and the season of occupation are shown. Normal text indicates settlement sites for which there is evidence. *Italics* indicate settlements that probably existed but for which we have no evidence.
● Settlements with shell middens   ● Settlements without shell middens

ILLUSTRATIONS: MIKE GORMAN

in the shells provides a nonacidic environment for all the other objects that ended up in the midden. As a result, organic items such as bones are preserved when they might otherwise not have been, and features such as cooking hearths and even dwellings and burials may also be well preserved within middens, built on the midden as it accumulated. In a sense, because of its volume and its preservative qualities,

a shell midden provides a three-dimensional view of a site that might otherwise consist only of a layer of charcoal and preserved flints 5 to 10 centimeters (2 to 4 inches) deep.

Shell middens can tell us a great deal about the people who accumulated them. The settlements at which they are found served various purposes. Two of the best-researched midden groups in

Europe come from the Late Mesolithic period of Denmark (the Ertebølle culture) and Portugal.

In Denmark, seasonality studies indicate that some of the settlements were occupied for most or all of the year. As is to be expected, these are usually the sites with the largest shell middens, and they are often in attractive sheltered locations on bays or estuaries. It appears that these were base camps occupied by at least some of the people for most of the time. Many smaller shell middens have also been found. Unlike the larger ones, they were occupied in particular seasons and usually have evidence of some specialized economic activity, such as hunting dolphins and porpoises.

When the evidence from various sites is combined, a general picture starts to emerge. During the winter, hunting parties headed inland, hunting deer and wild boar for their meat and animals such as pine martens for their pelts. Meanwhile, other groups stayed on the coast and hunted migrating sea mammals and birds, eating the shellfish that eventually formed the middens. In summer, fish was probably a major part of the diet. Because the central base camp was occupied all year, it is likely that food was brought in from the special-purpose camps, but such things are difficult to prove.

Research is less advanced in Portugal than in Denmark, but again, by combining the evidence from various areas, we are starting to get a different picture. Groups spent the winter at base camps near the inland ends of large estuaries, hunting deer and wild boar and supplementing their diet with shellfish. In spring and summer, people moved to camps nearer the open coast. As well as hunting large mammals, they caught rabbits, and they also set up fishing camps, a common catch being meagre (*Argyrosomus regius*—a large sea fish that comes inshore during the summer).

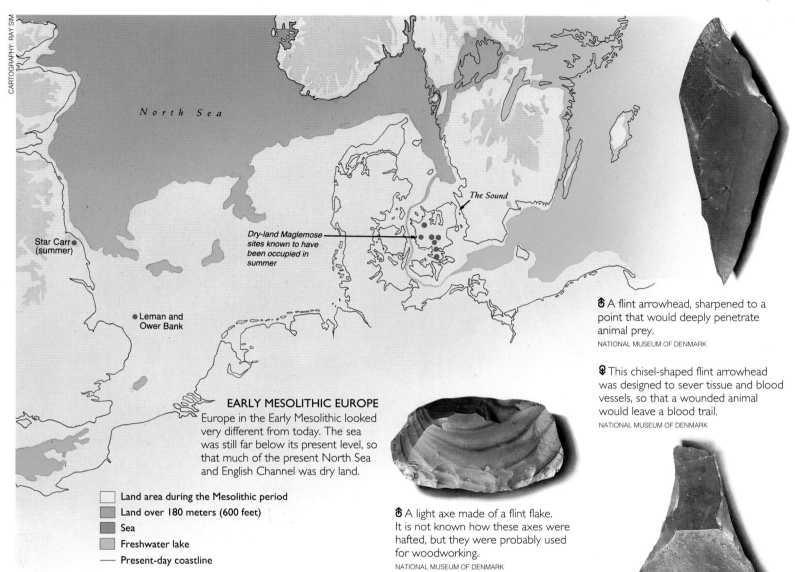

EARLY MESOLITHIC EUROPE
Europe in the Early Mesolithic looked very different from today. The sea was still far below its present level, so that much of the present North Sea and English Channel was dry land.

☐ Land area during the Mesolithic period
☐ Land over 180 meters (600 feet)
☐ Sea
☐ Freshwater lake
── Present-day coastline

⚱ A light axe made of a flint flake. It is not known how these axes were hafted, but they were probably used for woodworking.
NATIONAL MUSEUM OF DENMARK

⚱ A flint arrowhead, sharpened to a point that would deeply penetrate animal prey.
NATIONAL MUSEUM OF DENMARK

⚱ This chisel-shaped flint arrowhead was designed to sever tissue and blood vessels, so that a wounded animal would leave a blood trail.
NATIONAL MUSEUM OF DENMARK

⚱ Heavy axes made of flint, such as this specimen, were probably used by hunter-gatherers to make dugout canoes and other large wooden items.
NATIONAL MUSEUM OF DENMARK

nests in Finland, but spends the winter around the western Baltic and North Sea. Many bones of these swans have been found at the Late Mesolithic sites of Aggersund and Sølager, in Denmark, indicating that these sites must have been occupied in winter. Fish can provide similar evidence: the Late Mesolithic shell midden of Arapouco, in Portugal, contains many bones of fish that come inshore only during the summer and must, therefore, have been eaten then. The bones of migratory marine mammals such as seals and porpoises, and of the various land mammals that sometimes migrated in postglacial Europe, can tell a similar story.

But in most of Europe, large land mammals did not migrate over long distances, and the mere presence of their remains does not tell us when they were hunted. In these cases, archaeologists need to call upon more specialized techniques. If the jaws of young animals are found among the remains, we can work out fairly accurately from their stage of tooth development how old the animals were when they were killed. Modern red deer, for example, lose their milk teeth at about 24 to 26 months of age, and the same probably

applied to the red deer of Mesolithic times. If they were born in June, like their modern counterparts, a deer that had lost its milk teeth and was developing adult teeth in their place would have been killed some time during June, July, or August, when it was 24 to 26 months old.

When a number of sites are found in a region, we can start to see the overall pattern of settlement. The classic British bog site of Star Carr, on England's eastern coast, has yielded jaws of young red deer, roe deer, and elk, indicating that this Early Mesolithic site was a summer camp. Across the North Sea from Star Carr, Denmark has many bog sites that have preserved evidence of the so-called Maglemose culture. (The Danish place name Maglemose means "great bog".) These sites also date from the Early Mesolithic period, although from a little later than Star Carr, and several have yielded enough jawbones to indicate that they, too, were occupied in summer.

So where did these people spend the winter? While many other sites have been found, they have not yielded enough animal bones for firm conclusions to be drawn. Some of these may have been winter settlements, but there is another

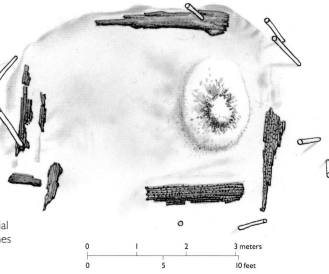

⚑ At Lepenski Vir, on the River Danube, in Serbia, archaeologists have excavated the remains of many trapeze-shaped houses. The reconstruction above shows the most likely method of construction. The inset plan shows the layout of the village. People would have been encouraged to settle here because of the abundant fish in the river.
ILLUSTRATION: RAY SIM

☞ Remains of a hut floor at the Early Mesolithic bog site of Ulkestrup, in Denmark. The outer edges of the floor were formed by large split planks, and the interior by a layer of small twigs. Thin poles formed the walls and roof. Only a small number of poles have survived, but they would have been more numerous and much longer, and probably supported a single ridgepole. No trace of any covering material has survived, but reeds and rushes were most likely used as thatch.
ILLUSTRATION: RAY SIM

possible explanation. At this time, the sea was still far below its present level: the modern Baltic Sea was a freshwater lake, drained by rivers into the North Sea across lowlands that are now flooded. If people had wintered near these rivers, their camp sites would now be under water, and this would explain why there are no known sites indicating winter occupation. While far from conclusive, other evidence also points to this.

Flint artifacts of the Maglemose type have been recovered by divers in The Sound (the

strait between Denmark and Sweden) at depths of between 5 and 23 meters (16 and 75 feet). A more remarkable find is that of an antler point, probably a spearhead, picked up by chance in a trawl net from a depth of 39 meters (128 feet) on the Leman and Ower Bank, off East Anglia. Similar to finds from Star Carr, it dates from the same period. We do not, of course, know whether these submarine finds come from winter settlements, but they may. The only thing we know for certain is how little we know of coastal life during the Early Mesolithic period, given that so much of the Maglemose shorelines have now been lost.

If we compare what is known of the Early Mesolithic Maglemose culture with finds from a Late Mesolithic Danish culture (which extended to southern Sweden) called the Ertebølle, after a major shell midden, we find considerable differences. As we have seen, all the surviving evidence of Maglemose times points to seasonal camps. By the Late Mesolithic, a different pattern had emerged in these coastal areas, and it is not difficult to see why. At this time, the sea had risen

Central house

Meeting place

River Danube

close to its present level, and marine resources, including fish, shellfish, seals, and waterbirds, would have become more plentiful, making it attractive for people to settle there all year round. With food in ready supply, they clearly had no need to move camp. And because the sea level has changed little from that time, the shell middens that bear witness to this change in the way of life—unlike so much of the evidence from Maglemose times—have been preserved.

Mesolithic Dwellings

Although many Mesolithic sites are known, traces of dwellings are rare. Many of the structures would have been lightweight and temporary, perhaps inhabited for only a single visit to a camp site, and little would remain after thousands of years. Sometimes traces of postholes survive, providing a ground plan, although it is often difficult to be sure what is a posthole and what is not. If a structure was altered or reconstructed during subsequent visits, the result can be very difficult to interpret. Even less is known about the sides and roofs of such dwellings, so any reconstruction can be nothing more than a "best guess".

When the remains of more than one structure are found at a site, the first question that arises is whether all the dwellings were occupied at once. If three huts are found next to each other, for example, this could indicate that three families lived there at the same time. Alternatively, one

family might have built a new hut every few years, but not on exactly the same spot. Dating methods such as radiocarbon are not precise enough to tell us which is the case. But if flint tools are found, together with the waste pieces that result from working flint, they can provide a vital clue. If the pieces found within a single hut can be fitted back together to form a single nodule, then that nodule was clearly worked there. If, on the other hand, pieces from two huts fit together, both huts must have been in use at the same time.

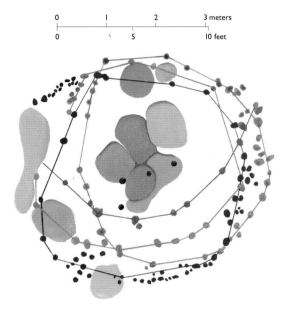

⚊ The angle of the postholes at Mount Sandel shows that the posts leaned inwards, suggesting that long, thin poles may have been bent over to form a hooped structure—although other interpretations are also possible.
ILLUSTRATION: RAY SIM

⚊ At Mount Sandel, huts were sometimes rebuilt several times, as the overlapping circles of postholes reveal. In the center lay several hearths, one belonging to each building phase.
ILLUSTRATION: RAY SIM

⚊ Mount Sandel, on the Bann River, in Northern Ireland, was an Early Mesolithic settlement, where people caught (and probably smoked) salmon, hunted wild boar, and collected hazel nuts. Animal skins may have been used to cover the huts, but no trace of this survives.
ILLUSTRATION: RAY SIM

☝ Bone fishhooks recovered from Early Mesolithic sites in Denmark are well made. At lakeside sites, bones of pike and other fish are very common, indicating that fish were an important source of food for the inhabitants.

Mesolithic Tools and Weapons

Mesolithic people used a wide variety of tools and other equipment, but the characteristic stone tool of this period is the microlith—the word simply meaning "small stone". Microliths are commonly found, and come in many types. They were apparently mass-produced as components of composite tools, including weapons, and are usually assumed to have been mounted as tips and barbs on arrows and spears. While they have occasionally been found still in position on hunting weapons, they may well have been used for a range of other purposes. They have been found mounted as sickle blade segments in Southwest Asia, but such tools are not known from the European Mesolithic.

Judging by the large numbers of animal bones found at well-preserved sites, these weapons must have been very effective. Mesolithic people were evidently capable of killing such dangerous quarry as wild boar and aurochs. A few bows from this period have been preserved in bog sites, including impressive specimens from Tybrind Vig, a Late Mesolithic site in Denmark, made of elm and measuring 160 centimeters (5 feet, 3 inches). The first evidence of domestic dogs dates from this period, and men armed with powerful bows and accompanied by dogs to track wounded animals would have been very effective hunters.

Other types of flint tools from this period include scrapers and burins for working wood, bone, and hide; larger blades, used as knives; and heavier items, such as axes and adzes. Bone and antler were also fashioned into a wide variety of tools. Being long, straight, and hard, cannon bones from the lower limbs of red deer and elk were often used, sometimes as mounts for microliths to form spearheads or daggers. Although wood must have been commonly used, wooden artifacts rarely survive, except in bog sites. These have sometimes

↦ Arrowheads are occasionally found still attached to parts of the arrow shaft. Sometimes, two microliths were used, one forming the tip and one the barb. Chisel-ended arrows are known from the Late Mesolithic period of Denmark. Bolt-headed arrows, carved entirely from a single piece of wood, were used to stun or kill small animals, so that their fur would not be damaged by the impact.

ILLUSTRATIONS: RAY SIM

yielded quite large items, such as bows. Further finds of paddles, some of them beautifully decorated, and, occasionally, of canoes, show that water transport and water resources were important in Mesolithic times, while a sledge runner recovered from the bog site of Sarnate, in Latvia, has given us a rare glimpse of another early form of transport.

Precious little cordage has survived. The German bog site of Friesack, not far from Berlin, has yielded many fragments of netting, along with a float made of birch bark, strongly suggesting that these fragments come not from a dip net on a handle but from something much larger. This was certainly the case with a find from the bog site of Antrea, in Karelia, where a collection of net fragments, floats, and sinkers indicate a net that hung vertically in the water and was about 30 meters (100 feet) long. The nets from both these sites were made of bast (the inner bark of certain trees). Plaiting and basketry must also have been common, but finds are rare. Fish traps of plaited twigs have occasionally been found—probably lost during use in streams and lakes, and preserved as sediments built up around them.

The hunting of land mammals leaves many traces in the archaeological record, in the form of animal bones and weapons and other technology. Fishing and related activities leave far fewer traces, although occasional finds of major pieces of equipment, such as boats and nets, indicate that they were equally or more important in some areas.

The third main food source is even less visible in archaeological terms: hardly any evidence of plant foods has come down to us, although early people must have eaten many types of fruits, nuts, roots, and tubers, and in considerable quantities. Vegetable matter survives only if charred or continuously waterlogged in anoxic conditions, and tools and other equipment can rarely be shown unequivocally to have been used to collect or process plants, although studies of wear patterns and organic residues on the edges of tools

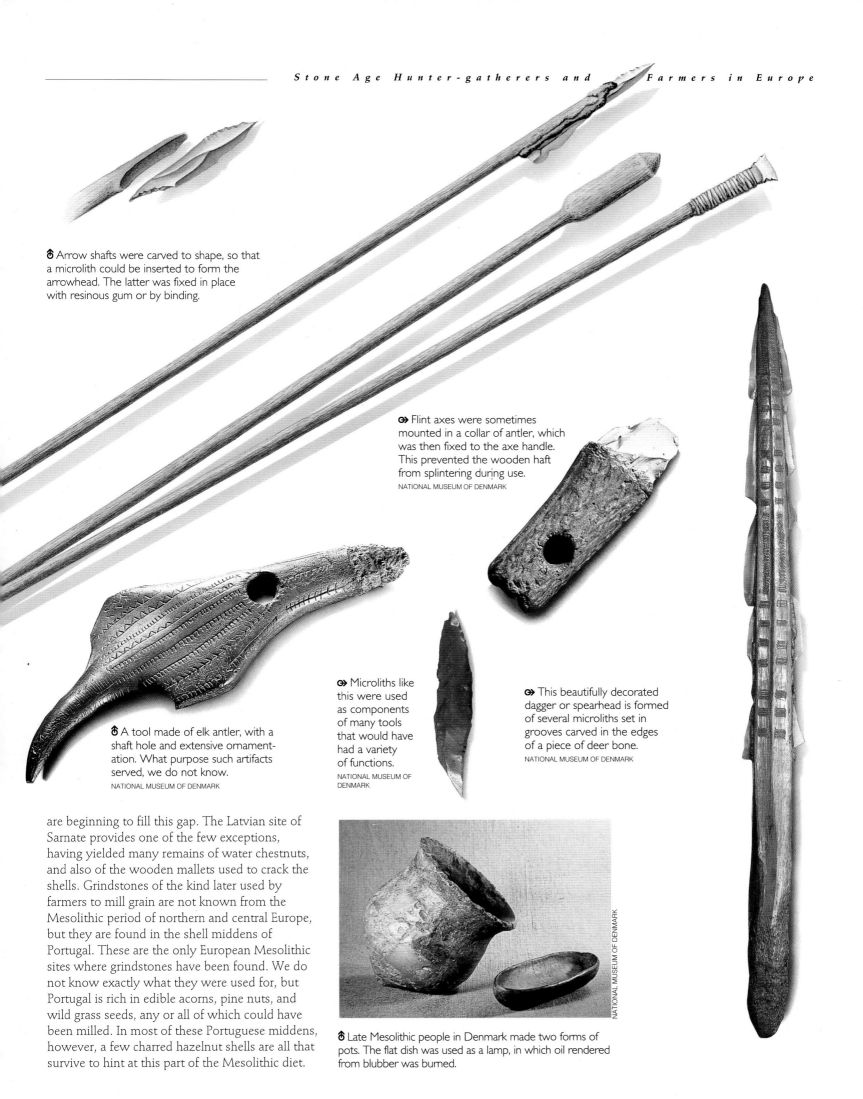

☝ Arrow shafts were carved to shape, so that a microlith could be inserted to form the arrowhead. The latter was fixed in place with resinous gum or by binding.

☞ Flint axes were sometimes mounted in a collar of antler, which was then fixed to the axe handle. This prevented the wooden haft from splintering during use.
NATIONAL MUSEUM OF DENMARK

☝ A tool made of elk antler, with a shaft hole and extensive ornamentation. What purpose such artifacts served, we do not know.
NATIONAL MUSEUM OF DENMARK

☞ Microliths like this were used as components of many tools that would have had a variety of functions.
NATIONAL MUSEUM OF DENMARK

☞ This beautifully decorated dagger or spearhead is formed of several microliths set in grooves carved in the edges of a piece of deer bone.
NATIONAL MUSEUM OF DENMARK

are beginning to fill this gap. The Latvian site of Sarnate provides one of the few exceptions, having yielded many remains of water chestnuts, and also of the wooden mallets used to crack the shells. Grindstones of the kind later used by farmers to mill grain are not known from the Mesolithic period of northern and central Europe, but they are found in the shell middens of Portugal. These are the only European Mesolithic sites where grindstones have been found. We do not know exactly what they were used for, but Portugal is rich in edible acorns, pine nuts, and wild grass seeds, any or all of which could have been milled. In most of these Portuguese middens, however, a few charred hazelnut shells are all that survive to hint at this part of the Mesolithic diet.

NATIONAL MUSEUM OF DENMARK

☝ Late Mesolithic people in Denmark made two forms of pots. The flat dish was used as a lamp, in which oil rendered from blubber was burned.

THE DOMESTICATION OF ANIMALS

RONNIE LILJEGREN

The domestication of animals has been one of most crucial things humans ever accomplished. In conjunction with the cultivation of cereals, it accounts for much of the increase in human numbers over the last 10,000 years. Not surprisingly, therefore, animal domestication has been a major area of archaeological study.

Taming and domestication are two very different activities. Individual animals of most species can be tamed, and hunter-gatherers without domesticates sometimes tame the occasional animal—usually a newborn or very young individual found during hunting. The reasons for this vary from curiosity, or the desire for a pet, to fattening the animal for a few weeks or months before eating it. All human groups are probably aware that individual animals can be reared in this way in a human society.

Domestication, on the other hand, involves not one but a group of animals, controlled and selectively bred by humans, usually with little or no interbreeding with wild animals. There are only two core areas where herd animals were domesticated: Southwest Asia (sheep, goats, cattle, and pigs) and the Andes (llamas and alpacas). Other herd animals, such as horses, camels, and various East Asian types of cattle, were domesticated in particular regions, but only after agriculture had been established nearby.

Identifying Domesticated Animals

Taming is very difficult to recognize archaeologically, but once separate domestic populations came into existence, genetic changes took place that can sometimes be seen. In addition, the age at which animals were killed can be determined from their teeth and bones. Thus, if animal remains are found of an age that is characteristic of killing for domestic purposes,

Cheviot

Four-horned Jacob

Merino

Mouflon

Lincoln

Syrian fat-tailed sheep

ILLUSTRATION: PETER SCHOUTEN

then the animals were probably domesticated.

The first animal to be domesticated was the dog. A grave at Ain Mallaha, in Israel, dating from about 13,500 years ago, contained the body of an old woman and the skeleton of a puppy some three to five months old. Whether this was a tamed wolf or a domestically bred dog is unknown, but domestic dogs are known by 9500 BC to 8000 BC from sites as far apart as Seamer Carr, in England, and Danger Cave, in Utah. Evidently, the wolf/dog was domesticated in a number of places, most probably for hunting purposes.

In Southwest Asia, genetic changes indicate that sheep and goats were domesticated before 8000 BC. Among goats, for example,

the horns change from scimitar-shaped to corkscrew-shaped, which is usually thought to result from domestication. At some sites, kill patterns related to domestication have been found, with many female goats surviving to old age but most males being killed at about two years of age. This shows that herders kept the females for breeding, but slaughtered the males when they reached their maximum weight. Cattle and pigs were domesticated rather later—before 7000 BC.

Breeding to Meet the Growing Demand

The need for a ready source of meat and hides is probably a sufficient explanation for the domestication of sheep, goats, cattle, and pigs. In Southwest Asia, cereals were

⟵ Animal domestication is a continuous process. It takes place over many generations, different races being developed to suit different environments. Sheep, with about 400 breeds, are a good example. Wild sheep, such as the mouflon, have a hairy outer coat and a woolly undercoat, and both sexes have horns. Modern sheep, such as the Lincoln, are often polled, or only the rams have horns, as in the case of the merino. Among Jacob sheep, animals with four, or even six, horns are common—a genetic defect, probably caused by inbreeding, which has been preserved as a decoration. Syrian fat-tailed sheep are adapted to a hot, dry environment, and use their fat as an energy supply. Wool differs considerably from one breed to another. It is long, coarse, and lustrous in the Lincoln; dense, with very fine fibers, in the merino; and quite coarse, and with little luster, in the Cheviot.

cultivated before sheep and goats were domesticated. Farmers were more numerous than hunter-gatherers, and the increased need for meat would have put pressure on local populations of wild animals. Breeding from tamed animals would have been an effective way of making up for the decreasing number of wild animals. Secondary products such as milk, blood, and wool, and the use of animals for traction, are usually thought to have been exploited only later. In some cases, this was certainly so.

Wild sheep have a hairy outer coat covering a woolly undercoat. Thick wool suitable for spinning and weaving resulted from long periods of selective breeding by farmers, which could only have been undertaken using domesticated sheep.

Milk, perhaps made into cheese, may have been exploited much earlier. Milking a goat for a year provides more energy than a goat carcass, and provides that energy by degrees, over a long period, rather than all at once: two good reasons why dairy products may yet turn out to have been utilized very early indeed.

As agriculture spread, other animals were domesticated, but remarkably little is known about them. Horses were probably domesticated in the grassy steppes north and east of the Black Sea. At the site of Dereivka, in Ukraine, which dates to a little before 4000 BC, there are more than 2,000 horse bones. For many years it was thought that these horses were domestic animals, but the kill ages do not support this assumption. Most of the horses were killed between five and eight years of age, just when they would have been most useful for both breeding and working if they had been domesticated. They were therefore probably hunted for meat—except for one animal, whose teeth had the characteristic beveling that results from long use of a bit. Perhaps humans used a few tamed or domesticated horses to assist them when hunting.

Even less is known about camel domestication. The earlierst claim comes from Shahr-i Sokhta, in Iran, dating to about 2700 BC. The evidence here is burned camel dung found in a pottery vessel—circumstantial, but not conclusive, evidence that the camel was domesticated!

Small Animals

Grain stores attract rodents, so it is not surprising that the first evidence for the domestication of the cat—at Khirokitia, in Cyprus—goes back to 7000 BC. The island has no native wildcats, so the cats must have been introduced in domesticated form.

Ferrets are useful when hunting rabbits, and the use of tame or domestic ferrets is mentioned in the writings of the Roman author Strabo at about the beginning of the first century AD.

Other small animals were domesticated for food—for example, guinea pigs in Peru, rabbits in Europe, and ducks and goldfish in China. All these animals were raised by societies that also kept larger herd domesticates. In Mexico, there were no larger herd domesticates, so smaller domesticated species were of considerable importance. The turkey was domesticated in this region, and specially bred fat dogs were the other source of meat, apart from that from hunted animals.

Sheep, goats, pigs, cattle, llamas, and alpacas are of vital importance to the cultures that herd them. Why, then, did people in the other early centers of cereal cultivation, such as Mexico, China, and West Africa, not domesticate local species such as deer and antelope?

While many species can be tamed, few are suited to being herd domesticates. Males in most deer and antelope species are territorial during the mating season and try to keep a group of females in their territory while fighting off other males. Herd structure is consequently weak or nonexistent, and the difficulties of domesticating such species are immense. In just a few species, however, there are a number of units within a herd, each consisting of a male with a number of females. Such herds do not range over the landscape during the mating season but are much more cohesive. All the major herd domesticates are of this second type: as we would expect, early farmers did not domesticate species at random but made effective use of those with the most potential.

THE ANCESTRY OF DOMESTICATED ANIMALS

DOMESTICATED ANIMAL	TIME	WILD ANCESTOR	PLACE
dog	>11,000 BC	wolf	many places?
sheep	8000 BC	wild sheep	Iraq, Iran, Levant coast
goat	8000 BC	bezoar (wild goat)	Zagros Mountains, Iraq
pig	7000 BC	wild boar	Southwest Asia (Anatolia)
cattle	8000 BC	aurochs	Southwest Asia and possibly Europe
horse	4000 BC	wild horse	southern Ukraine
one-humped camel	3000 BC	wild camel	southern Arabia
two-humped camel	2500 BC	wild camel	Turkmenistan/Iran
gayal or mithun	?	gauar	possibly India
bali cattle	3500 BC	banteng	Java or India
cat	7000 BC	wild cat	Southwest Asia
reindeer	?	wild reindeer	arctic Eurasia
ass	3500 BC	wild ass	Northeast Africa
yak	?6000 BC	wild yak	the Tibetan highland
water buffalo	>2500 BC	Indian wild buffalo	Indus Valley (Mesopotamia?)
llama	4000 BC	guanaco	Andean plateau
alpaca	4000 BC	guanaco	Andean plateau
guinea pig	>1000 BC	wild cavy	Peru?
rabbit	AD 1000	wild rabbit	southern Europe
duck	1000 BC	mallard	Southeast Asia
goose	3000 BC	greylag	southeastern Europe, Northeast Africa
domestic fowl	2000 BC	red jungle fowl	Indus Valley
peafowl	1000 BC	wild peafowls	India
turkey	500 BC	wild turkey	Mexico
budgerigar	AD 1840	wild budgerigar	Australia
canary	AD 1500	wild canary	Canary Islands
goldfish	AD 1000	Crucian carp?	China
mulberry silkworm	>2000 BC	wild silkworm	China
honeybee	>2400 BC	wild bees	Southwest Asia, Europe, Africa?

Cemeteries

While individual graves—and the occasional cemetery—are known from the Paleolithic period, it is not until the Mesolithic that we find evidence of the widespread use of cemeteries. About 20 cemeteries have now been found in Europe, some containing more than 100 graves. Disposal of the dead varied widely from place to place, reflecting regional variations in culture.

Cemeteries linked to the Ertebølle culture have been found in Denmark and southern Sweden, and several cemeteries have also been found beneath Portuguese shell middens. Thanks to these shell middens, we know quite a lot about the way of life of these two groups, but we know much less about that of the people of Brittany, England, the Baltic States, and Russia, where cemeteries dating from this period have also been found.

One striking aspect of these cemeteries is that most are in coastal areas. This has led some archaeologists to speculate that cemeteries were one of the means by which particular groups of people laid claim to certain territories. The presence of dead ancestors in a cemetery could legitimize such a claim and strengthen a group's sense of identity with its land. Clearly, this would be more likely to happen in areas where food resources were plentiful and stable, encouraging people to adopt a more settled way of life—such as along the coasts. The evidence from shell middens indicates that in Portugal, coastal people regularly moved from summer to winter camps within a limited area, while in Denmark, they seem to have lived in permanent settlements.

People living in the interior, without access to marine resources, would most likely have moved further, more frequently, and less predictably than coastal groups. They would, therefore, have been less likely to have identified with a fixed territory, and this may be why cemeteries are rarely found away from the coast. Significantly, the few exceptions have been found in places where resources would have been unusually plentiful and predictable, such as at

⚱ Cemeteries from the Late Mesolithic period are fairly common in coastal regions of Europe. Bodies were sometimes placed on red-deer antlers to be buried, and accompanied by various tools and pieces of jewelry.

☞ One young woman was buried in the Vedbæk cemetery, in Denmark, with a group of teeth, mostly from red deer, stitched or tied to the back of her belt or dress as a decoration. When her skeleton was excavated some 7,000 years later, the teeth were found still in place below her pelvic bone.
NATIONAL MUSEUM OF DENMARK

☞ *Opposite*: A grave in the Vedbæk cemetery, in Denmark, bears witness to a probable tragedy. The adult skeleton is that of a young woman aged about 18, and next to her lies the skeleton of a newborn child. We may speculate that they died in childbirth. The child was buried with a flint blade at its waist. Adult males in the same cemetery were similarly equipped, so perhaps the child was a boy. (It is very difficult to determine the sex of very young skeletons.) The red coloring is from ocher placed in the grave. The animal teeth near the woman's head were probably sewn as decoration onto a piece of clothing. The boy was lying on the bones of a swan's wing.

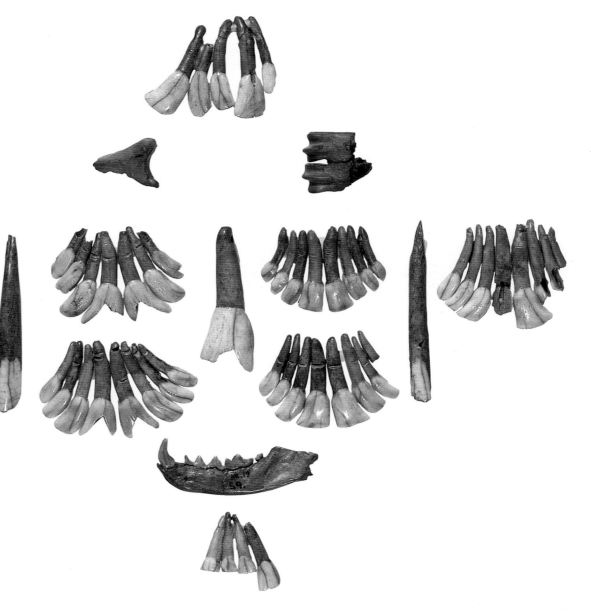

⚑ Lepenski Vir, in Serbia, lies where the River Danube flows through a gorge. This part of the river is particularly rich in fish, including sturgeon, which was a very important source of food in this area.

⚑ The sites of villages established by the earliest agriculturalists in southeastern Europe are marked by so-called tell mounds, formed by the repeated rebuilding of mudbrick houses.

MIKE ANDREWS/ANCIENT ART & ARCHITECTURE COLLECTION

Lepenski Vir, a prime fishing location in Serbia, on the River Danube. Fewer cemeteries are known from the Early Mesolithic and Paleolithic periods, but if most had similarly been in coastal regions, they would obviously have been flooded by the rising seas along with the settlements.

Whatever the truth of this, cemeteries are the only places where we can encounter individuals from these times. Limited though it is, the Danish and Swedish evidence indicates that these hunter-gatherers were quite tall and robust, comparable to modern Europeans, and very different from the shorter farmers of later prehistoric and Medieval times. Judging from this, Mesolithic diets, at least on the coast, must have been considerably better than those of these later peoples.

Ornaments are commonly found in graves in all these cemeteries. As the number of ornaments varies from grave to grave, it would seem that some people enjoyed a higher social status than others, but we know very little of the social structure of this time. Rich ornaments are occasionally found in children's graves, and it has been suggested that this may indicate that wealth and high social status were inherited. This could mean that there were hereditary chiefs. While this is certainly possible, burial customs are so varied

and difficult to interpret that it is very difficult to prove such a proposition one way or the other.

The First Farmers of Southern and Eastern Europe

Hunter-gatherers would probably have continued to pursue their various ways of life throughout Europe, with little change, but for one thing: the development of farming. How this development came about is an issue that is still hotly debated.

Most of the early crops and domesticated animals (such as wheat and barley, and sheep and goats) did not live wild in Europe, and so must have been introduced at some stage. Wild cattle and pigs, on the other hand, were found throughout postglacial Europe. These could have been domesticated locally, although current evidence suggests that they, too, came from outside Europe. All these species live wild in Southwest Asia, which is also where the earliest evidence of farming has been found.

The big question is, then, did immigrant peoples take farming to Europe with them, or did local Mesolithic groups somehow acquire the plants and animals and take up farming themselves? Obviously, there can be no single answer, since various combinations of immigrants and

ERICH LESSING/ARCHIVE/MAGNUM

local people would have been involved in different places. Opinions remain sharply divided as to which was the more important overall.

Some areas offer better clues than others as to the sequence of events. In southern Greece, for example, Franchthi Cave has yielded evidence of human occupation spanning thousands of years, so the sudden appearance there of wheat, barley, lentils, sheep, and goats, in layers dated to 7000 BC, could mean either that these things were introduced by immigrants or that local hunter-gatherers rapidly adopted practices and species that were passed between communities along existing contact routes. The island of Crete, on the other hand, was unoccupied during the Mesolithic period, so farming can only have arrived there with immigrants.

Throughout southeastern Europe, the way of life of the earliest farmers differed little from that established earlier in Southwest Asia. Numerous so-called tell mounds—mounds formed when houses made of sun-dried mudbricks collapsed, and new houses were later built on top of them—have been discovered throughout these areas, and have proved to be the sites of villages occupied by between 50 and 300 people. These communities were clearly too big to have been supported by hunting, gathering, and fishing, and lived quite close to one another. It was farming that supported populations of this size and density and made this pattern of life possible.

While the evidence from the eastern Mediterranean region tends to favor the immigration theory, that from the western region presents quite a different picture. More Mesolithic settlements have been found in the western basin than in the eastern, reflecting the more abundant resources in the west. This would suggest that the population in the west was larger. The earliest farming settlements here do not take the form of villages. The earliest sites have been found mostly in caves, many of which had previously been occupied by hunter-gatherers, as shown by the often abundant fish bones in these sites. Here, it looks much more as though local people took up elements of farming, while continuing to exploit coastal resources.

This proposition gains some support from the fact that not all elements of the farming economy spread from the eastern to the western basin at the same time. Instead, it appears that only sheep and wheat spread rapidly round the coastal fringe of the western Mediterranean. Perhaps Mesolithic hunter-gatherers found sheep easier to integrate into a part-farming, part-fishing economy, but the details remain obscure. The earliest bones of sheep found in northwestern Italy have been dated to about 6000 BC; those from southern France and Spain, to 5500 BC (earlier dates are claimed in both countries, but not generally accepted); and from Portugal, to 5200 BC. Goats

Early farming sites
Late hunter-gatherer sites
c. 7000 BC–5400 BC
c. 6500 BC–5200 BC
c. 5300 BC–5000 BC
Post-5000 BC

in northwestern Italy followed some 500 years later, and domestic pigs later still, but the dates for the introduction of these species elsewhere in the western Mediterranean are still debated. Wild animals and fish were caught in much greater numbers in the west, probably because they were more abundant. The fact that the earliest evidence of farming is found along the coast, as well as the difficulties of overland travel in those times, make it likely that farming spread by boat, whether or not migration was involved to any extent.

NEOLITHIC EUROPE

Farming did not spread across Europe at a slow and even rate. Sometimes it spread very fast indeed, but in between such periods, there were long pauses. Farming spread particularly fast in southeastern and central Europe and around the Mediterranean coasts, while it took longer to penetrate the coastal regions.

CARTOGRAPHY: RAY SIM

☞ The simplest form of plow is the ard, which scratches a shallow furrow in the soil. An ox-drawn ard can cultivate a field much faster than a person using a digging stick, but it is a more complex tool to make, and the oxen take a considerable time to train. An ard therefore represents a much bigger investment of human resources.

HISTORICAL-ARCHAEOLOGICAL RESEARCH CENTRE, DENMARK

C. M. DIXON

⚒ A polished stone adze and reconstructed haft. Tools like this were used to fell trees and work timber. They would have been vital to early farmers for clearing forest for agriculture, for building houses, and for making all kinds of wooden tools.

☞ The longhouses built by the first farmers in central Europe were substantial structures of considerable size. From the evidence of postholes, archaeologists can reconstruct the main timber elements with considerable accuracy. Finds of burned clay with impressions of sticks show that the walls and internal partitions were often made of wattle and daub—screens made of interwoven sticks covered with wet clay or cow dung, which hardened as it dried. Split planks were also used. The roofs were most probably thatched. We do not know whether there was an upper floor, as shown in this reconstruction, but it seems likely. The structure could certainly have supported one, and the farmers would have needed a place to store harvested grain and animal fodder for the winter.
ILLUSTRATION: OLIVER RENNERT

All European farmers made pottery, whereas very few hunter-gatherers did. The earliest farmers in Greece and south-eastern Europe produced well-made vessels in a variety of forms, often with geometric designs painted in several colors— mainly red, buff, and black. The pottery found in the western Mediterranean is different: it was not painted, and decorative bands were impressed or incised into the clay. Different styles of pottery cannot be used to distinguish different tribes, but they do suggest that there were major cultural differences between the two regions.

The Forest Farmers of Central and Northwestern Europe

Farming had not yet spread north of the Mediterranean, and most plants and animals, as well as farming methods, were adapted to the Mediterranean climate. Crops, for example, would probably have been planted in autumn. They would have grown throughout the cool, wet winter, and been harvested in May or June before the hot summer drought set in. This cycle mimics the natural cycle of wild grasses in the area.

Farmers moving out of this climatic zone and into central Europe faced a major challenge in that they had to turn the agricultural year on its head. In the colder regions, it was winter frost, not summer drought, that was the main threat to crops. Crops had to grow through the moist summer and be harvested in the autumn, so new crop strains and new agricultural techniques had to be developed. For farmers to have carried through these changes in less than a thousand years was a remarkable achievement indeed.

But farming did not spread across Europe at an even rate. Sometimes it spread quickly, and at others there were long periods when it did not spread at all. The unevenness of its advance is particularly marked in southeastern Europe. Farming spread through areas with a Mediterranean-type climate in just a few centuries—and then came to a halt in Hungary, where the climate is different and the wet, heavily forested soils of temperate Europe begin.

Farming reached the northern edge of the Mediterranean climate zone in southern Hungary

by 6000 BC, but only in 5300 BC did it spread any further into the cooler and wetter climates of central Europe. The next great leap took farming right across central Europe to the borders of Scandinavia and the North Sea in the space of just a few generations. Farmers had to make massive changes in their economy to be able to do this: wheat and barley were now almost the only crops grown, perhaps because pulses such as lentils and peas did not adjust so readily to the colder climate. Sheep and goats (the most common animals in the Mediterranean) were not well suited to the central European forests and so became less important. The animal bones found in settlement sites of this period are most often those of pigs and cattle, and animal products in general may have become a more significant part of the diet. It has been suggested that dairy products came into use at this time, and this seems likely.

These economic changes were accompanied by major social changes. No longer did settlements consist of compact villages made up of small houses. Instead, massive timber longhouses up to about 50 meters (164 feet) in length appeared all across central Europe, from Hungary to Poland and from the Netherlands to Ukraine. These longhouses were not grouped in villages but were spaced some way apart. We do not know how many people lived in these buildings, nor what activities went on inside them. Unlike later longhouses, there is no evidence that one end was used for stalling animals, but this does not necessarily mean that the whole of the interior was used as human living space.

After the rapid spread of this longhouse forest-farming culture, there was once again a pause. It was another thousand years before farming spread into southern Scandinavia. This, of course, was the area of the Late Mesolithic Ertebølle shell middens, which would explain the delay. Given the rich marine resources in this area, which were supplemented by other sources of food such as land mammals and plants,

there would have been little incentive for these coastal people to abandon their hunting-gathering way of life. A similar situation prevailed in Portugal, where hunter-gatherers living at the sites marked by their shell middens continued their traditional way of life for several centuries after farming had become established in the surrounding countryside. The attractions of coastal life in these areas would seem to be the most likely reason why farming spread into the Atlantic coastal fringes of Europe in a much more piecemeal way than it did into the interior of Europe.

These new farming groups, of course, developed vastly different technical skills from those of the Mesolithic hunter-gatherers. As noted, only a few hunting-gathering groups (the Ertebølle among them) made pottery, while all the farmers did. Farmers would obviously have to have cleared areas of forest, and the heavy stone axes they used for this purpose are commonly found. Less is known about the implements they used for cultivation. Only limited areas can be worked with a digging stick, and soon after 3000 BC, there is evidence that ards (simple scratch ploughs without wheels) were in use. Ards are sometimes found in bog sites, but the earliest evidence of them has come down to us in the form of furrows preserved as dark lines on the old soil surface beneath burial mounds. As farming began several centuries before people started to build these mounds, any earlier evidence of such furrows has not survived. Ards may be very old.

The development of agriculture was one of the most momentous changes that Europe has ever seen. It brought about a massive increase in population density, and this has continued ever since, as new farming methods and crops have been introduced. Without farming, the social and economic structures we call "civilization" could never have developed, and the Industrial Revolution is inconceivable. Europe was never the same again.

GÖRAN BURENHULT

⚒ Experiments have shown that substantial trees can be felled with stone axes in a remarkably short time. Bronze axes do not speed up the process. It was not until the coming of iron axes that farmers found a more efficient way to clear land of trees.

⚒ Grain was ground into flour with smooth grindstones. A handful of grain was placed on a large stone, and then ground with a small stone. Hunter-gatherers in some areas probably ground nuts by this method, but grindstones become much more common in early farming societies.
C.M. DIXON

☝ The mummified body was initially partly uncovered by the Alpine gendarmerie. It lay on its front on a large slab in the rock cleft.

THE ICE MAN OF THE TYROL

ANDREAS LIPPERT

☝ A view of the site from the north, with the Ortler mountains in the background.

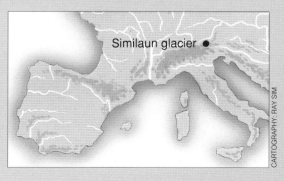

Similaun glacier ●

MORE THAN 5,000 years ago, a man was crossing a remote pass in the mountains of the Tyrol. As a storm approached, he sheltered in a hollow in the rock, some 3,200 meters (10,500 feet) above sea level, where he apparently froze to death. For several weeks his body was exposed to the wind and sun; as it dried out, it became mummified. The body was then covered by snow and finally entombed within the ice of a glacier that covered the site. There it lay, undisturbed, until September 1991, when it was discovered by hikers.

Pollen analyses in the alpine valleys and occasional finds of stone axes high up in the mountains have long indicated that people frequented the mountains and made use of the high pastures during the last stages of the Neolithic period. But the discovery of the remarkably well-preserved body of the "Ice Man", near the Tisenjoch pass, in the Otztal Alps, has permitted the kind of detailed investigation of life during this period that would otherwise never have been possible.

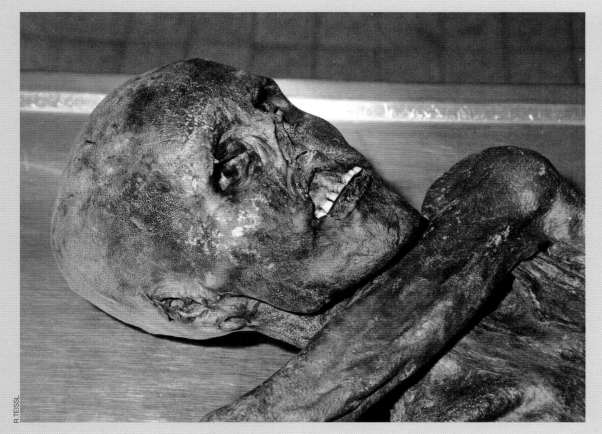

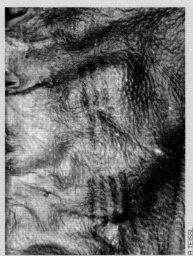

⚲ On the left side of the Ice Man's back, three groups of vertical lines are tattooed. These markings may have indicated his tribe or status.

⚲ The mummified head. Although considerably shrunken, the eyeballs and their pupils are still preserved.

The Ice Man—also known as Similaun Man, after the glacier in which he was found—was about 30 years old. He was dressed for the climate in fur and leather, patched together with thread made from sinew. A large, mat-like item woven from long grass may have been a shawl. His fur shoes were lined with hay and tied with laces made of grass and leather. On his knees, feet, hands, and back, groups of lines and crosses were tattooed in dark blue. These may have indicated his tribe or status.

A Neolithic Tool Kit

This Neolithic traveler was well equipped for his journey, with an axe, a bow and quiver, a backpack, a leather case containing several items, a firelighter and tinder, and a dagger. Before he settled down for refuge in his rocky hollow, the man had carefully deposited his quiver and axe, his bow and backpack, in two different places.

The shaft of the axe was made from a piece of yew wood about 80 centimeters (30 inches) long, with a short fork at one end, to which a very early type of copper-flanged axe, 9 centimeters (almost 4 inches) in length, was attached. The unfinished bow, roughly made of yew wood and unpolished, was about 1.8 meters (5 feet, 11 inches) long. The quiver was a fur bag stitched with leather and stiffened with hazelwood. It contained 14 arrow shafts, about 85 centimeters

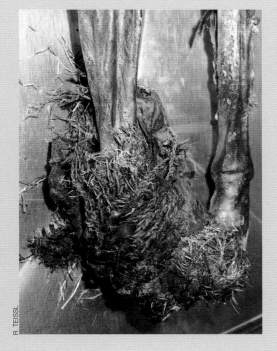

(33 inches) long, and made of dogwood and guelder rose. Two were notched and feathered ready for use, with arrowheads made of flint. The quiver also contained a pointed object made of bone or antler, possibly a tool for skinning animals. Finally, there was an animal sinew, the raw material for bowstrings or threads.

The frame of the backpack consisted of a thin piece of hazelwood bent in a U-shape and two small boards of larch tree with peg-

⚲ The remains of a fur shoe still surround his right foot. His roughly fashioned boots were lined with hay, obviously as insulation against the cold, and tied with laces made of grass and leather.

shaped ends. Nearby remnants of thick grass cord suggest that this was how the pack was attached. In the longish leather case was a flint scraper and a piece of tree-bark resin. On this resin were tiny fragments of pyrite. Together, these served as a firelighter. X-rays have revealed two flint points inside the container. These items obviously made up a repair kit for the arrows.

In addition, the Ice Man carried a tool used for sharpening flint artifacts, consisting of a small piece of bone set into a thick wooden peg. Two small tree fungi threaded onto a leather thong were evidently used as an antibiotic medicine. A dagger-like flint blade with a wooden hilt was probably a tool rather than a weapon; an oval bag of the same size, made of woven grass, presumably served as a sheath.

The earliest preserved prehistoric body ever found, the Ice Man is of immense significance for our understanding of the past. By studying his body and equipment, scientists have been able to provide answers to many questions about the social status, cultural level, health, and nutritional status of a native of the Alps in the Late Neolithic.

THE MEGALITH BUILDERS OF WESTERN EUROPE

4 8 0 0 B C – 2 8 0 0 B C

Stones, Tombs, and Temples along the Atlantic Coast

GÖRAN BURENHULT

THE GIANT STONE TOMBS that stand along the shores of the Atlantic have fascinated people for centuries. We know almost nothing about them, apart from their age and, in some cases, their ceremonial functions. Why were they built? What role did they play in society? Were they solely places in which the dead went to their final rest, or did they symbolize the life to come? Should they be regarded as dwelling places for dead ancestors? What role did astronomical observations play in the building of the monuments and in the ceremonies that took place at them? Why were most of them built in coastal areas of western Europe? Did they perhaps mark territories occupied by particular communities? The people who could have answered these questions vanished long ago, but recent excavations and research have brought us some way towards solving this enigma, surely one of the most intriguing of all archaeological puzzles.

◄◙ The Ring of Brogar, a huge stone circle in the Orkney Islands, north of Scotland, consists of gigantic, erect stone slabs. The function of this impressive monument is still unknown, but it may have served as a religious meeting point for a large number of settlements throughout the Orkney Islands, among them the famous Stone Age village of Skara Brae.

◙ A decorated stone slab from Antelas, at Oliveira de Frades, in the Viseu Valley, Portugal.

FABRICE ROULAND/RAPHO

☀ Life was easy for the Mesolithic hunter-gatherers of western Europe. Abundant coastal resources, including oysters, mussels, fish, and seals, as well as beached whales, supplemented by hunting and a rich supply of forest products, allowed these people to become more or less sedentary.

GÖRAN BUREN-HULT

☀ Thick heaps of prehistoric leftovers, such as this one at Culleenamore, in northwestern Ireland, dot the coasts of western Europe. These so-called kitchen middens consist mainly of oyster shells, and bear witness to the enormously rich food supply available to Mesolithic peoples.

More than 6,000 years ago, the Stone Age peoples of western Europe started to erect stone monuments over their dead—as tombs or as ceremonial places—and thereby introduced the megalithic tradition of the Neolithic period. Initially, archaeologists generally regarded these monuments as late offshoots of the monuments of Near Eastern civilizations, such as the pyramids of Egypt and the ziggurats of Mesopotamia. They were thought to have been introduced by the first farmers, who would then have spread along the Atlantic coast. Later on, it was suggested that a religious cult lay behind the appearance of these megaliths, and that Stone Age missionaries of some kind had spread by sea among the early farmers. Migration and the spread of ideas were key terms in this discussion.

In the 1960s and 1970s, however, excavations and a series of remarkably early radiocarbon datings at megalithic sites in western Europe finally threw these theories overboard. The oldest known megalithic tombs in France and Ireland were found to have been built about 4700 BC—2,000 years before Egypt's pyramids were erected. Every form of outside influence could therefore be ruled out. Today, we know that the idea of erecting megalithic tombs, and the need to do so, developed within the Stone Age societies of western Europe during the fifth millennium BC, but the meaning and function of the monuments still remain one of the great enigmas of archaeology. The megalithic tradition died out 5,000 years ago, so there is no traditional continuity, or "living link", in Europe that can answer our questions, and we know almost nothing of the social, psychological, and religious background that gave rise to them.

In Europe, the megalithic tradition reached its peak just before 3000 BC. Magnificent monuments—such as Stonehenge, in England, Newgrange, in Ireland, and the famous stone alignments a kilometer (more than half a mile) long at Carnac, in Brittany, France—were all built at this time. But what happened nearly 2,000 years earlier to give birth to this tradition?

A Land of Plenty

As a result of the dramatic improvement in the climate that occurred after the last Ice Age, people's living conditions changed entirely. As the forests advanced, hunting techniques altered, requiring new tools and hunting equipment. The axe, as well as the bow and arrow, came into use for the first time. For the most part, these developments occurred simultaneously over a vast area, from North Africa, in the south, to Scandinavia, in the north. But in one respect, the people along the Atlantic coasts of Ireland, France, and Portugal differed from their kinsfolk: they were the first people in the world to build megalithic tombs over their dead.

The climatic shift brought about sweeping changes in vegetation and landscape, and the so-called Atlantic period began about 6000 BC. As the average annual temperature rose, the open, boreal forests of pine and hazel gave way to dark, dense forests of deciduous species such as linden, oak, and elm, and the sun-loving undergrowth was replaced by ferns and ivy. This did not suit grazing animals, which in many places decreased markedly in numbers—some, such as the giant deer (*Megalocerus giganteus*), becoming extinct. Other animals, such as the wild boar, flourished. Europe boasted a much warmer climate 7,000 years ago than it does at the present time. Species such as the water chestnut and the European pond tortoise thrived in the far north of Scandinavia, whereas today we have to go as far south as southern central Europe to find them in their wild state.

At the same time, much of the ice sheets, which had been several kilometers thick, melted away, leading to a dramatic rise in the sea level. The North Sea was drowned, and the English Channel and the Irish Sea were created, turning England and Ireland into islands. Over a period of 2,000 years, almost half of western Europe was submerged. One might expect that such a dramatic reduction in land would have made it more difficult for humans to survive, but in fact, the countless newly created bays, inlets, and brackish lagoons provided one of the richest ecosystems on Earth for human subsistence.

Along the entire Atlantic coast, thick rubbish heaps, consisting primarily of mussel and oyster shells, bear witness to the importance of seafood for Mesolithic societies at this time. These heaps, known as kitchen (or shell) middens, are often more than 50 meters (164 feet) long, 20 meters (66 feet) wide, and sometimes more than 5 meters (16 feet) thick.

The people living along the coasts of Portugal, northern Spain, France, Ireland, western England, Holland, and southern Scandinavia all adapted to the changed conditions in the same way. The rich environment led to many of these societies becoming more or less sedentary, and while most groups in Europe's interior soon had to supplement the gathering of plants with farming, it took nearly a thousand years before the coastal peoples along the Atlantic were forced to do the same. This was in spite of the fact that inland and coastal societies were in close contact with each other: the appearance of pottery and polished stone axes among the coastal hunter-gatherers clearly demonstrates that they were influenced by the farmers of central Europe.

It is in the light of these facts that we may perceive the subsequent developments. As a result of their secure food supply and settled way of life, the coastal hunter-gatherers soon developed cultural practices typical of advanced farming societies. About 5000 BC, the first burial grounds appeared in southern Scandinavia. Sites such as Barum and Skateholm, in Sweden, and Bøgebakken, north of Copenhagen, in Denmark, have become legendary. A few centuries later, the first boulders were pulled into position over the dead on the west coast of Ireland and on the south coast of Brittany, in France. The megalithic tradition had begun.

The Social Revolution

When a group of people becomes sedentary, their way of life and mutual relations soon change considerably. The reason for increased sedentism within the Stone Age societies along the Atlantic coast is to be found in the presence of a wide range of foodstuffs that varied with the seasons and could be reached from the settlements in less than a day. In summer, the deciduous forests were filled with plants, fungi, roots, bulbs, and fruits; small game, larvae, and other edible insects abounded. Birds, birds' eggs, and fish supplemented this richly varied and nutritious diet. In the autumn, nuts and berries were eaten, whereas seafood and big-game formed the major part of the winter diet. Mussels, oysters, fish, and seals were vital foods for groups living in the year-round settlements.

In mobile societies, all members of a group probably performed the same activities. But as societies became sedentary, individual group members began to specialize in such skills as tool-making, food production, hunting, or fishing. At the same time, there was a growing need for greater social organization, and groups began to lay claim to resource areas in which other groups were not allowed to operate. Instead

of roaming freely, without territorial boundaries, more and more groups came to occupy specific regions, and the risk of conflict arose for the first time, although as long as populations remained small and resources were rich, there were probably few disputes. The first acts of aggression that can be traced in the archaeological record belong to the early, sedentary farming societies in central Europe: fortified settlements, battle-clubs, and ceremonial axes tell their own story.

The determining factor in this process of change was population growth. In present-day or historically known mobile societies, groups are not allowed to increase in size unless there is enough for all the members of the group to eat, even during the hardest of times; and in any case, it is impossible to carry more than one child during long migrations. Long periods of breast-feeding (which automatically reduces female fertility), abortion, and infanticide all serve to regulate population levels. As a result, starvation and

⚓ An infrared photograph showing Ballysadare Bay and the southern part of the Knocknarea Peninsula, in County Sligo, northwestern Ireland, in the middle of which lies the megalithic grave field of Carrowmore. The arrow indicates the kitchen midden area at Culleenamore. Infrared photography makes it possible to locate prehistoric remains that are not visible to the naked eye.

MEGALITH SITES IN EUROPE

BC	BRITTANY	IRELAND	BRITAIN	IBERIA	N. EUROPE
1500					
			Stonehenge III		
2000				Praia das Marcas	
2500					
3000	Gavrinis	Sliabh Guillion / Poulnabrone	Stonehenge II / Avebury / Giant's Hill / Skara Brae	Los Millares / Santa Cruz	Tustrup / Grønhøj / Carlshögen / Karleby / Drenthe
3500	Carnac / Kerléven	Newgrange / Knowth	Stonehenge I / Stones of Stenness / West Kennet		Gladsax
4000	Ile Carn / Ile Bono	Carrowmore 7	Fussell's Lodge / Lambourn	Orca das Seixas / Fragoas	
4500	Barnenez / Ile Gaignog / Kercado	Carrowmore 4			
5000					

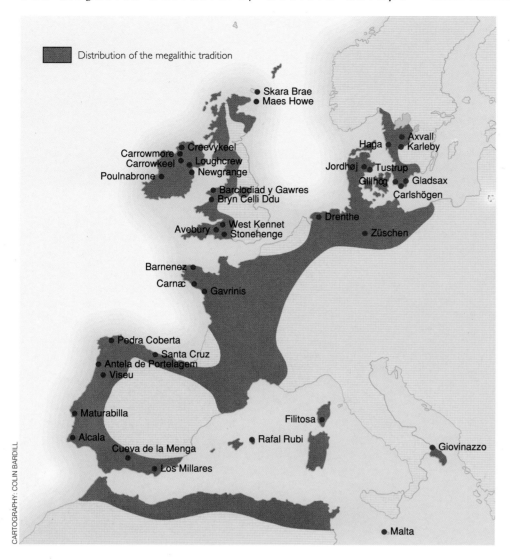

Distribution of the megalithic tradition

Skara Brae
Maes Howe
Creevykeel
Carrowmore
Carrowkeel
Loughcrew
Poulnabrone
Newgrange
Barclodiad y Gawres
Bryn Celli Ddu
Avebury
West Kennet
Stonehenge
Barnenez
Carnac
Gavrinis
Pedra Coberta
Santa Cruz
Antela de Portelagem
Viseu
Maturabilla
Filitosa
Alcala
Rafal Rubi
Cueva de la Menga
Los Millares
Giovinazzo
Malta
Haga
Axvall
Karleby
Jordhøj
Tustrup
Gillhög
Gladsax
Carlshögen
Drenthe
Züschen

CARTOGRAPHY: COLIN BARDILL

MEGALITHIC SITES OF WESTERN EUROPE

The distribution of the megalithic tradition in western Europe, showing major monuments and sites. Very similar monuments were erected from Portugal, in the southwest, to Scandinavia, in the north.

GÖRAN BURENHULT

⚱ A type of megalithic tomb known as a dolmen, at the grave field of Carrowmore, in northwestern Ireland. Together with some of the monuments in Brittany, France, this area has produced some of the earliest megalithic datings so far known.

malnutrition are almost unknown among mobile hunter-gatherers, despite the fact that they often inhabit areas with poor food resources.

When hunter-gatherers adopt a settled way of life, the balance changes. Tasks such as building houses, cultivation, and herding are done more easily by a large group. Large numbers of people are also an advantage when dealing with competing or even hostile groups. As a result, sedentism is closely connected with a heavy increase in population growth.

Paradoxically, the lavish coastal resources of the Atlantic coast forced the hunter-gatherers to engage actively in food production. Groups were tempted to settle in one place, and as time passed, the growing population could not support itself solely on what nature had to offer within the settlement area. A reduction in the salt content of sea water—which reduced oyster numbers, for example—accelerated this inevitable development. By about 4000 BC, most hunter-gatherer societies along the Atlantic coast had adopted a Neolithic way of life and had become part-time herders, although marine resources were still the main source of food for a long time. It was during this period of transformation, between 5000 BC and

4000 BC, that the first megalithic tombs were erected in western Europe.

Mobile hunter-gatherers seldom have permanent burial grounds, so grave fields, where a society's dead are all buried inside a defined area, are a sure sign of a population with a high degree of sedentism. While all known hunter-gatherers perform certain rituals or ceremonies in connection with burials, the burials generally take place wherever the group happens to be at the time, and such people rarely inter the dead below ground or erect lasting monuments above ground. Instead, the dead are often placed on platforms in the wilderness, and scavenging birds of prey restore the remains to the earth. It goes without saying that this kind of burial is seldom found in the archaeological record, and this explains why few graves have been discovered dating from the greater part of the time of the European Mesolithic hunter-gatherers. The first grave fields, which appeared about 5000 BC, thus testify to a considerable change in settlement patterns. The first megaliths are obvious examples of the same process.

The First Megaliths

In the Knocknarea Peninsula, in County Sligo, northwestern Ireland, about 40 stone monuments today overlook the Atlantic Ocean: dolmens, passage tombs, and stone circles. Clustered together in the interior of the peninsula, these monuments are all built of crude boulders torn loose from the surrounding mountains during the last glaciation and spread all over the area like meteors. The place is called Carrowmore, a Celtic name meaning "field of many stones". Originally, there may have been as many as 200 tombs, but during the past 100 years quarrying has destroyed many of them. Today, the area is protected against further destruction.

Between 1977 and 1982, a series of large-scale excavations was carried out at four of the undestroyed tombs at Carrowmore, and at a number of Stone Age settlements along the coast and on nearby Knocknarea Mountain. Many of these were kitchen midden settlements containing huge numbers of shells, predominantly of oysters. The dates of the grave field were startling. Carrowmore turned out to be one of the world's oldest known megalithic grave fields, its earliest monuments erected by about 4700 BC. The excavated settlements, as well as the large quantities of unopened mussels and oysters, the magnificent bone needles made from deer antler, and the ornaments made from sperm-whale teeth that were found in the graves, show that the monuments were built by people who were mainly hunter-gatherers but were increasingly turning to cattle breeding.

The situation in northwestern Ireland was far from unique. During the fifth millennium BC, similar social changes occurred more or less simultaneously in France, Spain, and Portugal. Some of the stone-built tombs in Brittany are among the oldest monuments known anywhere in the world. On the French Mediterranean coast, a farming economy was introduced into the Mesolithic Tardenoisian culture (named after the site of La Fère-en-Tardenois) during the sixth millennium BC, whereas the oldest known Neolithic settlements on the Atlantic coast did not appear until the beginning of the fifth millennium, about 4850 BC. The oldest layers of a settlement excavated at Curnic, in Guissény, have provided this early dating.

There are close similarities between the resource areas of the French regions, where megalithic traditions were first established, and those of Carrowmore. The populations along the Atlantic coast had access to a variety of apparently inexhaustible food resources, especially in the form of marine life. It is no coincidence that the central area of the megalithic tradition in France, the Bay of Morbihan, continues to be one of western Europe's best areas for oysters and other shellfish.

In addition, rivers abounded with fish, and the surrounding swamps teemed with birds. Further inland, the Atlantic deciduous forest offered an abundance of animal and plant foods. If farming was a part of a group's subsistence, it took place within a small enough area to allow megalithic traditions to develop. It has been argued that stone-built tombs served as territorial markers, and it cannot be ruled out that the monuments, apart from serving as graves and cult centers, also signaled a group's right to occupy a particular area.

An important find, showing that a pure hunting-gathering economy of the Mesolithic Tardenoisian tradition survived well into megalithic times, has been uncovered in a stone-built tomb at Dissignac, in St Nazaire. It consists of large numbers of microliths, small flint points, and barbs in the form of triangles, lancets, and microburins, found together with about 800 microliths of the Tardenoisian type. As at Carrowmore, large deposits of mussel shells have also been found in several graves. Whereas the Irish burials were always cremations, the communal burials of the French passage tombs took a different form.

⚱ Grave no. 4 at Carrowmore, during excavation. Erected about 4700 BC, it is the earliest known megalithic construction in Ireland.

⚱ The portal tomb of Poulnabrone, situated in the barren landscape of Burren, in County Claire, western Ireland, is one of Ireland's best-known and most impressive megalithic tombs. It was erected about 3000 BC. Originally, the roof-block was much larger, but recently part of it broke off, and now only two-thirds remain.

IMAGES OF OLD EUROPEAN RELIGION

Marija Gimbutas

THE PERIOD KNOWN as Old Europe—from about 6500 BC to 3500 BC—is characterized by a continuity of theme and style in its artifacts that represents an enduring view of the world. The richest materials come from southeastern and central Europe—present-day Greece, Bulgaria, Romania, Moldova, western Ukraine, Serbia, Bosnia, Croatia, Hungary, the Czech Republic, and Slovakia.

⚱ This terracotta bear, from the Greek island of Syros, carries a basin that opens into the animal's hollow body. The vessel may have been used in ceremonies connected with the worship of the birth-giving goddess.

NATIONAL MUSEUM OF ATHENS

Female statuettes proliferated, and have been found in what were temples, courtyards, and burial sites. Associations between objects and symbols painted or incised on these statuettes, and on shrine walls, ritual vases, and other cult objects, tell us much about the beliefs that prevailed in Old Europe. Connected with the cycles of nature and the female body, many of these symbols were adapted by farming societies from symbols developed by earlier hunting and gathering cultures. They indicate a matrilineal, custom-bound form of village life. Broadly, these symbols are associated with the giving and protection of life, fertility, death, and regeneration.

Life-giving and Life-protecting Symbols

As in the Upper Paleolithic period, a wide range of water symbols is linked with the giving of life, including zigzags, wavy or serpentine bands, and rows of vertical lines. There are also associations between the goddess and waterfowl, and the goddess is sometimes shown in the form of a waterfowl.

When this type of symbolism was first used, copulation was probably not known to cause pregnancy.

MARIJA GIMBUTAS

⚱ A clay model of a temple from a Macedonian shrine. It has T-shaped openings on each side and is topped by a bird-goddess mask standing on a cylinder in the roof. The goddess's necklace is shown in relief.

↩ A statue of the enthroned bird-goddess, from the Vinca culture, found at Bariljevo, near Priština, in Serbia. She is wearing an oversized mask with supernatural eyes and no mouth, and her status is shown by the medallion she is wearing, attached to a V-shaped necklace. Her legs and the throne are broken.
MIODRAG DJORDJEVIC

⚱ The face of a goddess, surrounded by meandering lines, peers from a stylized vulva on what was either an altar or a throne. This was found at Szegvár-Tüzköves, in southeastern Hungary, and dates from the fifth millennium BC.
HUNGARIAN NATIONAL MUSEUM

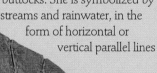

Since it was the female who gave birth, she was seen as the life-giver, and the breasts, buttocks, and belly were thought to be endowed with the power of procreation. The moisture in the goddess's uterus and internal organs was seen as the source of life, and breast milk was considered to be the substance that sustained life.

The goddess in a birth-giving pose is common in Paleolithic and Old European art, and she is sometimes symbolized solely by a vulva. The major animal forms she assumes are a deer, an elk, and a bear. In her madonna or nurse form, she wears a bear mask and carries a pouch for a baby or holds a child on her lap. She may also appear in such a pose as a snake or a bird.

The bird-goddess appeared, sculptured and painted on pottery vessels, from the Early Neolithic period—the seventh millennium BC. Vases in the form of birds and bird-women have also been found, as have models of temples topped with the image of the bird-goddess. She has a beak or a pinched nose, a long neck, an elaborate hairstyle or crown, breasts, wings, and, sometimes, protruding buttocks. She is symbolized by streams and rainwater, in the form of horizontal or vertical parallel lines respectively; V-shapes probably derived from the pubic triangle; and meandering lines.

The snake-goddess sits in a yogi-like position and has curved arms and legs, and a long mouth. She wears a crown, and her emblem is the snake coil. Thought to guarantee the continuity of life, she was worshipped in house shrines, and images of her continue into the Bronze and Iron Ages. In European folklore, snakes and birds are thought to be incarnations of ancestral spirits, a belief that goes back to Neolithic times.

⚨ This burnished clay figurine of a Neolithic snake-goddess comes from Crete. She has snake-like legs and a human face.
C.M. DIXON

Symbols of Fertility

The pregnant goddess, symbol of human and animal fertility, is portrayed as a nude with her hands on her enlarged belly. She predominates in the Early Neolithic period, and images of her are usually found on oven platforms and courtyard altars. She is associated with designs in the form of lozenges, triangles, snakes, and either two or four lines. With the advent of agriculture, she also became the deity that ensured soil fertility, and the sow became sacred to her.

There are also two male figures associated with plant regeneration and fertility: one is youthful and

⇦ One of the famous Cycladic figurines, this stiff nude, or white lady, from the island of Syros is carved from marble. Her arms are folded, and she wears a mask with a large beak-like nose and no mouth.
NATIONAL MUSEUM OF ATHENS/SCALA

strong and has an erect phallus; the other is ancient and peaceful. Both men are shown seated on stools. The old man sits quietly, his hands resting on his knees or supporting his chin. He is the god of dying vegetation—a major Bronze Age god in Southwest Asia and universally known throughout European history.

Symbols of Death

The goddess of death is shown as a rigid nude, her folded arms pressed tightly to her bosom and her legs together or tapering. She either has no face, her face being represented by a nose alone, or is masked, and her pubic triangle is supernaturally large. Sometimes she is shown as a finger-like object made of bone or bone-colored material that is either undecorated or has round, owl-like eyes. Her image is present from the Upper Paleolithic through the period of Old Europe, and extends to about 2500 BC in the Aegean area.

Throughout prehistory, symbols of death are found combined with symbols of regeneration. In the shrines at Çatal Hüyük, dating from the seventh millennium BC, breasts are shown enclosing boar tusks and vulture skulls. Megalithic graves, stelae, and burial urns carry images of the owl-goddess decorated with breasts, or with her body shown as a life-creating labyrinth, with a vulva at its center.

Symbols of Regeneration and Energy

The goddess of regeneration is shown as a bee; a butterfly; a triangle; an hourglass shape with human head and feet, or with hands in the form of bird claws; a fish; a frog; and a hedgehog. A bull with crescent horns, or a bull's head alone, was also one of the earliest and most common symbols of regeneration and energy. The egg, another universal symbol of rebirth, has been associated with the beginning of the universe since Paleolithic times.

The ideology that gave rise to this extraordinary range of symbols appears to have ultimately disappeared in the wake of the far-reaching social and economic changes that

occurred during the fourth and third millennia BC, which I believe are linked to successive waves of Indo-European pastoralists from the South Russian steppes. By degrees, the Old European world view, with its focus on the mother, gave way to an emphasis on the father.

MARIJA GIMBUTAS

⚨ White lady statuettes such as this one found near Sparta, in the Peloponnese, are always associated with death and are often found in Neolithic graves in southeastern Europe. The figure stands rigidly, with folded arms, and has an enormous pubic triangle.

⚨ The frog goddess is a major Old European archetype of birth-giving and regeneration. This black stone amulet from Thessaly is perforated, suggesting that it was intended to be attached to something else.
MARIJA GIMBUTAS

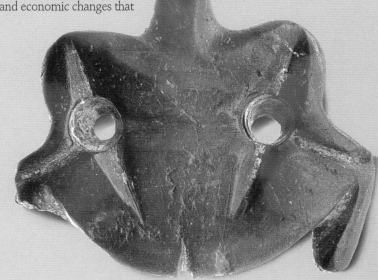

⚥ The famous mound of Barnenez, in northern Brittany, France, contains a tomb consisting of 11 chambers, which are reached by long, narrow passages. The earliest parts of the mound were built about 4500 BC.

C. CUNY/EXPLORER/AUSCAPE

⚥ Reconstruction of a long-barrow at Fussell's Lodge, in Wessex, England. The barrow was 51.5 meters (170 feet) long and was built about 3900 BC to 3800 BC.

ILLUSTRATION: KEN RINKEL, AFTER PAUL ASHBEE (1970): *THE EARTHEN LONG BARROW IN BRITAIN*, DENT, LONDON.

They were inhumations (burials of uncremated bodies), and the grave goods consisted mainly of necklace beads, stone axes, and pottery. Some of the oldest dated stone-built monuments in Brittany are the passage tombs of Barnenez, Ile Gaignog, and Kercado, which were all erected between about 4800 BC and 4500 BC. The material from Kercado comes from an early excavation, but its date closely corresponds with those of the other two. Like most megalithic monuments in western Europe, the French tombs were often rebuilt and enlarged a number of times, or were at least used continuously for long periods of time.

From Tomb to Temple

Almost all the European megalithic monuments were erected during the fourth millennium BC in what were by then well-established farming societies. Later, a handful of regions along the Atlantic coast developed into important ceremonial centers, which probably served ritual purposes for sizeable surrounding areas, far beyond the immediate territories. These early farming societies were characterized by rapid population growth, made possible by the production and storage of food. At the same time, a smaller number of food sources led to greater risks when fluctuations occurred in food production: bad harvests and sudden diseases among animals could have devastating effects on the population. Once the virgin forests of Europe had been occupied by farmers and herders and no further population expansion was possible, pressure on resources increased, forcing people to make better use of existing territories. Improved agricultural technology became necessary, resulting in the appearance of the plow and, during the Late Neolithic period, the two-wheeled cart. Pressures on resources apparently led to conflicts between

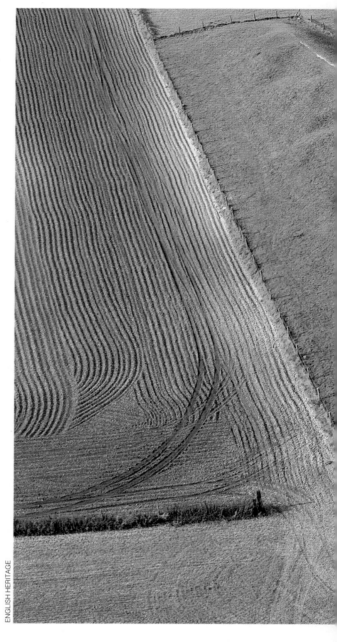

ENGLISH HERITAGE

neighboring groups of people. Many archaeological finds, such as fortified settlements of different kinds and ceremonial battle-axes, reflect increasing levels of aggression.

Jobs such as clearing new land and constructing fences are often beyond the abilities of a single family, and a considerable number of people would have been needed to build the large fortifications and ceremonial centers that early on became part of the first farming societies. During the fourth millennium BC, massive henges and palisades were erected across the continent, in England (in the form of causewayed enclosures), and through to southern Scandinavia—a henge being a circular monument built for ceremonial purposes, generally surrounded by a ditch. As a rule, groups of sizeable burial monuments were situated close to such constructions. The graves often consist of long mounds, a type of structure that is well known across Europe—from Kujavian graves in Poland

The long-barrow of West Kennet, in Wiltshire, southern England, is part of the ritual complex of Avebury. It is about 100 meters (330 feet) long and was built about 3500 BC.

The wall of stones in the eastern end of the West Kennet long-barrow blocks the entrance to a passage that leads into five burial chambers, where the remains of some 46 people have been found.
RONALD SHERIDAN/ANCIENT ART & ARCHITECTURE COLLECTION

The eastern end of the West Kennet long-barrow consists of a concave wall of huge sandstones, blocking an earlier entrance.

to English long-barrows. In western Europe, particularly in the English long-barrows, there is evidence of the practice of secondary burial after removal of the flesh, and the megalithic tombs thus served as ossuaries. Similar constructions have also been found in southern Scandinavia, and from about 3800 BC long-barrows and, occasionally, houses for the dead were erected in Denmark. Recently, however, an entirely new type of Scandinavian monument from this time has come to light: large fortified constructions of a ceremonial character.

At Sarup, on the Danish island of Funen, lies one of these imposing Early Neolithic structures. It consists of a system of moats or pits, each 20 meters (66 feet) in length, which together constitute a formation hundreds of meters long. Close by, a system of earthworks has been found on which a 3 meter (10 foot) high palisade of gigantic oak logs was erected. The whole site

ENGLISH HERITAGE

⚲ Stonehenge, in Wiltshire, is undoubtedly one of the world's most famous prehistoric sites and the most striking megalithic monument in Europe. For a long time, it was a major ritual center for megalithic western Europe. The oldest building phase has been dated at about 3300 BC, when the site consisted of a circular wall with ditches, along which ran a series of sacrifical pits, the so-called "Aubrey Holes". During the second phase, which occurred about 500 years later, the inner stone circle, the "Bluestone Circle", was erected. Today's magnificent stone circle with lintels was built during the early phases of the Bronze Age, about 1800 BC. During all of its long period of use, Stonehenge probably served as a temple that received the first rays of the summer solstice, on 21 June.

covers an area of about 4 hectares (10 acres) and dates from about 3400 BC. All the Danish ceremonial centers known today lie on spits of land in marshes and water systems, and groups of nearby stone-built tombs have been documented. A similar construction has also been found at Stävie, in southern Sweden.

These grand constructions, like the contemporary megalithic graves and temples, must have required joint efforts that would have demanded considerable social organization. Farming societies under the leadership of village chiefs were probably already in existence during the early phases of the European Neolithic period; probably, too, the farming societies behind the large megalithic centers were chiefdoms, with all that this implies in terms of paramount chiefs, specialization, social differentiation, and the redistribution of goods and services. In historically known chiefdoms, the subordinated village chiefs are often members of the royal family, or at least closely related to the paramount chief, and this creates close ties.

The paramount chief often serves as a religious head as well—a master of ceremonies or even a high priest—and in these societies there are objects and regalia that can be linked directly to official positions and duties, as well as temples and ceremonial centers. It is in this connection that we may be able to understand the reasons behind the erection of those remarkable megalithic monuments at that time, especially in England, Ireland, and France.

The Sun and the Stones

In Wiltshire, in southern England—one of the main areas for stone-built tombs in Europe—there are a number of huge circular monuments. The earliest constructions were causewayed enclosures, such as the one on Windmill Hill, where a system of ditches and earthworks with transverse passages provides the basic structure. Most characteristic, however, are the henges, which are the most common kind of construction in the area and are often equipped with circular ditches and one or more inner circles built of stone or wood.

ADAM WOOLFITT/ROBERT HARDING PICTURE LIBRARY

The biggest and most remarkable of these circular monuments is Avebury, in the middle of which now lies a whole village complete with church, pub, and petrol station; Woodhenge and Stonehenge are others.

The actual megalithic tomb at each of these sites is most often built into the short side of a magnificent long-barrow, and an almost complete lack of ornamental decorations on the graves and ceremonial monuments is characteristic of the region. The exception is Stonehenge, which boasts a series of carvings of bronze axes dating from early metal times, the period when the monument was last in use.

Modern excavations at Avebury have shown that polished stone axes were deposited there during religious ceremonies. By studying the shapes of these axes and the kinds of rock from which they were made, it is easy to determine where they came from, and it has been shown that they originated from practically every known megalithic area in southwestern England—from Cornwall, in the south, to Liverpool, in the north. Interestingly, no axes have been found that can be shown to have originated from the rich Neolithic districts further east, the reason being that megalithic burial and ceremonial traditions

CHARLES WALKER COLLECTION, LONDON

☝ The huge site of Avebury, in Wiltshire, with a diameter of more than 400 meters (1,300 feet)—in the middle of which lies a whole village— is the biggest henge monument in the region. It was used between about 3000 BC and 2000 BC, and forms part of a major ritual complex that also includes the West Kennet long-barrow, Windmill Hill, and Silbury Hill.

← The stone circle that surrounds Avebury originally consisted of more than 100 stones, many of which weigh about 40 tonnes (39 tons).

CAUSEWAYED ENCLOSURES

Richard Bradley

Farming communities in Europe first appeared mainly in two areas. On the fertile soils of central Europe and the Rhineland, we find evidence of large settlements with a productive agricultural economy; and here it seems as if people were moving into a largely unused environment. In the western Mediterranean, along the Atlantic coastline, and in southern Scandinavia, farming was adopted more gradually, and there is evidence of stable populations of hunter-gatherers. Each of the two areas is associated with one distinctive kind of monument: megalithic tombs originated along the Atlantic coastline and in Scandinavia; earthwork enclosures first developed among the Rhineland settlements and in neighboring areas.

The contrast goes even further. Some of the earliest burial monuments along the coastline copy the form of the longhouses in the agricultural heartland, and in these areas the houses of the living are rarely found. Where the large settlements of central Europe are discovered, especially those in the Rhineland, they are sometimes enclosed by earthworks consisting of between one and three banks and ditches. These can form continuous barriers, but in certain cases the ditches are interrupted at regular intervals by narrow causeways—hence the term "causewayed enclosures".

The earliest enclosures are poorly understood. They date from about 4800 BC and were built towards the end of the first period of farming expansion in central Europe. Often they were constructed near substantial settlements, and sometimes they occupy open spaces in between the main groups of houses and emphasize an area of ground that had already been important for some time. They were usually constructed towards the end of the period in which the settlement was in use, and sometimes even after any houses had been abandoned. These enclosures seem to have been used for a variety of communal activities,

GEORG GERSTER/JOHN HILLELSON AGENCY

including preparing food and making flint artifacts. On a few sites, new settlements have been built on old enclosures, and in these cases the earthworks were sometimes rebuilt on a larger scale. Sites that began as specialized enclosures within a heavily settled landscape sometimes themselves became fortified settlements. Among these were settlements whose inhabitants specialized in making fine pottery.

By about 4000 BC, there are signs of a more fragmented pattern of settlement. Major groups of longhouses no longer appear, and there are fewer signs of an expanding agricultural economy. While settlement sites are harder to discover, causewayed enclosures continue to be built, and their distribution extends to France. More of them adopt an extremely stereotyped ground plan. A few of these earthworks and ditches still enclose houses, but alongside these there is a range of quite new kinds of archaeological deposits. Some of the enclosures contained special kinds of artifacts, including unusual types of pottery normally found only with the dead. Meat joints, or even entire animals, have been found buried either within the filling of the ditches or in specially excavated pits inside the enclosure. Some appear to be the

remains of feasts, while others may be sacrificial deposits. There are also human burials. Although whole bodies are sometimes found, isolated bones are more common. This is consistent with the discovery of defleshed human remains, sometimes in elaborate formal arrangements, inside Neolithic funeral monuments. Some parts of the body are underrepresented in the monuments, suggesting that ancestral relics may have been circulated amongst the living. Human skulls are frequent finds and were often deposited in the ditches.

Causewayed enclosures were most widely distributed between about 3800 BC and 3200 BC. They extended from central Europe as far west as the Atlantic coast of France, as far south as Languedoc, and as far north as Britain, Denmark, and Sweden. As they did so, we find two major developments. Some enclosures were built in areas where there is little evidence of intensive farming. At the same time, the causeways in the ditches became the focus for more and more extravagant deposits of artifacts and human and animal bones. A growing proportion of the objects deposited were of nonlocal origin. The circulation of human remains became even more important, and it

◄◄ Hambledon Hill, in England, where the earthworks of a late prehistoric hill-fort overlie a complex of Neolithic causewayed enclosures and burial mounds. One enclosure was ringed by human skulls and may have been used for exposing the dead, while another was a defended settlement.

is only in this period that we find earthwork enclosures in the same areas as megalithic tombs—human bones may even have been moved between these monuments. Some enclosures were still constructed in the heart of the settled landscape, but in other areas they were in remote locations, sometimes in small woodland clearings. They took on important roles as communal meeting places, and there is still greater evidence that they were used for the exchange of exotic objects and for large-scale feasting.

Finally, in Britain and western France, a few of these monuments were reconstructed as defended settlements. Their earthworks were rebuilt without any causeways, and inside we find the remains of houses. Sometimes these defenses were not effective: a small number have been discovered that were attacked and destroyed. In Denmark, we find a similar sequence, but there the earthworks were abandoned and replaced by open settlements. In a sense, the history of enclosures turns back on itself. Some of the earliest sites had been enclosed settlements; so, too, were some of the last to be built. In between, they played a variety of more mysterious roles in prehistoric society, including the celebration of the dead.

The fact that the same kind of enclosure was built for considerably more than a thousand years, and across such large areas of Europe, is testimony to the strength of beliefs that we cannot understand in any detail today. But we do know that a basic continuity of ritual architecture has been maintained over a similar period in more recent societies—we might think, for example, of the stereotyped ground plans of mosques and Christian churches.

were not adopted in those regions. The area of origin of the axes found at Avebury thus corresponds exactly with the area of distribution of megalithic tombs in southwestern England. This gives an important dimension to the contemporary religious and social systems, in which an advanced religious organization apparently reached far beyond the borders of the individual megalithic farming economies scattered throughout this vast area. Furthermore, a very marked boundary line can be shown to have been drawn against societies that for some reason did not adopt the tradition of building megalithic monuments.

The sheer size of the megalithic structures in Wiltshire suggests that they were erected by a work force that could not have been called in from the immediate vicinity alone. The ditch and the large stone circle at Avebury boast a diameter of more than 400 meters (1,300 feet), and the circle originally consisted of more than 100 stones, many of which weigh about 40 tonnes (39 tons). Inside the circle were two smaller stone circles, each measuring about 100 meters (330 feet) in diameter, and from the southern part of the monument a system of stone alignments almost 2 kilometers (a little over a mile) long—the Kennet Avenue— leads in the direction of a huge mound known as Silbury Hill.

Silbury Hill is Europe's largest prehistoric mound. It is 40 meters (130 feet) high and covers an area of 2.2 hectares (5 acres). This huge hill is probably not a burial mound—the partly terraced hillside and the flat crest suggest that it once formed the foundation of a temple building. It may have been used in the cult ceremonies at Avebury

and Kennet Avenue. During the 1970s, a tunnel was cut into the middle of the mound. No grave was found, but it was established that the entire hill was man-made, and radiocarbon datings of peat found inside showed that it was built during megalithic times and was partly contemporaneous with Avebury. It has been calculated that if 500 men were to have been constantly engaged in building Silbury Hill, it would have taken more than 10 years to construct. A central leadership, or at least a concentration of religious power, would have been essential to ensure such a long-term effort. To a great extent, this also applies to the building of Stonehenge, where it is thought that the building material for the bluestone circle was transported to Wiltshire from the Preseli Mountains, in southern Wales, some 400 kilometers (250 miles) away.

It is likely that a similar religious "super-organization" existed, along with traditional tribal societies, in another important megalithic region in western Europe: Carnac, in France. The huge structures concentrated in the area around Carnac and Locmariaquer, in Morbihan, southern Brittany, are among Europe's most distinctive megalithic monuments. The most conspicuous are the menhir (standing stone) alignments erected in three main complexes: Le Ménec, Kermario, and Kerlescan, where some 3,000 menhirs still stand in rows. Most of them are colossal—up to 6 meters (20 feet) high—and together the alignments are nearly 4 kilometers (more than 2 miles) long. The complexes of erected stones are all composed of parallel alignments—at Kerlescan, no fewer than 13—and each complex is about 100 meters

⚑ The passage grave of Les Pierres Plates, at Locmariaquer, in Brittany, France. A large number of stones in this monument, notably the orthostats, are decorated with carvings.

⚑ Silbury Hill, in Wiltshire, is 40 meters (130 feet) high and 160 meters (525 feet) in diameter, making it the largest man-made mound in Europe. It was built some time during the third millennium BC. It contains no burial remains, and it is thought that it once served as the foundation of a temple building.

(330 feet) wide. Connected with these rows of stones are stone altars, stone circles, and a long series of megalithic tombs.

Many suggestions have been made as to the ceremonial function of the alignments, but no conclusive explanation has yet been given. Perhaps the individual stones represented deceased ancestors. Le Grand Menhir—a huge menhir at Locmariaquer, which today is broken into five pieces but was originally 21 meters (nearly 70 feet) high—may once have been used for astronomical observations or simply as a clearly visible center for the cult, as on clear days it could have been seen from many places around the Bay of Morbihan, including the stone alignments at Le Ménec, Kermario, and Kerlescan. Le Grand Menhir, probably the world's biggest menhir, is partly shaped and has an even, smoothed surface. It consists of a kind of granite that is not native to the area and must have been transported from the interior of Brittany to its final position by the water's edge—a remarkable feat, considering that it weighs 350 tonnes (345 tons).

In terms of megalithic ornamentation, Carnac is one of Europe's most important regions. At present, we know of 250 decorated stones from 75 different sites, mainly passage tombs, in Brittany alone. The earliest passage tombs, such as Ile Gaignog, date from the period between 4800 BC and 3700 BC. They contain simple depictions, such as yoke-like figures, sickles (or "hooks"), and axe blades with handles, and various kinds of anthropomorphic motifs— so-called "bucklers", which appear to represent divine figures.

The later passage tombs date from the period between 3700 BC and 3100 BC. By that time, megalithic monuments had become considerably

◄ The Le Ménec alignments, at Carnac, in Brittany, France, consist of 11 parallel lines of stones more than a kilometer long. We do not know what ceremonial function these alignments may have served, but it has been suggested that the individual stones may represent dead ancestors.

⬆ A large number of megalithic tombs, stone altars, and stone circles, such as this one, are found in association with the remarkable stone alignments of Carnac.

⬇ An historical drawing from *Archéologie Gaule*, showing the stone alignments at Carnac.

⤳ The large passage grave of Gavrinis, situated on an island in the Bay of Morbihan, near Carnac, is one of the large megalithic monuments in western Europe that contain decorated stones. The orthostats in both the chamber and the passage are decorated. Clear similarities can be seen between this site and Newgrange, in Ireland.

⚲ The carvings of Gavrinis are characterized by large groups of U-shaped patterns, snake figures, and zig-zag lines, as well as triangular axe blades in relief.

P. PLISSON/EXPLORER/AUSCAPE

P. PLISSON/EXPLORER/AUSCAPE

⚲ The passage grave of Antelas, at Oliveira de Frades, near Viseu, Portugal. This grave contains magnificent megalithic decorations in the form of schematic paintings in red and black.

GÖRAN BURENHULT

bigger, the tombs' interiors had been enlarged, and the passages extended. It was during this period that well-defined, inner compartments were constructed. The ornamentation, which originated from the earlier period, went through a remarkable development during this later phase, and it was at this time that some of the most splendid decorations in megalithic western Europe were created—equaled only by the art of the passage tombs in the Boyne Valley, in Ireland. There are close similarities between some elements of the decorations in the two regions, and contact between the two regions at this time of artistic perfection cannot be ruled out.

The peak of megalithic composition is represented by a passage tomb on Ile de Gavrinis, an island in the middle of the Bay of Morbihan. Here, both the stones in the chamber and those in the passage are decorated, and U-shaped images are boxed inside each other and placed in groups of differing sizes and in a variety of positions.

The anthropomorphic figures, which were among the original images in the early passage tombs in Brittany, developed from symbolic images into more and more marked, visual parts of the cult ceremonies. From very simple, frame-like images, these bucklers gradually became figures with marks indicating eyes and breasts, and in spite of their austere style, they appear to depict a divine figure. In megalithic monuments dating from the end of the Stone Age, these images appear to represent a female goddess. In gallery graves, which are the latest of the megalithic tombs, she is represented by a pair of breasts in relief, often with a necklace of beads placed either above or below the breasts. The worship of this female deity is also reflected in freestanding anthropomorphic stelae (upright slabs) or menhir statues in western France, which have eyes, a nose, and marks clearly indicating breasts: there is no doubt as to their sex. Some of these figures, usually those with necklaces, also have stylized hands, usually placed below the breasts.

Along with the magnificent stone-built tombs in Brittany, the Irish passage graves represent some of Europe's most imposing and grandiose monuments. Most of them are clustered in groups in the northern and, especially, the eastern parts of the island, and they are often dramatically situated high on mountain ridges. Loughcrew, in County Meath, and Carrowkeel, in County Sligo, are among the important grave fields, and there are also magnificent constructions at Tara and Fourknocks, in County Meath, and at Baltinglass, in County Wicklow. The most outstanding, however, are Newgrange, Knowth, and Dowth, in the Boyne Valley, County Meath.

Some 25 kilometers (16 miles) from its mouth at Drogheda, by the Irish Sea, the Boyne River makes a sharp bend, in the middle of which lie three giant 5,000-year-old mounds. Two of them, Newgrange and Knowth, have for many years been the subject of systematic excavations. Newgrange has been reliably dated at about 3200 BC to 3000 BC, and thus represents the end of a 1,500-year-old megalithic tradition in Ireland. Knowth is somewhat older and has been dated to about 3700 BC to 3500 BC.

Newgrange is gigantic. It measures 85 meters (279 feet) in diameter and covers an area of almost half a hectare (1 acre). A passage 19 meters (62 feet) long leads into the cruciform chamber, which has a corbeled roof and a ceiling 6 meters (20 feet) high. Almost every stone in the kerbstone circle, as well as in the passage, is covered with ornamentation. The people who built this monument clearly had a sophisticated knowledge of astronomy: the entire grave is constructed to receive the first rays of the winter solstice on 21 December through a separate roof-box above the long passage. Newgrange is a gigantic observatory that was erected to serve a megalithic cult. (See the feature *Newgrange: Temple of the Sun*.)

Cannibals in the North

The stone-built tombs in northern Europe are known for their rich finds of burial deposits. These consist mainly of splendidly decorated pottery of many different shapes, but there are also large numbers of amber amulets in the form of miniature clubs or battle-axes. Often, these finds have been made outside the entrances to the chambers, and it was once assumed that they were the remains of grave goods that had been removed before later burials had taken place. In the 1930s, however, it was shown that most of these finds had never been placed inside the chambers but were simply the remnants of sacrificial food offerings made in connection with burials and

other recurring ceremonies. That an ancestor cult predominated is clearly indicated by these megalithic rituals.

The burials always took the form of inhumations. Large numbers of bodies were placed on the floor of the chamber, with space often being left for later burials. During the time they were in use, the graves must have been filled with bodies in varying stages of decomposition. In some places, the burial chambers were divided into smaller units separated by stone slabs. As a rule, these compartments are too small to accommodate a body lying prone, yet the bones of complete individuals have been found within them. It is possible that the flesh was removed from the bodies before they were buried, as in long-barrow burials in England, perhaps by boiling or decomposition. However, since there are no traces of cutting on the bones, and since not even the smallest bones of the feet are missing, it seems likely that the bodies were placed in a sitting position in the compartments, with their arms and legs tied together, and that they were left to decompose.

Cremated human bones have often been found during excavations of dolmens and passage graves, particularly outside the entrances to the chambers, and this has been taken as clear evidence that human sacrifices took place in connection with megalithic burial ceremonies, as cremation was never practiced in northern Europe during the Stone Age. Furthermore, the excavation of a dolmen at Fosie, in southernmost Sweden, has shown that a series of cremated human bones, which were all placed beneath separate stone slabs, was the result of cannibalism. Probably only the brains were eaten, as the bones consisted of the deliberately broken cranial parts of 22 people.

⚡ The megalithic decorations in the Viseu region, in Portugal, as well as those in Galicia and Cantabria, in Spain, consist mainly of paintings, which are often on stones in the chambers. Fortunately, many of these 5,000-year-old works of art are very well preserved, including this one in the passage grave of Antelas.

REPRODUCED BY PERMISSION OF OXFORD UNIVERSITY PRESS FROM ELIZABETH SHEE TWOHIG (1981): *THE MEGALITHIC ART OF WESTERN EUROPE* [AFTER ALBUQUERQUE E. CASTRO *ET AL.* (1957): *COMM. SERV. GEOL.* 38].

⚡ The first signs of aggression and war in northern Europe appeared as people began to adopt a settled way of life and to take up farming. This 35-year-old man from Porsmose, outside Naestved, in Denmark, was pierced by two bone arrows. One of them had pierced his breastbone, the other had gone through his nose and into his brain. The man lived about 3000 BC, during the time of the megalithic tradition.

NATIONAL MUSEUM OF DENMARK, DEPARTMENT OF ETHNOGRAPHY

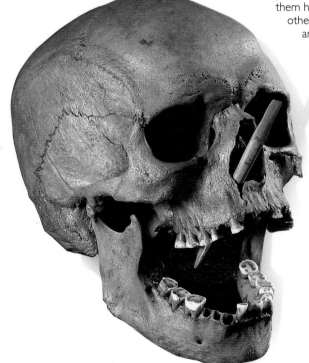

NEWGRANGE: TEMPLE OF THE SUN

GÖRAN BURENHULT

JUST ONCE EVERY YEAR, at 9.54 am on 21 December, a growing light spreads gradually in the pitch-dark burial chamber. Six minutes later, the sunbeam is at its broadest and bathes the chamber, situated 22 meters (72 feet) from the entrance, in a dazzling light. Then the light starts to fade, and by 10.15 am it has disappeared altogether.

This amazing scene lasts for 21 minutes, and after that the burial chamber remains in total darkness for a further 364 days, until the next winter solstice. The place is Newgrange, in the Boyne Valley, in Ireland, one of the most splendid megalithic monuments in Europe—a passage grave with a cruciform chamber, situated deep in a magnificent mound. Newgrange and the nearby mounds of Knowth and Dowth are grand monuments of a Stone Age society in western Europe and bear witness to an astonishing knowledge of technology and astronomy.

The graves represent the peak of an almost 2,000-year-old megalithic tradition in Ireland, and have been dated at about 3200 BC, making them more than 500 years older than the Pyramid of Cheops, in Egypt. It is well known that the sun played an important part in the cult ceremonies of the Stone Age, the best example being Stonehenge, in southern England, which was designed to predict the summer solstice. But it was not until Michael J. O'Kelly's excavation of Newgrange at the end of the 1960s that it became clear that the winter solstice, the rebirth of the year, had also been of great importance in cult ceremonies and rituals among Ireland's Stone Age farmers.

The chamber has a corbeled roof, and is thus held together by the weight of the soil above. Each roof-stone is pushed in a little more than the one below, so each layer of stones reduces the diameter of the roof. During construction, the roof must have been supported from within by stanchions. Neither the

↩ Once a year, on 21 December, at 9.54 am, the burial chamber of Newgrange is illuminated by the rising sun. At 10.15 am, this dwelling of the dead once again rests in total darkness for a further 364 days.

⚲ The excavator, Michael J. O'Kelly, beside the entrance stone at Newgrange, which is considered by many to be the most exquisite example of megalithic art known. The stone slab to the right of the passage entrance is the sealing stone that once blocked the entrance and thus separated the world of the living from the world of the dead. The roof-box, through which the first rays of the winter solstice penetrate, is clearly visible above the entrance.

chamber nor its vaults has ever been rebuilt or even repaired, so the construction has withstood the ravages of time for more than 5,000 years.

In 1963, during the excavation of the monument, a notable discovery was made above the passage entrance. There is a rectangular opening, 90 centimeters (about 3 feet) high, on top of the passage roof-block, and this roof-box runs the entire length of the first passage and leads into the chamber. An elegant triangular pattern is carved on the front of the first roof-block. On the ground below the opening, two quartzite cubes were found, both of which were scored horizontally on the underside. These cubes fitted exactly into the opening, and furthermore, the first roof-block had the same kind of horizontal scores. It was obvious that the quartzite cubes had been used to seal the opening of the upper passage, and judging from the scoring, this passage had been opened and resealed frequently.

When Newgrange was completed at the end of the fourth millennium BC, the chamber and passage were sealed with a stone block, and at subsequent cult ceremonies no one was admitted to the monument's interior. Clearly, the opening and the narrow tunnel above the passage served as a "channel of communication" between the living, outside the sealed chamber, and the dead, inside.

Professor O'Kelly made some calculations relating to the function of the roof-box. These showed that the summer solstice could not have had any significance at Newgrange, but that the winter solstice, on 21 December, could possibly explain the complicated construction above the passage. In the early morning of 21 December 1969, O'Kelly made his way into the dark chamber to see if his calculations were correct. He sealed the entrance of the monument with a black cloth, just as the sealing stone had once blocked the opening, but the narrow tunnel above the passage was left open.

With his camera ready, he sat down in the middle of the floor of the chamber and waited for the sun to rise. He switched off his torch, and everything turned pitch-black. The rest is best described in O'Kelly's own words:

"At exactly 9.54 a.m. (BST) the top edge of the ball of the sun appeared above the local horizon and at 9.58 a.m. the first pencil of direct sunlight shone through the roof-box and right along the passage to reach across the tomb chamber floor as far as the front edge of the basin stone in the end-chamber. As the thin line of light widened to a

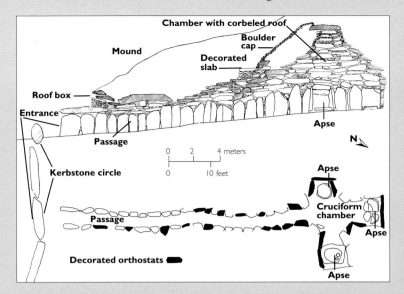

17 cm [7 inch] band and swung across the chamber floor, the tomb was dramatically illuminated and various details of the side and end-chambers as well as the corbelled roof could be clearly seen in the light reflected from the floor. At 10.04 a.m. the 17 cm band of light began to narrow again and at exactly 10.15 a.m. the direct beam was cut off from the tomb. For 17 minutes, therefore, at sunrise on the shortest day of the year, direct sunlight can enter Newgrange, not through the doorway, but through the specially-contrived narrow slit which lies under the roof-box at the outer end of the passage roof."

So the roof-box was opened before sunrise on 21 December every year to let the first sunbeams of the year into the chamber, but what happened then? Were the spirits of the dead consulted about the coming year? Or did the living report on what had been done during the past one? Were people sacrificed—

⊕ Plan and profile drawings of the passage and chamber of Newgrange. The stones marked in black are decorated. The passage that leads into the chamber extends for 19 meters (60 feet) and is lined with more than 40 monoliths, 15 of which are decorated with carvings.
AFTER O'KELLY, 1975

⊕ Newgrange has a diameter of between 79 and 85 meters (260 and 280 feet). It is bordered by a kerbstone circle consisting of 97 boulders, each more than 3 meters (about 10 feet) long, and almost all of them are richly decorated with megalithic carvings.

⊕ A majority of the weight-bearing monoliths in the burial chamber and the apses are exquisitely decorated, mainly with spirals and zigzag patterns, the finest ornament of all being the famous triple spiral.

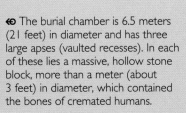

⊕ The burial chamber is 6.5 meters (21 feet) in diameter and has three large apses (vaulted recesses). In each of these lies a massive, hollow stone block, more than a meter (about 3 feet) in diameter, which contained the bones of cremated humans.

or only animals? Which individuals in society went to their final rest in Newgrange? Many small megalithic tombs in Ireland contain the bones of hundreds of cremated people, but only a small number have been found in Newgrange. These few may have been chiefs who also served as priests, but it is also possible that the bones are those of people sacrificed at the inauguration of the monument and that Newgrange was never used as a burial chamber. Clearly, it was primarily a cult center—not a burial place.

Newgrange provides a splendid example of the intellectual sophistication of our illiterate, Stone Age ancestors. Advanced social systems probably existed in many regions in Europe as early as 5,000 years ago. Certainly, there were powerful chiefdoms that maintained close contacts with each other over wide areas. There is evidence in southern England that the stone circles at

Avebury were used for cult ceremonies that were common to the whole southwestern part of the country, from Cornwall in the south to the north of Wales. While the sun played a central role in these ceremonies, it is not clear what additional astronomical observations may have been made at the ceremonies. Behind this monument—one of prehistory's most advanced constructions—lie centuries, even millennia, of astronomical observations and cult ceremonies, the forms of which would have been transmitted orally from generation to generation.

GÖRAN BURENHULT

⚓ The stone-built tombs in the district of Drenthe, in northern Holland, are some of the most impressive in Europe, both in terms of length and the size of the stones used. This dolmen at Borger, on the road between Assen and Emmen, is one of the most outstanding examples in the region.

GÖRAN BURENHULT

⚓ A well-preserved, stone-built tomb at Drouwen, north of Borger, in the district of Drenthe.

Remains of people from megalithic times who were sacrificed and eaten have also been found in bogs. One such find was made in a bog at Sigersdal, in Zealand, Denmark, consisting of the remains of two naked young girls (probably sisters) who had been strangled, clubbed, and drowned about 3500 BC. A clay pot, the bottom marked by the imprints of emmer grains, was found with them. The pot had probably contained food offerings, a common type of sacrifice during Neolithic times. Further out into the bog, 13 magnificent polished flint axes had been lowered into the water as well.

It seems likely that some form of fertility cult was behind the sacrifice at Sigersdal. By making such an offering, people believed that they would secure the right conditions for continued existence and for the return of the seasons, with new crops and new human and animal offspring. These rituals were probably linked to the winter and summer solstices, a connection that, in megalithic Europe, is clearly seen in monuments such as Newgrange and Stonehenge, whose main function was related to these important annual events.

There are several examples of cannibalism from the period around 3500 BC, when the sisters were sacrificed at Sigersdal. At Troldebjerg, in Langeland,

Denmark, the remains of at least three people have been found, together with votive offerings in the form of flint axes, battle-axes, and pottery containing food. The human offerings included a 13-year-old child and a 40-year-old woman, both of whom had been killed by violent blows to the head. Sacrificial animals, including five young steers, four pigs, a goat, and a dog, show traces of having been killed in the same way.

The Surviving Evidence

Megalithic traditions have survived in many societies in various parts of the world, and in some places stone-built tombs are still erected over the dead. Studying these more recent cultures can help us understand some of the elements that gave rise to megalithic traditions, the beliefs of megalithic people, and the function of the monuments. For a start, it is clear that such tombs were never built by mobile hunting-gathering societies. While this may seem self-evident, the building of the tombs themselves can be related to many factors, such as social ranking, group size, and a degree of territorial control, which would often have led to increased aggression.

In all such peoples studied, all members of a society are well aware of which person or family has built and uses a certain monument, and the social rank of an individual is generally reflected in the size, appearance, or placing of the tomb or the erected stone. Another distinctive trait of most of these societies is the fact that many people or families are not entitled to erect any monument at all over their dead. In some societies, every man, or at least a majority of the men, can, by way of complicated and costly ceremonies, work his way up to a sufficiently high rank for this to become possible. In other societies, however, this is not possible, because the traditional hereditary lines cannot be broken.

It is clear, therefore, that megalithic monuments are erected only by settled societies with a relatively high population density, and the right to such a monument is associated with high social rank, either inherited or acquired. Without exception, the leaders of those societies are chiefs. In addition, human sacrifices, and sometimes the eating of individuals from enemy tribes, played a crucial role in all historically known megalithic societies. This corresponds with the archaeological record of the European Neolithic period, and suggests a society in which aggressive actions were thought necessary to ensure continued existence, and in which these actions were part of religious ceremonies. Outside pressure and warfare demand powerful leaders, and it is perhaps unsurprising that all known megalithic societies are dominated by men. This does not necessarily imply that women have a low status, but only that the men hold the political power and perform the cult ceremonies.

In historically known megalithic societies, monuments never serve primarily as territorial markers, nor do they depend on the society's technological level, as they appear in societies resembling those of the Stone Age, the Bronze Age, and the Iron Age. But societies that depend on stone-built tombs for their cult ceremonies have many features in common. The cult is almost always associated with the worship of ancestors. In some heavily stratified societies, including most of the Polynesian chiefdoms in the Pacific, some megalithic monuments were associated with the worship of gods, but these are the exceptions that prove the rule. Usually, the different graves and menhirs represent ancestors whose spirits are considered to be always present and to take part in the ceremonies. Sacrificial offerings are made to appease ancestors and secure admission to the kingdom of the dead, where the final reunion takes place. In societies that erect tombs with entrances, similar to the European dolmens and passage graves, the entrance generally represents the gates of the kingdom of the dead. Clearly, people's motives in erecting megalithic monuments seem similar, irrespective of time and place.

The reasons for the decline of the megalithic tradition in Neolithic western Europe are not well understood. Economic and social collapse has been suggested as a possible explanation, but a religious upheaval probably also played a crucial part in the social changes that occurred across the continent about the middle of the third millennium BC. The changes were also partly a consequence of the appearance of metal and other innovations, such as the wheel, the cart, and possibly also the use of horses for riding. Behind this change in tradition lies the appearance of the so-called Battle-axe cultures, which were once thought to have been a part of the Indo-European migrations. It can be shown, however, that these new societies had their beginnings in the old, megalithic ones because of the continued and widespread use of the old burial grounds and, above all, because of the continuity of settlement that has been revealed by modern excavations.

From about 2800 BC, no new stone-built monuments were erected in Europe. The megalithic priests had had their day.

⌂ The world's oldest monumental entrance, the entrance to the Hagar Qim temple, on the island of Malta, is a magnificent example of early megalithic architecture.

⚲ The megalithic temple of Mnajdra, which lies on the south coast of Malta, is characterized by a complicated inner construction and the presence of high altar stones of different kinds.

NEW LIGHT ON DEATH IN PREHISTORIC MALTA: THE BROCHTORFF CIRCLE

DAVID TRUMP, ANTHONY BONANNO, TANCRED GOUDER, CAROLINE MALONE, AND SIMON STODDART

⚱ A large, headless, standing statuette from the temple of Hagar Qim, carved from soft limestone. Although they are often referred to as "mother goddesses", the sexuality of these stone figures from Malta is ambiguous.

RONALD SHERIDAN/ANCIENT ART & ARCHITECTURE COLLECTION

THE SMALL MEDITERRANEAN ISLANDS of the Maltese archipelago are famous for their temples built between 3500 BC and 2500 BC, which are some of the earliest free-standing stone buildings in the world. These complex, lobed structures, with altars, doorways, and a great deal of decorated, carved stone, bear witness to the elaborate rituals and beliefs of prehistoric peoples.

Rituals connected with the dead were carried out in one of the most impressive of all prehistoric sites, the Hal Saflieni hypogeum. This extraordinary underground chamber was once the burial temple of an estimated 6,000 to 7,000 people. Carved out of soft limestone, it has many elements in common with the other temples, including megalithic doorways, and has steps leading into some 30 major rooms, arranged on three main levels. Salvage excavations undertaken in the early 1900s resulted in most of the skeletal material within the hypogeum being discarded and lost, and few records survive even of the layout of the finds.

An Underground Burial Monument

Recently, however, excavations have been carried out on the Brochtorff Circle, a monument on the island of Gozo similar to Hal Saflieni, and this work is providing valuable information about prehistoric burial customs, enabling researchers to fill in many details that were lost at Hal Saflieni. The Brochtorff Circle was first excavated in the 1820s, but, fortunately for posterity, these excavations were not completed. The only useful

⚱ The innermost excavated area of the Brochtorff Circle, showing the limestone cave system, embellished by architectural features.

CAROLINE MALONE/SIMON STODDART

☞ The details of this reconstruction of the Brochtorff Circle are based on recently excavated evidence. Many of the cavities would originally have been roofed.

AFTER STEVEN ASHLEY

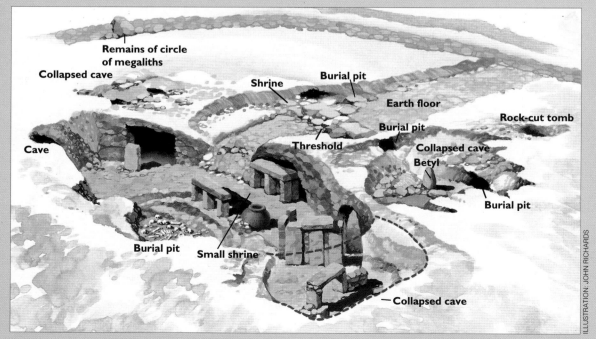

Remains of circle of megaliths

Collapsed cave

Shrine

Burial pit

Earth floor

Rock-cut tomb

Burial pit

Cave

Threshold

Collapsed cave

Betyl

Burial pit

Burial pit

Small shrine

Collapsed cave

ILLUSTRATION: JOHN RICHARDS

Eight limestone figures found in a bundle at the small shrine—perhaps the tools of trade of a ritual specialist. Some appear to be at varying stages of manufacture.

quite distinct from other forms of Mediterranean sculpture. The figures had distinctive hairstyles, with pigtails. The surviving head shows an elaborate "bob", with a pigtail at the back. One holds what may be a smaller representation of itself, and the other holds a small vessel. The attractive honey-colored stone was originally painted in many colors, and traces of black, red, and yellow can still be made out today. What was the significance of these two figures? Only by analyzing the context of the shrine in the course of future excavations can we hope to answer this question.

Immediately next to this shrine, a natural pit full of bones shows that the site was primarily a place of burial. Small "mother goddess" figurines of baked clay accompanied these burials. Bodies were not interred complete, but were evidently the subject of a series of rites that have left their traces throughout the caves and niches on the site. Bundle burials (bundles of bones), scorched burials (partly burned bones), partly articulated bodies, stacks of skulls, and numerous other configurations have been recorded, some of them buried alongside domestic animals, including pigs, sheep, and even a small puppy.

This burial site appears to have been the focus of an entire community, and preliminary analysis of the human bones suggests that people of all ages, both male and female, were buried here. Whereas there are several temples on the plateau, there is only one monumental cemetery, situated strategically on slighly higher ground between two temples.

records of this early work are two watercolours by a local artist.

The Brochtorff Circle was first used about 4000 BC, and stands on a plateau of rough coralline limestone. A vertical shaft opened into a rock-cut tomb consisting of two chambers about 2 meters (6 feet, 6 inches) in diameter. This tomb contained the partial remains of at least 63 people, deposited in a burial rite in which many of the long bones and skulls of earlier occupants were removed and disposed of to make room for new arrivals. The bodies were placed in the chambers together with shell necklaces, pots of ocher, and small stone and bone pendants. A curious carved stone figure of type known as a statue menhir stood in the entrance of one chamber, and a large seashell in a jar of ocher stood in the other.

The Ceremonial Heart

In time, these small-scale burial tombs, which were possibly used for individual families, were superseded by a much larger communal cave cemetery. This

cemetery was established in a natural cave system that was transformed through the use of blocks of softer stone, improving its appearance and adding to its architectural qualities. A circle of megaliths was set up surrounding the site, two larger, upright stones flanked the entrance, and a large temple-structure filled a roofless cave at the center of the circle. This temple was the ceremonial and ritual heart of the site. The excavations have recently un-

covered a small shrine, flanked by a standing megalithic screen, where someone, perhaps a shaman, appears to have left the tools of his trade: a bundle of figures with flat, schematic bodies, a pottery strainer, a small pot of yellow ocher, a large stone vessel and, most remarkable of all, a stone sculpture representing a pair of obese figures sitting side-by-side on a wicker couch.

These seated figures are unique in the Maltese islands and

Seated side-by-side on a couch, these limestone figures (one with the head broken off) were found together with the figures shown above. The one on the left holds a smaller figure; the other, a small cup.

BRONZE AGE CHIEFDOMS AND THE END OF STONE AGE EUROPE

4 5 0 0 B C – 7 5 0 B C

The Rise of the Individual

ANTHONY HARDING

THE AGE OF BRONZE in Europe was, in truth, a kind of Golden Age—an age in which a number of major advances occurred that were to transform the Neolithic world of "Old Europe" into the home of the Celts, the Italians, the Etruscans, the Thracians, and the Dacians, along with all the other people of the region known from historic times. The years between 3000 BC and 700 BC therefore represent a crucial transitional stage of development for society, technology, and the economy.

Although the alloys used in copper metallurgy may seem a relatively minor matter compared with the other important developments that took place during this period, metalworking for the production of tools and weapons became a major preoccupation for the people of those times. The changes that occurred in this technology over time have enabled archaeologists to develop a chronological framework for the period, and to see the period within the broader context of human development between the last Ice Age and the rise of the Greek and Roman civilizations.

◄● Sheet bronze body-armor molded to the contours of the human torso, and decorated with bosses. This fine cuirass was found at Marmesse, in France, and dates from the Late Bronze Age—the ninth or eighth century BC.

◐ This beaten sheet gold ornament in the form of a cross with spiral terminals, from the Moigrad Treasure, Romania, is from the Late Neolithic period, about 5000 BC to 3000 BC.

C. M. DIXON

BRONZE AGE SITES

The major Bronze Age sites mentioned in the text are shown, together with mining areas. There were major Bronze Age centers in many other areas as well.

CARTOGRAPHY: RAY SIM

⚘ **Mine sites**

⚲ Two gold earrings from Boltby Scar, Yorkshire, England. The use of gold to adorn the head and hair is a sure sign that this metal was highly valued.

BRITISH MUSEUM

⚲ The entrance to one of the Bronze Age mine shafts at Mount Gabriel, County Cork, in southwestern Ireland.

WILLIAM O'BRIEN

The Quest for Metal

Metals came into regular use, in the sense that ores were mined and smelted, back in the Neolithic period. By 4000 BC, technology had advanced to the stage that large numbers of tools were being made by the technique of smelting and hammering. The casting of copper tools became common practice after 3000 BC. Gradually, various substances, notably tin and lead, were added to the copper to harden it and so make it easier to cast; sometimes this appears to have been done simply to extend the quantities available. True bronze—copper with an admixture of about 10 percent tin—came into popular use about 2000 BC and was from then on the commonest alloy of copper. The history of gold exploitation was comparable, although alloys were much rarer. Sheet gold was more commonly used than solid gold, and was often used to cover everyday objects, such as buttons—a sure sign that this metal was regarded as something special.

The quest for metal ores must have been a major preoccupation for Bronze Age industrialists. Once sources were found, their mining methods were efficient and exhaustive. In the Austrian Alps (such as the Mitterberg area, near Bischofshoven), on the Great Orme's Head, in North Wales, and elsewhere, deep shafts and adits some hundreds of meters long were cut into solid rock to reach the veins of ore. Fires were lit to crack open the rock, and the ore was prized out with wedges and picks. At Mount Gabriel, in southern Ireland, there is also evidence of Bronze Age mining—albeit sketchy, because the miners of those times removed every trace of ore.

These early mines were predominantly worked between about 3000 BC and 750 BC. Although the methods used to date these sites have been questioned, techniques derived from the natural sciences, together with archaeology, can provide a consistent chronological framework.

The traditional approach—relying on the evidence of artifacts that link Europe with Greece, and Greece with Egypt—provides a chronology that is generally agreed upon, with certain exceptions, and in many instances the timber used in construction can be dated by means of tree-ring analysis. It is an extraordinary achievement to be able to date the building of a settlement to an exact year in the remote past: for instance, the major part of a settlement discovered in Switzerland at Mozartstrasse, near the Opera House, in central Zürich, was built about 1600 BC. Much of the timber used came from trees felled between 1604 BC and 1573 BC, but an especially large number of trees were felled in 1602 BC and between 1599 BC and 1598 BC. It is rare that artifacts themselves can be dated so precisely, but the techniques of tree-ring dating are now so well developed that they will very likely have been perfected by the year 2000.

Burial Rites and the Individual

Had you entered a burial chamber in Neolithic Europe, you would have found an extraordinary and frightening scene of disarray, with bones scattered about and newly arrived corpses lying in compartments or on shelves on either side. Burial was collective in the sense that the same space was used again and again. When one body was reduced to bare bones, it was swept aside to make room for another. One of the most remarkable changes that heralded the arrival of new beliefs and practices after 2500 BC, and marked the beginning of the Bronze Age, was the shift to individual burial throughout much of central and western Europe. Just as the nature of the new culture varied from place to place, so, too, did the timing of this change in burial practices.

Across much of continental Europe, the characteristic pottery found with these individual burials is known as corded ware, being decorated by impressing cord into the wet clay, and is most commonly in the form of tall drinking cups. Often, a stone battle-axe, so called because these axes apparently had a military and/or ceremonial function, is found with the pots. (See the feature *The Battle-axe People: Europe's First Individualists.*)

⚔ The grip of a solid-hilted, Late Bronze Age sword from Switzerland. The metal grip has been cast onto the blade and secured by a set of rivets.
SWISS NATIONAL MUSEUM

⚲ A large burial mound on Overton Hill, near Avebury, Wiltshire, in southern England. Such barrows covered individual burials of the Early Bronze Age in many parts of Europe, and were clearly intended to be highly visible monuments to the dead.

ROGER VLITOS/JANET AND COLIN BORD

THE BATTLE-AXE PEOPLE: EUROPE'S FIRST INDIVIDUALISTS

MATS P. MALMER

In the first centuries of the third millennium BC, a surprising change occurred in Europe. Most people appear to have begun to follow a single religion, and a new social system seems to have evolved, giving greater freedom and rights of personal ownership to the individual. The preceding thousand years had been very different, with the European peoples favoring a collective approach. At the same time, Europe's cultural map had been extremely diverse.

A variety of megalithic tombs built from heavy boulders were constructed for communal burials, offerings, and worship on the Iberian peninsula and in France, the British Isles, the Netherlands, and Scandinavia. In Germany, Poland, and Hungary, the first farmers built villages comprising communal houses up to 45 meters (148 feet) long. In the Alpine region and northern Italy, villages and other extensive wooden structures were built on moors or lake shores. In eastern Europe, hunters and fishers also lived in large villages. Although pottery was being produced all over Europe, every region seems to have had its own types of pots. They were often extremely well made, in many different shapes, and were, so archaeologists believe, of symbolic significance. It is thought that each region, with its own pottery, monumental graves, and distinctive type of village, constituted a social unit of some kind, perhaps with its own language.

In the third millennium, the situation changed radically. No more megalithic tombs were built. Instead, we find individual burials, usually in pits or wooden coffins, which were either left as flat graves or were covered by a low earthen mound. The body was always placed in a crouched position, as if sleeping. Thousands of such graves have been excavated in many parts of Europe, from Spain in the west to Ukraine in the east, and from Sicily in the south to central Norway in the north.

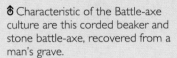
Characteristic of the Battle-axe culture are this corded beaker and stone battle-axe, recovered from a man's grave.

LANDESMUSEUM FÜR VORGESCHICHTE, HALLE

BRITISH MUSEUM

EUROPE AT THE TRANSITION FROM STONE AGE TO BRONZE AGE

The continent was dominated by two mutually related cultures, the Bell Beaker culture and the Battle-axe culture. Remains of one or both will probably be found in the future in most areas that now seem empty. We do know, however, that they did not extend to the Balkan peninsula.

- ▨ Bell Beaker culture
- ▨ Battle-axe people/Corded Beaker culture
- ▨ Overlap of Bell Beaker and Corded Beaker cultures

The houses, too, changed. They are as wide as before, about 6 to 7 meters (20 to 23 feet), but they are much shorter, usually 10 or 12 meters (33 to 39 feet), being suitable for a single family rather than a group.

Beakers and Battle-axes

As grave goods, we now usually find only one type of clay pot, a gently S-curved beaker, obviously intended for drink. This is in sharp contrast to the preceding age, with its variety of pottery shapes. There are, however, two slightly different types of beakers, one found mainly in western Europe and the other in eastern Europe. The former is called a bell beaker, because it looks like an upside-down bell, and the latter a corded beaker, because a cord was often used as an instrument for decoration. Both are well made and neatly decorated with

horizontal lines or bands. It may seem strange that archaeologists have bothered to distinguish between the two, for the main difference between them is that the bell beaker is decorated from rim to base, whereas only the upper part of the corded beaker is decorated. But, in fact, they have been thought not only to have come from two different cultures, but from two entirely different ethnic groups.

In a man's grave, a bell beaker is sometimes found with a copper dagger, while a corded beaker is often discovered with a stone battle-axe. This is why archaeologists refer to the people who lived in those parts of Europe where corded beakers are found—from central Russia and Ukraine to the Rhine—as the Battle-axe people. The Bell Beaker people are found throughout western Europe, while in the border zones, and especially the Rhine

Linköping

CARTOGRAPHY: RAY SIM

area, the two cultures were mixed. The Bell Beaker culture appeared a little later than the Corded Beaker culture, but the two coexisted for a long period.

A Man, a Woman, a Dog, and the Rising Sun

One example of the many thousands of graves from this period was found in Linköping, in southern Sweden. It contains two skeletons, one of a man, the other of a woman, both of them in a crouched position. Double graves such as this are sometimes found in Battle-axe cultures, but no evidence has been found to indicate that either of the people was sacrificed. Possibly, both died of the same disease.

The woman is at the northeastern end of the grave, lying on her left side, and the man is at the southwestern end, lying on his

In graves of men from the Bell Beaker culture, a bell beaker is sometimes found with a copper dagger. The grave find shown here also includes amber beads and a bowman's wrist guard made of stone, with gold studs to fasten it to a leather strap.

right side. Thus, both are looking to the southeast, towards the rising sun. The man is 25 to 30 years old and about 180 centimeters (5 feet, 9 inches) tall; the woman is 18 to 20 years old and about 162 centimeters (5 feet, 4 inches) tall. They are racially similar to modern Swedes.

In front of the man's face lies his stone battle-axe. It is a very beautiful weapon, but not very practical, since it would easily break at the shaft-hole; a wooden cudgel would be much more reliable. There is also a fine dagger of deer antler and a bone needle for fastening his dress.

The woman's grave goods are even richer. By her head are two low beakers—a typical Swedish variant—with bell beaker decoration. So the Battle-axe culture is represented in this grave by the man's axe, and the Bell Beaker culture by the woman's beakers. Near the beakers are sheep bones—the remains, no doubt, of a piece of mutton. Sheep were typical livestock during the third millennium, whereas cattle predomi-nated in the fourth. Three small adzes, suitable for carpentry, are also near the woman. Adzes have been found in many women's graves, so there can be little doubt that women did woodwork. Near the woman's feet is a lump of brown paint, and behind her back there are a few small objects, which were probably originally contained in a small skin bag. There are two small copper spirals, most likely very costly items. Copper objects are occasionally found in the Battle-axe culture, but occur more commonly in the Bell Beaker culture. The woman's skin bag also contains an amber bead, a fine needle for fastening her dress, and a few other household items. At her back there is the skeleton of a dog—a medium-sized spitz— obviously buried together with his master and mistress.

The Linköping grave provides a "snapshot" of the Battle-axe people. We see a young couple. They are tall, noble, and rich. Since they are living in one of the best agricultural regions of Scandinavia, they are probably landowners. He has an exquisitely worked battle-axe, but it is more a status symbol than a weapon. We may guess that he

🔥 The double grave from Linköping, in southern Sweden. The man's skeleton is on the left. In front of his chest are his stone battle-axe and a dagger made of deer antler. The woman's skeleton is on the right. On each side of her head, there is a pot; and at her back, the skeleton of a dog.
ÖSTERGÖTLANDS LÄNSMUSEUM

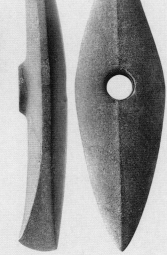

🔥 One of the pots found in the Linköping grave, with bell beaker decoration.
ÖSTERGÖTLANDS LÄNSMUSEUM

↪ Side and front view of the battle-axe from the Linköping grave.
ÖSTERGÖTLANDS LÄNSMUSEUM

likes hunting and has refined manners. She is well dressed and paints her body, but she is also accustomed to doing practical work.

Possession Becomes Personal

How is the massive change in Europe at the beginning of the third millennium to be explained? Many scholars think that the Bell Beaker culture originated on the Iberian peninsula and spread to Britain, Scandinavia, and Ukraine. The idea has been put forward that these people were prospectors, looking for copper and tin ores. The Battle-axe cultures are thought to have come from Russia or eastern Germany and to have spread as far as Scandinavia and the Rhine, but cord-decorated beakers are also found in the Bell Beaker culture of England, France, and Spain.

Many scholars maintain that the Battle-axe people introduced Indo-European languages and conquered the whole of Europe. But to do this they would have needed a warlike spirit and military skill and technol-ogy surpassing that of the Romans, and this was certainly not the case.

The encounter in the Rhine area of eastern Battle-axe people and west-ern Bell Beaker people could hardly have occurred peacefully. No doubt, the megalith builders and other peoples of an earlier age would also have defended themselves against the Battle-axe invaders.

A more reasonable explanation seems to be that the change in Europe occurred when people became acquainted with metal and realized its economic importance. Before metal entered their lives, there was no reason for them to possess a piece of land; land was

probably owned by the village or the tribe, and both houses and graves were communal. But when a man could hold a piece of metal in his hands that was worth as much as a large field, then the moment for personal ownership had arrived. And since, in a primitive society, economics, social relations, and religion are very closely con-nected, it is likely that the economic change had exactly those effects that we can observe in the Battle-axe and Bell Beaker peoples. They were the first individualists in the civilization of temperate Europe.

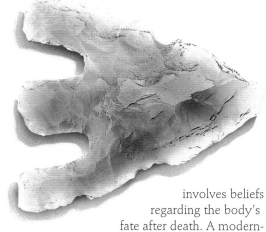

⟿ This barbed and tanged flint arrowhead of the Early Bronze Age is typical of many found with burials of the late third and second millennia BC, indicating the importance of the bow and arrow for hunting and warfare.
B. WILSON/ANCIENT ART & ARCHITECTURE COLLECTION

⚲ An Early Bronze Age bell beaker pot and several metalworker's tools—two cushion stones, an awl, and a wrist guard—from Lunteren, in Gelderland, Holland. The find also included six flint arrowheads, a flint axe, a stone hammer, and a whetstone, and represents a typical set of tools from the earliest stages of the Bronze Age. The triangular, flat copper dagger is from a different site.
RIJKSMUSEUM VAN OUDHEDEN, LEIDEN

By contrast, in western Europe and parts of central and southern Europe, individual burials coincided with the appearance of bell beakers—drinking cups shaped like an upside-down bell. These beakers are often accompanied by arrowheads and stone or bone rectangular plates that are perforated at the corners. The plates are believed to be guards worn to protect an archer's wrist from the slap of the bowstring.

In central Europe, people were usually buried in a simple pit or a stone-lined grave in the ground, but in the west, it was more common to bury the dead under a great mound of earth or stones, known as a barrow or tumulus. Cemeteries containing dozens of such graves are to be found in many parts of Europe; and in some areas of south central England and Denmark, prominent mounds litter the landscape. Not all of these mounds date from the period when corded ware or bell beakers were in use, for the custom of building them became a trend that extended over hundreds of years. Sometimes, the dead were richly provided for, as evidenced by several graves in central Europe, including Leubingen, in Sachsen-Anhalt, Germany, and the graves associated with the Wessex culture, in England; sometimes they were given little or nothing. What is important is the fact that an identifiable individual was buried in his or her own purpose-built space.

Individual interment was not the only major change in burial customs during the Bronze Age. While burial in a pit or under a mound was standard practice throughout most of Europe until about 1300 BC, after that date it became increasingly common to burn the dead and deposit the ashes in an urn, which was then buried in the ground—hence the term urnfields to describe these cemeteries. The period of the urnfields continued down to the start of the Iron Age, about 750 BC. The change from burial to cremation has been interpreted as evidence of a major shift in beliefs. In most societies, treatment of the dead is imbued with symbolic significance and involves beliefs regarding the body's fate after death. A modern-day example of this is the wide-spread opposition to the reintroduction of cremation in Britain voiced in the nineteenth century: only after a number of well-publicized court cases did it become evident that cremation was not an illegal practice, merely a socially unacceptable one.

From the time of the urnfields, both burials and cemeteries are much more numerous, cemeteries commonly containing several hundred graves. It therefore seems likely that Europe's population increased dramatically during the urnfield period—the Late Bronze Age. Whether this came about as a result of improved agricultural methods is unclear. From an archaeological point of view, however, the urnfields present a problem, in that the practice of cremating the dead destroyed much of the evidence that would enable us to reconstruct the society and population of the period.

Nevertheless, much has been learned from the detailed study of certain cemeteries, such as that at Przeczyce, in Poland, where 874 graves were found. Most of these were burial sites, only about 15 percent containing cremated remains. Because of this, grave goods had usually survived intact (whereas in cremations they are often destroyed or damaged), making it possible to correlate an individual's age and sex with the richness of the grave goods. At Przeczyce, such status distinctions were minimal, but this does not mean that they did not exist in Przeczyce society. The production of fine metal products during the Late Bronze period indicates that significant wealth was attainable, but this wealth was not often displayed in death. Only in rare cases can we confidently identify a burial as that of a local chieftain or princeling—such as the great mound of Seddin, in Mecklenburg, Germany, which contained a rich find of gold and bronze objects. Elsewhere, we can only speculate.

Thus, although Bronze Age burials have provided a large quantity of material, they have often provided little information. In such cases, we need to turn to other sources of information, such as settlements, evidence of warfare, exchange of goods, industry, ritual, and belief, in order to construct a picture of the times.

Lakeside Settlements

Life in the Bronze Age, as in all traditional societies, revolved around the common needs of subsistence, production, and shelter. People worked, ate, slept, socialized, and died within the environment of a simple agricultural village. Since most of these villages were built with organic materials, few traces of them are left. Our knowledge of Bronze Age housing is therefore limited, and only where stone was used regularly can we confidently reconstruct the form and function of these buildings. Fortunately, in several areas settlements have been found that are surprisingly rich in archaeological remains.

It is on lakes in the Alps that traces of settlement are most apparent. Numerous well-preserved villages have been found in their shallow waters, especially in Switzerland. There are two reasons for this. First, periodic flooding resulting from high rainfall, or rapidly melting snow in spring, caused water levels to fluctuate, which meant that these settlements were periodically occupied and abandoned. Secondly, the house timbers have been well preserved in the waterlogged ground. This occupation pattern recurred regularly at many lake sites from the Early Neolithic to the end of the Bronze Age. During the Bronze Age, there were phases of occupation during the corded ware period

(about 2700 BC to 2500 BC), during the late Early Bronze Age (between 1650 BC and 1500 BC), and during two periods of the Late Bronze Age (1050 BC to 950 BC, and about 850 BC).

Piles were driven into the soft mud of the lake shores, creating a platform on which super-structures could be erected. The precise way in which this was done varied; indeed, there is controversy about how and where along the lake edges the houses were built. Certainly, the ground was wet and would have to have been stabilized. The thousands, even millions, of wooden posts that were used for this purpose strongly suggest a highly organized effort. Since trees were felled in large numbers, the environmental effects must have been drastic.

Auvernier, on Lake Neuchâtel, was a typical settlement, with rows of rectangular houses ranged within a surrounding palisade. The houses probably had a timber framework, with wattle-and-daub infilling. Each house had a hearth, and no doubt other standard fittings as well, although in most cases it has been impossible to identify individual pieces of furniture.

Similar houses may well have been built on dry-land sites along the Swiss alpine valleys. In these regions, a series of glacially formed knolls and hillocks—either on the valley floor or, less commonly, high on the valley sides—were chosen for high-density, long-term settlement. A site such as Padnal, near Savognin, in the Engadin, was occupied more or less continuously from the Early Bronze Age to the start of the Late Bronze Age, the form of the houses changing very little throughout this period. Occupation of the same site for hundreds of years led to a build-up

The site of Padnal, near Savognin, in the Engadin, southeastern Switzerland. The flat top of the mound is the result of people leveling off accumulated debris each time new buildings were erected on the site.

A reconstruction of the Late Bronze Age settlement at Zedau, in eastern Germany. The houses are framed by upright posts, and have wattle-and-daub walls and thatched roofs.
ILLUSTRATION: JOHN RICHARDS

☞A gold disk from a burial at Kirk Andrews, on the Isle of Man, Britain.
TOWNLEY COLLECTION/BRITISH MUSEUM

of debris, which significantly raised the surface level, not unlike the tell sites of Southwest Asia or eastern Europe. Among these rare stratified sites are some on the Hungarian plain, which are typically 150 to 200 meters (500 to 650 feet) in diameter and up to 10 meters (33 feet) high. Excavation of one of these sites at Tószeg, near Szolnok, in central Hungary, has revealed a dense succession of rectangular houses, built from daub on wooden frames, which filled the interior of the mound.

Sites such as these, however, represent a minority of those known to have existed in Bronze Age Europe. Much more common is the simple open site, usually occupied once or twice only, with a scatter of post-built houses, the sole remains of which are traces of wooden uprights. A Late Bronze Age site (from the urnfield period) at Zedau, in eastern Germany, illustrates the pattern well. Here, no less than 78 small rectangular and square post-built houses were constructed. Most had six or four posts, wattle-and-daub walls, and a thatched roof. Hearths and ovens lay outside. There is little evidence of planning, the structures appearing to have been built by individual social groups with the requirements of day-to-day living in mind.

These structures took various forms, according to local economic and social circumstances. On the downlands of southern England, a characteristic formation was a group of round, post-framed houses, often built on platforms, with a number of stock pens nearby. The earthen banks surrounding these enclosures merge with the fields stretching between one site and the next. A site such as Black Patch, near Newhaven, in Sussex, is a good example. Several hut platforms were located on the slope of a hill, each supporting two to five round huts. The excavator of this site has

♀ A reconstruction of Bronze Age life at Tanum, Bohuslän, in western Sweden, with post-framed, thatched-roof houses.

JENS RYDELL/BRUCE COLEMAN LTD

suggested that the size of the huts indicates that each was probably occupied by only one person. It is likely, therefore, that a group of huts was occupied by a family, including, perhaps, retainers or other dependants.

Most of the sites described so far were open, undefended farming hamlets. At times, however, there was a need for defense. Defended sites occur only at particular times in particular areas. Presumably, their existence indicates a need

DUSCHER/BRUCE COLEMAN LTD

to retreat into relatively inaccessible areas for protection, perhaps against organized groups of marauders from neighboring territory. We can see this trend developing most clearly during the Late Bronze Age, and in some places even earlier. Ram's Hill, in Berkshire, southern England, for instance, was protected first by a palisade and later by a fully developed wooden rampart. Complex ramparts were built during the Late Bronze Age at many German sites, although

these sites seem to have been occupied only briefly. Little is known about the nature of the houses inside such hill-forts, but at the Wittnauer Horn site, in northern Switzerland, what looks like a main street is faced on both sides by rows of rectangular houses. At Ram's Hill, the remains of round houses were found inside a palisade, and it seems likely that when other sites are excavated extensively enough, comparable remains will come to light.

⚓ Numerous settlements were established along lake shores such as this, at Neuchâtel, beside the Jura Mountains, in western Switzerland. Their foundations were secured by driving wooden piles into the mud.

111

OAK COFFIN GRAVES IN DENMARK

GÖRAN BURENHULT

A SERIES OF EARLY BRONZE AGE mounds in southern Jutland, in Denmark, holds a very special position in the history of European archaeological research. The remarkably well-preserved finds from these burial sites, notably clothes and wooden artifacts, are unique for this period, providing a detailed picture of everyday life and death in northern Europe nearly 3,500 years ago.

These great mounds are those of Muldbjerg, Egtved, Skrydstrup, Borum Eshøj, Trindhøj, and Guldhøj. They were usually built of turf, which formed a massive, wet cover over the grave site. Iron salts, which occur naturally in turf, leached and soon turned into a layer of iron sandstone. This protective cover prevented air from entering the mound's interior. The oak coffins and their delicate contents were thus enclosed within a preservative environment very similar to that of bogs.

The degree of preservation of the skeletal remains varies greatly from mound to mound. In some cases, the grave is empty, nothing being left of the mortal remains. In others, even the brain and heart are preserved. The hair is often very well preserved, even in the armpits and around the genitals, and sometimes even facial features can be discerned.

In one man's grave at Guldhøj, some remarkable wooden artifacts were unearthed, including bowls and a folding chair made of ash-wood and otter fur. The folding chair is very similar to chairs found in contemporary Egyptian tombs. In the man's belt was a dagger in a wooden sheath. As in most of the other graves, the body had been placed on a cow's hide.

Male Fashion before the Age of Trousers

It is the well-preserved clothes, however, that make the Danish oak coffin graves one of the most notable Bronze Age finds in Europe. The graves of two men discovered in Muldbjerg and Trindhøj have provided detailed information about the clothes and ornaments worn by men at that time. Both were dressed in long loincloths held in place by leather straps. Trousers were not yet being worn. These plain-weave clothes consist of nine pieces of cloth sewn together with whipstitch. Both men carried a kidney-shaped cloak over their shoulder and wore a round cap. Swords, fibulas, double buttons, and belt adornments completed their outfit.

Two burials of women are particularly interesting, because they provide information not only about the clothes and ornaments of the time, but also about the social structure of northern Europe 3,500 years ago.

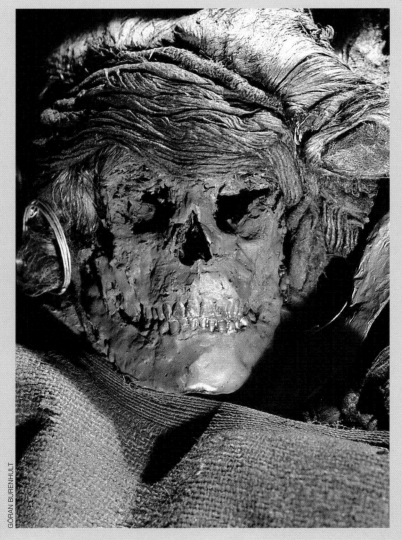

GÖRAN BURENHULT

◐ A drawing of the burial of an old man from Borum Eshøj, as he was found during an excavation in 1875. This giant mound contained three oak coffins with the well-preserved remains of an old man, a young man, and an old woman. These people were probably members of the same family.

◐ The well-preserved skin of the young woman from Skrydstrup reveals beautiful facial features. She has a unique hairstyle, with a net of black horsehair. Rings of gold were placed by her ears.

Married or Unmarried Women?

The Egtved mound contained the remains of a slender 20 to 25-year-old woman about 1.6 meters (5 feet, 3 inches) tall. The well-preserved facial skin revealed a beautiful profile. Her hair was short and light blond, her teeth were in perfect condition, and her nails were neatly trimmed. She wore a poncho-like sweater and a knee-length skirt held by a woven belt. Flowers found in the grave indicate that she was buried in summer. A rolled-up piece of cloth by her feet contained the burned bones of an 8 to 9-year-old child—possibly the remains of a human sacrifice. A birch-bark container with the remnants of an alcoholic drink made from wheat and cranberries, flavored by bog-myrtle and honey, was found nearby.

The girl from Skrydstrup had died at the age of 18. She was slender, and about 1.7 meters (5 feet, 6 inches) tall. Her hair was about 60 centimeters (24 inches) long, elaborately arranged, and held with a hairnet and a headband. Gold earrings were placed in her hair, by her ears, and from her facial features we can guess that she was very pretty. Unlike the woman from Egtved, she was dressed in a remarkably long skirt measuring 1.45 by 4 meters (about 4 feet, 9 inches by 13 feet).

The finds from Egtved and Skrydstrup have provided evidence of two different kinds of female clothing during the Bronze Age. It has been suggested that the different styles reflect differences in the dress of married and unmarried women.

Braids of hair found in Danish bogs may indicate that young Bronze Age women sacrificed their hair when they married. The complicated hairstyle of the Skrydstrup woman possibly indicated her social status and that she was unmarried. Judging by its size, the cloth she wore as a skirt may have served as a dowry. The short hair and elegant skirt of the Egtved woman would then represent the outfit of the married woman. Together, these finds from Jutland allow us an unparalleled, if tantalizingly brief, glimpse into Bronze Age society.

⚱ The well-preserved outfits provide detailed information about Bronze Age clothing in northern Europe 3,500 years ago. Trousers had not yet come into use. Instead, the men wore loincloths and wide, kidney-shaped cloaks.
NATIONAL MUSEUM OF DENMARK

◄ Many of the Danish oak coffin graves, like these two from Trindhøj, were plundered soon after the burials had taken place—an interesting sign that this Bronze Age society was not able to exercise total control over antisocial elements.
NATIONAL MUSEUM OF DENMARK

⬧ This unique sheet gold cape from Mold, in North Wales, dates from the Early Bronze Age. The cape is decorated with bosses of several different shapes.
BRITISH MUSEUM

⬀ The solid, cast-on grip and swelling, leaf-shaped blade of this sword from Switzerland are characteristic of certain weapon types from the Late Bronze Age.
LAUROS-GIRAUDON

⚲ This sheet bronze helmet from southern France is decorated with large bosses, and has a prominent crest of sheet bronze running from side to side.
MUSEES DE NICE/LAUROS-GIRAUDON

⬀ *Opposite:* Gold from a grave at Varna cemetery, near the Black Sea coast of Bulgaria. The numerous objects include sheet metal bulls, horn symbols, disks, beads, an armring, and a solid gold axe with a shaft.

Warfare: Shining Armor and Deadly Weapons

The picture that emerges is one of people carrying on a centuries-old agricultural tradition whose peace is periodically shattered by the attacks of marauders. This impression is reinforced by the trappings of war that are so prevalent in Bronze Age sites. Weaponry is found at all stages of the period, both in graves and in hoard finds. In the earlier years of the Bronze Age, the standard weapon was the bow, supplemented by the dagger for those few who could gain access to this weapon. People presumably fought first with bow and arrows, followed by hand-to-hand combat when the need arose.

Nothing is known about the defensive armor used in the Early Bronze Age. In the Middle Bronze Age, daggers evolved into rapiers and, eventually, swords. The spear was also invented at this time and rapidly became widespread. These weapons continued to be used, with refinements, throughout the Late Bronze Age and into the Iron Age, with the main addition being defensive armor. The history of the sword is of great importance in understanding how Bronze Age combat developed. At first, the sword seems to have been used entirely as a thrusting weapon, and it was therefore slim and light. As the demand arose for it to deliver cutting or slashing blows as well, it became much heavier, with a broad, leaf-shaped blade. Great attention was given to the method of attaching the handle to the blade. This was one of the weak points in the design of early swords, and improvements were constantly sought.

Armor was then required to ward off the blows of the heavier weaponry. Although the armor that survives is made of sheet bronze, it is more likely that the functional armor of the day was made of leather or, in the case of shields, wood. Experiments have shown that sheet bronze is easily penetrated by arrows or by sword blows. Body armor consisted of the cuirass (covering the torso), greaves (over the shins), and helmet, with side pieces to cover the cheeks. A magnificent cuirass found at Marmesse, in France, illustrates the care that went into these creations. The sheet bronze is molded to the shape of the torso, and the musculature and other features are shown schematically. Early helmets were basically conical, with a knob at the top for the addition of a plume.

One can well imagine that the Bronze Age warrior, when fully dressed in high-quality armor of this sort, was an impressive and fearsome sight—no doubt the aim of the exercise. Shining armor, fearful war-cries, and deadly weapons—as we can imagine from the description of Achilles in *The Iliad*—were intended to be an irresistible combination. It is doubtful, however, whether such warriors ever attacked fortified sites. Perhaps, instead, they challenged their enemies to single combat on open ground.

Industry and the Exchange of Goods: The World beyond the Village

For most people, life in the Bronze Age consisted of agricultural labor to ensure the provision of daily bread, but they were aware of a world beyond their own. During the period, many commodities in raw or finished form were transported over short and long distances, to service the needs of those who had no local access to them. This movement had both economic and social implications. We need only consider the distribution of raw materials across Europe, and it is immediately evident that access to these materials varied considerably. Thus, gold was obtained from well-known deposits such as the Wicklow Mountains of Ireland or the Muntii Metalici in the Carpathians, in Transylvania, and moved to Britain and western Europe; amber came mainly from the Baltic area and western Jutland;

⚈ An Early Bronze Age necklace of jet beads from Scotland, consisting of six spacer beads, perforated longitudinally, and a larger number of spindle-shaped small beads. The necklace imitates the decoration on crescent-shaped neck ornaments made of sheet gold.
THE TRUSTEES OF THE NATIONAL MUSEUM OF SCOTLAND, 1993

⚈ A necklace of faience beads from a cemetery at Košice, in eastern Slovakia, dating from the Early Bronze Age. Bronze Age faience is a primitive form of glass.
ANTHONY HARDING

tin came from Cornwall, Brittany, Spain, and perhaps from distant Turkey and Afghanistan; and copper itself came not only from major sources such as the Austrian Alps, Cyprus, and Transylvania, but also from many small sources in the British Isles, the Alps, Iberia, and the Balkans.

Advances in methods of determining the composition patterns of copper and other metals, of amber, and of manufactured materials such as glass and its primitive form, faience, have enabled archaeologists to reconstruct the movement of goods across large distances within Europe—although, of course, many goods were moved only a short distance. (The word "trade" has connotations that may not be appropriate for a period of whose economic organization we know little or nothing.) This kind of analytical approach has to be combined with typological studies (relating to the form and function of objects) if a true picture is to emerge. Where artifacts are specifically and unambiguously different in form, such methods can be decisive. If we examine the pattern of bronze production and distribution, for example, we can reconstruct something of the mode of operation of Bronze Age smiths from the ways molds were formed and reused. In addition, the distribution of objects from their presumed points of origin sheds light on the location of smithing workshops. We are thus well placed to determine how and when goods were moved, and to advance reasonable theories about why they were moved.

One of the most striking pieces of evidence for long-distance contact is provided by amber. Amber is a resin, derived from fossil pine trees. While it is found quite widely across the world, by far the greatest quantities in Europe come from what are called Baltic sources, although not all Baltic amber actually comes from the shores of the Baltic Sea. Baltic amber can be identified by analysis, and was present in Bronze Age Greece, Italy, Hungary, and the Balkans, as well as in the countries north of the Alps. What is more, the amber found in Greece, almost exclusively in high-status graves, includes flat, rectangular beads known as "spacer-plates" (designed to keep the strands of a multiple-stranded necklace in position) that are perforated in a curious V-shaped pattern found on amber in central, northern, and northwestern Europe. In all likelihood, these beads were manufactured in Britain or Germany and transported to Greece—a journey of several thousand kilometers.

This is not as far-fetched as it might seem, as we can also point to the example of Greek Bronze Age pottery, which was taken to many parts of Italy, to Sardinia, and also, it seems

(from a single certain identification), to Spain. It has not yet turned up north of the Alps, in France, or on the shores of the Black Sea, but it would come as little surprise if it did, since the Mediterranean was the scene of much international exchange of goods between east and west. A number of spectacular finds, including several shipwrecks, graphically illustrate how far imperishable goods, at least, traveled. From these cargoes, we can be sure that metals were one of the main items to be moved about the Mediterranean in the Bronze Age, and that the people of Cyprus were significantly involved in this process. Scientists have been less successful in tracking down the movement of goods in continental Europe by analytical means, but the distribution of so-called ring ingots—copper alloy neck rings, thought to be a means of transporting copper—indicates that Alpine copper was transported around large areas of central Europe. It is likely that Irish copper and gold also had a wide circulation.

But simply to identify the sources of such commodities is to ignore another critical factor: how desirable particular commodities were for the communities that used them. Although we may take it for granted that gold was a desirable resource, this has not always been the case. It was only when the need developed to express status differences by specially created wealth divisions, and objects and commodities were used to express those divisions, that gold became a prestige item. It has been suggested that gold was not at first regarded as being especially valuable, but by the time of the Copper Age cemetery at Varna, in Bulgaria, about the middle of the fifth millennium BC, this view had presumably changed. Here, gold was the preferred adornment for the parts of the body associated with power: the head, hands, and genitalia. Certainly, by the time the great gold neck ornaments known as lunulae, and the ornamental collars known as gorgets, which are found somewhat later in Ireland, were created, gold was prized. There are grounds, too, for thinking that all kinds of exotic materials—such as seashells, boars' tusks, and glass and faience beads—came to acquire a special cachet in the eyes of Bronze Age craftspeople and their patrons.

Of course, not all goods were exchanged over long distances. It is likely that most of this activity took place between neighboring communities and involved locally available materials. The movement of metal and pottery objects can be tracked in this way, but it is not always easy to say what this movement might represent. A recent study has shown how particular types of female ornaments moved freely within a radius of 100 kilometers (60 miles) from their sources, suggesting the existence of a series of communities that favored similar styles of objects. A striking

MICK SHARP

feature is that objects found outside their own immediate area of distribution are found only within neighboring communities. It seems likely that they belonged to women who married into these communities.

Ritual and Belief: Stone Rings and Carved Ships

What did Bronze Age people believe about life, death, the supernatural, and the place of humans in the natural world? Although we cannot answer these questions directly, we can look at a range of sites that reflect the influence of their beliefs. Stonehenge, for example, attained its developed form during this period, although it had been begun many years earlier, in the Neolithic period. During the Bronze Age, people brought massive stones to the site—both local sarsens and imported bluestones (probably from the Preseli mountains of southwestern Wales)—and erected them in a variety of shapes and patterns, culminating in the present arrangement of rings and horseshoes.

Judging from the number and richness of the barrow groups around it, Stonehenge was

a major center, and it remained unique even though its basic elements—a circular bank and ditch—are repeated many times across the length and breadth of Britain. Whatever else it was, Stonehenge undoubtedly served as an important center of ritual and ceremonial activity. Although it is popularly associated with the Druids, we know nothing specific about the rites that were practiced there or the ethnic background of the people who constructed it. The same is true of the cup and ring marks carved onto exposed rock surfaces in various parts of Britain, mainly in the north and west.

Equally remarkable, and more informative of aspects of Bronze Age ritual life, are the many carvings that adorn rock faces in parts of Scandinavia and the southern Alps. Unlike British examples, many are of recognizable forms—people, animals, and ships, and artifacts such as plows, axes, and lures (trumpets)—although there are also many kinds of symbols that cannot be directly interpreted. Great panels of rock bearing such art have been found, especially in western Sweden. As they have no apparent utilitarian purpose, the carvings are believed to

⚓ A rock art panel at Ormaig, near Kilmartin, Argyll, in Scotland. As well as numerous cup marks, the panel includes the rare ringed rosette design, which is also known from Galloway (southwestern Scotland) and Ireland.

⚉ Rock art in Argyll, western Scotland: part of the panels at Achnabreck, near Lochgilphead. On the left is a cup with two rings; and on the right, a rare example of a horned or double-ended spiral.

MICK SHARP

reflect belief systems, and possibly people's preoccupation with the daily tasks of subsistence, including contact with other groups by means of water travel.

There are numerous carvings of ships, and because Scandinavia has since been uplifted as a result of geological processes, they are often in places that are now far from the sea. Originally, they would have been created within sight of creeks and bays. Such carvings, a regular part of Bronze Age life in the area, may have been undertaken as a propitiatory act before people set out on a voyage. The main means of communication between neighboring communities was by sea, and these journeys are unlikely to have been very long ones. The images raise the interesting question of who owned the ships, since it would have required a good deal of valuable labor to build them. It has been suggested that this was one of the means by which some individuals sought to obtain power over others, and that such boats were the tangible expression of this power.

The Individual Comes of Age

We have looked at the bare bones of the period that we call the Bronze Age. What inferences can we draw about society in that period? To understand the changes that occurred, we must remember that in the preceding Neolithic period, an individual's death was hardly ever marked by the provision of special grave goods, even though the resting place itself was often large and elaborate. The Neolithic period in western Europe saw the construction of large numbers of great stone monuments that demanded enormous amounts of labor and great architectural skill, and it is unlikely that they could have been erected without leadership in the form of chiefs. In the absence of any direct evidence for individual chiefs, the chiefdoms have been termed "group-oriented", meaning that they relied upon and reflected the abilities of a whole group. By contrast, the Bronze Age recognized the contributions of individuals, and the leaders of that period

⚉ Stone molds for casting double-winged bronze pins, from eastern Switzerland.

SWISS NATIONAL MUSEUM

have therefore been termed "individualizing". The Iron Age saw the appearance of supremely powerful and rich leaders who possessed enormous quantities of material wealth, fortified centers of power, and political control of large tracts of territory.

Chronologically and, presumably, socially, the Bronze Age falls between the extremes of the Neolithic period and the Iron Age. It is unfortunate that the material evidence does not give us a better idea of the conditions that Bronze Age leaders inherited and developed, but there is some evidence to show that even in the earliest

phases of the period, definite, if simple, social divisions existed. The remarkable developments in agricultural technology, and the massive increase in industrial production, enabled the powerful to maintain and enhance their position by exploiting people who relied on these occupations for their livelihood. Such a system was self-perpetuating, and it is not surprising to find it had been carried to extreme lengths by 500 BC. But we must not forget that climatic and environmental deterioration would also have played a major role in bringing about economic and social change.

The Bronze Age was a period of remarkable technical mastery and great technical advances— a time when the foundations were laid for the Iron Age world, which, in turn, brought forth the great civilizations of the Classical period. The Bronze Age impressed itself on the landscape of parts of western Europe, and its monuments remain visible to this day. Shadowy though this period may at times appear, the shadows are from time to time dispersed by shafts of sunlight glancing off the gold and bronze its warriors wore, and the Bronze Age emerges as a true harbinger of the spectacular developments that took place in Europe after 800 BC.

⚔ Dating from the early first millennium BC, this rock art at Emelieborg, near Tanum, in Bohuslän, western Sweden, depicts figures in horned helmets, probably engaged in ritual fighting, together with animals.

VALCAMONICA: A CENTER OF CREATIVITY

Emmanuel Anati

V ALCAMONICA, in the Italian Alps, is a narrow valley 70 kilometers (45 miles) long, between Switzerland and Lake Iseo, north of Brescia. More than 300,000 rock engravings have been discovered there to date, which makes it the richest concentration of rock art in Europe. The areas of rock art are spread along the valley for more than 25 kilometers (16 miles) and are from 20 meters (660 feet) to about 1,400 meters (4,600 feet) above sea level. These areas have been classified by UNESCO as "World Cultural Heritage".

The earliest rock art in Valcamonica was produced by hunters in the Proto-Camunian period, some 12,000 years ago. This art is characterized by large animals drawn in contour, spears, fishing traps, and some symbols. The elk, which became extinct in this region at the beginning of the Holocene period, is the main animal depicted. The art relates to hunting rituals and practices and indicates that the peoples of Eurasia had traditions in common.

In the sixth millennium BC, a change occurred in both the style and content of the rock art, and compositions of the Proto-Camunian type were no longer produced. Stylized human figures in a praying position, with upraised arms, featured during the Neolithic period (5500 BC to 3300 BC) and were often combined with symbols and such subjects as sun disks, axes, and dogs. Depictions of

plows, hoes, and idols, which appear to have been derived from Danubian prototypes, testify to contacts that influenced the now-stable Camunian community. Towards the middle of the fourth millennium BC, a new iconography, based upon highly abstract symbols, such as concentric circles, zigzag patterns, and masked images, foreshadowed major social and ideological changes.

Several compositional changes took place in Neolithic periods I and II. In period I, the human praying image was associated mostly with single depictions such as a sun disk, an axe, an animal, or another human being. The first domestic animal to be represented was the dog. Oxen and goats were added in period II, and the number of items per composition increased, with symbols and representations of ceremonies and collective social, economic, and cult activities. Weapons and tools included spears, boomerangs, bows and arrows, spades, and agricultural objects.

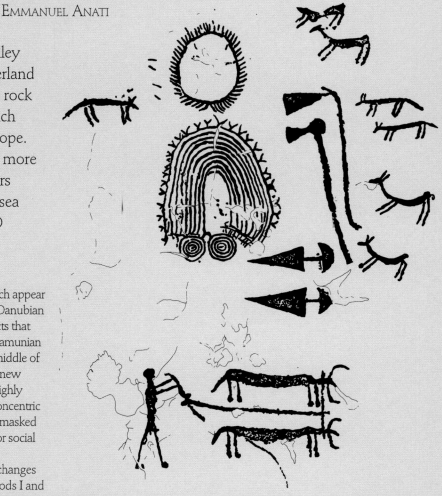

⚱ A tracing of the stele known as Bagnolo II from Valcamonica, showing triangular copper daggers of the Remedello type, axes, animals, a sun disk, spectacle-spirals under a necklace-like element of parallel lines, and a plow scene. The carving can be dated to the Chalcolithic period, 3200 BC to 2500 BC.

Periods I and II are also characterized by images of technological acquisitions, such as plows, bows, traps, and weaving looms. The main economic activities of hunting and fishing are represented, in conjunction with agriculture and animal-rearing and objects suggesting that organized trade was developing. Religious beliefs included a sun cult, a cult of the dead, and a cult of dogs and other animals; and towards the end of the period, anthropomorphic "idols" appeared. Symbols and patterns engraved during these periods, such as masked faces, zigzags, concentric circles, meandering lines, and axes, are similar to the decorations of megalithic cultures.

During the Chalcolithic (the beginning of period III), from the end of the Neolithic to the begin-

ning of the Bronze Age (3200 BC to 2500 BC), new figurative patterns appeared on menhir statues and in monumental compositions in Valcamonica, including double-spiraled pendants (spectacle-spirals), sun disks, triangular copper daggers, and perforated axes and halberds, accompanied by human and animal figures. The sun is shown as the head of a cosmological being, and the river is its belt. Such compositions, more than 5,000 years old, are the earliest known that can be attributed to a typically Indo-European world view.

Apparently originating in eastern Europe, these symbolic–religious elements reached the European Alps along with economic and technological innovations that resulted in profound cultural change. The most important of these innovations

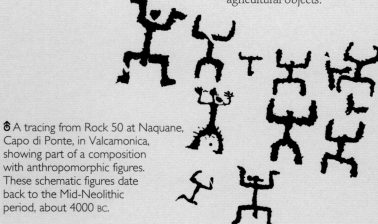

⚱ A tracing from Rock 50 at Naquane, Capo di Ponte, in Valcamonica, showing part of a composition with anthropomorphic figures. These schematic figures date back to the Mid-Neolithic period, about 4000 BC.

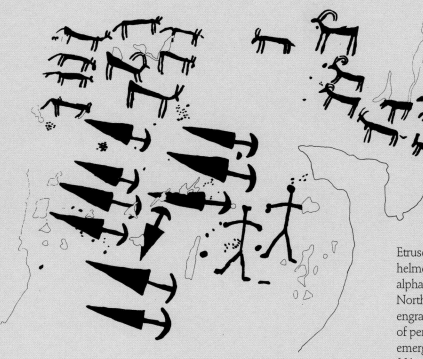

⚉ This section of the Chalcolithic carvings at Massi di Cemmo no. II, Capo di Ponte, in Valcamonica, shows triangular copper daggers, animals, and human figures.

were metalworking (with the first copper tools), the introduction of the wheel, and the use of wheeled vehicles. In the European Alps, the first evidence of metal tools and wagons occurs in the form of images depicted in rock art and on menhir statues, about 3200 BC. At this time, there is also evidence of socio-economic changes: a hierarchy with chiefs and priests, and more complex commercial production by artisans.

During the Early and Middle Bronze Age (2500 BC to 1200 BC), there was a consolidation of the changes bought by the Chalcolithic revolution. Mining, metalworking, and centers of specialized production evolved, and became integrated within a commercial network that covered large parts of Europe and the Mediterranean basin. These changes were reflected in the rock engravings of Valcamonica: new, increasingly complex compositions that represented a way of life based on economic production. Axes and daggers predominated for a long period, being replaced during the final phases by scenes of warriors engaged in duels and other warlike activities.

Weapons, other objects, and topographical maps were typical of the Early and Middle Bronze Age (the middle and end of period III). Mythological scenes and anthropomorphic figures became more numerous in the Middle Bronze Age, and the horse appeared, along with other domestic animals. Metalworking and weaving were shown, and religious beliefs related to a cult of objects and weapons. During the Late Bronze Age, there is evidence in the engravings of a growing cult of spirits and heroes.

In the second and first millennia BC, political entities emerged from tribal societies, and this eventually led to the formation of nations. Societies became more complex as economic structures and relationships among various groups evolved. Towards the end of the second millennium BC, in the Final Bronze Age (the beginning of period IV), the Camunians depicted figures and objects that related to the urnfield cultures of central Europe. In the first half of the first millennium BC, economic and cultural contacts with the area encompassed by the Hallstatt culture became increasingly evident. The subject matter and figurines from bronze and pottery

objects find many parallels in the rock art of the Early Iron Age.

From the seventh to the fifth century BC, Villanovian and Etruscan influences were apparent. It is likely that Etruscan traders reached Valcamonica during this period and introduced a new style of rock art featuring muscled warriors with Etruscan-style daggers, shields, and helmets. They also introduced the alphabet: more than a hundred North Etruscan inscriptions were engraved on the rocks in the middle of period IV. Celtic characteristics emerged somewhat later, in the late fifth and in the fourth century BC, and

period IV ended with the Roman occupation of Valcamonica in 16 BC.

Period IV is characterized by realistic scenes of daily life and magical–mythological figures. A range of engravings that is very useful in establishing chronology shows people holding shields, helmets, spears, axes, and items of personal adornment; and numerous engravings of structures, huts, and temples provide much information relating to the history of architecture. Agricultural tools such as plows, scythes, sickles, hoes, and pickaxes are shown, and there are scenes of metalworking and wheel-building. The domestic animals depicted are those found on a modern farm: dogs, oxen, horses, pigs, goats, ducks, chickens, and geese.

In the Post-Camunian period, after the Camunians' territory had been incorporated into a Roman province, there were sporadic expressions of rock art. There are some Roman engravings, including a few Latin inscriptions, and a large number of medieval and later scribblings. Unlike the prehistoric engravings, these did not have a religious motivation, and appear to have been the games of shepherds. They are mostly personal impressions, ranging from depictions of hangings to heraldic emblems.

The rock art of Valcamonica is characterized by continuously changing style and subject matter over the course of 10,000 years, and this enables us to use the engravings as historical documents. They form one of the largest known archives of European history, and art history, stretching from the end of the Ice Age to the Roman conquest and beyond.

◄◙ Some of the youngest examples of rock art in Valcamonica show Etruscan influence, probably through traders from the south. In this carving from Naquane, the warriors are dressed in Etruscan helmets and can be dated to between 550 BC and AD 450.

STONE AGE FARMERS IN SOUTHERN AND EASTERN ASIA

6 0 0 0   B C   –   A D   1 0 0 0

Farmers, Potters, Fisherfolk, and Navigators

PETER BELLWOOD AND GINA BARNES

Today, SOUTHERN AND EASTERN Asia are home to more than half of the world's population. The biological and cultural patterns that make this region such an ethnic kaleidoscope owe a great deal to the achievements of its earliest agriculturalists, whose first major settlements can be traced back to before 5000 BC.

The prehistories of the various regions of southern and eastern Asia followed different, if overlapping, courses. For example, much of the cultural development of Southeast Asia, Japan, and Korea was linked to that of China. India's culture, on the other hand, developed partly under the influence of western and central Asia. Despite this, both India and Southeast Asia shared many aspects of language and culture because of communication between northeastern India and the Southeast Asian mainland.

◄◑ Rice terraces in Bali, Indonesia. In much of monsoonal Southeast Asia, rice is grown in lowland areas in bunded fields, often fed simply by summer rainfall. Hillside terraced and irrigated systems such as these are found especially in Java, Bali, and the northern Philippines.

☖ A Taiwan jade earring from a grave in Peinan in the form of a human figure. Numerous jade earrings in a variety of styles were recovered from graves at this Neolithic site in Taiwan, together with many other finely crafted items.
CHAO-MEI LIEN

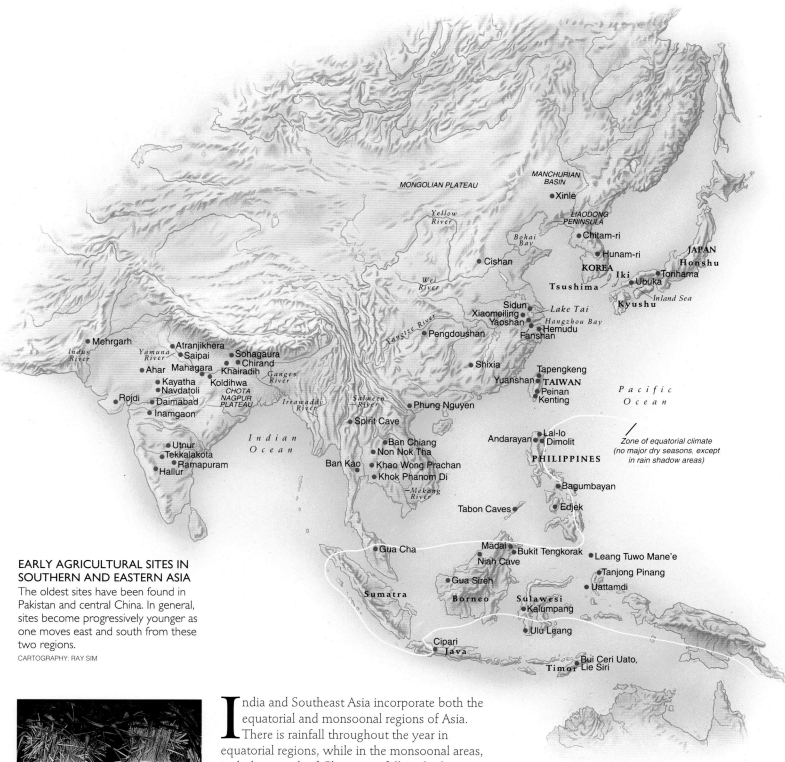

EARLY AGRICULTURAL SITES IN SOUTHERN AND EASTERN ASIA

The oldest sites have been found in Pakistan and central China. In general, sites become progressively younger as one moves east and south from these two regions.

CARTOGRAPHY: RAY SIM

☝ Bundles of harvested rice panicles stored for drying before being threshed, in Bali, Indonesia. Evidence of rice cultivation in prehistoric times comes from impressions or husks in pots and bricks, from charred grains in hearths, and, occasionally, from waterlogged deposits.

India and Southeast Asia incorporate both the equatorial and monsoonal regions of Asia. There is rainfall throughout the year in equatorial regions, while in the monsoonal areas, including much of China, rain falls only during summer. The agricultural prehistory of this huge and diverse area was dominated by summer-growth cereals such as rice and the various millets. This contrasts with the winter-growth cereals and legumes (pod-bearing vegetables) that were grown at that time in western Asia and Pakistan. In addition, Southeast Asia and neighboring Melanesia offered early cultivators a number of important tropical tubers, fruits, and other edible plants, particularly bananas, sugar cane, yams, taro, coconuts, and breadfruit.

Despite this wealth of plant food, the archaeological and linguistic records of India and Southeast Asia give no indication that early hunter-gatherer communities in these areas had independently begun to cultivate plants to any significant extent. There is evidence, however, that this occurred in two neighboring regions: western Asia and China. Both regions were to exert a considerable influence on India and Southeast Asia.

By 7000 BC, western Asian agriculture—based on winter wheat and barley, and domesticated cattle, sheep, and goats—had spread into western Pakistan, where it is particularly well documented at the site of Mehrgarh. By 2500 BC, this complex had given rise to the Harappan civilization on the plains of the Indus and in neighboring Gujarat, Rajasthan, and Haryana.

Far to the east, agricultural communities based on rice cultivation in the Yangtze Valley and millet cultivation in the Yellow River Valley were well established by 6000 BC. These people kept domestic pigs, dogs, chickens, and, perhaps, (along the Yangtze) water buffaloes. At the same time, other communities, about which rather less is known, were controlling the water levels in swamps in the New Guinea highlands, probably in order to grow taro and other native noncereal plants. These three regions—western Asia, central China, and New Guinea—can all be regarded as primary and indigenous centers of early agricultural activity.

Until 4000 BC, most of India and Southeast Asia, with the possible exception of some regions of northern Southeast Asia close to China, were still occupied by hunter-gatherers. Over much of India and Sri Lanka, these peoples developed stone tool industries featuring small blades and microliths. Similar industries developed in parts of central Indonesia (especially Java and southern Sulawesi) and the Philippines, whereas on the Southeast Asian mainland, pebble and flake tools of a type known collectively as the Hoabinhian industry were in vogue. There is no convincing evidence that any people in this region before 4000 BC lived in settled communities, systematically practiced agriculture, or made pottery.

❦ This stone knife from the Tembeling River valley, in Pahang, Peninsular Malaysia, is of uncertain age.

❦ A stone bracelet from Peninsular Malaysia, probably dating from the last two millennia BC.
ZALEHA TASVIB/KUALA LUMPUR MUSEUM

❦ A Hoabinhian biface tool from Peninsular Malaysia. This type of tool was used by hunter-gatherers in the Malay Peninsula between about 8000 BC and 2000 BC.
ZALEHA TASVIB/KUALA LUMPUR MUSEUM

❦ A polished quadrangular-sectioned stone adze from Peninsular Malaysia, probably dating from the last two millennia BC.
ZALEHA TASVIB/KUALA LUMPUR MUSEUM

❦ An undated edge-ground axe from Gunung Cheroh, in Ipoh, Malaysia. Similar tools appear earlier than 20,000 years ago in northern Australia and Japan.
ZALEHA TASVIB/KUALA LUMPUR MUSEUM

❦ The watery landscape of the Yangtze basin, in southern China, was host to experiments in the domestication of rice and other aquatic plants.

INDIA

 A Malwa jar from the Chalcolithic village of Inamgaon, Maharashtra, dating from about 1500 BC. Malwa ware is the finest of the early painted pottery styles found in northwestern India.
DECCAN COLLEGE, INDIA

 This pottery kiln excavated at Inamgaon has a firing chamber, clay "cushions" to support the pots, and an outer stoke-hole. It dates from the Early Jorwe period, about 1300 BC. Kiln-firing technology for pottery is known from sites in northern Iraq as early as 6000 BC, and spread into India via the Harappan culture.

Between 4000 BC and 2000 BC, a number of important developments took place that heralded significant cultural changes on the Indian subcontinent. By about 3000 BC, there are indications that a cattle-based pastoral economy was spreading southwards from Rajasthan into the western and central Deccan. For example, the site of Utnur, in northern Karnataka, incorporated an oval enclosure surrounded by a palm-trunk stockade big enough to accommodate perhaps 500 cattle. Huts were constructed between the corral and a separate outer stockade. The inhabitants made pottery, some of which was painted. Accumulated cattle dung was periodically burned, forming large ash mounds, which are still visible today. On present evidence, this pastoral way of life seems to have been restricted to only a few regions in western and south central India.

Agricultural Beginnings

Hard on the heels of these early pastoralists appeared the earliest agricultural societies of northwestern India and the Deccan. By about 2500 BC, as agriculture expanded out of the Indus region into Gujarat, a major change had occurred. The Harappan culture here had come to depend

 Harvested sorghum. A type of millet, sorghum was grown by the early agriculturalists of the Deccan Peninsula, along with other monsoon crops. It was probably brought to India from sub-Saharan Africa, via southern Arabia, about 2000 BC.

less on winter-growth crops such as wheat, barley, and legumes as summer-growth cereals such as millets and sorghum were introduced. This change is especially well documented at the Mature and Late Harappan site of Rojdi, in central Gujarat. Although some sites well south of Rojdi show that the people here retained an economy based on western Asian crops until after 1000 BC, the partial shift to millets and sorghum undoubtedly advanced the process of the agricultural colonization of the Deccan.

Two of the plants involved in this process, finger millet (*Eleusine coracana*) and sorghum (*Sorghum bicolor*), are believed by some archaeologists to have originated in Africa, although certain botanists dispute this in the case of finger millet. The two cereals could have been spread by trade contacts—extensions, perhaps, of the historically documented trade between the Indus civilization and the inhabitants of the Persian Gulf area during the late third millennium BC. Two other millets, *Panicum miliaceum* (common millet, perhaps domesticated in northern India) and *Setaria italica* (foxtail millet, which may have been first domesticated in eastern Europe or central China), also played a part in this spread of agriculture.

Millets never became as important on the Ganges plains as in the Deccan. On the Ganges plains we see, after 3000 BC, a mix of wheat and barley, with rice at many sites. As early as 4500 BC, rice may have been cultivated at Koldihwa, in Uttar Pradesh, but the evidence for this has not been confirmed. The oldest confirmed dates for rice in India are from about 2500 BC at Chirand and Khairadih, in Bihar. Rice was also known to the Harappans well before 2000 BC.

The cultural materials associated with the oldest farming settlements in India are extremely varied—there is certainly no single cultural source. The spread of agriculture from the northwest towards Maharashtra and the Deccan was

DECCAN COLLEGE, INDIA

PETER BELLWOOD

associated from the start with a number of artifacts and activities that may reflect Harappan antecedents. For example, these people produced painted wheel-made pottery fired in true firing chamber kilns, and copper and bronze axes. They carried on a stone blade industry and made clay figurines of humans and animals, particularly cattle. Their economy was based on various combinations of summer and winter cereals, along with domesticated cattle and, to a lesser extent, sheep, goats, pigs, buffaloes, and fowl. Cotton and flax were used to make woven fabrics and cordage. Houses were rectangular, with walls of wattle and daub or stones set in clay, lime-plastered floors, clay ovens, storage pits, and storage platforms. A few circular structures have also been found, probably used for storage.

Excellent examples of such sites, dating from about 2600 BC onwards, are found at Ahar, in Rajasthan; Kayatha and Navdatoli, in the Malwa region of Madhya Pradesh; and Inamgaon and Daimabad, in Maharashtra. At Inamgaon (about 1400 BC), an area of 5 hectares (12 acres) was partly fortified by means of a bank of earth and stones, with the houses laid out on a roughly rectangular grid and separated by lanes. One area of the site was fed by an irrigation ditch, which suggests that crops (mainly barley and legumes in this instance) were probably cultivated all year round.

Further to the south, in Karnataka and Andhra, the oldest agricultural sites, dating from the late third millennium BC, contain circular houses, some of which have stone foundations and mud-plastered floors. While copper tools were used from the time of the earliest agricultural expansion, stone axes and blade tools were still being produced. At sites such as Hallur and Tekkalakota, in Karnataka, and Ramapuram, in Andhra Pradesh, the economy was firmly based on cattle husbandry and the cultivation of millets (including pearl millet, *Pennisetum typhoides*, which may also have originated in Africa). Surprisingly, little is known of early agricultural developments in the far south of India. In Sri Lanka, the first cultivators do not appear to have arrived until the Iron Age, between 1000 BC and 500 BC.

The Ganges Plains

During the late third millennium BC, a north-westerly (possibly Harappan) influence is found in the form of red-slipped (ocher-colored) and black-on-red painted pottery at sites on the Ganges plains. These pottery finds extend from the Yamuna River eastwards toward Bihar and, ultimately, Bengal. Contemporaneous with these red wares (and excavated together with them at Saipai, in Uttar Pradesh) are a number of hoards of copper implements—axes, swords, harpoons, spearheads, and human-shaped plaques (so-called anthropomorphs)—found since 1822 at the junction of the Ganges and Yamuna rivers and

in Chota Nagpur. Ocher-colored pottery was also found with both barley and rice at Atranjikhera, in Uttar Pradesh, but by 1000 BC rice had become the dominant crop in most of the Ganges basin.

The importance of rice suggests that early agriculturalists with a cultural tradition derived from the northwest were not the only settlers in this region. At many sites in Uttar Pradesh and Bihar, there are signs of earlier occupation by settlers who grew rice, made the cord-marked and rice-husk-tempered pottery typical of Southeast Asia, and built circular huts of wattle and daub. They had already colonized the plains before 2000 BC, and their traces, usually also associated with western-type crops and domestic animals, can be seen at Koldihwa, Mahagara, Sohagaura, and Chirand.

Many of these early agricultural settlements in the Ganges basin, especially those showing northwesterly influences, probably mark the arrival of Indo-European-speaking peoples from a linguistic homeland in western or central Asia. Similarly, Neolithic finds in the Deccan are probably associated with early Dravidian languages, traceable to a joint homeland with the Elamite language, in Iran or Pakistan. The early spread of both these language families within India may not have occurred completely independently. Elements of both, for instance, may have been represented in the Mature and Late Harappan civilization, just as the contemporary Mesopotamian civilization incorporated at least three ethnolinguistic elements: Sumerian, Akkadian, and Elamite. Both groups, especially the Dravidians, intermarried and ultimately assimilated with the numerous hunter-gatherer communities that preceded them on the subcontinent.

The Indo-Europeans and the Dravidians, however, did not determine the whole course of Indian prehistory after the development of agriculture. As noted, peoples with cultural and linguistic affinities with the Southeast Asian mainland also played a part.

Peter Bellwood

BO-GIRAUDON

☉ This anthropomorphic figure of cast copper from Shahabad, in Bihar, probably dates from the second millennium BC. Such figures are often found in hoards with copper implements. They may have served as ritual axes, as some show signs of sharpening around the head and shoulder regions.

♀ A carinated pot from the Peninsular Malaysian Neolithic period, which lasted from about 2000 BC to 500 BC. It was excavated from the Neolithic cemetery in the cave of Gua Cha, in Kelantan, Malaysia.
ZALEHA TASVIB/KUALA LUMPUR MUSEUM

NEOLITHIC JADES OF THE LIANGZHU CULTURE

Tsui-mei Huang

N THE 1970s AND 1980s, a large number of Late Neolithic sites, now known collectively as the Liangzhu culture, were discovered in the Lake Tai area of the Lower Yangtze Valley, in China. These sites have been radiocarbon-dated to between about 3400 BC and 2000 BC. More than 5,000 pieces of jade, including a large number of perforated disks known as *bi* and tubes known as *cong* have been found in graves here.

According to the ancient Chinese text *Zhou Li* (*Rites of Zhou*), which dates from about 400 BC or 300 BC, *bi* and *cong* were widely used by the court in the Zhou dynasty (which lasted from about 1000 BC to 221 BC). Little is known of how they were used, but they were described as ritual objects given by the king to his subjects. They were associated with homage paid to Heaven and Earth, from which came the king's mandate to rule.

Jade Grave Goods

In October 1982, the tomb of a man of about 20 years of age was unearthed in a field to the east of an oval earthen mound called Sidun, in Wujin, Jiangsu province. The tomb was profusely furnished, containing 4 pottery vessels, 14 stone and jade implements, 49 jade ornaments, 24 *bi*, 33 *cong*, and 3 jade *yue* axes that showed no signs of wear. (*Yue* axes are broad-bladed and were usually used as weapons.) The two largest and most highly polished *bi* were resting upon the man's abdomen and chest; the remainder had been placed above his head, and beneath his head, body, and feet. Twenty-seven large *cong* surrounded the body; others rested above the man's head and next to his feet. Such an arrangement of *bi* and *cong* corresponds with descriptions given in the *Zhou Li* of how these jades were arranged on and around the corpses of the elite.

In 1986, more than 3,200 pieces of jade—constituting more than 90 percent of the grave goods—were found in 11 grave mounds arranged in two lines on an artificial hill at Fanshan, in Yuhang county, Zhejiang province. The next year, another 1,000 jade objects were excavated from 12 graves scattered

in two tiers within a rectangular earthen platform on the top of Yaoshan (Mount Yao), 5 kilometers (3 miles) northeast of the Fanshan site. The platform, about 400 square meters (4,300 square feet) in size, consisted of three layers. The inner layer, at the eastern end, formed an altar, and was built of red earth. The second was a ditch filled with gray earth surrounding the altar. The third layer (the foundations), to the west, north, and south of the ditch, consisted of yellowish brown earth scattered with pebbles. The goods found in the graves partly built into the red soil of the altar were more lavish than those in the more distant graves.

The structure of the platform and the way the graves had been grouped show that as well as being a cemetery, Yaoshan was used for ceremonial purposes. In addition, the positioning of the graves, and the way they differ from each other, show that there were privileged social groups within the culture.

Monster-like Creatures

Most of the Liangzhu jades consist of nephrite, a type of jade that is extremely hard and tough. All the *cong* and various other jade objects are decorated with designs of monster-like creatures. In addition, some are carved with human and animal images in the form of intaglio, relief, and openwork, and decorated with exquisitely incised spiral patterns. Since there is no evidence that metal was in use at the time these jades were made, it is thought that they may have been carved with sharks' teeth.

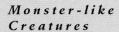 Carved from jade, *cong* are circular inside, square outside, and vary in length. They are thought to have been ritual objects used by the court to symbolize the Earth. *Cong* and *bi* are also described in ancient Chinese texts as symbols of rank.
WENWU PUBLISHING

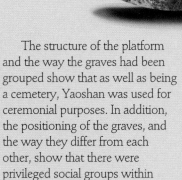 A *bi* is a flat jade disk, ranging from about 10 to 30 centimeters (3 to 9 inches) in diameter, with a small hole in the center. *Bi* are thought to have been used to symbolize Heaven.
WENWU PUBLISHING

These jades were both ritual symbols and symbols for legitimating social differentiation and political relationships, but nothing is known about how they were distributed. The monster-like motif constantly reinforced the social structure, reiterating a supposedly divine message of social and political inequality.

The manufacture of such technically sophisticated jades strongly suggests that there was a social hierarchy, with the rulers having a monopoly of the supply of jade and control over a group of specialized craftspeople. The recent discovery of a deposit of tremolite—a stone resembling nephrite—in the village of Xiaomeiling, in Liyang county, not far from Lake Tai, suggests that there may have been nephrite mines in the region.

The Liangzhu excavations are significant. By showing the importance of jade along the southeastern coast of China in the Late Neolithic period, they challenge the orthodox view that civilization developed in the north of the country.

KUALA LUMPUR MUSEUM

Sites of this period in Southeast Asia are best known in Thailand, although claims of evidence of agriculture as early as 7000 BC in Spirit Cave, in the far northwest of the country, are now being questioned. Certainly, rice agriculture was established at Ban Chiang, in northeastern Thailand, by 3000 BC, along with domesticated pigs, dogs, fowl, and cattle. This culture was also characterized by the production of cord-marked, burnished, and incised pottery placed in graves. Similar collections of items, less well understood, have been found in Vietnam.

Thai Burials

Unfortunately, unlike India, there are no detailed settlement plans for early agricultural sites anywhere in Southeast Asia, but a number of burials with considerable collections of offerings have been unearthed in the region, such as at Ban Chiang and Non Nok Tha, in northern Thailand, and at Khok Phanom Di, to the east of Bangkok. At this latter site, a cemetery dating to between 2000 BC and 1500 BC has been excavated within a massive 5 hectare (12 acre) occupation mound. The bodies were mostly wrapped in barkcloth (a felted fabric beaten out of the inner bark of trees, weaving apparently being unknown this far south at this time), dusted with red ocher, and buried with a range of items including pottery, shell ornaments, bone fishhooks, stone adzes, and, possibly, rice offerings. One wealthy woman, thought to have been a potter, was buried under a large pile of the clay cylinders from which pots were made, together with more than 120,000 shell beads, which had probably been sewn onto a barkcloth jacket. Her grave also contained numerous finely incised and burnished pottery

The skeleton of a young woman buried at Gua Cha, central Peninsular Malaysia, about 1200 BC. A single pot had been placed above her head and five pots over her legs (one of which contained a rat skull). She was wearing a polished nephrite bracelet, and two stone adzes were buried with her.

The surface design of this four-legged vessel from the Early Period at Ban Chiang (third millennium BC) was made using a technique known as rocker stamping.
LUCA INVERNIZZI TETTONI/PHOTOBANK

Red-on-buff painted pots from the Late Period at Ban Chiang, about 200 BC to AD 200. With their intricate curvilinear patterns, these pots are world renowned.

SOUTHEAST ASIA

The agricultural prehistory of Southeast Asia is inseparably linked to that of China. Indeed, until the southward conquests and colonizations of the Chinese after 1000 BC, there was no marked cultural separation between Southeast Asia and what is now China. Both regions were home to culturally related people who spoke the Tai, Austroasiatic, and Austronesian languages. The Yangtze River formed the northern boundary of Southeast Asia.

By the sixth millennium BC, societies with an economy based on rice cultivation and domesticated pigs, dogs, and chickens (plus, perhaps, cattle and water buffaloes) already existed in the Yangtze basin of China. By 3000 BC, this way of life had spread over the coastal regions of southern China and into Vietnam and Thailand, and by 2500 BC, into northeastern India.

LUCA INVERNIZZI TETTONI/PHOTOBANK

⊕ These glass ornaments from Ban Chiang are undated, but are presumably later than 400 BC. Glass does not appear in Southeast Asia until after that date.

LUCA INVERNIZZI TETTONI/PHOTOBANK

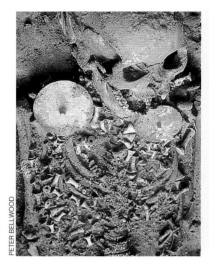

PETER BELLWOOD

⯅ The burial of a 35-year-old woman at Khok Phanom Di, in central Thailand, dated to about 2000 BC to 1500 BC. More than 120,000 shell beads were found around her upper body, and had probably been sewn onto a jacket. She had shell disks at her shoulders, a shell bangle on her left wrist, and about 10 pottery vessels were placed over her legs. Clearly a person of high status in the community, she was evidently a potter.

⊕ A tripod pot from Ban Kao, dated to about 1800 BC. The legs are cord-marked, and perforated to allow air to escape during firing.

LUCA INVERNIZZI TETTONI/PHOTOBANK

vessels. A 15-month-old child was buried with similar items nearby, possibly indicating that this was a hierarchical society, in which wealth was inherited. Graves were placed in fenced enclosures reserved for family groups and maintained over many generations.

Khok Phanom Di yielded no metal artifacts, although people living in the Khao Wong Prachan Valley, near Lopburi, in central Thailand, knew how to cast bronze to make socketed axes and

bracelets as early as 1500 BC. In central Thailand, as in much of India, the technology for copper and bronze working appeared soon after the beginnings of agriculture. Strangely, however, metalworking did not spread to Indonesia for another thousand years.

Agriculturalists spread down the peninsula of southern Thailand into Malaysia after about 2500 BC, but there are no signs of metalworking in the region until about 500 BC. These peninsular agriculturalists made a distinctive type of burnished or cord-marked pottery, often with pedestals or hollow tripod legs. Pottery of this sort has been widely found in sites from Ban Kao, in Thailand, southwards into Malaysia.

The Move South

In the islands of Southeast Asia (Indonesia, the Philippines, East Malaysia), as on the mainland, the record of agricultural societies begins later the further southwards one moves. Between 3000 BC and 2000 BC, early agriculturalists from southern China settled Taiwan. By 2000 BC, some of their descendants in eastern Indonesia came into contact with western Melanesian horticulturalists, with whom, in time, they assimilated. By 1500 BC, their descendants, in turn, were poised to colonize the Pacific islands, beyond the Solomons.

The early agricultural record in the islands of Southeast Asia is restricted mainly to small collections of pottery and stone tools from rock shelters and caves; dense vegetation and heavy erosion in this region make it difficult to find open sites with clear evidence of agriculture. In some upland regions, though, the start of agriculture has been dated by analyzing pollen and charcoal in core samples taken from lake and swamp sediments. The results show that forests had been cleared, presumably for agriculture, by at least 3000 BC in Taiwan, and some time before 2000 BC in Sumatra and Java. The available archaeological, linguistic, and ethnographic data suggest that the crops grown in this region in prehistoric times included rice, yams, taro, sugar cane, bananas, coconuts, other fruits and tubers, and, in rare instances, millet. It is likely that rice cultivation was less important in the equatorial regions and never extended as far as the Pacific islands beyond western Micronesia.

Taiwan Transition
The early agricultural archaeology of Taiwan reveals a transitional phase between southern China, on the one hand, and the islands of the Philippines and Indonesia, on the other. The early cord-marked pottery of the Tapengkeng culture was soon partly replaced by the plain or red-slipped wares of the Yuanshan and Peinan cultures. Other artifacts found in Taiwan's Neolithic sites include stone adzes and barkcloth beaters, slate reaping knives (probably used to harvest rice and millet), and slate spear or arrow points. Rice was certainly grown. At the site of Peinan, near Taitung, in southeastern Taiwan, recent excavations have uncovered more than 1,500 graves lined with slate slabs associated with a settlement consisting of dry-stone–walled houses and storage pits laid out in lines. The jade grave goods from this site, most of which dates to about 1000 BC, reflect an astonishing level of stone-working skill. (See the feature *Peinan: A Neolithic Village.*)

Southwards from Taiwan, approaching the equatorial zone, a number of sites have been found in the Philippines and in central and eastern Indonesia (Lal-lo, Andarayan, Dimolit, Leang Tuwo Mane'e, Uattamdi). Dated to between about 2500 BC and 1500 BC, they have yielded collections of red-slipped pottery, perhaps derived from that in Taiwan, with occasional shell or stone adzes. In the rock shelter site of Bukit Tengkorak, in Sabah, red-slipped pottery dating to 1000 BC has been found together with obsidian from New Britain, which lies far to the east in the Lapita homeland region of western Melanesia. Unfortunately, this region has not produced much direct evidence of agriculture owing to the relatively poor conditions for preservation and the lack of good sites for settlements. There is, however, evidence that pigs were introduced into Timor about 2500 BC.

Elsewhere in the islands of Southeast Asia, the oldest pottery in Sarawak, also dated to about 2500 BC in the Niah Caves and Gua Sireh, is quite different from the red-slipped wares of eastern Indonesia. It was impressed with a carved wooden paddle and sometimes tempered with rice husks, resembling the pottery of Malaysia and Thailand. Virtually nothing is known of early agricultural

archaeology in Kalimantan (southern Borneo), Java, Bali, or Sumatra, but agriculture was presumably introduced to these regions at about the same time as to the other Indonesian islands.

Agricultural Colonizations
As in India, the early agricultural record of Southeast Asia tracks the colonizations of agricultural peoples and the concomitant spread of their distinctive languages, rather than the simple spread of agricultural techniques between settled communities of hunter-gatherers. (See the feature *The Austronesian Dispersal and the Origin of Language Families.*) It is probable that before 2000 BC, most of the languages of mainland Southeast Asia were Austroasiatic, extending into northeastern India and the Ganga plains, and possibly even into Borneo and Sumatra. These languages probably spread with the beginnings of rice agriculture from an area spanning much of southern China and northern Southeast Asia, from Burma across to Vietnam. Since 2000 BC, other speakers of Tai and Tibeto-Burman languages have replaced some of these Austroasiatic populations as they spread out of their linguistic homelands in southern China.

In the islands of Southeast Asia, the Austronesian speakers colonized southwards from Taiwan after 3000 BC, finally settling the whole of the Philippines and Indonesia and assimilating the people who lived in the areas west of Timor and the Moluccas. This expansion came to a halt in and around New Guinea, but continued after 1500 BC into the previously uninhabited islands of the Pacific. Ultimately, during the first thousand years AD, this migration extended as far as Madagascar and Easter Island.

Peter Bellwood

⚭ This elaborately incised and red-slipped pottery from Bukit Tengkorak, in Sabah, northern Borneo, dates from about 1000 BC. It was found with obsidian imported from the Pacific island of New Britain, 4,000 kilometers (2,500 miles) to the east.
PETER BELLWOOD/SABAH MUSEUM, KOTA KINABALU

⚭ A stone cist grave at the megalithic cemetery of Cipari, on the eastern slopes of Mount Ceremai, near Kuningan, in West Java, Indonesia. Neolithic dates at an age of 4,000 years have been claimed for the earliest constructions at this site, although megalithic traditions in island Southeast Asia are generally thought to have developed much later, during the Iron Age.

GORAN BURENHULT

PEINAN: A NEOLITHIC VILLAGE

CHAO-MEI LIEN

THE IMPORTANCE OF the Peinan site, in Taiwan, is twofold. First, it may help us to better understand the Neolithic culture of the island. Secondly, it may shed light on links between this culture and the forebears of the Austronesian peoples of today.

The Peinan site is located in southeastern Taiwan. It was identified as a site of archaeological importance at the end of the nineteenth century, but was not fully investigated until 1980, when graveling operations began in preparation for the construction of a new railway siding at Peinan. A series of intensive archaeological salvage excavations was then carried out from 1980 to 1989. These revealed that Peinan was the largest prehistoric site in Taiwan, measuring more than 80,000 square meters (95,000 square yards).

◄● A carved jade earring from Peinan, in southeastern Taiwan, in the form of two human figures and an animal. More than 13,000 finely crafted objects have been recovered from graves at this Neolithic village.
CHAO-MEI LIEN

The archaeological finds excavated from within an area of 10,000 square meters (12,000 square yards) included an enormous number of artifacts, at least 50 units of architectural foundations, 1,530 burials and graves, and more than 13,000 items of beautifully crafted objects recovered from graves, which together provide us with a clear picture of village life in eastern Taiwan between about 3000 BC and 1000 BC. This collection of finds is known as the Peinan culture.

A Village Life

The people of the Peinan culture lived a settled village life. On the evidence of the stone tools found in the habitation levels of the site,

⚱ This woman was buried wearing jade earrings and slate bracelets. Examination of her upper jaw showed that her lateral incisor and canine teeth were missing, owing to the custom of extracting these teeth at puberty.

◄● In the left foreground is the cover of one of the slate-lined graves. The surrounding ground floor is paved with slate slabs, showing that the grave is 20 to 30 centimeters (8 to 12 inches) beneath.

they appear to have relied mainly on the cultivation of hill rice and millet for their subsistence; and the stone tools and animal remains indicate that they also hunted wild boar and deer quite intensively. The site was repeatedly occupied, which may be related to a system of shifting cultivation. They were skilled in procuring slate slabs, which they used to build houses and graves and to make various kinds of tools.

Village Layout

The village was located at the foot of the Peinan Hills, on the southern terrace of the Peinan River. Within the village, houses were built side-by-side in a line following the direction of the hill. The houses were rectangular, and built directly on the ground surface. The average size was about 11.5 meters by 5.5 meters (38 feet by 18 feet). Doorways could not be identified with certainty, but they most likely faced east, towards the delta of the Peinan River. Front yards and most house interiors were paved with slate slabs or split boulders. Each house was adjacent to one or two outside storage structures, which adjoined those of neighboring houses. Graves were located underneath the house floors rather than in a separate village cemetery, and had the same orientation as the houses.

Graves and Burials

A total of 1,530 burials and graves were found in the excavated area. The graves were lined with slate slabs, and the burials ranged from fetuses to the elderly. Most of them were single burials, but about 21 percent of the graves held more than one skeleton, usually because they had been opened at a later date and reused. In most cases, the bodies were buried in an extended posture, with the head towards the south-west. The burials revealed a high fetal and infant mortality rate.

Analysis of the skeletal remains provided evidence of several customs, including chewing betel nut, tooth extraction, and headhunting. These practices are common to almost all other Neolithic cultures in the region.

About 75 percent of the adult graves and 23 percent of the infant graves yielded beautifully crafted grave goods, the most abundant and refined being made of a local material called Taiwan jade, or tremolitic nephrite. The items included necklaces made of tubular pieces of varying lengths; other items of adornment such as earrings, hair ornaments, and bracelets; and delicate examples of blades and adzes. Some of the ornaments were decorated with unique zooanthropomorphic and/or geometric designs, among them being earrings that would impress any connoisseur of jade.

CHAO-MEI LIEN

⇐ Fifteen grave pots were found in this grave, indicating that at least that number of people had been buried here. Most burials at Peinan were single burials, but about 21 percent of the excavated graves had been opened and reused.

⚱ Tools such as this Taiwan jade arrowhead were made with great skill. Fine examples of blades and adzes, made from the same stone, were also found in graves.
CHAO-MEI LIEN

☛ An example of Peinan grave pottery.
CHAO-MEI LIEN

☛ The graves at Peinan were densely distributed and lined with slate slabs. The bodies were usually buried with their heads towards the southwest.

CHAO-MEI LIEN

CHINA

Fields terraced into the yellow soils of the loess plateau of northern China. The oak forests that once grew here were cleared for millet cultivation.

China's two great river basins nurtured the development of two very different types of agriculture. In the north, millet was grown in the Yellow River basin, while in the south, in the Yangtze River basin, rice was cultivated. These crops provided China's staple food for thousands of years, although today rice is the more important. This division of the agricultural landscape was the result not of custom and culture but of climate and geography, combined with the constraints of a primitive agricultural technology.

In southern China, abundant water is available to irrigate fields for wet-rice cultivation. This scene, in Jiangsu province, in the Yangtze River basin, shows the sculptured landscape characteristic of rice-growing regions.

Agricultural Contrasts

The northern mainland consists of loess—fine particles of soil, blown in from the central Asian deserts during the Ice Age. This soil settled like a mantle, hundreds of meters thick in places, over the region drained by the upper reaches of the Yellow River. Although rainfall is sparse in the north, in the course of time erosion riddled the loess plateau with gullies and gorges, and sediments have been carried eastwards and deposited across the great plains of northern China. It is this sediment that gives the Yellow River its name. Pollen analysis suggests that the plateau was once forested, mainly with oaks, but the plains were subject to large-scale seasonal flooding which continuously deposited new sediment. Flooding not only discouraged settlement of the area, but also deeply buried whatever early occupational remains there may have been.

With an annual rainfall limited to 250 to 500 millimeters (10 to 20 inches), falling only in summer, and no irrigation technology to raise river water to field level, the earliest agricultural methods used in the loess country were designed to conserve moisture. Millet, a drought-resistant plant, was the ideal crop, and foxtail millet (*Setaria italica*) and common millet (*Panicum miliaceum*) were both grown in Neolithic times. Forests were probably cleared to permit cultivation, but judging from early writings on agricultural methods, it appears that the typical slash-and-burn techniques of burning the forest cover to create ash fertilizer and long fallowing to restore fertility were unnecessary. The capillary action of loess soils brought both moisture and nutrients up from the depths. This process was encouraged by turning the soil with plant matter intact, and then leaving it to lie fallow for a year, allowing the plant matter

The Yellow River picks up its load of yellow sediments in the loess lands of northern China. These sediments are later deposited by floodwaters, which were more feared than welcomed by early farmers, across the great central plains.

The earliest evidence of farming in China reveals the presence of domestic animals. Early on, cattle were harnessed to work in the fields. V-shaped stone implements dating from the Middle Neolithic period are thought to have been plowshares. From this time, draft animals were important to agriculture in both the north and south.

P. STEVENS/ANCIENT ART & ARCHITECTURE COLLECTION

Within historic times, land has been terraced to grow both millet and rice. As population growth put pressure on land resources, terracing brought increased areas of land under cultivation but required a greater investment of human labor, both to construct and to maintain the terraces.

FRANZ J. CAMENZIND/PLANET EARTH PICTURES

to decompose and form a cover under which moisture could collect. Crops were planted only in the second and third years of a three-year cycle.

In contrast, the agriculture practiced in the south was based on an abundance of water. The lower Yangtze River winds through flat alluvial plains past numerous marshes and lakes. Rice was at home in this watery landscape, needing to be inundated for several months during its growing period. Because rice also needs dry conditions for ripening, early agriculturalists drained their rice fields by digging ditches. The construction of drainage works was probably the first step in altering the environment; later, canals were dug for irrigation purposes. This led to the creation of specialized field systems for growing rice outside its natural, seasonal, marshy habitat. Because the water depth must be kept constant, which is difficult over large areas, paddy fields have been,

⬥ Dating from 2500 BC, this rare anthropomorphic jar lid from Banshan, in Gansu province, measures only about 20 centimeters (8 inches) in diameter.

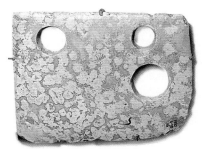

⬥ This Late Neolithic hardstone blade may have been a hoe used both vertically and horizontally, as indicated by the perforations made to fit different hafts.

RONALD SHERIDAN/ANCIENT ART & ARCHITECTURE COLLECTION

until modern times, necessarily small—40 square meters (430 square feet) or less. With the development of terracing, which radically transformed the natural landscape, much greater areas became available for rice cultivation.

Thus, the patchwork of small paddy fields in the south and the extensive unstructured fields in which millet was cultivated in the north were both designed to maximize the amount of water available for growing crops. Each system influenced the local culture. For example, rice growing required a significant investment in the field system, and demanded a degree of cooperation between the various groups living along the irrigation network to ensure that the rice was adequately watered. The development of small, dispersed landholdings spread the risk. As the census conducted during the Han period (206 BC to AD 220) shows, the population of the rice-growing south grew much more rapidly than the population in the north.

The Early Chinese Neolithic

Unlike other areas of the world, China has not yet yielded the secrets of its transition to an agricultural society. Recent excavations have pushed back the earliest dates for crops far beyond the traditional Yangshao period (about 4200 BC to 2900 BC), which now has the status of Middle Neolithic only for northern China. The earliest agricultural sites known belong to full-scale agricultural societies, but no evidence has yet emerged regarding the processes of domestication, except, perhaps, in the case of the chicken.

Sites with evidence of the earliest millet farming in the north are generally attributed to the Peiligang culture. These sites are scattered in clusters along the eastern foothills of the loess highlands, to the north and south of the Yellow River, and on terraces of the Wei River flowing into the Yellow River from the west. Dated to between 6500 BC and 5000 BC, the sites consist of villages with cemeteries and storage pits. Millet remains have been excavated from the pits and found in storage jars. Remains of a jungle fowl found at the site of Cishan suggest that it is an ancestor of the domestic chicken. Pigs and dogs were also domesticated, but the many remains of various kinds of deer that have been found indicate that people continued to hunt wild game. The artifacts associated with these early villages are of an extremely advanced type, including highly crafted, polished stone hand mills with legs, serrated stone sickles, several functional ceramic items, and numerous bone implements, some of which have engraved decorations. Clearly, these belonged to a fully developed agricultural village society. What remains to be explained is how this culture developed out of the microlithic, nonceramic cultures known from the early postglacial period in northern China, where wild millet varieties are assumed to have originated.

In southern China, fewer village sites have been discovered, chief among them being Hemudu, dating to about 5000 BC. A mysterious layer of rice remains, 50 centimeters (20 inches) thick, consisting of stalks, leaves, grains, husks, and chaff, was found covering this site. Judging by the architectural finds, these rice remains may have resulted from granaries collapsing. Hemudu stood at the edge of a marsh on the coast of Hangzhou Bay, and waterlogging has preserved both the rice remains and the remains of a number of wooden buildings. These buildings had been constructed using sophisticated techniques, including mortise and tenon joints, and raised above the marshy ground on stilts.

This area would have been ideal for growing rice. Remains of aquatic plants used as food were also found, suggesting experiments in aquaculture. As at the Peiligang sites in the north, the remains of wild game, both from the forest and the water's edge, suggest a continued reliance on hunting. An elaborate range of artifacts was also found at Hemadu, with carved and engraved bone implements, wooden objects for a variety of purposes, and distinctively shaped ceramics often incised with decorations. The main agricultural tool was a bone spade made from a water buffalo's shoulder blade, the water buffalo having been domesticated locally, along with dogs and pigs.

The discovery and excavation of Hemudu in the 1970s dealt the final blow to the idea that agricultural societies originated in the north and spread southwards (the so-called "nuclear hypothesis"). Remains of rice in the south have now been dated to between 7000 BC and 8000 BC at Pengdoushan, in Hunan province. Both Hemudu and Pengdoushan are in the region where the wild ancestors of rice are assumed to have grown. It is now thought that rice was probably domesticated at several times and places within this region in the early Holocene period, about 8000 BC.

The Spread of Rice Agriculture

Since rice originated in the south, rice grain impressions on northern Yangshao pottery, first identified in the 1920s, can be considered as evidence that rice was introduced to this region. But it is still not clear how far north rice was cultivated during the Neolithic period. Rice grains are compact, nutritious, and store well. Though heavy, they also travel well, and have been used in bulk as currency in historic times. For this reason, it cannot be assumed that rice discovered in an archaeological deposit was grown in that region. Although field systems are the best documentation of rice growing, as yet none have been excavated in northern China. Nevertheless, historical literature suggests that by the Han period rice was being grown by ethnically distinct groups in the swampy coastal lowlands of Bohai Bay. A major research problem today is to determine how and when the practice of rice growing was transmitted further east to the Korean peninsula, although its arrival and spread in the Japanese islands is relatively well documented.

Gina Barnes

⚫ Even within the Yangshao tradition, painted pots are less numerous than unpainted ones decorated only with surface finishing techniques such as cord-marking, pricking, or paddling. The painting on this pot is in vertical sections that do not entirely cover the surface.
RONALD SHERIDAN/ANCIENT ART & ARCHITECTURE COLLECTION

♀ A human stick figure forms part of the painted design on this short-necked Yangshao urn. Recovered mainly from burial sites, both short-necked and long-necked urns were painted with designs specific to different regions.
WERNER FORMAN ARCHIVE/ART & HISTORY MUSEUM, SHANGHAI, CHINA

THE AUSTRONESIAN DISPERSAL AND THE ORIGIN OF LANGUAGE FAMILIES

Peter Bellwood

Comparative linguists divide the majority of the world's languages into families, some of which extend over huge geographic areas. For instance, in the Old World, the Indo-European, Afro-Asiatic, Niger-Kordofanian, Sino-Tibetan, Elamo-Dravidian, Austroasiatic, and Austronesian language families have spread over enormous distances, reaching more than halfway around the world in the case of Austronesian.

The known history of the spread and replacement of languages indicates that societies can sometimes assimilate their neighbors in a linguistic sense, particularly if they have expansive tendencies or aspire to conquest or to control by an elite. Such processes, however, cannot explain the spread of the great language families just listed. They can only have reached their present extents through thousands of years of linguistic diversification combined with large-scale population growth and dispersal.

LANGUAGE FAMILIES IN THE OLD WORLD

Areas of early agriculture are outlined in black. The African region outlined represents the postulated homeland region for the Niger-Kordofanian and Nilo-Saharan language families. That in western Asia represents the homeland region for Indo-European, Caucasian, Sumerian, Elamite, Dravidian, and, possibly, Afro-Asiatic. That in eastern Asia represents the postulated homeland region for Austroasiatic, Tai, Austronesian, Hmong-Mien, and, possibly, Sino-Tibetan. New Guinea was the homeland of many diverse families of Papuan languages.

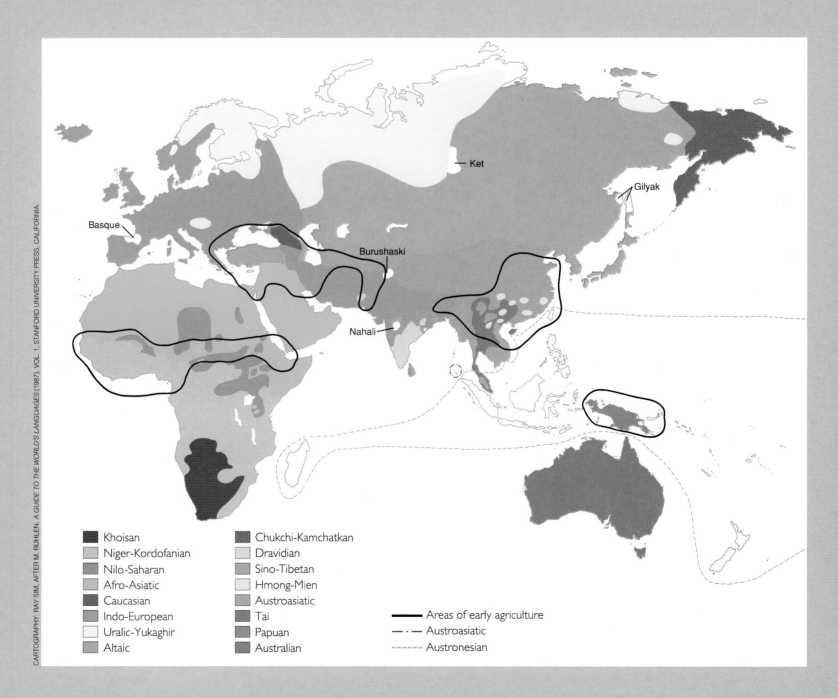

CARTOGRAPHY: RAY SIM, AFTER M. RUHLEN, *A GUIDE TO THE WORLD'S LANGUAGES* (1987), VOL. 1, STANFORD UNIVERSITY PRESS, CALIFORNIA.

Ket

Gilyak

Basque

Burushaski

Nahali

- ■ Khoisan
- ■ Niger-Kordofanian
- ■ Nilo-Saharan
- ■ Afro-Asiatic
- ■ Caucasian
- ■ Indo-European
- □ Uralic-Yukaghir
- ■ Altaic
- ■ Chukchi-Kamchatkan
- □ Dravidian
- ■ Sino-Tibetan
- □ Hmong-Mien
- ■ Austroasiatic
- ■ Tai
- ■ Papuan
- ■ Australian

— Areas of early agriculture
— · — Austroasiatic
- - - - - Austronesian

Language Homelands

Because the component languages of families such as Indo-European and Austronesian have so many features of grammar, vocabulary, and sound in common, it is thought that they must be derived from an ancestral form of those languages, a so-called "protolanguage", that originated in a specific and quite circumscribed homeland. On the basis of comparative studies, linguists can suggest likely areas for these homelands.

One of the key features of such homelands is that they are areas where there is evidence of the language family in question having developed over a longer period of time than is the case in peripheral regions. In general, a language family becomes more diverse with time, so the greater the degree of diversity to be found within a language family in a given region, the longer the period over which that family of languages has developed in that region.

The homeland regions currently favored by linguists for many major language families coincide with regions that the archaeological record indicates were early centers of agriculture. Such centers include New Guinea; central and southern China; western Asia; the southern borderlands of the Sahara, in Africa; central Mexico; and the northern Andes, in South America. In these areas, linguists have traced not only the greatest internal degree of diversity within the major language families, but also unusually large numbers of language families existing in close proximity. The picture suggests a pattern of outward spread in several

INITIAL EXPANSION OF AUSTRONESIAN SETTLEMENT

Archaeological and linguistic evidence indicates that early Austronesian speakers spread out from southern China and Taiwan, generally skirting the large island of New Guinea, whose interior was already occupied by agricultural populations. While current finds suggest that there was a gap of 1,000 years between their reaching western Polynesia and their subsequent spread into central Polynesia, some archaeologists believe that this gap will be eliminated as research proceeds. Madagascar, not shown here, was settled in the first millennium AD.

☐ **PAPUAN LANGUAGES**

directions, much as the petals of a flower spread from their central point.

Such movement, and the overall spread of these major language families, cannot be explained simply by linguistic diffusion through contact between different populations or by people switching, for whatever reason, to a secondary language and, in time, abandoning their own. We are left with only one sensible conclusion. Early populations must have spread the "protolanguages", and the most likely time in prehistory for this to have taken place is at the interface between hunter-gatherers and early agriculturalists. This is not to claim that all language expansion occurred at this interface—clearly, this would fly in the face of history. But the extent to which languages spread in the early phases of agricultural development appears to have been unparalleled until the period of European colonialism after AD 1500.

Agriculture, even in the earliest phases, would always have supported substantially higher population densities than did hunting and gathering, and given the chance, agriculturalists would generally have sought new land to cultivate. More recently, as the

world has become more "packed" with people, such pancontinental spreading of languages and populations has become more difficult, as the historical record indicates. Not even the mightiest empires known in historic times have been able to spread their language permanently over a wide area, replacing all previous languages, unless they colonized substantial parts of those areas. The history of Latin, Mongol, Spanish, Dutch, and English bears eloquent testimony to this.

The Spread of Austronesian Languages

If this perspective is applied to the Austronesian language family, to take an example that is of great significance for Southeast Asian prehistory, the linguistic and archaeological evidence suggest that, in essence, the Austronesian languages originated in southern China before 3000 BC, in a zone of early rice agriculture that was also the homeland of the Austroasiatic and Tai languages. The early Sino-Tibetan languages probably evolved to the north, in the Yellow River basin, in an adjacent region of millet agriculture.

During the two millennia after 3000 BC, the early Austronesian speakers continually colonized areas away from those regions of the Asian mainland populated by early Austroasiatic, Sino-Tibetan, and Tai speakers who were similarly expanding. This expansion—through regions occupied by small forager groups only, according to the archaeological record—took them first into Taiwan, then into the Philippines, then into Indonesia, and eventually, via Melanesia, into the uninhabited islands of the Pacific. Austronesians, in general, skirted New Guinea, where separate agricultural populations (the ancestral speakers of the Papuan language families) were already in occupation.

Ultimately, by AD 1000, the Austronesian languages had spread throughout the islands stretching from Madagascar to Easter Island—more than halfway around the world. This was achieved by people moving into new areas and colonizing them. While language diffusion as a result of contact and interaction between peoples can explain localized linguistic variations, only colonization can explain the very widespread distribution of major language families.

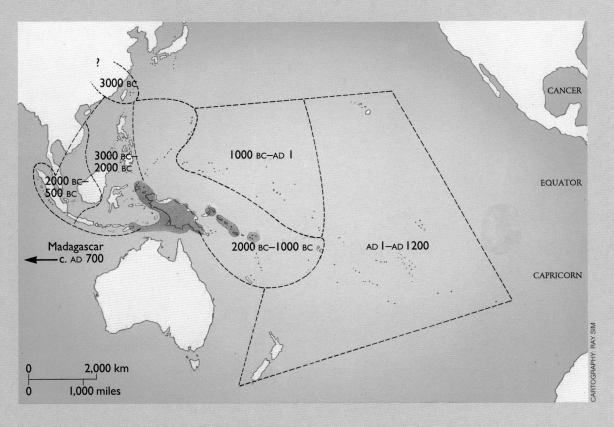

KOREA AND JAPAN

E arly farmers of the Korean peninsula and Japanese islands grew millet, barley, wheat, and rice. Of these cereal crops, only millet was native to the region. Barley and wheat were brought from the west through the Chinese mainland, and rice spread towards the northeast from the Yangtze delta. The introduction of wet-rice agriculture from 1000 BC was a clear departure from other subsistence methods. Growing an irrigated crop requires scheduling and regular maintenance, as well as a sophisticated technology—all of which had a significant social impact. How was this technology transmitted, and how did its introduction change society?

Chulmun and Jomon

While there is no debate as to the methods of rice cultivation used in Korea and Japan, where rice was an introduced crop, this is not the case with millet and a range of vegetable crops. There are numerous questions as to how communities in this region domesticated these plants, and how this process was coordinated with the hunting and gathering of wild food resources before wet-rice technology was adopted. The people of the

ALBERT NORMANDIN/THE IMAGE BANK

postglacial Chulmun culture, who occupied the Korean peninsula from 6000 BC to 1500 BC, and those of the Jomon culture, who occupied the Japanese islands from 10,000 BC to 300 BC, were hunter-gatherers. Red deer, wild boar, salmon, shellfish, and nuts were the main food items. Not only was the environment generally rich, but these people had developed reliable storage facilities in the form of underground pits and ceramic containers, enabling them to live a settled existence. Both Chulmun and Jomon societies were characterized by the construction of substantial pit houses, although burial remains from either culture are rarely found.

Perhaps because of the richness of the forests, salmon runs, and coastal shellfish grounds of northeastern Honshu, the first evidence of domesticated vegetable crops comes from western Honshu, an area that was poorer in natural food resources. Red beans and gourds have been recovered from the Torihama site (dated to between 5000 BC and 3500 BC), and buckwheat pollen has been recovered from Ubuka bog (dated to about 6500 BC). Charred layers have been identified in western Jomon excavations. These unrelated data have stimulated theories that slash-and-burn agriculture may have been practiced. The main slash-and-burn crop, however, is thought to have been millet rather than buckwheat, and no certified remains of either of these crops have been recovered from Jomon sites.

MARK J. HUDSON

⚓ Excavations continue year-round in Japan, shedding light on such pre-agricultural subsistence practices as collecting shellfish, as well as on early methods of rice cultivation.

↪ Jomon fisher-peoples living on the rocky northeastern coast of Honshu did not take up rice cultivation until two centuries after it was introduced to Japan, in 500 BC.

↪ The pre-agricultural Jomon made a wide variety of ceramic artifacts, from incense burners to "teapots". Deep, highly decorated pots such as this were used for cooking.
LAUROS-GIRAUDON

The Chulmun sites of the Korean peninsula tell a similar story. Most sites are on river banks or the coast and have yielded considerable evidence of fishing and shellfish collecting as well as of hunting deer and boar and gathering nuts. Only from the site of Chitam-ri, in the north, has a grain, tentatively identified as millet, been recovered in clear association with Chulmun pottery. This raises the question of the relationship between the northern Chulmun societies and the millet agriculturalists of the Chinese mainland. An important link between them is the Xinle culture of the Liaodong peninsula, in the southern Manchurian basin.

The Xinle Culture

Dates for the Xinle culture range between about 5500 BC and 2500 BC, and the Xinle site itself was occupied between 5500 BC and 4500 BC. Although carbonized millet has been found at Xinle, other sites in the vicinity have yielded evidence related to fishing. Thus, the Xinle culture was not only diversified, but represents a true halfway house between the fully agricultural societies of the North China plain and the hunter-gatherer societies of Korea and Japan. This description fits, because Xinle has textured pottery that is very similar to the Chulmun and Jomon ceramics and totally unlike the painted pottery of the Yangshao millet agriculturalists on the Chinese mainland. The Xinle people used flint tools, as did the people of the postglacial cultures of the Manchurian and Mongolian regions. Their range of polished stone tools, including mortars and pestles, and polished axes or adzes, resembles that associated with the Chulmun and Jomon cultures.

Who Was First?

From 1500 BC, there is increasing evidence of the use of agricultural products in Korea and Japan. The earliest date for rice is 1300 BC, coming from what is now North Korea. Millet has been recovered from several Korean sites, including Hunam-ri, in the south, dating to between about

1500 BC and 250 BC; foxtail millet was stored in jars together with rice, sorghum, and barley. With all these grain finds in archaeological sites, however, it is not always clear whether the crops were grown in the region or traded in, through some process of exchange. The Korean finds are associated with Mumun pottery, which succeeded Chulmun and continued on into the Bronze and Iron Ages, from 1000 BC.

In the Japanese islands, sporadic evidence of different types of grains has been recovered from Jomon sites as early as 3500 BC. We know, therefore, that peoples of the Late and Final Jomon cultures were familiar with certain grain crops and perhaps grew some themselves. Nevertheless, there is little archaeological evidence that they relied on cereals until the beginning of wet-rice agriculture about 1000 BC. Most of this evidence—in the form of paddy field systems—is found in Japan, although similar remains are expected to be found in Korea. (See the feature *Wet-rice Cultivation*.)

☝ Amsadong is a village consisting of reconstructed Chulmun pit houses near Seoul, in South Korea. The people who once lived here fished in the river and processed nuts, but the find of a stone "plowshare" suggests that they may also have grown millet, as was done in northern China.

← Chulmun fisher-peoples used notched pebbles to weight their nets, but from Mumun times, in the Korean Bronze Age, clay cylinders were specially made for this purpose. These are still used today.

← The first millennium BC in Korea is usually called the Bronze Age, and is marked by dolmen burials, such as this. The dolmen tradition is thought to have started among the Chulmun peoples of the north at the time they began to cultivate millet.

Thus, the first people to engage in farming in Korea and Japan were Chulmun and Jomon villagers who learned about cereal grains, perhaps through trade and exchange with their neighbors on the Chinese mainland and maybe even through migration. But heavy reliance on such cereal crops emerged only with the bronze-using and iron-using cultures that succeeded Chulmun and Jomon between 700 BC and AD 300 on the Korean peninsula and between 300 BC and AD 300 (the Yayoi period) in the Japanese islands. Information about the agricultural practices used by these peoples on the Korean peninsula is extremely scarce: one engraving on a bronze object shows a person wielding a forked foot plow, and some historical documents mention crops and domestic animals. Remains of actual field systems are confined mainly to the Japanese islands, where the Yayoi people constructed substantial paddy fields in the western coastal lowlands.

Island-hopping to Japan

The northwestern half of Kyushu Island, in westernmost Japan, is dotted with mountain clusters separated by large stretches of alluvial plains. From the northern coast, one can see the island of Iki, then the Tsushima islands; and from Tsushima, the southern coast of the Korean peninsula is visible on a clear day. Wet-rice technology is thought to have reached Kyushu by island-hopping across these straits. Perhaps migrating rice farmers from the Yangtze delta region of China brought it to the Jomon people. Perhaps Jomon seafarers visited the southern coast of the Korean peninsula, where they learned about rice growing.

There is no doubt that Kyushu rice technology came directly from the peninsula, because with it came characteristic peninsular artifacts: beveled adzes made from peninsular rock, polished stone daggers and arrowheads, and cylindrical beads—all previously unknown in the Japanese islands. The new technological "package" included such implements as stone reaping knives and wooden rakes for preparing the fields.

In northern Kyushu, the local Jomon people took up rice farming. These people used Yamanotera and Yusu-style ceramics. Deep, wide-mouthed bowls typical of this kind of pottery have been found in excavations of paddy fields and canals. The alluvial flats were well suited for conversion to rice fields, although people continued to collect plants and shellfish in the traditional way, as well as to hunt and fish. Harvested grain was kept in a style of storage jar inspired by peninsular ceramic traditions. Gradually, the range of artifacts of the Final Jomon farmers in northern Kyushu was transformed by the requirements of grain production. The population also expanded considerably. By 300 BC, the period of "incubation" in northern Kyushu had

☝ The Yayoi people of Japan were once thought to have been peaceful, rice-growing villagers, but it is now recognized that warfare traditionally played an important part in their life. Within 600 years of their adopting agriculture, about AD 300, the Yayoi spawned an elite who controlled the resources necessary to make such elaborate artifacts as this gilt-bronze sword pommel.
COURTESY OF THE FREER GALLERY OF ART, SMITHSONIAN INSTITUTION, WASHINGTON, DC

♀ Bronze and iron arrived in Japan with wet-rice technology, so the Yayoi were not mere Stone Age farmers. Intricately decorated bronze bells such as this would not have been personal possessions but may have played a role in seasonal agricultural rituals performed by the whole community.
COURTESY OF THE FREER GALLERY OF ART, SMITHSONIAN INSTITUTION, WASHINGTON, DC

☝ Yayoi villages consisted of thatched pit houses and granaries raised on stilts. A wide ditch is often found around the settlements, as a form of protection, while nearby cemeteries housed jar burials, coffin burials, and precincts for important families marked off by moats. The house shown here is a reconstruction.

ended. A new pottery style—the Yayoi, combining the peninsular and local styles—emerged, and the populace exploded out into the Inland Sea area.

Within a hundred years, rice farming and its attendant Yayoi culture spread throughout the western Japanese islands, and migrants even made "spot" landings on the northern Honshu coast. This rapid transformation is very similar to the expansion of the Early Neolithic farmers of Europe's Linear Bandkeramik culture.

In both cases, it is not yet known exactly how the migration occurred and what happened to the existing hunter-gatherer communities in the areas that were taken over. Were they converted to an agricultural way of life? Were they eliminated through warfare and disease? How many people actually migrated out of Kyushu, and were they of a different ethnic composition owing to their long contact with the Korean peninsula?

These questions lie at the center of current scholarly debate on the earliest farmers of the eastern Eurasian fringe. The outcome of this debate is sure to shed light on how the Asian people made that momentous transition from mobile hunters to farmer settlers.

Gina Barnes

WET-RICE CULTIVATION

Mark J. Hudson

JAPAN IS SO FAR the only country in East Asia where paddy fields have been identified archaeologically. About 500 such sites have been excavated, a fifth of them dating to the Yayoi period (300 BC to AD 300), which saw the emergence of Japan's first full-scale farming culture. Since wet-rice cultivation did not begin in Japan until this time, we cannot be sure when the technology represented by these field systems was first developed. However, many of the problems posed by growing rice in paddy fields are the same today as they would have been in the Early Neolithic period throughout East Asia, and the Japanese sites afford us a unique insight into how those problems were resolved.

In wet-rice cultivation, water supply is more important than soil type or climate. Rice can be cropped continuously on the same land if the field is kept inundated until shortly before harvest. Water is usually retained through a careful process of leveling and bunding (or embanking) fields. The water supply can come either from flood, ground, or rain water, or else via irrigation channels. Although its origins are unclear, this basic paddy technology has existed in East Asia for thousands of years. The photographs show the seasonal round in modern Japan.

☝ Rice seedlings are transplanted into flooded fields. In Japan, this method, which has several advantages over direct seeding, probably dates to the Yayoi period.

☝ After the rice is transplanted in May or June, it is left to ripen. Careful attention is given to weeding over the summer months.

☝ Harvesting in the late autumn is now done by machine in Japan, but more traditional iron tools are still used in some parts of Asia.

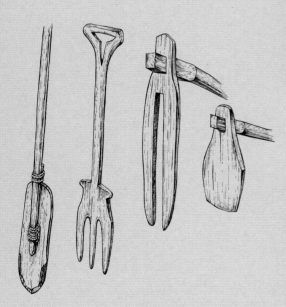

☝ Wooden agricultural tools from Yayoi sites. Although iron tips were added to some tools in later centuries, the basic shape of many implements remained more or less unchanged until early this century.
ILLUSTRATION: DAVID WOOD

☞ Stooks of rice left to dry in the field after harvest.

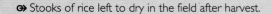

143

144

PACIFIC EXPLORERS

Highlanders and Islanders

J. PETER WHITE

TWELVE THOUSAND YEARS AGO, only the larger islands of the western Pacific knew the tread of human feet. People lived in the Bismarck Archipelago, on the Solomon Islands, and on the great island of New Guinea—from which one could still walk across Torres Strait to Australia and, ultimately, Tasmania.

People had lived on these lands, through all the climatic changes of the last Ice Age (here most noticeable through the lowering of sea levels, as sea water was frozen into the ice sheets of the northern hemisphere), for 30,000 years or more. And even after the end of the Ice Age, until about 2000 BC, they remained confined to these larger islands, which we now call Near Oceania. The smaller islands of the Pacific, or Remote Oceania—from the modern countries of Vanuatu, New Caledonia, and Kiribati eastwards—were explored only after that date.

Three aspects of human history in this part of the Pacific are sufficiently well known to allow at least the outlines of a story to emerge and problems to be recognized: the development of agriculture and the production of stone axeheads in the New Guinea highlands, and the spread of Lapita pottery in the islands. Much of the rest of Pacific prehistory can still only be glimpsed through the finds from a few excavations. This is the case particularly with both Irian Jaya and the Solomon Islands. Parts of Papua New Guinea are better explored, but a coherent story is still being pieced together. For instance, the origins, age, and real uses of stone figurines, as well as mortars and pestles, found in both highland and lowland areas are still not known.

◄ Intensively cultivated gardens of root and tree crops mingle with patches of managed forest throughout much of Papua New Guinea's central highlands.

⬥ A rim sherd of Lapita pottery. The characteristic geometric decoration is made with toothed stamps—like combs with short teeth—applied in horizontal bands.

R. BOLZAN/AUSTRALIAN MUSEUM

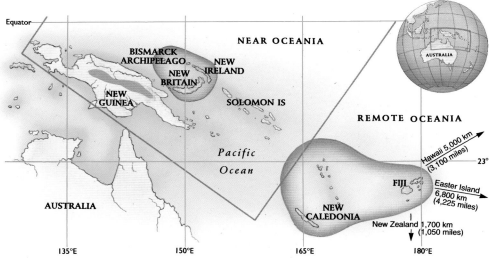

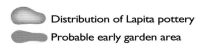

Distribution of Lapita pottery

Probable early garden area

NEAR AND REMOTE OCEANIA

Near Oceania comprises the islands of the Southwest Pacific that are relatively large and close together. Most consist of continental rocks and host a diverse range of plants and animals. The islands of Remote Oceania are further apart, mostly small, and have simpler environments.

CARTOGRAPHY: RAY SIM

One major theme emerges from the research discussed in this chapter. This is that change and development in this part of the world are not the result of innovations brought by waves of migrants. Although contacts with Southeast Asia have brought some new things to the area, most of the changes have developed internally. Near and Remote Oceanic cultures today are the creations of the people whose ancestors have been there for tens of thousands of years.

The New Guinea Highlands

The central mountain range of New Guinea is formed by the edge of the Pacific plate crumpling as the Indo-Australian plate pushes north and beneath it. Running northwest-southeast, the mountains rise to a maximum height of some 5,000 meters (16,500 feet), so there is snow and ice on the highest peaks. Between the mountains, in both the central highlands of Papua New Guinea and parts of Irian Jaya, there are wide, flat

valleys at altitudes of about 1,500 meters (5,000 feet). It is here that more than a million highlanders live, people whose existence was completely unknown to the Western world until the early 1930s.

At the time of this first contact with Europeans, all these highlanders were agriculturalists. Their primary crop was sweet potato, grown in carefully prepared garden mounds, often with water-control ditches. While the form of gardens varied somewhat from area to area, especially in respect of the shape and size of garden mounds, their basic structure did not, and their produce fed dense populations of people and pigs. The tools these highlanders used were simple—wooden digging sticks and spades shaped like canoe paddles, as well as stone axes—but they nonetheless succeeded in controlling their environment, especially in steep, swampy, or frosty areas, to a considerable extent. They used drains to take away excess water or cold air (both of which flow downhill), terracing to prevent soil creep, and, in some areas, wooden irrigation pipes to carry water to dry areas.

In their essentials, these highlands gardens of roots, vegetables, and tree crops were similiar to gardens found throughout the Pacific and in many parts of tropical Southeast Asia at that time— indeed, such gardens are still common today. There are no grain crops, and people rarely store harvested crops, year-round harvesting being the norm. Many theorists have seen this form of agriculture as a "simpler", and therefore earlier, form of cultivation. It may well possess a longer history than do grain crops such as rice, but recent research shows that it is far from simple. In the New Guinea highlands and many other parts of the Pacific, the main crop today is sweet potato

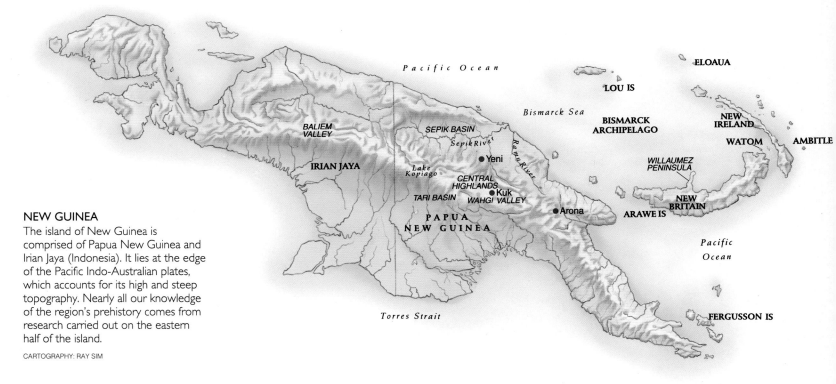

NEW GUINEA

The island of New Guinea is comprised of Papua New Guinea and Irian Jaya (Indonesia). It lies at the edge of the Pacific Indo-Australian plates, which accounts for its high and steep topography. Nearly all our knowledge of the region's prehistory comes from research carried out on the eastern half of the island.

CARTOGRAPHY: RAY SIM

The Wahgi Valley is the largest valley in the New Guinea highlands, with fertile soil on both the floor and the surrounding slopes. At an altitude of 1,600 meters (5,200 feet), there is little malaria, and the valley is densely populated.

(*Ipomoea batatas*), a plant undoubtedly of American origin, which arrived in the region only within the last 1,200 years. Most other crops are local domesticates—including taro, bananas, and sugar cane—with the occasional import, such as yams, from Southeast Asia.

Early Agriculture at Kuk

The site that has told us most about the history of highlands agriculture is situated in the Wahgi Valley. Known as Kuk, it is part of a very large swamp that has preserved evidence of a 9,000-year-long tradition of gardens and drainage systems, along with some evidence of vegetation changes over this period. Long-term research by Jack Golson of the Australian National University has yielded some important results.

First, although the swamp can be very productive, some form of water control has always been necessary for agriculture to be possible here. This has been achieved by digging ditches up to 2 kilometers (one and a quarter miles) long and 3 meters (10 feet) deep to channel water from its inlet point across the swamp to a river outlet. Radiocarbon dating shows that the first of these ditches was dug about 7000 BC.

Secondly, the form of gardens was not always as described by Michael Leahy in the 1930s (see opposite). Golson has been able to identify six major periods when swamps were used for agriculture, and it is only during the last 2,000 years or so that people have made square garden beds. Before that, the pattern of garden mounds and small ditches was much less regular, suggesting that the area was used less intensively.

Thirdly, during the later part of the Pleistocene period, until some 12,000 years ago, much of the valley floor was forested, whereas it is now entirely covered with grass. The gradual environmental change over this time has been caused by generations of people clearing the land

Michael Leahy, with his brothers and Jim Taylor, were the first white people to visit the Wahgi Valley, in 1931. The photograph above was taken on an early visit.

The gardens we saw west of the Chimbu were laid out in neat squares, each bed being eight or ten feet square and surrounded by drainage ditches from one to two feet deep. Soil taken from the ditches had been heaped up on the beds, so as to raise them above the general ground level. The gardens were fenced mainly with wooden slabs. We saw some of them on steep hillsides that showed evidences of laborious terracing, rows of slabs being driven in the ground to keep the soil from washing away...The level valley floor between the gullies was intensively cultivated, all the land being covered with neatly fenced gardens, or deeply scored with the drainage ditches of former years.

The green garden patches were a delight to the eye, neat square beds of sweet potatoes growing luxuriantly in that rich soil, alternating with thriving patches of beans, cucumbers and sugar cane. Some of the gardens had picket fences, the pickets being made of straight branches two inches thick, neatly hacked off to the same height. Others were stoutly fenced with rails, each section of the fence consisting of eight or ten rails laid horizontally between stakes driven in the ground.

There were no villages, the whole valley as far as we could see being one continuous settlement, with groups of oblong houses spaced every few hundred yards. Each group of houses had a clump or two of the beautiful, feathery bamboo, a few banana trees and a grove of casuarinas, and invariably flowers and ornamental shrubs.

From M. Leahy and M. Crain, *The Land That Time Forgot*, Hurst & Blackett, London, 1937.

⚘ Taro is an edible root native to Southeast Asia, Near Oceania, and, probably, northern Australia. It requires careful cooking to remove bitterness, but people have been eating it for at least 25,000 years.

⚘ A native of America, sweet potato has been grown in Near Oceania for perhaps the last 1,200 years. Today, it is the staple food for millions of people in the region.

for gardens and using the timber to make fences, houses, and fires. The casuarinas Leahy mentions are still regularly planted to provide timber— a practice that goes back at least 1,200 years.

Fourthly, evidence of one crop grown from about 4000 BC until the present has been found in the ditches in the form of phytoliths characteristic of one kind of banana. (Phytoliths are plant cells filled with opaline silica deposited from ground water, which survive in the ground for thousands of years.) Remains of other crops have so far proved elusive, but this is not surprising, given that the root crops grown in the highlands— including sweet potato, taro, and yams—produce none of the hard evidence in the form of phytoliths, pollen, seeds, or shells that might survive in the archaeological record. We can, however, be reasonably sure that the main crop was taro, a root crop native to the western Pacific and Southeast Asia.

The history of agriculture at Kuk is partly paralleled elsewhere in New Guinea. Other swamps in the same area were cultivated in a similar way, although, as far as we know at present, only from about 3500 BC. At the eastern edge of the highlands, where the climate is more

seasonal, people near Arona made their gardens in the flat shores of very old lakes, now dry, modifying them by digging ditches to retain water during the dry season. This technique was used from before 1000 BC, probably to grow taro. Nowadays, sweet potato is grown in these areas, and because it tolerates drier conditions, the gardens overrun these old systems, the ditches no longer serving any purpose. In the upper Sepik Valley, in the Yeni swamp, at an altitude of only 500 meters (1,600 feet), an increase in the quantity of grass relative to tree pollen has shown that forest clearance had started by at least 3000 BC. At the same time, the people in this lowland area also hollowed out small basins and built low ridges suitable for wet and dry crops. Today, the area is uncultivated grassland, perhaps abandoned during the last century because of a disease epidemic or warfare, both of which are frequent causes of local depopulation.

From Forest Cultivation to Gardens

Any discussion of New Guinea highlands prehistory must take account of the probability that people living in these areas had cultivated

wild food plants for tens of thousands of years. For at least as long as *Homo sapiens* has existed, people living in tropical areas have tended particular kinds of plants that were useful for food, tools, medicine, or decoration, rather than just foraging opportunistically. Thus, what we are seeing at Kuk is not a sudden recognition by wandering hunters and gatherers that plants could be cultivated (sometimes called the "Aha!" theory of agricultural origins). Rather, Kuk shows the transition from tending useful plants where they grew naturally, or had been planted, in areas scattered throughout the landscape to grouping them in a convenient location and preparing the ground for them. The evidence for this, dating from 7000 BC, occurs at about the same time as that of similar agricultural developments elsewhere in the world. These highlands gardeners may also have fenced their plots.

Like many made at present in highland areas where the population is less dense, these early gardens are likely to have mimicked the diversity of the local environment, with a range of plants growing in close proximity. In this, they differed from the gardens Leahy describes, most of which were devoted to a single crop and were located in areas of high population. That change came later, in the last 5,000 years, as the population increased and larger crops were required.

In considering why people started to grow crops in gardens, we must start from what we know to have happened: the fact of people grouping together the plants they cared for. One obvious explanation of this change is that it was to protect plants, which represented people's livelihood, from some threat. Threats may have included other people, animals such as pigs, and such natural occurrences as floods and cold weather. Pigs are native to Southeast Asia, not New Guinea, and were probably brought by boat. Very limited archaeological evidence—a mere handful of teeth in dated sites—suggests that they may have been imported as early as 8000 BC, although some radiocarbon dates for the teeth themselves suggest that they may be much younger. If pigs were present, however, they could have been significant competitors for the fruits and roots people ate, thereby encouraging the development of fenced gardens.

An alternative view is that the changes occurred for more positive reasons, such as to create a more regular food surplus to provide for ceremonies or to exchange with neighbors for other goods. Population increase is likely to have played a part, as may a change in the climate, such as increased rainfall.

Our problem lies in testing these proposals. Some, such as whether pigs were present at this time, or whether the climate changed, can be tested; others rely more on comparative studies of similar societies from the more recent past.

CLAIRE LEIMBACH

J. PETER WHITE

PETER FOX/THE QUALITY IMAGE

◀◉ Stone axes were the major tools used to clear forest for gardens and to cut timber for fences and houses. In the extensive Baliem Valley (in the Irian Jaya highlands), axes were hafted by inserting them into a carefully shaped hole in a handle made of solid wood. Elsewhere, handles took on a more complex form, and axeheads were bound in with flexible cane.

⬆ Gardens on the edge of Kuk swamp. Squared-off beds growing sweet potato are in different stages of production. Bananas and tall casuarina trees (for timber) are also cultivated.

◀◉ Forest has to be cleared to make gardens, and the timber is often used to fence the gardens against feral pigs. Some useful trees are left standing— here pandanus, the leaves of which are used for house thatch—and the rest of the litter burned to return nutrients quickly to the soil.

THE LAPITA SITE AT NENUMBO, IN THE SOLOMON ISLANDS

ROGER C. GREEN

MORE THAN A HUNDRED sites with sherds of the distinctive Lapita pottery—pottery made by the first people to settle the smaller islands of Remote Oceania, dating from 1300 BC—have now been identified by archaeologists, but less than half of them have been tested by excavation. Major investigations have been carried out at a dozen sites, of which Nenumbo, on the low-lying coral island of Ngaua, in the Outer Eastern Islands of the Solomons, is one of the most thoroughly examined so far.

The distribution of potsherds at 36 Lapita sites shows that hamlet-sized settlements ranged in size from 500 square meters to 4,500 square meters (5,400 square feet to 48,500 square feet). Nenumbo, being about 1,000 meters (3,300 feet) square, is among the smaller of these hamlets.

At Nenumbo, the distribution of potsherds was analyzed, and excavations made in areas where sherds were most concentrated. The discovery of large postholes confirmed that there had been a structure 7 meters by 10 meters (22 feet by 33 feet) in the center of the hamlet, and smaller postholes showed that there had been several post and thatch structures nearby.

Radiocarbon tests carried out on charcoal from several fireplaces, supported by tests made on a number of obsidian artifacts, show that the hamlet was occupied for a relatively short time about 1100 BC. The site was then covered by ash from the nearby (and still active) volcano of Tinakula to a depth of about 30 centimeters (1 foot), and was subsequently used for gardening.

The people of Nenumbo fished and gathered shellfish on the inshore reef and in the lagoon, and caught the occasional bird. They also caught two kinds of rats, one of which was a Polynesian variety, and raised domesticated pigs and chickens. Given the presence of these domestic animals, pots and earth ovens for cooking, storage pits, implements for food preparation, and a relatively small amount of debris from meat and shellfish consumption, it seems likely that they also grew root and tree crops.

Imported Items

The sophistication of the Nenumbo people's economy and their voyaging skills are also reflected in numerous imported items. They imported obsidian from their Lapita homeland in the Bismarck Archipelago, some 2,000 kilometers (1,250 miles) to the northwest; and a few pieces of glittering micaceous rock, one piece of obsidian, and some sedimentary sandstone came from the D'Entrecasteaux Islands, a similar distance to the west. Numerous chert pieces, finished adzes, and the occasional pot came from islands in the south central Solomons, several days' sailing northwest. Most of the pots, additional pieces of chert, and a number of volcanic ovenstones came from islands within a day's sailing (in several directions); and a few obsidian items were brought from the Banks Islands, several days' sailing southwards.

Specialized chert and obsidian tools were found at the site of the large building, along with a considerable quantity of decorated sherds, many of which formed flat-bottomed dishes or open or carinated (shouldered) vessels. In the area where the post and thatch structures stood, excavations revealed cooking ovens, storage pits, a well, and pots with restricted necks.

Decorations on the more complex of the pots range from a human mask face to rectangular and curvilinear patterns in panels repeated around the upper portion of the carinated vessels. More than a hundred motifs are found on these pots, similar to motifs found on pottery at sites further west and, to a lesser degree, to the east. Nenumbo has proved a key site in furthering our understanding of the Lapita culture.

⚫ Several potsherds making up a portion of an anthropomorphic face design, found at the hamlet site of Nenumbo, on the coral island of Ngaua, in the Solomons.
ROGER C. GREEN

⚫ A reconstruction of the complex face design that decorates some of the Nenumbo pots, as shown in the sherds above.
ROGER C. GREEN

Powerful Axes

Another aspect of highlands archaeology that has been extensively researched is the manufacture and distribution of stone axe blades. Stone axeheads are found in sites from Late Pleistocene times onwards. They range in length from 4 to about 35 centimeters (one and a half to 14 inches), with the smaller ones usually being the result of much resharpening. Axeheads are oval or rectangular in cross-section and were hafted in short wooden handles. Most prehistoric Pacific axeheads are made of river pebbles of tough stone, flaked and ground into shape. Quarries in areas of high-quality stone were developed during the last 3,000 years, and finds of axes from these sources can be used to determine trade routes and other links between people. The development of quarries in itself points to changes in social organization at this time.

In the early twentieth century, nearly every highlands man owned a stone axe, and some owned several. Women used axes and had rights to them, but whether they owned them is less clear. Axes were used to chop trees and for other gardening tasks; to make wooden tools, fences, and houses; and to split firewood. But some were also regarded as being valuable objects that could only be used in exchanges involving such valued items as women, pigs, and imported seashells. In some areas, each man made his own axehead from local river stone, but in others the finished product was imported. At Lake Kopiago, near the Strickland River, for example, axeheads came from a quarry several days' walk away. Each head changed hands several times on the way and ended up costing a pig or a large container of salt. Because they were socially distant from the process of axe production, local Duna people did not know how axes were made, or where they came from.

In the central highlands, around the Wahgi Valley, many axeheads were produced at a small set of quarries along the Tuman River. John Burton's extensive research into early twentieth-century practices has shown that these quarries were particularly important to the clans who owned them as a source of large axeheads—20 to 30 centimeters (8 to 12 inches long)—which were considered to be a sign of prestige and commonly formed part of so-called bride prices. In the course of mining these out of a band of stone some 2 meters (6 feet, 6 inches) thick lying some 8 to 15 meters (25 to 50 feet) underground, clansmen also produced quantities of smaller pieces of stone. Unlike the larger axeheads, which were ground into shape by the mining clans, these smaller pieces of stone were traded with neighbors, who ground them down into everyday work axes.

Quarrying expeditions, Burton suggests, took place every three to five years, on average, and involved up to 200 men for a period of several

months. Each expedition may have produced 10 to 25 axeheads per man—a total of 2,000 to 5,000. If this seems a small return for the investment of time and labor—and only a few of these axes would have been large—it must be realized that not only did the rock seam dip into the mountain, which meant that much overburden had to be cleared away to expose a rock face, at which only a few men could then work, but all the axe stone was extracted by heating the seam with fires and then hammering it with handheld stone hammers until it cracked and chunks of stone could be wedged out. In this way, 40,000 to 100,000 axeheads per century were produced, to be exchanged within the wider community. (This scale of production was probably achieved only in the last few centuries.)

A few axeheads from these quarries, usually small ones resulting from larger ones breaking during use or resharpening, traveled as far south as the southern coast of New Guinea, well beyond the highlands; but the majority were used within a radius of some 50 kilometers (30 miles) by the half-million people who lived there.

Axeheads, or chips off them, from the Wahgi Valley quarries are not found in archaeological excavations, even at nearby sites, earlier than 500 BC. Quarrying began, in fact, at

M.J. LEAHY COLLECTION/NATIONAL LIBRARY OF AUSTRALIA

⚑ In many parts of the New Guinea highlands, large stone axes were carefully bound into wooden handles with elaborate decorative bindings. Such axes were used for display and so-called bride prices rather than as a chopping tool—as shown in this photograph, taken at a sing-sing in the 1930s. (A sing-sing is a ceremony that includes dancing and singing.)

◄ The axehead in this axe from Simbu Province is some 30 centimeters (12 inches) long, and the whole tool is designed to be a valuable item, fit only for display.

C. BENTO/AUSTRALIAN MUSEUM

☞ Clubheads are made in the shape of disks, stars, triangles, and even "pineapples". They were shaped by sawing and grinding and were then mounted on a straight handle, being held in place by carefully woven fiber bindings. They were in widespread, though not common, use within the last century, and a few were still being made in the 1930s.

C. BENTO/AUSTRALIAN MUSEUM

☞ *Opposite:* This carving of a woman is unusual in depicting a complete human form. The hands and legs are crossed, and she appears to be wearing a head covering. The figure is about 40 centimeters (16 inches) high and was acquired in the Ramu Valley, in the lowlands of Papua New Guinea.

R. BOLZAN/AUSTRALIAN MUSEUM

☙ Some pestles are highly elaborate in form, but what is portrayed is open to interpretation. This one, from southwestern Papua New Guinea, has been likened to a bird, a reptile, a penis, and a woman!

R. BOLZAN/AUSTRALIAN MUSEUM

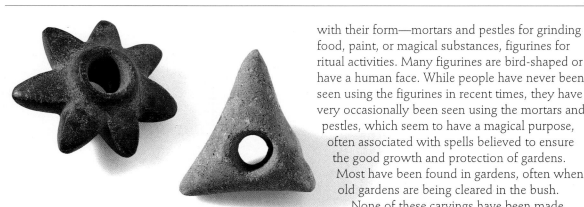

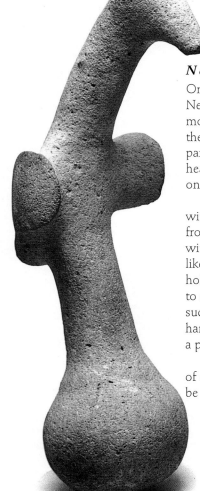

about the same time as square garden beds—representing a more intensive form of soil tillage and, presumably, a growing population—came into use at Kuk. The archaeological evidence from rock shelter sites suggests that it was only after these developments had taken place that people started to raise and eat pigs to any extent. Axe quarrying, that is, can be seen as one aspect of increasing economic intensification within central highlands societies. Other, social, changes would have accompanied such developments. The social dominance of "big men", for example, who achieved their eminence by hard work, many marriages, and managing increasing quantities of exchangeable goods rather than by birth, may well date from this time. Larger-scale societies usually develop some more visible form of hierarchy.

New Guinea Stone Carvings

Only four types of stone carvings are found in New Guinea, all of them quite small objects: mortars, pestles, figurines, and clubheads. On the main island, the first three have been found particularly in parts of the highlands, but clubheads are more common and have been found on most islands within Papua New Guinea.

Stone-headed clubs were used in some areas within the last century. In shape, they vary widely, from a flat disk, through a flat star shape, usually with four or five points, to something that looks like a knobbed hand grenade. All, however, have a hole through the center to allow them to be bound to a long handle. Mostly made of a tough stone such as basalt, they were pecked (with a stone hammer), ground, and drilled into shape over a period of some weeks.

More puzzling are the other three kinds of carvings, which have never been seen to be used in a way that seems compatible with their form—mortars and pestles for grinding food, paint, or magical substances, figurines for ritual activities. Many figurines are bird-shaped or have a human face. While people have never been seen using the figurines in recent times, they have very occasionally been seen using the mortars and pestles, which seem to have a magical purpose, often associated with spells believed to ensure the good growth and protection of gardens. Most have been found in gardens, often when old gardens are being cleared in the bush.

None of these carvings have been made since the time of European contact. New Guineans today usually regard these objects as being natural rather than having been made by humans. A few fragments have been found in archaeological sites dated between 3000 BC and 1000 BC, but whether most are as old as this is unclear.

Archaeology in the Lowlands

We know much less about the prehistory of coastal New Guinea. On the north side of the island, recent excavations in caves and shell mounds have shown, as expected, that settlement dates back into the Late Pleistocene period. Pottery was being made from at least 3000 BC. People continued to live in the area when the Sepik River basin was flooded by the sea about 4000 BC and subsequently refilled with sediment washed down from the highlands. No sites of similar age have been found on the south side of the island, not because people did not live there, but most likely because these early sites have been destroyed by erosion of the hills or buried deeply by soil filling the river valleys.

In the recent past, pottery was made and exchanged over much of lowland New Guinea, especially along the coasts. While older pottery has been found in parts of the north coast, most of this lowland pottery was made after 1300 BC, and its source is sometimes traced to the widespread style known as Lapita.

☞ Mortars are usually made of a tough volcanic or metamorphic rock such as basalt or hornfels. They may be plain bowls, or have a fluted shape—like this one from Siane, in the Papua New Guinea highlands—or even be mounted on a pedestal.

JENNY MILLS

THE SEPIK RIVER PEOPLE OF PAPUA NEW GUINEA: CULTURE AMID CATASTROPHES

PAUL GORECKI

The Sepik basin is one of the most culturally diversified regions in the world. Ever since the mighty Sepik River was first explored by Europeans, in 1887, both the art and the material culture of the Sepik people have attracted enormous interest from museum and private collectors all round the world. Many have wondered how old this "primitive" art is, but no one can yet offer a definitive answer. Serious archaeological research in the Sepik started only in the 1980s, and the results so far indicate that the region has undergone far-reaching environmental changes over the past 10,000 years—changes that must have had a considerable impact on the people living there.

Earthquakes, Floods, and Volcanoes

The Sepik and north coast of the island of New Guinea can aptly be described as regions of catastrophes. Prehistoric coastal societies clearly had to cope with major and sudden changes in their immediate surroundings, as people in these areas still have to today. We know that the coast is constantly uplifting through tectonic activity, with the result that coral reefs and their fish and shellfish resources are periodically destroyed. In the Vanimo region, substantial uplifts

occurred in 1600 BC, 500 BC, and AD 700—at an average rate of 1.5 meters (5 feet) per 1,000 years. Coastal and inland regions are also affected by severe earthquakes from time to time. An earthquake recorded in 1907, for example, changed the Sissano lagoon from fresh to salt water. Another, in the Torricelli mountains in 1935, caused large-scale landslides and loss of life, as well as destroying garden and forest resources. In addition, the coast has regularly been hit by the aftermath of volcanic eruptions, and a number of volcanoes are still active today.

⚑ This pottery sherd from Seraba Cave, decorated with incised parallel wavy lines, is dated to 700 BC.
PAUL GORECKI

PAUL GORECKI

⚑ Located behind Fichin village (shown here) in equatorial rainforest, Lachitu Cave has evidence of human occupation dating back to 35,000 years ago.

PAUL GORECKI

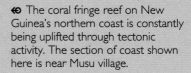

⚏ The coral fringe reef on New Guinea's northern coast is constantly being uplifted through tectonic activity. The section of coast shown here is near Musu village.

Prehistoric people living in the Sepik River basin have also had their share of major catastrophes. In fact, it seems that the basin itself may have been formed only recently. Although results are still preliminary, there is growing evidence that a large part of what is now the Sepik River basin may once have been a huge marine inlet. In 4000 BC, the sites of such townships as Angoram and Pagwi may have been on the coast; while the sites of present-day Ambunti and Amboin would have been on islands surrounded by the sea, and those of all present-day river villages, including Timbunke, would have been under the sea. Assisted by tectonic uplift, the basin may have been gradually formed after the last rise in sea level about 4000 BC. It would have started out as a brackish, mangrove-dominated environment, becoming a vast freshwater swampland perhaps less than 2,000 years ago. Even today, the Sepik River and all its southern tributaries are still searching for a permanent bed to settle in and in the process causing regular large-scale flooding—another natural disaster affecting people's way of life.

GERRY ELLIS

⬅ Sepik people canoeing on the mighty Sepik River. Canoes are the only means of transport between villages in the Sepik River basin, and fishing is the river people's main economy.

➡ Prehistoric pottery sherds with incised and appliqué decoration found on the surface on Koil Island. Traditionally, there was contact between Koil, in the Schouten Islands, and the island of Manus, 350 kilometers (215 miles) to the north.
PAUL GORECKI

Ancient Sepik Cultures

Despite these clearly hostile conditions along the coast and in the basin, people have lived here for more than 35,000 years, developing a number of cultures that have culminated in what can be seen today. Lachitu Cave, near Vanimo (on the northern coast, near the Indonesian border), has evidence of human occupation going back 35,000 years. Deposits from this cave have shown that by 14,000 years ago these coastal people were relying heavily on shellfish from reef areas for food, the dominant species harvested being *Turbo argyrostoma*.

By 4000 BC, more extensive areas of the Vanimo coast seem to have been inhabited. Deposits in Lachitu and nearby Taora Cave dating from this time indicate that local people were still relying mainly on marine foods, supple-

mented by a few land mammals. A specific, notched type of stone tool appears in these caves at this time, which, according to studies of wear patterns and organic residues, may have been used specifically to make bows and arrows. Strange slate artifacts dating from about 3400 BC have also been found in these caves. While their function is still unknown, they seem to be ceremonial rather than utilitarian. Similar, but undated, artifacts have been found elsewhere in New Guinea, including in the Sepik River basin.

Melanesia's Earliest Potters

At about the same time, pottery makes its first appearance not only along the Vanimo coast but also in the Lower Ramu and Middle Sepik basins. In both Lachitu and Taora caves, near Vanimo, it first appears between 3600 BC and 3400 BC in the form of undecorated vessels, with coral sand added to the clay to prevent cracking during firing. In the Lower Ramu, the earliest pottery has been found in the open sites of Beri and Akari, also dating to about 3600 BC. Some of the vessels found here have decorations incised into them or notched into their lips. In the Middle Sepik, pottery has been found in Seraba Cave in layers dating from 4000 BC, and by 700 BC pottery-making was clearly a flourishing tradition in the Middle Sepik region. The dominant decoration on these Seraba vessels consists of two parallel wavy incisions around the circumference. What all this means is that

pottery—one of the traditional arts for which the Sepik people are world famous—has a much longer history in New Guinea than in any other part of Melanesia.

An Early Exchange Network

Another remarkable aspect of Sepik prehistory is the complex network of exchange these early people set up. It seems that over the past 10,000 years Sepik people not only established an exchange network within the region but also extended it to areas far afield. For instance, the tiny island of Koil, off Wewak, near the mouth of the Sepik River, was visited by long-distance sea traders from the island of Manus within the last few thousand years. These traders introduced the volcanic glass known as obsidian into the local exchange systems, and we know that more than 1,000 years ago it was already regarded as a valuable commodity by those living along the Vanimo coast, more than 700 kilometers (430 miles) from its source. All the obsidian flakes so far found between the mouth of the Sepik River and the Irian Jaya border come exclusively from Manus.

Archaeological research in the Sepik has just begun, and yet it is already yielding fascinating results that have a significant bearing on the prehistory of Melanesia in general. There is no doubt that Sepik societies, with all their complexity and their remarkable kaleidoscope of traditional art, have roots that go back deep into the remote past.

THE SEPIK REGION

The Sepik basin is regularly flooded, while the northern coast and the adjacent islands are subject to periodic earthquakes and volcanic eruptions.

CARTOGRAPHY: RAY SIM

Taora
Lachitu • Vanimo

Bismarck Sea

TORRICELLI MOUNTAINS

KOIL IS

• Wewak

SEPIK BASIN

Pagwi
Sepik R • Seraba • Angoram
Ambunti • Timbunke • Beri
Akari
Ramu R

• Amboin

CENTRAL HIGHLANDS

☝ The precision of the geometric designs characteristic of Lapita pottery was often accentuated by an infill of powdered lime.

H. GALLASCH/JIM SPECHT

Lapita Pottery

Lapita pottery is central to much of the research that has been carried out in the Pacific islands, at least as far east as Tonga and Samoa. It is important for several reasons.

The first is that the people who made this pottery were clearly the first to settle the smaller islands of Remote Oceania—and probably the earliest inhabitants of any Pacific island east of the Solomons. They almost certainly voyaged as far as South America, for which the presence of the sweet potato is the only evidence. Their descendants eventually reached Hawaii, Easter Island, and New Zealand, while some moved north and west into what are now the central and eastern island nations of Micronesia.

Secondly, an extensive region was settled in a very short time. This implies both that exploration was purposive, not accidental, and that voyagers had good sailing canoes and navigation skills. The settlement of Remote Oceania is the earliest large-scale maritime colonization to have occurred anywhere in the world.

Thirdly, despite some intensive investigations over the last two decades, there is still major disagreement among researchers about the origin

NATIONAL MARITIME MUSEUM, GREENWICH

☝ The artists who sailed with Captain Cook and other European explorers showed the islands of Oceania to be beautiful, and life in these parts to be generally carefree. Some of the Pacific island vessels they portrayed were faster and more maneuverable than those of the Europeans. This view of Tahiti was painted by William Hodges on Cook's second voyage in 1773.

of Lapita pottery and associated cultural materials such as shell ornaments, the central issue being whether they were of local origin or made by migrants from Asia.

Lastly, the story of this research tells us much about how Westerners, both scientists and laypeople, have interpreted the history of the Pacific Ocean peoples over the years.

Lapita pottery was first discovered on Watom Island, just off New Britain, in 1909. How it came to be named after a site on the west coast of New Caledonia, is something no one seems to know. It has since been found over an area ranging from near the Irian Jaya border, in the west, to Samoa, and possibly even the Marquesas, in the east (the sherds here being few, small, and not highly

characteristic)—a distance of some 8,000 kilometers (5,000 miles).

Lapita ware is characterized by being coarsely handmade and poorly fired, but very finely decorated with bands of geometric designs impressed into the clay by stamps consisting of a single row of teeth—probably like short combs with short teeth (although none have ever been found). This decoration can be extremely elaborate, sometimes incorporating stylized faces and decorative plugs fitted into ear lobes. Geometric decoration is found on a range of pot shapes, including round-based, narrow-necked bowls and flat platters. Other pots have similar geometric designs incised rather than stamped into the clay, although this form of decoration is never as fine.

The significance that has been attached to the distribution of Lapita pottery needs to be understood in the context of Pacific history in general. The early northern European sailors, such as Captain James Cook, who brought news of the Pacific islanders to Europe in the eighteenth century, described Remote Oceania in glowing terms—the wonderful climate, easy way of life, and beautiful, friendly islanders—an image that many Europeans, Americans, and Australians still cherish. These explorers contrasted the tall, fair, friendly Polynesians with the inhabitants of the larger islands such as the Solomons further west, who were shorter, dark-skinned, and much less friendly towards unknown intruders. They were also surprised at the similarity of language and customs between many islands, from Hawaii to New Zealand, attributing this to the inhabitants' evident ability to sail between these islands. From these and other observations, the idea took root among Europeans that these islanders could not be the descendants of islanders living further west and must, therefore, have migrated into the Pacific from somewhere else. Where that somewhere else might be has never been entirely clear. Guesses have included India, China, South America, and everywhere in Southeast Asia; one of the lost tribes of Israel has also been considered. Within the last few decades, however, Southeast Asia has become the favored area, largely because language studies have pointed in this direction.

All Remote Oceanic languages are of Austronesian stock. Other Austronesian languages are spoken in Taiwan, the Philippines, throughout Indonesia, in some coastal areas of New Guinea, on the smaller islands of Near Oceania, and even in Madagascar, far away across the Indian Ocean. Austronesian languages are quite similar to each other, and linguists have accordingly argued that they must have developed in one part of this area quite recently (otherwise they would be more different) and spread as people migrated to other regions. It is difficult to date these migrations, as there are no written records and there is as yet no general agreement among scholars as to the

PAUL GORECKI

linguistic methods that might be used for this purpose. But it is generally agreed that the original Austronesian language (proto-Austronesian) originated between 6000 BC and 3000 BC— probably, most linguists believe, in Taiwan.

Within Remote Oceania itself, the relative closeness of the languages of different islands has been paralleled, in recent decades, by the relationships demonstrated through archaeology. Radiocarbon dates show, for example, that Hawaii was settled well before New Zealand, and we know that the Hawaiian language has diverged more from that of the central Pacific than the Maori language has. It is this demonstrated link between archaeology and language history that has become a model for the rest of Pacific history. Lapita pottery, it has often been argued, provides tangible evidence that Austronesian speakers from Southeast Asia migrated through the islands of Near Oceania and out into the Pacific.

There are some problems with this view, the main one being, perhaps, that Lapita pottery has not been found in any quantity west of the islands of Near Oceania. Only a handful of sherds has

been found on the main island of New Guinea, for example. Nor has any pottery been found that is clearly its ancestor.

More tellingly, although Lapita was long thought to be the oldest form of pottery in Near Oceania, pottery recently found on the north coast of New Guinea has been dated to about 3000 BC— making it about 1,700 years older than the earliest Lapita pottery. Unlike Lapita ware, this early New Guinean pottery has almost no decoration on it, and increasingly, researchers are coming to the view that the geometric designs characteristic of Lapita ware may be derived from designs already being used on contemporary barkcloth (used for clothing) and in tattooing, for example. Moreover, the generally rough quality of Lapita ware, which is often made with large amounts of coarse shell temper and poorly fired, is not what would be expected if it derived from Southeast Asian pottery. While the craft of pottery-making may originally have come from Asia, it seems unlikely that Lapita pottery did so, and its distribution is therefore unlikely to reflect the migratory routes of early Austronesian speakers.

⬆ Nearly half of this pot (later reconstructed) was dug up at Lamau, on the west coast of New Ireland, in 1985. The design is geometric, but the decoration is not as fine or as elaborate as the dentate-stamped form of Lapita pottery. Lapita bowls commonly take this shape.

PAUL GORECKI

⬆ The decoration on the Lamau pot is incised—cut into the damp clay with a sharp shell or stone—rather than stamped into the clay.

⚓ The first recorded find of Lapita pottery was made in 1907 by Father Otto Meyer, on Watom Island, near Rabaul. His specimens, including these four sherds, were sent to the Basel Museum, in Switzerland. The next two finds were made in Tonga, in the 1920s, and in New Caledonia, in the 1950s.
MUSEUM FÜR VÖLKERKUNDE/J. SPECHT

⚲ Rings, beads, and armbands from the Talepakemalai site, Papua New Guinea. Made of *Conus* and *Spondylus* shells, they were found on an old lagoon floor, where they had been dumped, along with broken Lapita pottery, shells, and animal bones, from houses built on stilts over the water.

Lapita Sites and Early Exchange Systems

Excavations in Near Oceania within the last decade have revealed small quantities of Lapita pottery in most New Britain and New Ireland sites occupied between 1300 BC and 0 BC. In some sites, however, including the small offshore islands of Eloaua, Watom, and Ambitle, and several islands of the Arawe group, it has been found in considerably larger quantities. The Talepakemalai site on Eloaua, in particular, has preserved not only quantities of pottery but also a wide range of stone and shell artifacts, the latter including fishhooks, bracelets, rings, armbands, beads, and pendants. It has also yielded evidence that these Lapita potters commonly fished in lagoons and gathered shellfish, were engaged in agriculture,

and kept domestic pigs, dogs, and chickens. The bases of some house posts have also been found. The site appears to have been a village built on stilts over a tidal lagoon, and radiocarbon dates suggest (as do those from some other sites) that people lived here continuously for some hundreds of years. Analyses of clays, tempers, and decorative motifs suggest that pottery or clay was moved between some sites, but research as to the extent to which this occurred is still under way. The clearest evidence of the transport of materials comes from the presence of obsidian. (See the feature *Obsidian Tools: A Study in Prehistoric Melanesian Trade.*)

Obsidian is a volcanic glass, usually black. It is known to occur in only three areas of Near Oceania—on Lou and Fergusson islands, and on the Willaumez Peninsula of New Britain—with several possible sources in each area. Some progress has been made in distinguishing obsidian from different sources, and material from both the Willaumez and Lou quarries has been found in Lapita sites. It is found not only in Near Oceania, but as far east as Fiji, although only in small quantities in these Remote Oceanic sites. Willaumez obsidian has also been identified far to the west, in sites on the small Talaud Islands, in Indonesia, and on the northeast coast of Sabah. The finds from the eastern islands of Near Oceania and in the west date to within the Lapita period, but not—as we might expect if the traffic in obsidian had been initiated by Southeast Asian migrants—to its earliest stages.

Obsidian was clearly important to the people who made Lapita pottery, but why they wanted obsidian is not well understood, since locally available stones or sharp-edged shells could have been used in its place. However, they evidently valued it, flaking it into very small pieces once it was away from its source, using some of these pieces for cutting and scraping vegetable foods and making a few into points and engraving tools.

It may be that the sites that have yielded quantities of Lapita pottery were centers of distribution networks. They were often located on deep-water bays, with good but protected sea access, although the inhabitants of these villages drew most of their food supply from the land nearby. In some ways, they seem very like the settlements of traditional traders in these regions, who until the early twentieth century made their living largely by moving a wide range of goods—pottery and feathers, pigs and axes—around local areas. What distinguishes the Lapita period is the fact that such similar pottery is found over such enormous distances, suggesting that it was the physical expression of some as yet unknown ideology. How obsidian was distributed—whether through one large-scale trade network that linked Lapita potters, or through a series of such networks, or through some other mechanism such as small-scale, hand-to-hand trade—remains to be determined.

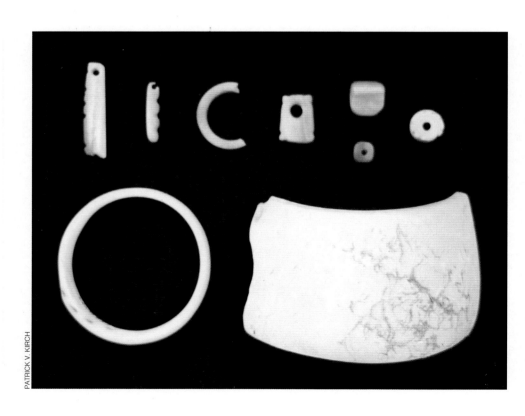

PATRICK V. KIRCH

The People Who Settled Remote Oceania

We can also look to biological evidence, both modern and ancient, for clues to the identity of the first people who settled Remote Oceania. The modern evidence includes such studies as finger and palm prints, tooth size and shape, the genetics of various blood groups, and mitochondrial DNA analysis, all of which have a component of inherited characteristics and can therefore be used to establish relationships. Ancient evidence comes from burials and consists mostly of the shape and size of various bones and teeth, which can be compared with each other and with those of different modern groups.

The modern evidence faces the difficulty that evolution (random biological changes acted on by selective forces), genetic drift (random changes that become established by chance), and mixing between different populations, as well as the small size of original founding populations, must be assessed and their effects excluded before long-ago links can be proposed. The main problem with the prehistoric evidence is simply that so little of it has survived. There are, for instance, fragmentary remains of only about 15 people from sites that contain quantities of Lapita pottery, and that is too few to enable us to draw any firm conclusions.

None of these problems has prevented researchers from putting forward carefully qualified interpretations, but it is not surprising that workers in the two different fields have come up with rather different results. A recent survey by geneticists Sue Serjeantson and Ron Hill concluded that although Pacific islanders showed unmistakeable evidence of Near Oceanic forebears, some genetic markers linked them quite closely also with Asian ancestors. On the other hand, anatomist Phil Houghton points out that the large, muscular bodies of many Polynesian people are physiologically well adapted to ocean voyaging, and that people of similar build have been found in burials associated with Lapita pottery. Houghton further claims that this physiological type is unsuited to living on tropical landmasses such as Southeast Asia or New Guinea, is therefore unlikely to have evolved there, and is, moreover, not found there. He believes that such people can only have evolved in the island environment of Near Oceania. In part, such differences result from the fact that different researchers use different methods and different theoretical frameworks—the usefulness of which will become more apparent as further research is carried out.

Pasts Yet to Be Written

As our knowledge of Pacific history and prehistory unfolds, two things become clear. The first is that large-scale changes have occurred in the Pacific world, for the most part independently of what was happening elsewhere in the world at that time. Until recently, histories of Pacific peoples have been written largely in terms of waves of migrants. Each wave was thought to have brought with it some cultural attributes that are still found in the area, such as agriculture, pottery, and axes. By contrast, current studies of Pacific prehistory show that many developments originated locally. Highlands agriculture, for example, was based on locally developed techniques and predominantly local crops and supported populations as dense

◄◙ A woman and child of Tanna Island, Vanuatu, drawn by William Hodges in 1774. The woman is wearing earrings, probably of shell, and a necklace made of shell disks and a whole shell. Her cap is made of barkcloth, and the child is carried in a kind of bag made of the same material and slung over her shoulders.

NATIONAL LIBRARY OF AUSTRALIA

as in any other rural society of the time. Lapita pottery evolved in the islands of Near Oceania, and its makers carried it far afield in the Pacific, colonizing on a scale unmatched until the European voyages of the last 500 years. People in the newly independent countries of Near Oceania can lay claim to a long and vigorous history of cultural independence.

But the recognition that Near Oceania has an independent history is also important to the rest of the world. In Western accounts in particular, there has been a strong tendency to see traditional Near Oceanic cultures as "living fossils", examples of what the whole world must have been like before cities and industrial societies developed. But no society has been static. The past is not exactly like the present: everywhere it is a foreign country, to be explored through history and archaeology.

OBSIDIAN TOOLS: A STUDY IN PREHISTORIC MELANESIAN TRADE

ROBIN TORRENCE

EUROPEANS TRAVELING in the Pacific islands about 200 years ago observed elaborate trading networks operating throughout Melanesia. In some places, specialist traders distributed a broad range of utilitarian goods and foodstuffs, as well as ceremonial items, such as shell necklaces and armbands of various types, between widespread settlements. In other areas, large groups of men left their village for months at a time to undertake long-distance trading expeditions, carrying large cargoes across dangerous seas.

A Noncommercial Economy

Melanesian trade had a very different character from the commercial and market-based economies we know in modern times. In Melanesia, there was no "money" or universal medium of exchange: exchange rates varied from place to place, but at any one point they were fixed, so that, for example, a certain amount of fish was always given in return for a particular quantity of sago, or a special kind of shell ornament was exchanged for another of a particular type. Value was determined by arbitrary cultural rules and not by scarcity or the amount of labor invested in goods. An important aim of Pacific archaeology is to trace the history of trading systems, in order to better understand the development of these noncommercial economies, so different from our own.

The task is not an easy one. Many items that were probably traded—such as fish, garden crops, feathers, and baskets—are perishable and would leave few traces for archaeologists to discover. Fortunately, however, tools made from a black, glassy volcanic stone called obsidian are commonly found at prehistoric sites in Melanesia. Obsidian occurs naturally only in a few, very restricted localities, but it has been found over a wide area, in sites far from its source. Trade seems a likely explanation for this distribution. Certainly, in recorded history, specialist traders carried obsidian nodules and tools along established trade routes.

Prehistoric Trade

Archaeologists study prehistoric trade by looking at both the distribution and production of items. Since obsidian from each of the five source areas known in Melanesia has a slightly different chemical composition, obsidian artifacts can be readily traced to their geological source. Distribution patterns are studied by making maps showing where obsidian tools derived from each source area have been found. By about 18,000 years ago, obsidian from outcrops around Talasea and Mopir, on New Britain, had found their way to Matembek Cave, on New Ireland. Between about 1500 BC and AD 500, obsidian from Talasea is found in sites stretching from Malaysia in the west to Fiji in the east, the most extensive distribution of a good known anywhere in the prehistoric world.

The second approach to studying trade is to look at production—that is, how obsidian artifacts were made. Research being conducted in the province of West New Britain by archaeologists from the Australian Museum provides a useful case study of this kind of analysis. The first stage of the research focused on the obsidian outcrops themselves. Exploration in the Talasea region revealed that sources of obsidian are scattered over an area of at least 100 square kilometers (38 square miles) and so would have been within easy reach of anyone living in the area. No one group of people could have held a monopoly over supplies of the raw material. But not all potentially useable sources were exploited. People

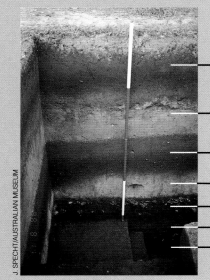

J. SPECHT/AUSTRALIAN MUSEUM

PHASE 4

Volcanic eruption c. 1,100 years ago

PHASE 3

Volcanic eruption c. 3,500 years ago

PHASE 2

Volcanic ash undated

PHASE I

☝ Stratigraphic layers excavated at Bitokara Mission. The darker layers, representing different phases of obsidian tool manufacture and use, are separated by yellow layers composed of volcanic ash from two major eruptions.

always preferred outcrops where large nodules of obsidian could be obtained with little effort, but they selected different locations at various times during at least the past 5,000 years. The choice of sources, therefore, cannot completely be explained by economic reasons, as would be the case in a commercially based economy. It seems likely that social factors have long played a role in establishing rights of access to obsidian sources.

Changing Patterns of Use

The second stage of the Australian Museum project has concentrated on how obsidian artifacts were made and used in the period from somewhere before 1500 BC up to the present day. An exciting site was discovered in 1981 at Bitokara Mission, near Talasea, when an archaeologist noticed abundant quantities of obsidian artifacts at the base of a freshly dug toilet pit. The Mission is perched on top of a cliff containing obsidian deposits and overlooks the nearby harbor. The setting was created by a very

thick and viscous volcanic lava that flowed slowly down the slopes of a volcano and stopped at this point. A team returned in 1988 and carried out systematic excavations. The Bitokara Mission excavations revealed a sequence of levels containing abundant quantities of waste by-products from artifact production, as well as discarded, used tools. Layers representing four periods of manufacturing activity are neatly separated by layers of volcanic ash, which have sealed the material beneath them.

In the earliest two phases, which have not yet been precisely dated but are earlier than 1500 BC, blocks of obsidian were dug up or collected from obsidian flows located on slopes just slightly uphill

RICHARD FULLAGER

☝ When viewed under very high magnification, fragments of plants cut or scraped about 1500 BC can be observed still adhering to the edge of an obsidian stemmed tool found at Bitokara Mission.

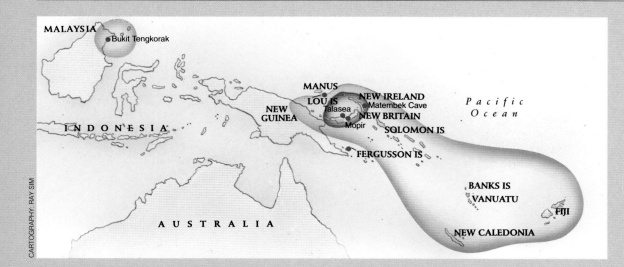

CARTOGRAPHY: RAY SIM

PREHISTORIC OBSIDIAN
The widespread distribution of obsidian from Talasea and Mopir demonstrates regular contact among seafaring peoples. The different patterns reflect different trading systems in these two periods.

Known distribution

about 1000 BC

about 8000 BC

HISTORIC TRADE ROUTES
Obsidian traveled overland between trading partners in adjacent villages, and by sea with specialist traders.

CARTOGRAPHY: RAY SIM

from the Mission. Large flakes were struck off them and were carried downhill to a level spot for the final stages of manufacture. The artifacts made at Bitokara varied greatly in shape and size, but many had a protrusion, or stem, which was probably wrapped with plant material and used as a handle. Microscopic analysis of wear patterns and residues preserved on their edges show that the stemmed tools were mainly used to cut plants, possibly root crops.

In the second of these two periods, as well as stemmed tools, many small flakes were made by hitting an obsidian cobble repeatedly and turning it over several times during the process. The resulting "rotated core" has a very distinctive shape. Analysis has revealed that most of the flakes were used for cutting and scraping plant material, but a few were used on animal tissues. The cores were not used as tools but are merely a waste product.

The division of labor between quarrying on the hillside above Bitokara Mission and the manufacture of tools lower down the slope, combined with the evidence that large quantities of stemmed tools were made, suggests that production in these two earliest periods was at least partly geared toward exports. Unfortunately, sites elsewhere in island Melanesia dating to before 1500 BC are extremely rare, so we do not yet know much about where the obsidian artifacts were going.

About 1500 BC, the entire area was completely devastated by ash from a major volcanic eruption. It seems likely that it would have been abandoned for at least a generation. When people once again began to exploit obsidian at Bitokara Mission, in the third period, they no longer quarried on the hillside or made stemmed tools. Only small flakes were made, using the technique of rotated cores from the previous period. From the fact that quite a few flakes can be fitted back together on their core, it seems that many of these small tools were made and used at the same spot, therefore suggesting that few, if any, tools were exported.

These results are puzzling, since it was during this third period at Bitokara that obsidian from Talasea is most widely distributed. Possibly, the hillside outcrops at Bitokara Mission were abandoned because they had been buried by the ash, and people chose instead to gather lumps that had eroded out and could be found in stream courses or on beaches. At this stage of research, however, we do not know why people stopped making stemmed tools for export. It seems likely that unworked pieces of obsidian were traded during this period. This change in exports from Talasea suggests that the nature of trade during the third period also differed from earlier times.

About AD 900, another volcanic eruption occurred. In the subsequent, fourth period of occupation, rotated cores are no longer found. The greatly reduced number of artifacts present indicates that production had declined considerably at this site, and, again, there is no evidence of quarrying on the hillside. It seems that in the fourth period the site at Bitokara Mission was used only occasionally. Since it is known from observations made by Europeans during the past hundred years that unmodified pieces of obsidian from Talasea were systematically being traded throughout West New Britain and across to mainland New Guinea, other outcrops in the area may have been exploited at this time. Old people living in the region today do not remember obsidian from Bitokara Mission being traded, but they do know of other places where obsidian is said to have been collected for trade.

A Key to the Past

The Australian Museum project at Talasea shows that the processing of obsidian at one source area has changed several times in the past. The variations observed at Bitokara in how obsidian was acquired (quarried or collected) and exported (in the form of tools or raw material) suggest that prehistoric economic systems operated in a different way from the trading systems seen at the time of European contact. These initial results are exciting, but a great deal more needs to be learned before archaeologists can reconstruct how these early trading systems worked.

Already, further excavations are in progress at other source areas in the Talasea region to find out if the patterns that have emerged at Bitokara are repeated more widely. Studies of how obsidian was used at sites where it had to be imported are also under way. Finally, archaeologists are studying the trading system of the last several hundred years both by talking to people who remember how it worked and by comparing their stories with contemporary archaeological remains.

162

FARMERS OF THE NEW WORLD

10,000 BC – AD 1492

An Enduring Native American Gift to the World

DAVID HURST THOMAS

By the time Europeans began exploring the Americas, all but a handful of the indigenous societies relied, to some degree, on domesticated plants for their livelihood. The list of New World domesticates includes a diverse range of grains, root crops, vegetables, spices, nuts, and fruits. Although initially wary of new foods, the European interlopers soon learned first hand the potential of Native American agricultural products. The new crops were quickly exported to European ports, and from there, the New World bounty reached around the globe.

Today, the result is amazing. Sixty percent of the food that now supports the world's population was originally domesticated by Native Americans—maize, potatoes, manioc, beans of several varieties, squash and pumpkins, sweet potatoes, vanilla, tomatoes, chili peppers, pineapples, avocados, gourds, sunflowers, and amaranths. American cottons paved the way for all modern commercial varieties—and, for better or worse, Native Americans were also responsible for domesticating the still-sought-after stimulants of tobacco and coca (the source of cocaine).

◄ An Anasazi ruin inside a sheltered cave, overlooking the Green River and Canyonlands National Park, in Utah. The canyon walls offered countless flat surfaces for prehistoric artists to paint their pictographs and peck their petroglyphs. Much of this rock art survives today.

⚱ Maize (Indian corn) was developed through thousands of years of experimentation. So extensive was the genetic manipulation that today, modern maize requires human intervention to spread its own seeds.
D. DONNE BRYANT STOCK

MIDDLE AMERICA
The area known as Mesoamerica was one of the first regions in which plants were domesticated. From their early agricultural base, the Mesoamerican people forged one of the New World's two great civilizations.
CARTOGRAPHY: RAY SIM

☝ The earliest people in Mexico's Tehuacán Valley cooked seed pods from the screwbean mesquite (*Prosopis pubscens*) into a rich syrup. Later, the Cahuilla Indians of California carefully pruned the thorny wild mesquite trees to make it easier to harvest the pods.

☞ Chili peppers have a high tryptophan content. Used as a condiment, they complement maize, which provides little of this important amino acid.

Clues from the Tehuacán Valley

Our modern understanding of American agriculture draws heavily on the innovative archaeological investigations of Richard "Scotty" MacNeish in the 1960s. After years of searching for early evidence of maize in places like Mexico's Sierra de Tamaulipas, MacNeish was finally drawn to the caves and rock shelters of the arid and mountainous Tehuacán Valley, in central Mexico. Having investigated 38 of the Tehuacán caves, MacNeish dug several test pits into the deposits of Coxcatlán Cave, where the remains of six tiny corncobs had been preserved, all more primitive than any discovered previously. Radiocarbon dating put their age at about 3600 BC, older than any domesticated corn yet discovered. Even earlier remnants of maize have been found since.

Buoyed by his results, MacNeish launched a major interdisciplinary project in the Tehuacán Valley. After excavating 9 sites intensively and testing 18 others, he was able to trace a sequence of cultural developments from about 9500 BC to the arrival of Europeans in AD 1531. This research still forms the basis of our understanding of early American agriculture. More recent excavations, by Kent Flannery and his colleagues, at Guilá Naquitz, in the Mitla area of the Oaxaca Valley, in Mexico, have corroborated the early part of the Tehuacán sequence.

The earliest people of the Tehuacán Valley lived in small, mobile family groups which probably consisted of between four and eight people. Familiar with the range of local environments and with the foods seasonally available in each area, they survived by hunting the native American horse, antelope, and deer, and by gathering the fruits, seeds, and nuts that grew around them. They roasted century plants, cooked up syrup from mesquite pods, and leached tannic acid from bitter acorns to make them palatable. These early foragers sometimes lived in caves, and sometimes camped in the open—fanning out when food was scarce and converging on favored camp sites when times were better.

When these first Tehuacanos arrived, at the end of the Pleistocene period, the climate was colder and drier than it is today. But as central Mexico became warmer, both the grasslands and the water supply began to shrink, ultimately driving some animals, including horses and antelopes, to extinction. In time, smaller game, such as deer and cottontail rabbits, became more important as a source of food, as did gophers and even rats.

About 7000 BC, the Indians of central Mexico, while continuing to range widely in search of food and other resources, began to collect plants more intensively, particularly those that were eventually domesticated—such as squash, beans, and the wild ancestor of maize (probably teosinte).

Some time before 5000 BC, the people of the Tehuacán Valley started to make use of a considerably wider range of plant foods. Bottle gourds may have been the first plants domesticated in the New World, but people also began to plant and tend squash, amaranths, chili peppers, and, perhaps, avocados. These initial gardens required minimal care and contributed little to the food supply. Neither seasonal foraging trips nor settlement patterns were much affected.

Agriculture may have arisen in response to the changing climatic conditions during the Late Pleistocene period that culminated in the end of the last Ice Age and the beginning of the period we know as the Holocene. With the changes in vegetation this brought about, supplies of important plant foods would have become less predictable.

Later, as the population grew, hunter-gatherers became increasingly less mobile and more territorial. Plant cultivation proved to be a good way to increase the food supply, and food storage a logical way to even out the differences between good and bad years.

Tiny maize cobs like the ones MacNeish discovered at Coxcatlán Cave appeared in Tehuacán Valley gardens some time before 3400 BC, along with beans, chili peppers, squash, gourds, and amaranths. By about 2500 BC, agriculture provided perhaps 25 percent of the Tehuacán food supply. A thousand years later, this proportion had increased to about 40 percent. The evidence from Tehuacán and Oaxaca indicates that permanent villages may have been established by 2500 BC. MacNeish believes that people may have been living in villages all year round by this date, although other archaeologists suggest that the earliest permanent villages did not appear in Middle America until about 1700 BC.

The Maize Debate

Considerable debate also surrounds the introduction of maize into South America. (See the feature *On the Trail of Maize: Mother of Corn*.) Although evidence of maize existing before 4000 BC occasionally turns up in South America, maize finds continue to be sparse for the next 2,500 years, until about 1500 BC.

Robert McC. Bird, who has examined most of the prehistoric maize recovered in South America, suggests that maize arrived in Middle America about 3000 BC. Numerous varieties of maize developed and gradually moved southwards. With an extremely wide range of maize types in existence, the rate of both evolution and dispersal had accelerated by 1000 BC. Rapid hybridization took place, making maize an even more adaptable and versatile plant and increasing its yield. This also accounts for the complex mosaic of maize varieties found across South America.

Bird also stresses that after a period of localized evolution and differentiation, certain varieties of maize were taken north, back into Middle America. This process may have been repeated many times, producing new genetic varieties that often resulted in specialized kinds of maize adapted to local conditions.

MICHAEL S. THOMPSON/COMSTOCK

⚨ Amaranths were among the earliest wild plants to be domesticated in the Americas.

⚨ These three large ceramic figures from Nayarit, in western Mexico, depict Native American women making tortillas from ground maize. They date to between about 200 BC and AD 600.

AMERICAN MUSEUM OF NATURAL HISTORY

Relying heavily on new data from Ecuadorian plant phytoliths —microscopic silica particles contained in plants—Deborah Pearsall argues that because early maize is so varied, it must have been introduced to South America some time before 5000 BC. At this early date, however, maize was neither widespread nor an important part of the diet. Evidence from Peru indicates that maize did not become widespread until about 1500 BC, or slightly later.

Many archaeologists, such as Pearsall, have come to rely heavily on the evidence provided by the distribution and analysis of microscopic plant phytoliths. Distinctive silica phytoliths occur in plants of the grass family and are also found in groups such as rushes, sedges, palms, conifers, and deciduous trees.

Although phytoliths have been identified in archaeological sites for decades, it was rare for archaeological deposits to be systematically analyzed for phytoliths before 1970. Since then, interest in this unusual technique has exploded, and today the identification and analysis of phytoliths recovered from archaeological sites hold great promise for reconstructing paleo-environments and for tracking the process of plant domestication.

The difficulties of basing taxonomy (plant classification) on phytoliths have meant that phytolith analysis is still not widely accepted as a valid method of archaeological research. Considerable progress has recently been made in the area of taxonomy, however—in particular, Pearsall's breakthrough in identifying maize phytoliths, which pushed back the date for the introduction of maize to Ecuador by several thousand years. The next step is to develop reliable criteria for identifying teosinte phytoliths, which would represent a major advance in our understanding of how maize was domesticated.

Apart from such systematic problems, some archaeologists remain reluctant to accept phytolith data when they conflict with more traditional evidence, such as kernel impressions, maize motifs that appear on ancient ceramics (as at Valdivia, in Ecuador), actual maize parts, and traces of maize on metates (grinding slabs).

Plant Domestication: The Beginning of Agriculture

Plants were domesticated at many different times and in many areas throughout South America. Although much remains to be learned, it seems clear that the range of plants cultivated in South America did not evolve in isolation. Cultivars (plant varieties produced from a naturally occurring species) were exchanged across large regions almost from the time they originated.

Regardless of when they first arrived—surely some time before 14,000 years ago—the earliest South Americans followed a Paleoindian way of life, hunting now-extinct Pleistocene animals and smaller game, and gathering wild plants. Then, about 8000 BC, a shift occurred. Evidence from a number of Andean sites shows that a new way of life was adopted: the so-called Archaic adaptation, based largely on hunting llama, alpaca, and deer, and gathering a range of wild plants.

This period also saw the beginnings of plant domestication in South America. Domesticated potatoes were present in northern Bolivia by 8000 BC; beans and chili peppers in highland Peruvian valleys by about 8500 BC. By 6000 BC, the list of domesticated plants had expanded to include squash, gourds, and guavas. These earliest

Painted by renowned artist Diego Rivera, this mural at the Palacio National, in Mexico City, shows the importance of maize to ancient Mexican communities.

finds are still in question, mainly because of the nature of the archaeological sites where they were found. Most of the early cultigens have been recovered from dry caves, many of which, unfortunately, had been disturbed by later burials. The deposits in such caves also attract rodents, which tend to scatter food remains, mixing them with other material.

Coastal and lowland cultivars, including cotton and squash, appear in central sierra sites between 4200 BC and 2500 BC. From about 4000 BC to the end of the Peruvian Preceramic period (1800 BC to 1200 BC), there is increasing evidence, from sites such as Huaca Prieta, that plants were extensively cultivated, including many that had been domesticated previously (such as beans, gourds, squash, chili peppers, and, of course, guavas). New crops also appear about this time, particularly cotton, avocados, sweet potatoes, peanuts, and manioc. Despite this diversity, root crops were the main source of carbohydrates in the diet until maize spread through the mid-altitude and low-altitude zones.

How Were Plants Domesticated?

Such are the apparent facts of the initial domestication of plants in Middle and South America. But how do we explain the processes that were involved?

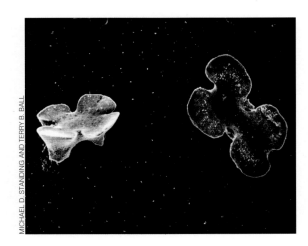

One cogent explanation has been offered by archaeologist Kent Flannery. Survival of the earliest human communities in the Mexican highlands depended upon certain key food resources—maguey, cactus fruits, mesquite pods, wild grasses (such as *Zea*), white-tailed deer, and cottontail rabbits. Many of these plants and animals were available for only a few months of the year, and when more than one resource was available at one time, hunter-gatherers had to decide which had priority. Since these two factors—seasonal availability and what is often referred to as scheduling—meant that no particular resource predominated, this

way of living proved flexible and relatively resistant to change.

Flannery argues that the origin of agriculture can be traced to genetic changes in only one or two of the many plants that humans exploited. For example, the wild ancestor of maize might have undergone genetic alteration as a result of natural crossbreeding and subsequent evolution, with some assistance in the form of human intervention. Whatever the reason, the upshot was an increase in the size and number of cobs and the number of kernel rows, and the loss of the outer leaves—known as glumes—that enclosed the individual kernels.

Beans, on the other hand, might have evolved independently from maize, becoming larger and more permeable to water and therefore easier to process as food. They may also have evolved limper, less brittle pods that did not disintegrate when mature, making harvesting easier. These minor genetic changes would have set further changes in motion, for as these plants began to provide better harvests, they would have become the preferred source of food. This, in turn, would have helped along the process of genetic change. People would have begun to alter their way of life to take advantage of these cultigens.

Biologist David Rindos has suggested another explanation, emphasizing evolutionary processes independent of human enterprise and initiative. His theory, the so-called coevolutionary perspective, plays down any linear, cause-and-effect relationship.

⚜ Ecuadorians harvesting potatoes, which were first domesticated about 8000 BC.

⬅ The identification and analysis of phytoliths (microscopic silica particles occurring in plants) is providing new information about early plant domestication. This scanning electron photomicrograph shows the morphology of the phytoliths characteristic of maize.

⚜ The Hopi Indians of eastern Arizona used wooden tweezers to collect the edible fruit of the prickly pear, and rolled the fruit in sand to remove the spines. They also collected prickly pear joints. The large thorns were burned off; then the joints were boiled, dipped in a rich syrup made from baked sweet corn, and eaten.

ON THE TRAIL OF MAIZE: MOTHER OF CORN

David Hurst Thomas

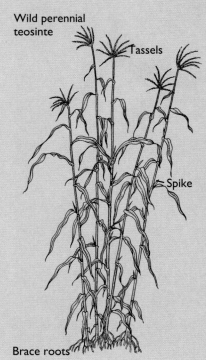

Wild perennial teosinte

Tassels

Spike

Brace roots

Modern maize (*Zea mays*, below) and wild perennial teosinte (above) are closely related. They have the same number of chromosomes and hybridize freely. The main difference between the plants is in their seed-bearing female organs: whereas teosinte has numerous small, brittle spikes that shatter when they mature, maize has two or three large ears, enclosed by husks. Teosinte also has numerous side stalks (tillers). The tassels are the male flower clusters.

☝ These drawings of Aztec methods of planting, tending, and harvesting maize, attributed to sixteenth-century native artists, were published in the *Codex Florentino*.

O f the more than 100 plant species domesticated by Native Americans, none is more familiar or widespread than maize (*Zea mays*), also called Indian corn. Maize was the staff of life for much of pre-Columbian America, from Argentina to Canada, from sea level to the slopes of the Andes. For more than 7,000 years, the people of the Americas domesticated hundreds of kinds of maize, from the ancient thumbnail-sized wild cobs to the formidable ears of corn sold today throughout the world.

The combination of maize, beans (*Phaseolus*), and squash (*Curcurbita*) is commonly considered to be America's agricultural triumvirate. Not only can all three crops be grown together in the same field, but they complement one another nutritionally. Although rich in starch, maize is deficient in lysine, an essential amino acid. Beans are rich in protein, and contain large amounts of lysine. Eaten together, beans, maize, and squash combine to create especially valuable plant protein.

Modern maize

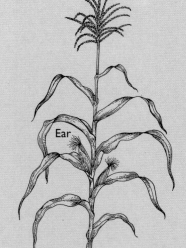

Ear

Brace roots

↪ Important stages in the evolution of teosinte to maize, resulting from selective harvesting and planting of transitional stages of teosinte.

Stage 1: In wild teosinte, long canes are borne near the base, terminating in an all-male tassel. The upper spikes are predominantly male, while the lower spikes tend towards a female state.

Stage 2: As branches become shorter, the degree of femaleness increases.

Stage 3: The branches continue to condense. (Stages 1 to 3 are still found in wild populations growing in Guerrero, Mexico.)

Stage 4: A husk begins to enclose the fruit cases.

Stage 5: The husk fully encloses the ear. The form of teosinte shown here was ancestral to Tehuacán soft-cob maize.

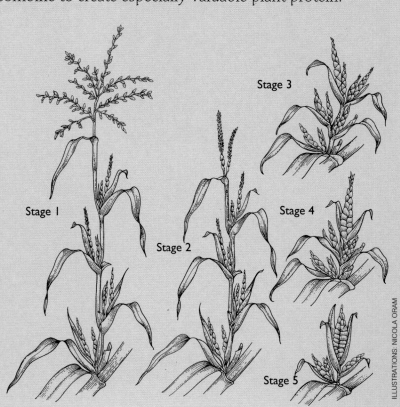

Stage 1
Stage 2
Stage 3
Stage 4
Stage 5

☞ Modern ears of maize (corn) exhibit a fantastic degree of diversity in size, shape, and color, as a result of centuries of selective breeding and crossbreeding. Because domesticated maize also hybridized with wild teosinte, a huge gene pool became available to Native American farmers. The maize ear in the lower right-hand corner is US Corn Belt dent, the world's most productive maize. To the left is an ear of Cuzco Gigante, a Peruvian race with the world's largest kernels. Above the Cuzco is a tiny Lady Finger popcorn, and above that is the whitish ear of a Brazilian pod corn, its kernels enclosed in chaff.

The precise origin of maize is controversial: the literature on this subject is vast and sometimes contentious. The prevailing view is that modern maize evolved through natural mutation and hybridization (or interbreeding) and frequent backcrossing with its nearest wild relative, teosinte (*Zea mexicana*). This explanation is supported by several lines of evidence. For example, frequent hybridization occurs between maize and teosinte under natural conditions; maize and teosinte have the same number of chromosomes; there are several key anatomical similarities between the two; and there is an overlap in the size range of pollen spores found in the two species. Teosinte derives from the Nahuatl word *teocintli*, which means "God's ear of maize". In many parts of Mexico, teosinte is still called *madre de maiz*, "mother of maize".

A little-supported alternative view, championed in particular by botanist Paul Mangelsdorf and his colleagues, is that cultivated maize is descended from a now-extinct form of wild pod popcorn, which bore individual kernels enclosed and protected by chaff. These botanists hold that wild teosinte resulted from the hybridization of maize with *Tripsacum*, a type of wild grass.

⚘ Gourds (*Curcurbita*) are among the oldest cultivated plants in the New World. Archaeological specimens dating from 8800 BC to 7250 BC have been recovered from Guilá Naquitz Cave, in Oaxaca, Mexico.

Instead, he sees domestication not only as an evolutionary stage, but as a process resulting from coevolutionary interactions between humans and plants.

The process of plant domestication began when people started to disperse and to protect key wild plant resources. For example, by favoring larger seeds over smaller ones, people have, over the centuries, brought about significant genetic changes. Assuming that people also planted these larger seeds, such economically desirable genetic traits as superior size would have been encouraged, leading to total domestication of the species. In other words, the relationship between plants and human beings both promoted and preserved a "conservative" ecological liaison.

Specialized domestication took place as new types of relationships between plants and people developed. Plants being used as food became increasingly common in areas where people lived, and so population movements were to indirectly benefit domesticated plants.

Over time, people came to rely on the plants they needed for food to such an extent that people and plants became interdependent. People also selectively destroyed various plant species in the vicinity of their communities, setting the stage for the development of complex agricultural systems. Full-blown agriculture began when practices such as weeding, irrigation, and plowing created new opportunities for plant evolution, thereby increasing the rate at which domesticated plants evolved.

⚘ Beans (*Phaseolus*), an important source of protein, on sale in a modern Ecuadorian market. Cultivated in the Peruvian Andes at least 8,000 years ago, American beans reached the Old World during Columbus's second voyage of 1493, and then rapidly spread across Europe, Africa, the Mediterranean basin, and Asia.

Not all archaeologists are comfortable with the Rindos model. Darwin's evolutionary theory holds that living things evolve by means of natural selection. Although Darwin's principles have been further developed by geneticists, plant ecologists, and, more recently, molecular plant biologists, Rindos rules out human intervention, considering it to be irrelevant. Many others, Flannery included, feel uncomfortable about excluding human intentions from early agricultural enterprise. Understandably, anthropologically oriented scholars seek cultural explanations for cultural behavior, and become concerned when human behavior is reduced to biology. Flannery puts it this way: "… anthropologists know that human hunter-gatherers are mammals, primates and predators, but that is not what anthropologists find most interesting about them."

Highland and Lowland Systems of South America

The agricultural system of the high-elevation Andes—from just below 3,000 meters (10,000 feet) to slightly above 3,500 meters (11,500 feet)—is ancient. Remains of domesticated potatoes—the only high-elevation crop also found to any extent

SOUTH AMERICA
Key archaeological sites yielding evidence of the early domestication of plants in South America. Botanical remains recovered from Ayacucho and Guitarrero Cave provide evidence that maize, beans, gourds, squash, and potatoes were being cultivated by the fifth millennium BC.
CARTOGRAPHY: RAY SIM

in lower zones—have been recovered from archaeological deposits as old as 8000 BC.

Paleobotanical evidence is more sporadic in the mid-elevations of the Andes— between about 1,500 meters and 3,000 meters (5,000 feet and 10,000 feet). It is clear, however, that agricultural activity extends back to between 8000 BC and 7500 BC at Guitarrero Cave, where people grew chili peppers and two species of beans. Even at this early date, people in the mid-elevations were in contact with farmers from other areas.

The Guitarrero Cave site also contains a number of legumes, including peanuts, common beans, and lima beans. Apparently, these plants did not evolve in the area, but were probably introduced from lower elevations, along with squash and gourds. Fruit trees, including guava, were also important at the mid-elevations. The use of coca can be traced archaeologically to an ancestral form that grows wild on the eastern Andean slopes. Coca was probably first cultivated on the Peruvian montaña, and then spread to the Amazon.

The lowland agricultural systems of South America pose many problems for archaeologists. Most of the crops were initially domesticated in the tropical forest, where sites are difficult to find and even more challenging to excavate. In addition, plant remains are usually poorly preserved. As a result, most of the archaeological evidence comes from elsewhere, such as the deserts of coastal Peru, where plants cultivated earlier in the lowlands were incorporated into floodplain (and later irrigation) agriculture.

The starchy dietary staple of most Amazonian and Caribbean tribes at the time of European contact was manioc or cassava (*Manihot esculenta*), the source of tapioca and without doubt one of the dozen most important food plants in the world today. Both bitter and sweet forms of manioc contain various levels of prussic acid, the source of cyanide. Removing the poison requires a substantial effort—peeling, grating, washing, squeezing, and toasting—but flour from bitter manioc can be stored for months, as can bread made from the flour.

Current research suggests that manioc originated as a domesticated plant in northeastern Brazil and was introduced into Middle America from South America. Because manioc is grown from cuttings, however, little direct evidence of its cultivation has survived in the archaeological record, and the dates for both its initial domestication and its later distribution across the continent remain in dispute.

Some argue that the first evidence of the domestication of manioc can be traced archaeologically through the appearance of small stone flakes set as blades in early grater boards, used to convert the manioc tubers into pulp, and pottery griddles (*budares*), used to roast the processed manioc. These griddles have been tentatively dated to about 2100 BC along the Middle Orinoco River, and they become common after 1000 BC. Other archaeologists believe manioc was domesticated much earlier—perhaps by 5000 BC—in the tropical forests of lowland Colombia, Venezuela, and Ecuador.

Despite the antiquity and importance of manioc, archaeological evidence indicates that sweet potatoes may have been cultivated even earlier, at least in Peru. Apparently, these two tuber crops were not introduced to the coast together, which probably means that they were initially domesticated in different places.

⊕ Agricultural terraces at the Inka citadel of Machu Picchu, in Peru, perched some 2,400 meters (8,000 feet) above sea level. These astonishing stone terraces were so skillfully constructed that it seems they will last forever. Laborers added layers of rock and clay as subsoil, and then hauled up rich alluvial soil from the river far below, over steep embankments 800 meters (half a mile) deep. At the time of the Spanish conquest, Native American farmers were producing 3,000 kinds of potatoes in the Andes.

◄⊙ A manioc (*Manihot esculenta*) plantation near Loreto, in Peru. Also known as cassava, manioc is the source of tapioca.

☙ Cotton bolls beginning to open in the San Joaquin Valley, California. Cotton was probably first domesticated in western South America about 3100 BC, with a secondary center of domestication in Amazonia.

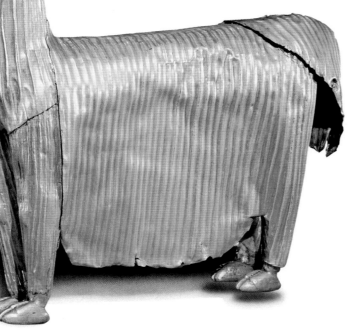

☙ High-altitude pastoralists in the central and southern parts of the Andes relied heavily on domesticated camelids. The alpaca was kept mostly for its wool, and llamas were used primarily as beasts of burden. Of the domesticated animals, only the guinea pig seems to have been a significant food source. This handsome silver long-haired llama dates from the Inka period.

Evidence is particularly sparse for the domestication of the numerous tree fruits important to lowland agriculture. Avocados can be traced to the Late Preceramic or Initial period of Peru, with guanabanas (soursops), pineapples, and papayas appearing somewhat later. Cotton was probably domesticated in western South America, either in the northern coastal region or in southwestern Ecuador. Amazonia was a secondary center of domestication. The earliest cotton has been found in the Ayacucho caves, dating from 3100 BC to 1750 BC; finds later than 2000 BC are commonplace.

Maize arrived in Mexico from the tropics some time before 4000 BC, as food-producing populations expanded into Amazonia, moved down into the eastern slopes of the Andes, and then spread westwards across the Andes.

The Domestication of Animals

Although a wealth of plant foods was domesticated in the Americas, domesticated animals were of little importance, except in the central Andes. In this region, the domestication of camelids—llamas and alpacas—is particularly interesting. The hides were made into clothing and rope; the wool was woven to make warm clothes; the meat was eaten fresh, or sundried as *charki*; the entrails and bones were stewed; and the tallow was used to make candles.

The earliest evidence of animal domestication comes from sites at elevations above 4,000 meters (13,000 feet), where the altitude makes the cultivation of food crops much less effective. This evidence raises an intriguing question about the relationship between the domestication of plants and animals in the High Andes. At Panaulauca Cave, Pearsall found evidence dating back to the second millennium BC linking the corralling of camelids with the increased use of *Chenopodium* and *Lepidium*, both plants that thrive on disturbed soil, such as the

pits, mounds, and middens surrounding American Indian camp sites. The proximity of domesticated plants and animals may have reinforced a pattern of incipient farming that eventually led to full-scale cultivation.

Elsewhere in the Americas, ancient dog bones have been found in the caves of the Junín region of the Peruvian Andes, dating back to about 6000 BC. In fact, it may be that domesticated dogs accompanied the first Americans across the Bering Strait. Archaeological and documentary evidence also suggests that, at times, dogs were eaten, providing an important source of protein.

The guinea pig, domesticated from its wild Andean ancestor, provided another food source, and in Middle America, people supplemented their largely vegetable diet with muscovy duck and turkey.

and permanent wetlands. This method, called drained field agriculture, was a sophisticated form of intensive wetland agriculture carried out on specially designed fields. The construction of these fields varied tremendously, from the sunken fields and canals found in arid areas along the Peruvian coast to the *chinampas* (incorrectly called "floating gardens") built in shallow lakes near Mexico City. The overriding objective was to produce patches of well-drained, aerated, well-structured, and fertile soil that would produce high crop yields over long periods of time. Indeed, some of the highland Mexican fields in use during the time of the Spanish conquest are still being cultivated today.

The earliest examples of these fields may be as old as 1000 BC, but most date to between AD 300 and AD 1000, a time of major population growth. It was during this time, when food was in high demand, that the largest number of terraced and drained fields were being cultivated.

The simplest, and apparently the most ancient, practice was simply to cut canals from a wetland area into an adjacent swamp, with the intervening field only slightly raised. This style of construction was eventually modified by piling up nutrient-rich muck from the canal beds to create raised fields of extremely rich soil, in which multiple crops could be grown year after year. Because the fields were elevated above the floodplain, crops were not flooded out during the rainy season.

Drained field technology became a critically important aspect of New World agriculture, providing sufficient food for the dense populations that lived in areas such as the Maya lowlands. On the basis of archaeological evidence from Pulltrouser Swamp, in Belize, Middle America, B.L. Turner estimates that the construction of raised fields took between

⚭ These freshly harvested cocoa pods are the fruit of the cacao, or chocolate, tree (*Theobroma cacao*). Chocolate is made from the beans.

⚭ An early stage of archaeological excavations at Coxcatlán Cave, in the Tehuacán Valley, Mexico. This extraordinary site contained 28 stratified zones, with 42 distinct cultural occupations that yielded abundant artifacts, animal remains, and botanical specimens spanning the period from 10,000 BC to the present.

⚭ Aerial view of Pre-Columbian raised fields near Lake Titicaca, Peru. Some 80,000 hectares (198,000 acres) of the lakeside marshes surrounding Lake Titicaca were reclaimed for agriculture. Between 400 BC and AD 1000, potatoes and other crops grown in these artificially drained fields supported from 20,000 to 40,000 people living at the nearby city of Tiahuanaco.

Mayan Engineering: Raising the Fields

Plants were domesticated in places such as the Tehuacán Valley over thousands of years, but elsewhere, under very different circumstances, agricultural change came about much more abruptly.

The Maya began cultivating maize some time before 2000 BC, presumably in dry-land fallow (plowed land that has remained unsown) and orchard gardens. Early fallow practices ranged from forest and bush rotations, with slash-and-burn techniques, to short, annual rotations which probably involved weeding, tilling, crop mixing, mulching, and so forth. Dry-land fallow required only 19 to 25 working days per hectare per year.

But like many other Native American people, the Classic Maya (AD 300 to AD 900) of the Yucatán Peninsula, in Mexico, eventually developed a method for cultivating seasonal

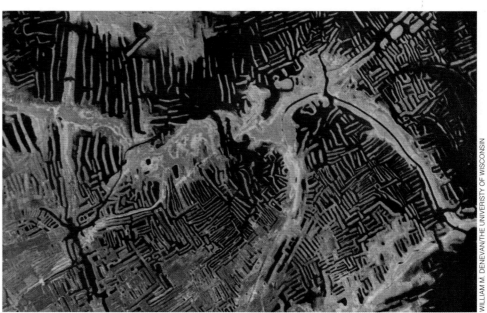

☞ One of the Hohokam irrigation canals excavated at the Snaketown site, in Arizona. Such major canals were interlinked with vast networks of lateral ditches and diversion areas. Although corn was the most common crop to be irrigated, archaeological excavations have shown that beans, squash, bottle gourds, cotton, possibly barley, and amaranths were also widely grown in these systems.

ARIZONA STATE MUSEUM

⚲ Aerial view of Anasazi fields and gardens, located in the central Rio Grande Valley of New Mexico. These were solar gardens of sophisticated design. The lines and grids are formed of aligned stones of various sizes. The dark stones retained the sun's heat into the night, warming nearby plants and extending their growing time. The squares were commonly filled with gravel, which helped to trap rainwater and runoff. The interspersed "waffle gardens" were usually enclosed by clay adobe ridges or walls, and then irrigated.

833 and 3,116 work days per hectare. Clearly, the output from the fields must have justified this considerable effort.

This ancient system of intensive, year-round cultivation sustained high-yield crops such as maize, beans, squash, cacao, and cotton. In modern Mexico, these fields support such diverse crops as manioc, cabbages, squash, rice, corn, watermelons, alfalfa, chili peppers, carrots, turnips, and salad vegetables. A newly constructed canal system near Villahermosa, in Mexico, is being used for intensive fish

farming, and it is likely that the ancient canals of Middle America that were built to drain the fields were similarly used to add vital protein in the form of fish to the pre-Columbian diet.

After AD 900, the Maya went through a period of social upheaval, during which they suffered major population losses throughout much of their territory. As the demand for agricultural products declined, the higher-cost systems were abandoned, and dry-land fallow agriculture once again prevailed.

Agriculture Comes to North America

As in highland Mexico, the evidence from North America clearly indicates that the domestication of plants was a long-term process. For thousands of years, nonagricultural Native Americans had a varied impact on wild plants without actually domesticating them. For instance, before the arrival of Europeans, Californian foragers modified the natural environment in a variety of ways. The people of the interior commonly torched underbrush, directly improving the habitat for the valued acorn crops they depended on. Further south, the Cahuilla, another Californian group, carefully pruned thorny mesquite trees to facilitate harvesting the edible pods. The Paiute, who lived in the Owens Valley, irrigated large stands of Indian ricegrass and other wild plants, even though most of the plants they ate grew completely wild. Although the oak tree, mesquite, and Indian ricegrass were never domesticated in California, practices such as these set the stage for the development of complex agricultural systems elsewhere in the Americas.

Plant macrofossils have been recovered from various rock shelter sites, leading many archaeologists to believe that maize first appeared in western North America about 1000 BC. Others, citing as their evidence maize pollen detected in Chaco Canyon sediments, suggest that cultigens arrived in the Southwest a thousand years earlier.

Despite the tremendous amount of research that has gone into establishing such "first dates", the question is less important than it may first appear. Whichever date ultimately proves to be accurate, organized farming did not develop overnight in the American Southwest. For at least a thousand years, the cultivation of maize and other plants was combined with the traditional hunting and gathering way of life.

This is perhaps best illustrated by the Western Apache of east central Arizona, where some of the earliest examples of plant cultivation in the American Southwest can be found. The Western Apache had a balanced economy. Men hunted large game animals, but meat was not eaten to the extent that game were driven from their territory altogether. They farmed, but not to the extent that they depended on crops alone to

TOM BAKER

GEORGE H.H. HUEY

TOM TILL

⇧ Anasazi farmers of the American Southwest built intriguing cliff dwellings and multiroom apartment structures, called pueblos. Here, at Spruce Tree House, in Mesa Verde National Park, Colorado, the ladders coming up through the floor mark the entrances to two subterranean kivas (ceremonial rooms).

↞ A modern pathway leads visitors through the circular ruins at Tyuonyi (Bandelier National Monument, New Mexico), one of the most impressive Anasazi pueblos in the Rio Grande drainage area. Tree-ring dating shows that the 400 rooms were built between AD 1383 and AD 1466. When the population was at its peak, Tyuonyi was three stories high.

↣ This original Anasazi ladder still stands in place, leading into a Utah kiva.

TOM TILL

☝ An Anasazi petroglyph from southeastern Utah, dated to between AD 700 and AD 800, depicting a prehistoric bear hunt.

☝ Manos (hand stones) and metates (grinding slabs) were used to process maize in these Anasazi grinding bins at Betatakin (Navajo National Monument, Arizona).

☞ A chilly winter morning at Spruce Tree House, a well-preserved Anasazi cliff dwelling in Mesa Verde National Park, Colorado.

sustain them throughout the year. They gathered wild plant foods and small game, but not enough to obviate the need for big-game hunts.

The Western Apache moved regularly. Their winter camps were in the south, and in spring they moved higher up into the mountains to the north to plant, hunt, and collect food from the wild. From late August until October, they also harvested piñon nuts, acorns, and juniper berries, before moving back to their winter homes.

For the Western Apache, farming provided a buffer against a possible shortage of naturally available foodstuffs. Because maize could be stored, it was readily available in such times of shortage. The earliest varieties of corn were not very productive and required relatively little effort to cultivate, which meant that traditional hunting and gathering activities were not disrupted. Perhaps 25 percent of the Western Apache diet came from domesticated plants, hunting supplying another 35 to 40 percent.

During the late nineteenth century, the basic social unit among these Western Apache farmers was the relatively autonomous household. Individual households could move from one group to another at will, although members of each group tended to be from the same clan. In some years, such groups lived almost entirely by hunting and gathering; in others, they relied almost exclusively on farm products. The same applied to the Hopi of eastern Arizona. When crops failed, as they did occasionally, Pueblo communities broke up into smaller family foraging groups, which were capable of living off foodstuffs available in the wild.

Farming in the Southwest Comes of Age

By 1000 BC, casual agriculture was well established in the Mogollon Highlands of the American Southwest. At sites such as Bat Cave, New Mexico, we can see that people had come to rely on agriculture for a significant part of their food supply. By about AD 200 to AD 700, the ecology of the Southwest had changed forever, for both farmers and nonfarmers.

In arid regions, people would have needed a strong incentive to persist in cultivating maize. The adoption of agriculture was by no means an inevitable process, and the archaeological record shows that populations expanded and contracted in cycles over a period of 2,000 years. When a population outgrew its territory, people migrated to other areas. Sometimes, the migrants succeeded in establishing stable farming societies that lasted for centuries. At other times, they failed, and the land was temporarily abandoned. But once agriculture took a firm hold in the Southwest, hunting and gathering became less important.

Although maize, settled village life, and ceramics were once thought to have arrived as a "package" from Mexico, it is now clear that

⚡ Zuni people have farmed their homeland, just west of the continental divide in western New Mexico, for centuries. Here, Zuni farmers tend their "waffle gardens": small agricultural plots for growing fruit and vegetables such as melons, herbs, chili peppers, and onions. Enclosed by ridges of clay earth, the rectangular compartments retain water diverted from the nearby river.
THE BETTMAN ARCHIVE

⚡ Although it is difficult to establish continuities between archaeological complexes and modern Pueblo people, some archaeologists think that the ancient Anasazi of Chaco Canyon can be linked to the modern Zuni people. This large Zuni jar from the late nineteenth century is decorated with numerous stylized plant, bird, and deer motifs, together with repeated geometric units, painted on a white slipped background. The "heartline" extending from the deer's mouth to its heart is a distinctively Zuni motif.
AMERICAN MUSEUM OF NATURAL HISTORY

these characteristic features of the local culture arrived separately. Taken together, they greatly enhanced an already rich Native American heritage in the Southwest. Archaeologists conventionally divide this late pre-European period into three major cultures: the Mogollon, the Hohokam, and the Anasazi, each occupying a distinctive ecological niche within the mosaic of Southwestern environments.

The highland Mogollon farmed the forests and upland meadows along the border between Arizona and New Mexico. They are best known as the makers of the legendary Mimbres pottery, painted with complex geometric designs and intricate human forms, birds, bats, bighorn sheep, rabbits, and insects. The earliest Mimbres pottery, in the classic black-on-white tradition, dates from about AD 750 to AD 1000. Then, between about AD 1050 and AD 1200, the tradition shifted to more colorful designs, featuring, in particular, different shades of black and red.

The early Mogollon people lived in villages of randomly spaced pit houses (in which the floor is dug down to a depth of half a meter, or about 18 inches, to facilitate sealing the walls against wind and rain). After a time, they shifted to apartment-like structures built above ground, with interconnected storage and living rooms, similar to Anasazi pueblos. The Mogollon culture began to decline in AD 1100, and had been completely eclipsed by AD 1250.

The scorching Sonoran Desert to the west was home to the Hohokam. Archaeologists originally thought that the Hohokam migrated from Mexico about 300 BC, but it is now believed that they were native to the area. The Hohokam were accomplished desert-dwelling farmers who constructed hundreds of kilometers of irrigation canals throughout central Arizona. Today, more than 2,000 years later, a canal system that has been virtually superimposed on the early Hohokam plan diverts water from the Salt River for the city of Phoenix, Arizona.

By about AD 1450, the classic Hohokam culture had declined, perhaps as a result of drought or increased soil salinity. Many believe that the modern O'Odham (Pima and Papago) people are descended from Hohokam pioneers.

The Anasazi homeland lay to the north, in the high deserts of the Colorado Plateau. Although the earlier Anasazi lived in pit houses, between AD 700 and AD 1000 their descendants began constructing the distinctive multiroom apartment (pueblo) complexes that were to give their descendants, the Pueblo Indians, their name. About AD 900, the Anasazi people of northwestern New Mexico experienced a sustained burst of cultural energy, giving rise to what is known as the Chaco Phenomenon. (See the feature *The Chaco Phenomenon*.)

Farmers of the North American Plains and Woodlands

Traditional textbooks on the history of Western civilization often suggest that primary agricultural inventions originated independently in three places—in the so-called Fertile Crescent of Southwest Asia, in Southeast Asia, and in highland Mexico. Now, archaeologists recognize that plants were domesticated many times, in many places—including an important and newly discovered center in northeastern America. Although early explorers recorded extensive maize cultivation throughout eastern North America, new archaeological evidence makes it clear that the full-blown cultivation of maize began only five centuries before Europeans arrived.

The transition from foraging to farming along the rivers of the eastern woodlands involved three key steps: first, native North American seed plants were domesticated about 2000 BC; second, horticultural economies based on these local crops began to emerge between 250 BC and AD 100 (maize arriving on the scene about AD 100); and third, maize finally became a major crop between AD 800 and AD 1100.

From 6000 BC to 700 BC, the foraging people of eastern North America followed the same basic seasonal pattern, moving from one part of their home range to another in pursuit of grasses, fruits, nuts, fish, and game, as they became available. They traveled in small bands, which gave them the flexibility needed to respond quickly to fluctuations in the local food supply.

After about 4000 BC, the changing climate enriched many river valley environments. Shoals and lakes developed, and the abundance of wild seed plants, shellfish, fish, and animals such as deer and raccoons encouraged people to form permanent settlements. Men hunted; women collected wild plants. Shellfish, so abundant in shallow waters, were available to all.

Over countless generations, people had become familiar with the life cycles and habits of the nut trees and seed plants so important to them, and in the rich soils of their settlements the women began the great experiment that would ultimately produce domesticated plants. They probably tried out many types of plants, but, in the end, it was weeds from the floodplains that produced results. Sunflower and its distant cousins marshelder, goosefoot, and a wild gourd (the ancestor of summer squash) became the success stories. These aggressive, weedy plants, which colonized the areas swept clean by spring floodwaters, all produced highly nutritious seeds and were important sources of food. They readily invaded the rich soils surrounding human settlements and were the subject of early experiments aimed at increasing yield and dependability. There is evidence that these seed crops were being deliberately planted in 2000 BC, at which time they were beginning to yield a dependable, managed food supply that could be stored for use in late winter and even into early spring.

People and plants became interdependent to the point that human groups began to reoccupy certain areas because they offered favorable farming conditions. Despite this, however, current archaeological evidence shows that domesticated crops were not a substantial source of food before 500 BC, and that agriculture did not play a major role until about AD 100, a full thousand years after the first plants were domesticated.

The First Farmers of Eastern North America

So it was that Native Americans began domesticating plants in eastern North America. Local crop plants became important economically during the so-called Hopewell period, which extended from 100 BC to AD 400. This period is named after a huge Ohio mound that was excavated in the nineteenth century. These people—some of the earliest of North America's Mound Builders—built large, impressive geometrical earthworks and conical burial mounds for what must have been elaborate burial ceremonies. Hopewell became the "umbrella" name for a Pan-Indian religion, to describe a situation in which linguistically and culturally distinct people shared the same basic beliefs and symbols. For centuries, Hopewell was a dominant force across eastern North America.

Because both burial mounds and domesticated plants are found earlier in Mexico than in southeastern North America, archaeologists once thought that the practice of mound building and

agriculture must have arrived together from Middle America. But, as in the American Southwest, there is no direct evidence that any group ever moved north from Mexico. Maize and beans arrived in the east from the American Southwest at different times, so it seems unlikely that they were introduced directly from Mexico.

For years, most archaeologists considered the Hopewell economy to be strictly based on maize. Now, however, with more precise dating methods available, we know that the earliest maize in eastern North America dates from only about AD 100. These new insights are important, because they make it clear that neither the development of Hopewellian society nor the rapid shift towards agriculture that took place in eastern North America can be attributed to the importation of corn from Mexico. For centuries, maize was only a minor, almost negligible, addition to already well-established food resources. The extraordinary Hopewellian accomplishments in the areas of agriculture, religion, and culture must have been solely the result of local ingenuity and inventiveness—the culmination of thousands of years of human experience.

How did such a remarkable agricultural system evolve? The use of any particular plant crop was extremely localized, depending on the ecology of the local area. In some places, foragers relied little

EASTERN NORTH AMERICA
Key archaeological sites of eastern North America. The massive earthworks at Poverty Point date to about 200 BC. The earliest burial mounds were raised by the Adena culture, after about 500 BC. The remaining sites date from the Mississippian tradition (AD 700 to AD 1500).
CARTOGRAPHY: RAY SIM

☝ The sunflower (*Helianthus annuus*) was domesticated in eastern North America by 2000 BC.

households located along a stream or river valley. In some parts of the fertile floodplains, such as those surrounding the lower Illinois River, small settlements formed loosely knit villages.

But the cultivation of food plants that could be stored simply provided a buffer against food shortages. Foraging and the hunting and gathering way of life remained important and were by no means replaced by agriculture.

At the time that Hopewellian societies began to extend the boundaries of their river valley fields, their horizons expanded dramatically in other ways. Across the eastern woodlands, small farming settlements were clustered around centrally located ceremonial sites, where various seasonal rites took place. These sites varied considerably in form. Today, the only archaeologically visible clues to the location of such places are the low earthen domes built over the graves of revered people.

⚓ The flawlessly modeled Serpent Mound, an earthen religious effigy extending for 210 meters (690 feet) in Adams County, Ohio. The serpent is wriggling northwards, mouth agape, trying to swallow a massive egg.

⚘ A carved stone animal effigy from the Hopewell period, found in Ohio.
HILLEL BURGER/ROBERT S. PEABODY MUSEUM OF ARCHAEOLOGY

⚘ A Hopewell snake effigy made of mica, from Hamilton County, in Ohio.
HILLEL BURGER/ROBERT S. PEABODY MUSEUM OF ARCHAEOLOGY

on cultivated plants, but in general the broad mid-latitude riverine zone, stretching from the edge of the Appalachian Mountains west to the prairie margin, became a homeland to these early food producers, who cultivated several high-yield, highly nutritious local crops. These people grew squash, marshelder, sunflower, and goosefoot, as well as erect knotweed, maygrass, and a little barley. Modern experiments have demonstrated the economic potential of these indigenous eastern North American crops.

From about the beginning of the first century AD to AD 200, Hopewellian settlements remained small, generally comprising one to three

But these sites were not just places of death. They were also the scenes of lavish feasts and other activities that brought together families scattered across the countryside. Along the rivers of northern Mississippi and northern Alabama, people built and maintained flat-topped earthen mounds that elevated the ceremonial above the everyday world. These mounds foreshadowed the later and much larger Mississippian pyramids. Elsewhere, earthen embankments, often very large and testifying to remarkable engineering skill, surrounded such ceremonial platforms, setting them apart. In south central Ohio, elaborate earthen banks extended for hundreds of meters, forming octagons, circles, and squares, at once defining and protecting these sacred precincts.

The Ascendancy of Maize

The centuries between AD 800 and AD 1100 saw a dramatic shift in American agriculture. The Mississippi people began to look beyond the traditional cultivation of native plant crops and to focus on a single, nonindigenous species— maize. In time, corn would come to dominate both their fields and their lives at such places as Etowah, Moundville, Angel, Hiwassee Island, Spiro, and Cahokia.

Across eastern North America, this concentration on growing corn led to the emergence of more complex sociopolitical structures. Maize would support the evolving Oneota peoples of the Great Lakes, the Iroquoian confederacy of the Northeast, and the Fort Ancient settlements along the middle Ohio River Valley, as well as the diverse range of Mississippian chiefdoms that emerged along the river valleys of the Southeast and Midwest. It would be maize that later sustained the Creek and Choctaw to the south, the Mandan and the Pawnee of the Plains.

Maize had dominated agriculture in the Southwest from the time it was introduced via Mexico, but in the east, more than six centuries elapsed between the time that maize was introduced as a minor cultigen and its becoming a major crop. This lag can be partly explained by genetic modifications to the plant itself. About AD 1000, a new variety of corn, known as eight-row maize, was developed in eastern North America. Frost-resistant and specifically adapted to the short growing seasons, this new breed of corn quickly spread to the northern latitudes, and by the time of European contact, it dominated Native American agriculture across the Northeast, the Ohio Valley, and the Great Lakes.

Imported or Homegrown?

One critical question remains: was agriculture in the New World invented completely independently, or was the idea in some way imported from the Old World?

Most archaeologists would agree that New World farmers developed in relative isolation from Old World influences. With two exceptions, all New World cultigens were domesticated from native American species, which strongly suggests that American agriculture developed independently. These two exceptions—gourds and cotton—are important and instructive. Possibly Old World imports, they became extremely important in the Americas.

The bottle gourd is one of the most ancient cultivated plants in the New World, perhaps because of its usefulness as a container for transporting food and water during preceramic times. The problem lies in identifying the wild ancestor of bottle gourds. Many botanists argue that gourds are native only to Africa. Specimens that were either gathered from the wild or cultivated have been found in very early Mexican and Peruvian sites, so it may be that gourds arrived in South America with African explorers in very early times. Alternatively, because gourds can float in sea water for nearly a year, they may have drifted across the Atlantic from Africa.

The archaeological evidence reveals that cotton was domesticated in Mexico some time before 3000 BC, and cotton textiles were being produced along the Peruvian coast by 2500 BC. Mexican and Peruvian cottons are different species, and were probably domesticated independently from local varieties. But there is a genetic complication: both Mexican and Peruvian cottons can be explained only as hybrids of local varieties and African cotton. To some investigators, cotton provides clear-cut evidence of deliberate trans-Atlantic contact. Others, seeking more "independent" explanations for Old World and New World agriculture, point out that African wild cotton could have drifted across the Atlantic and hybridized with New World species without human intervention, perhaps even before humans arrived in South America.

Setting aside bottle gourds and cotton as possible exceptions, current evidence clearly indicates that American Indian agriculture was an indigenous New World achievement, in which outside influences played no significant part.

An autumn assortment of squash and gourds from New England. Recent research has shown that some of today's curcurbits were domesticated in Mexico. Others, including virtually all the summer and acorn squashes, were first domesticated in eastern North America, about 2000 BC.

Looking across the prehistoric landscape at Mound City Group National Monument, near Chillicothe, Ohio. This is the most famous Hopewell site, where ancients buried their dead beneath these earthen mounds, often accompanied by fine pottery, elegantly carved stone pipes, and opulent jewelry. The 5 hectare (13 acre) compound is surrounded by a rectangular earthen embankment.

THE CHACO PHENOMENON

DAVID HURST THOMAS

NEARLY A THOUSAND YEARS AGO, the Anasazi people living in the Chaco Canyon of northwestern New Mexico developed one of the most progressive and prosperous social systems in prehistoric North America. By means of a complex ritual and economic network, dozens of formerly autonomous communities united to pool their strengths in this precarious environment.

Archaeologists now estimate that perhaps 6,000 Anasazi people lived in Chaco in AD 1100. For six generations, this now-remote region was the heart of the Anasazi world. By AD 1130, nine towns, each containing hundreds of rooms, dominated a 15 kilometer (9 mile) stretch of Chaco Canyon. The largest of these, Pueblo Bonito (Beautiful House), was once five stories high and could house a thousand people. America would

⌖ Black-on-white ladles from Pueblo Bonito.

P. HOLLEMBEAK/J. BECKETT/ AMERICAN MUSEUM OF NATURAL HISTORY

THE SOUTHWEST
Important archaeological sites and culture areas in the southwestern United States. The three major cultural traditions, Anasazi, Hohokam, and Mogollon, can each be subdivided into numerous time periods, and several local variants have also been identified.
CARTOGRAPHY: RAY SIM

☞ From the twelfth century, Chaco architects had tried to shore up the cliff behind Pueblo Bonito. But on 21 January 1941, a massive limestone slab known as Threatening Rock tumbled downwards, the rubble crushing 65 excavated rooms in the northeastern section of the site.

☞ This black-on-white pitcher, about 18 centimeters (7 inches) high, was found at Pueblo Bonito. Pitchers such as this were produced between AD 1075 and AD 1200.
P. HOLLEMBEAK/J. BECKETT/AMERICAN MUSEUM OF NATURAL HISTORY

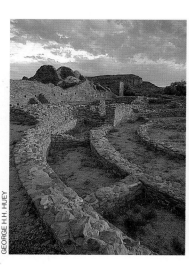

GEORGE H.H. HUEY

⌖ Construction of this unusual triple-walled, circular structure behind Pueblo del Arroyo has been tree-ring-dated to AD 1109. Some archaeologists think that it may have been built by migrants from the north, who brought Mesa Verde-like architecture to Chaco Canyon.

TOM TILL

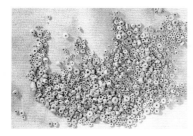

⚸ Although Chacoan society lacked money, turquoise beads probably served as status symbols and items of portable wealth. These are some of the 2,300 beads and small pendants recovered from a single room at Pueblo Bonito.
P. HOLLEMBEAK/J. BECKETT/AMERICAN MUSEUM OF NATURAL HISTORY

☞ One of the 12 kivas (ceremonial rooms) at Chetro Ketl, just down the road from Pueblo Bonito. The great curving wall had special niches, each filled with strings of stone and shell beads and then sealed with masonry. In the center of the floor is a raised square firebox flanked by a pair of rectangular masonry vaults (perhaps foot drums). Constructed between the early eleventh and early twelfth centuries AD, Chetro Ketl, at its peak, had several stories, with 200 to 225 ground-floor rooms and a total of 550 rooms.

STEVE MULLIGAN

AMERICAN MUSEUM OF NATURAL HISTORY

not witness a larger apartment building until the Industrial Revolution of the nineteenth century.

The Chaco people built arrow-straight roads running hundreds of kilometers into the surrounding desert, the longest and best-defined of which—probably built between AD 1075 and AD 1140—are more than 80 kilometers (50 miles) long. In places, the Chacoans constructed causeways, and elsewhere they cut stairways into sheer cliffs. The

◄◙ The ages of these black-on-white pitchers, all found in a single room at Pueblo Bonito, vary considerably.

generally straight bearings of these constructions suggest that the works were carefully planned and engineered.

Because the Chaco Anasazi did not use wheeled carts or draft animals, one wonders why the roads were so wide and straight, and what they were used for. Although some of the shorter roads connect Chaco Canyon with quarries and water sources, the function of the longer roads—whether for trade, processions, hauling building materials, defense, carrying food, or simply ease of travel for what must have been a great deal of traffic—remains unknown.

More than 600 kilometers (400 miles) of well-built roads connected Chaco to outlying settlements, probably reflecting extensive regional alliances. Several related mesa-top signal stations have been found, which provided line-of-sight communication, presumably by smoke, fire, or reflected light.

Archaeologists believe that the Anasazi systematically packed up their possessions and left Chaco Canyon about AD 1150. Various reasons for this have been put forward, but it probably resulted from a complex interaction between such factors as drought, soil erosion, crop failure, human overpopulation, disease, and low-level warfare.

Modern Pueblo people believe that the Anasazi left Chaco because the serpent deity—the god in charge of rain and fertility—mysteriously abandoned them. Helpless without their god, the people followed the snake's trail until they reached a river, where they once again built houses.

Four centuries later, the incursions of the Spanish explorers were witnessed by 50,000 Pueblo people living in more than a hundred towns along the margins of the San Juan Basin and the Rio Grande drainage area. These Pueblo people were the descendants of the Chaco Anasazi.

⬆ The frog was a symbol of water in Anasazi culture. This jet effigy is 8.5 centimeters (about 3 inches) long.
AMERICAN MUSEUM OF NATURAL HISTORY

GEORGE H.H. HUEY

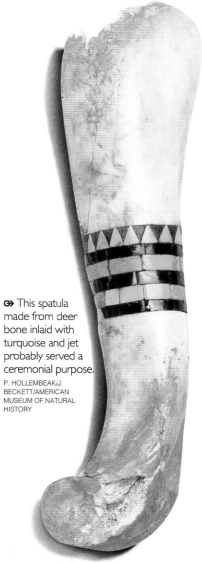

⊕ This spatula made from deer bone inlaid with turquoise and jet probably served a ceremonial purpose.
P. HOLLEMBEAK/J. BECKETT/AMERICAN MUSEUM OF NATURAL HISTORY

⬅ Doorways in Pueblo Bonito, with the original roof beams still in place. More than 200,000 such support timbers were used in buildings throughout Chaco Canyon, each beam having been carried by hand from the mountains, a distance of at least 65 kilometers (40 miles).

WHY ONLY SOME BECAME FARMERS

1 1 , 0 0 0   B C   –   A D   1 5 0 0

A Global Overview

Noel D. Broadbent, Göran Burenhult, and Moreau Maxwell

THE TRANSITION FROM hunter-gatherer to farmer was one of the most sweeping events in the history of humankind. Most experts today agree that the impetus for this transition came from need rather than desire. Such a fundamental shift in the way of life led to major changes in social structures, and to the development of new religious systems—farmers' gods were different from those of hunter-gatherers. Increased sedentism created entirely new settlement patterns, and at the same time, population growth increased. Mobile hunter-gatherers have to restrict their group size, both for practical reasons—you cannot carry more than one child at a time during long journeys— and in order to be able to survive when times are harsh. In a farming economy, on the other hand, as long as virgin land is available, more hands mean that more crops can be grown and more cattle raised, thus starting an endless circle of population growth leading to a demand for more food.

◄◙ The people along the mighty Sepik River, in Papua New Guinea, are one of the few New Guinean populations that do not depend on farming for their livelihood. Instead, these settled riverine people subsist by gathering plants, fishing, and hunting, sago being their main source of food.

◙ A Sub-Neolithic flint arrowhead from Finland.
NATIONAL BOARD OF ANTIQUITIES, FINLAND

⚲ Traditional hunter-gatherer societies still exist on the remote Andaman Islands, in the Bay of Bengal. Here, a man of the Onge tribe, on Little Andaman Island, is fishing with bow and arrow. The ocher paste on his face serves as both a decoration and an insect repellant. At the turn of the century, there were 672 Onge; now, they number only about 100.

The developing farming tradition was accompanied by a number of new phenomena. With increased population pressure came the need to control personal territory, and this created the risk of conflict. For the first time, evidence of aggression appears in the form of fortified settlements and ceremonial combat weapons—symbols of power and dominance. With this new emphasis on strength and aggression, women's status declined. In many places, inequality between the sexes had its roots in the social organization of the established farming societies.

With large numbers of people living in the same area for long periods, problems of hygiene arose that were unknown to mobile hunter-gatherers. As time went on, the farming way of life also led to a far less balanced and less nutritious diet than that enjoyed by hunter-gatherers. The quality of stored food deteriorated as a result of infestation by rats and other vermin, creating a breeding ground for new, deadly strains of bacteria. Epidemic disease appeared for the first time.

At the Crossroads

Farming communities were much more vulnerable to climatic fluctuations than were hunter-gatherers. The possibility of storing grain and keeping domesticated animals led to a false sense of security. There was, of course, a reserve if crops failed; but this meant drawing on next year's seed for sowing, thus depleting stocks and paving the way for future catastrophe. Being dependent on a limited range of foodstuffs, farming communities found it difficult to withstand times of adversity. Farming and herding were also vastly more labor-intensive than hunting and gathering. Why, then, did people become farmers at all? And why did a number of peoples around the globe never adopt any form of farming? Only by understanding why people in certain parts of the world became farmers, can we understand why others didn't.

At the end of the nineteenth century, it was thought that farming emerged as a way of life during the period known as the Neolithic for the simple reason that it was in every respect a superior way of life to hunting and gathering. Some individual, so it was believed, hit upon the brilliant idea of planting a seed in the ground in order to avoid having to wander around to find food. In the 1930s, the Australian archaeologist V. Gordon Childe put forward what appeared to be a more credible explanation in his so-called Oasis Theory, which postulated an event of such profound significance that he called it the Neolithic Revolution. He suggested that a period of extreme drought in Southwest Asia at the end of the last glacial period forced people to gather at the few oases and river valleys that remained, where their close association with animals and plants led to the process of domestication. Thus agriculture was born.

But Childe's theory was not supported by later studies of Neolithic settlements, which were established in a range of different climatic and environmental settings. Robert Braidwood's work during the 1940s paved the way for a less rigid approach. He suggested that farming emerged largely in response to the ever-increasing cultural differentiation and specialization within different populations—in short, it was a matter of people adapting to local conditions. The oldest farming communities known are found in the so-called Fertile Crescent of Southwest Asia (the region stretching from the Levant, through the present-day states of Syria and Iraq, to the Zagros Mountains). In the early stages of these settlements, Braidwood found clear signs that people had specialized in hunting aurochs and wild sheep, and in gathering the wild grasses that were the prototypes of the later cultivated cereals, as far back as glacial times.

Barbara Bender, on the other hand, has argued that it was predominantly social factors that lay behind the changes characteristic of the Neolithic period, such as the development of more complex, hierarchical societies with a wide-ranging network for the exchange of goods between different regions. Parallel to the rise of food production, status symbols and other artifacts came to play a crucial role in these societies.

In various places throughout the world, a series of farming communities developed independently of each other, according to local conditions. In Southwest Asia, for example, wild prototypes of barley and wheat provided

ANTHONY BANNISTER/NHPA

the basis for an emerging agricultural economy. Corresponding developments in North Africa were based on millet; in South and East Asia, on rice, and in central America, on corn. Similarly, different types of animals were domesticated in different parts of the world.

The Crisis That Never Was

The fact that the transition from hunting and gathering to farming took place at roughly the same time in many parts of the world indicates that similar factors lay behind the process. But one thing is certain: the late glacial and Mesolithic hunter-gatherers had a much more complex social system (one that had its roots in the Upper Paleolithic period), and engaged in much more specialized subsistence activities, than was previously assumed. It was in these Mesolithic hunting-gathering communities, with their relatively limited tribal territories, that the conditions for developing a system of food production were most favorable. Their knowledge of local food resources was very sophisticated. For example, there is evidence that Mesolithic hunter-gatherers in western Europe cleared forests

to facilitate the hunting of deer as early as about 6000 BC. At the same time, the dog was domesticated, and even different species of deer may have been kept as domestic animals.

It is a common misconception that hunter-gatherers must live in straitened circumstances, on the brink of starvation and malnutrition. One should keep in mind that present-day hunter-gatherers are restricted to regions such as semideserts and arctic areas—the least hospitable regions on Earth. Modern studies of such societies have shown that the opposite is the case, and that they normally have a very stable supply of food, often with a large surplus. The !Kung Bushmen of the Kalahari Desert, in Botswana, whose technology is similar to that of the Mesolithic hunter-gatherers of Europe, provide a good example. In this dry desert area, they not only successfully manage their food supply, but can also afford to be very selective when gathering edible plants. It has been estimated that the !Kung collect and eat only about one-quarter of the plant species available, and that they spend only two or three hours a day searching for food—less than 20 hours a week.

⬧ A Bushman aiming his poisoned bone arrow at an animal in the dry grass stands of the Kalahari Desert, in southern Africa. The Bushmen, sometimes called the San, live in small, scattered, mobile bands. Their most common prey are antelopes, including gemsbok, springbok, wildebeest, and eland.

JOHN DOWNER/PLANET EARTH PICTURES

⬧ In front of a dome-shaped grass hut, a Kalahari Bushman collects plants. Bushman bands number between 30 and 60 people.

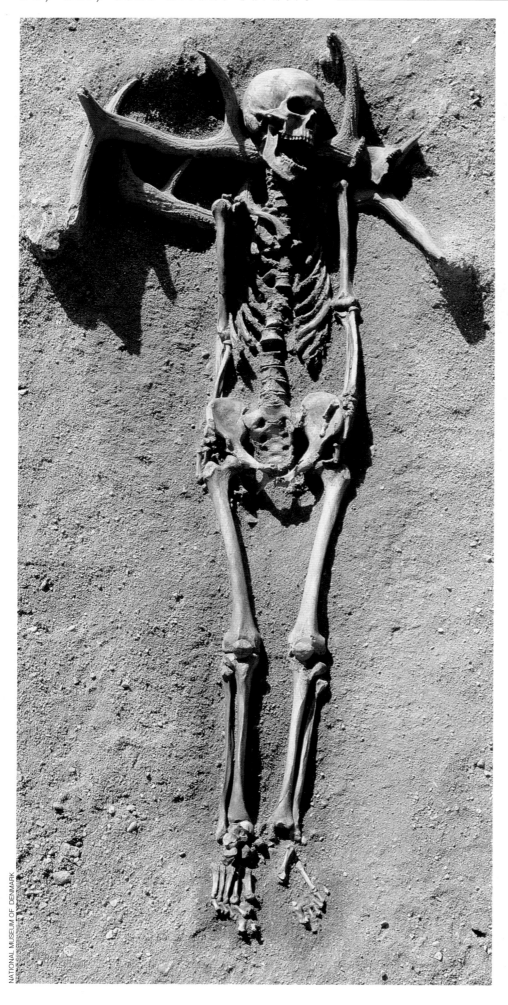

It is clear that the changed climatic and environmental conditions at the end of the last glacial period were one of the main reasons for the rapid development of new economic systems all over the world. In most cases, this process was probably not voluntary. A combination of many different factors gradually forced people to actively produce food to meet the demands of growing populations. In particular, the Mesolithic hunter-gatherers who lived along the coasts of northwestern Europe can give us an insight into the reasons why people left their hunting, fishing, and gathering way of life, and became farmers.

From Mesolithic to Neolithic

About 6000 BC, the so-called Atlantic period began in western Europe. This was the warmest period after the last glacial, with average temperatures reaching several degrees above those of today. Dense deciduous forest covered the land. There was an abundance of big game, including boar, deer, and bears, as well as smaller animals. Lakes and rivers teemed with fish, and in coastal regions, fish, seals, mussels, and shellfish were plentiful. These were some of the richest resource areas on Earth. Having such a rich and varied supply of food, these people were less vulnerable to fluctuations in the availability of any one foodstuff.

The territory within which these Mesolithic societies moved shrank in size once they no longer needed to cover great distances in pursuit of big game. It has been estimated that the population density during this period was about 1 to 20 individuals per square kilometer (less than half a square mile). Contrary to earlier beliefs, then, the shift to farming did not represent an improvement in people's living conditions. A few hours of gathering per day was replaced by perhaps 10 hours of toiling in hard soil. In addition, gathering food for domesticated animals demanded a great deal of work. As supplies of food became uncertain, people began, for the first time, to suffer from starvation and disease. Yet within 2,000 years, these Mesolithic peoples had become farmers.

◄● One of the spectacular Mesolithic burials at Vedbæk, near Copenhagen, in Denmark, dating back some 7,000 years. An old woman, aged about 50, had been placed on her back, with her head and shoulders resting on two red-deer antlers—possibly reflecting an association between age and high status in the Mesolithic communities of northern Europe.

DAVID BEATTY/COMSTOCK

Paradoxically, it was mainly in resource-rich areas of the world that farming communities developed. Arctic regions were obviously unsuitable for farming and herding, as were desert areas and tropical rainforests. The only way to survive in these areas is to adapt to the existing environment. As a rule, this requires people to live in groups small enough to be sustainable, and to undertake long seasonal migrations.

The abundant food supply enjoyed by European Mesolithic communities usually led them to adopt a completely settled way of life, a combination that always leads to population growth. By about 5000 BC, the first farming communities had been established all over central Europe, with the exception of coastal western Europe. In spite of close contacts between farmers inland and hunter-gatherers on the coast—as evidenced, for example, by the latter's adoption of pottery and polished stone axes—it was almost another thousand years before these coastal

PETER JOHNSON/NHPA

⚕ Numbering between 150,000 and 200,000, Pygmies live in small bands scattered across the rainforests of equatorial Africa. They subsist by hunting and gathering, but have developed a close system of cooperation with their farming neighbors.

↩ Members of a Bushman band on the move through the Kalahari Desert, carrying their few belongings with them.

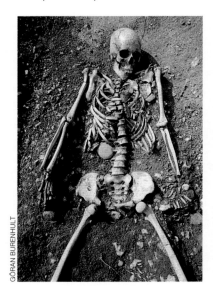

⚱ Dating from about 2800 BC, this Pitted-ware grave at the settlement of Ajvide, on the island of Gotland, in Sweden, contained the remains of a 20-year-old woman. She was dressed in a skirt that had been decorated with seal teeth. Five left sides of hedgehog mandibles were found on her chest, together with the leg bones of cormorants.

peoples started to cultivate their land and herd animals. Until then, they clearly had not needed to exert themselves in time-consuming farming activities. By about 4300 BC, however, the Neolithic era was firmly entrenched, bringing to an end the agreeable life of the Mesolithic.

The same scenario was repeated in many parts of the world. Lending support to the ecological explanation is the fact that some farming communities, for ecological reasons, actually reverted to a hunter-gatherer economy. For instance, the first farming community in eastern Sweden, the so-called Vrå culture, was established shortly after 4000 BC. About 3000 BC, a cooler and moister climate (known as the subboreal period) led to a marked increase in the supply of marine foods, especially seals, in the Baltic Sea. The early farming economy that had been established in this region disappeared, and its practitioners instead founded a rich hunting-gathering community, known as the Pitted-ware culture, after their distinctive pottery. This was based mainly on fishing and seal hunting, but some elements of the earlier farming economy were retained, notably domestic pigs.

This very clear-cut Scandinavian example shows how rapidly people adapted to changing ecological conditions in order to secure their food

⚱ Seals, mainly harbor and gray seals, were the mainstay of the Pitted-ware economy. Enormous amounts of seal bones have been unearthed in the settlements, along with quantities of pig, fish, and wildfowl bones.

⚱ As the name implies, Pitted-ware pottery is characterized by deep pits in the surface. Some researchers have suggested that these pits had some practical purpose, while others think that they were simply decorations.

☞ The limestone cave of Stora Förvar ("Great Repository") on the island of Stora Karlsö, off the coast of Gotland, in the Baltic Sea. During Pitted-ware times, some 5,000 years ago, the cave was used as a seasonal settlement, where seals, fish, and birds' eggs were the main sources of food.

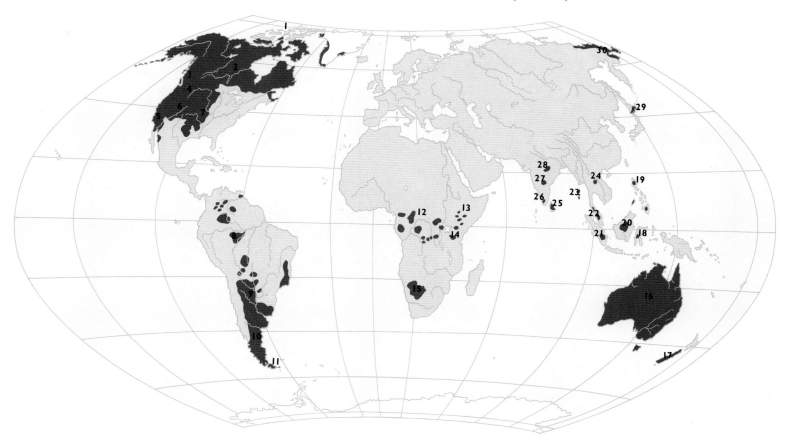

CARTOGRAPHY: RAY SIM

supply. We are thus able to understand not only the complex and richly varied Neolithic process that took place throughout the world, but also the survival of those hunter-gatherer communities that managed to live in a state of ecological balance, not expanding beyond the land's capacity to support them in their traditional way of life—a situation that at the same time fostered social stability.

The majority of the hunting-gathering peoples that have retained their original way of life are to be found in isolated marginal areas, where climatic conditions are extreme. What characterizes all these societies is that they have adapted to their particular environment in highly specialized and often sophisticated ways. Such peoples include the Bushmen of southern Africa and the Pygmies of the central African rainforests, as well as a number of peoples on the Indian subcontinent and in Southeast Asia, such as the Birhor, the Andamanese, and the Semang.

Two regions, where hunter-gatherers with richly varying economies have existed into modern times, stand out as exceptions within this scattered picture: Australia and North America. For thousands of years, the Australian Aborigines have adapted both to some of the world's most arid deserts and to resource-rich coastal areas, notably in northern Australia. Similarly, the North American Indians and Inuit (Eskimos) have shown a remarkable ability to adapt to a range of different environments, from coastal areas in the Pacific northwest to forests, deserts, and arctic tundras.

GÖRAN BURENHULT

⚭ The aboriginal populations of the Malay Peninsula include the Semang, the Senoi, and the Jakun. They still subsist mainly by hunting and gathering, but in recent times, the Jakun, in particular, have partly adopted agriculture. The main hunting weapon is a wooden blowpipe, such as this one used by a Jakun hunter at Tasek Chini, in Peninsular Malaysia.

HUNTER-GATHERERS

The areas marked are those where hunter-gatherer populations have existed in historic times—generally in extreme environmental conditions.

1	Eskimos
2	Subarctic Indians
3	Northwest Coast Indians
4	Plateau Indians
5	California Indians
6	Great Basin Indians
7	Plains Indians
8	Amazon basin hunter-gatherers
9	Gran Chaco Indians
10	Tehuelche
11	Fuegians
12	Pygmies
13	Okiek
14	Hadza
15	Bushmen
16	Australian Aborigines
17	Maori
18	Toala
19	Agta
20	Punan
21	Kubu
22	Semang
23	Andaman Islanders
24	Mlabri
25	Vedda
26	Kadar
27	Chenchu
28	Birhor
29	Ainu
30	Chukchi

The Jomon: Fishers and Potters

The comparatively late arrival of farming along Europe's Atlantic coast, where the climatic changes at the end of the last glacial period ensured an abundant supply of marine foods for the taking, has direct parallels in many other parts of the world. The salmon-fishing Indians along North America's northwestern coasts developed a complex system of chiefdoms (which is uncharacteristic of hunter-gatherer societies, most of which are not hierarchical), and never adopted any form of farming or herding. In northern Japan, an abundance of marine resources shaped one of the earliest and most distinctive fishing cultures known.

The people who crossed the Beringia land bridge during the last glacial period and settled the New World originated from the eastern Siberian hunter-gatherer communities that roamed the harsh tundras around the valley of the Aldan River. Between 18,000 and 12,000 years ago, the so-called Dyukhtai tradition evolved there. But not all of these Siberians made their way northeast towards the Chukchi Peninsula and Alaska. About 13,000 years ago, when the melting ice sheets raised the sea level, drowning many coastal areas, a number of peoples settled along coasts and lakes

☝ Ainu men in front of their settlement in Hokkaido, Japan. The vanishing Ainu have followed their traditional hunting-gathering way of life until recent times. Some anthropologists believe them to be the descendants of Jomon peoples who lived in Hokkaido and northern Honshu, while others have suggested that they constitute an independent Paleoasiatic ethnic group.

☞ Dating from the late Jomon period, this elaborately ornate clay mask may have had some ritual significance.
UNIVERSITY MUSEUM/UNIVERSITY OF TOKYO

further south, in eastern Asia. As the land area shrank, coastal regions became more important, and the warmer climate also allowed deciduous forests to spread, providing additional sources of food. As in Europe, in areas where food resources were abundant, people settled within limited territories. The Jomon were one of these peoples.

The Jomon communities, including those on the island of Honshu, largely depended on the abundant local supplies of shellfish and salmon, supplementing their diet with animals such as red deer and wild boar, and plant foods such as nuts, acorns, and edible seeds. This hospitable environment led them to adopt a settled way of life as early as 13,000 years ago. As a result, the Jomon were the first people to make pots—and somewhat later (about 11,000 years ago), also figurines and masks—of burned clay. The tiny clay figurines usually depict female figures, so-called *dogu*, and were probably used in some kind of fertility cult.

To date, more than 10,000 Jomon settlements have been discovered. Most are in Honshu, and such sites as Fukui, Kamikuroiwa, and Sampukuji have yielded some of the oldest finds of pottery. All of the settlements bear witness to similar cultural traditions, but there is also a marked degree of regional adaptation to different environments. Subsistence was tightly linked to the changing seasons. The earliest settlements are found beneath rock shelters or consist simply of pit houses. These were replaced after about 5000 BC with larger wooden houses, which were well built and had elaborate fireplaces.

During the course of the long-lasting Jomon tradition, plants were cultivated to a limited extent in some areas, primarily different species of *Echinochloa* and *Perilla*. Other kinds of domesticated plants, such as bottle gourds and mung beans, were probably introduced from the south. These Neolithic introductions mainly occurred in western Honshu, whereas the communities in the richer coastal regions of the northwest maintained their original way of life.

About 3000 BC, the colder climate of the subboreal period began to affect Japan. Coastal resources once again became increasingly important, and cultivation in western Honshu declined. About 1500 BC, the Jomon people of Kyushu, in the south, started to cultivate wet rice and buckwheat, whereas the original Jomon tradition survived until as late as about 300 BC in northern Honshu and Hokkaido. In Hokkaido, some populations continued their 14,000-year-old way of life until about AD 800.

Göran Burenhult

⬳ This Jomon clay figurine, or *dogu*, dates from the third or fourth century BC. Most of these *dogu* depict female figures, and it has been suggested that they were used in some sort of fertility cult.
LAUROS-GIRAUDON

☞ A late Jomon ritual site at Tabara, in Tokyo, Japan.

MARK J. HUDSON/AUSTRALIAN NATIONAL UNIVERSITY

ARCTIC HUNTERS AND FISHERS OF EURASIA

A drawing of a rock carving at Zalavruga, near Belomorsk, in Karelia, Russia, showing three men on skis. Settlements in the vicinity of this rock art site have been dated to about 2000 BC to 1500 BC.
GÖRAN BURENHULT

FENNOSCANDIA,
c. 8500 BC TO 3500 BC
The arrows indicate the earliest migration routes into northern Norway, Sweden, and Finland. The early sites mentioned in the text are shown, and the shaded areas indicate cultures.
CARTOGRAPHY: RAY SIM

Early settlers favored sites such as this shallow lake in Finnish Lapland, where waters rich in oxygen and nutrients provided a reliable supply of fish, one of the Arctic's most important food sources.

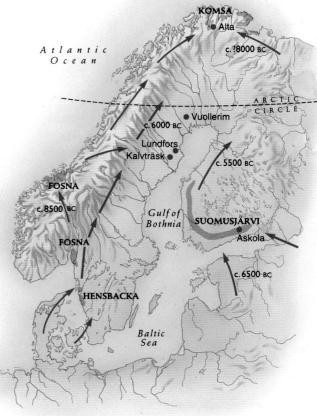

Human cultural adaptation to arctic conditions developed during the Paleolithic period, more than 20,000 years ago. Vast numbers of Pleistocene (Ice Age) animals supported human populations at the southern margins of the continental ice sheets in Europe. From Siberia, which was largely untouched by these ice sheets, there was an open route to North America across the Bering land bridge—the gateway to the New World.

The Arctic Environment

The key to survival in arctic regions was not merely obtaining food, but being able to withstand temperatures as low as minus 46 degrees Celsius (minus 50 degrees Fahrenheit) for weeks at a time. Without minutely sewn, watertight, and insulating clothing made from animal skins, humans could never have done this. This kind of clothing was made possible by the invention of the bone sewing needle during the Paleolithic period. Technology in general (housing, transport, heating, and so on) also had to be adapted to treeless environments that were covered by snow and ice for most of the year. The Arctic is, in fact, a vast desert surrounding a frozen ocean, and for these reasons arctic cultures are among the most specialized that humans have ever developed.

Arctic regions have low temperatures throughout the year, with average summer temperatures of no more than 10 degrees Celsius (50 degrees Fahrenheit). Under such conditions, the ecosystem is characterized by low productivity, with few species of plants and animals. People settled where supplies of fish and game were good, close to rivers and estuaries rich in oxygen and nutrients, and along coasts that were free of ice for part of the year. The most important sources of food in the Arctic were fish, seals, whales, and reindeer (caribou in North America). In the Subarctic, elk (moose in North America), beaver, and birds were more important, although reindeer, which migrated into the forests after grazing on the tundra or in the high mountains during the summer, were also hunted.

Remarkably, farming was introduced to a limited extent as early as 2500 BC in areas with maritime climates, such as northern coastal Norway, Sweden, and Finland. But hunting, fishing, trapping, and berry collecting remained the economic mainstays in these regions well into the twentieth century.

Early Settlement in Scandinavia and Finland

Scandinavia and Finland, which were deglaciated less than 10,000 years ago, became the last stronghold of European hunters who depended on arctic and subarctic resources. While these hunting societies were in some respects similar to those that had disappeared thousands of years earlier in Europe, it must be kept in mind that these northern cultures coexisted with, and were influenced by, the Neolithic, Bronze Age, Iron Age, and Medieval cultures evolving in western Europe and European Russia at that time.

NATIONAL BOARD OF ANTIQUITIES, FINLAND

⚭ Mesolithic spearheads or knives from Finland made of polished slate. Flint does not occur naturally in northern Scandinavia and Finland, so quartz and slate were utilized instead.

The earliest settlements in Scandinavia are found along the western coasts of Sweden and Norway. These cultures—known as Hensbacka in Sweden, and Fosna and Komsa in Norway—go back as far as 9000 BC to 8000 BC. Although reindeer were hunted in the highlands of southern and northernmost Norway, the people who lived in these settlements depended largely on marine resources, such as seals, whales, fish, and sea birds. In this regard, they were similar to the Paleoeskimo societies that spread across arctic areas of North America some 3,000 years later.

By 6000 BC, hunters had penetrated the interior of the Scandinavian peninsula as far north as the Arctic Circle. The remains they left behind in the archaeological record are similar to those of the Mesolithic peoples of northwestern Europe. They made microliths and small axes of flint and flint-like stones, and larger tools of bone and elk (moose) antler, including fishing harpoons and fishhooks, as well as wooden and bark equipment, such as net floats, bows, traps, and dug-out canoes.

The Nordic region was also settled from the east and southeast. As in Norway, the oldest sites in Finland are associated with ancient beaches. In southern Finland, the Askola and Suomusjärvi cultures were based primarily on seal hunting, which became the economic foundation of coastal societies throughout the Baltic region.

In northern Sweden, indigenous inland and coastal cultures developed during the period from 5500 BC to 2000 BC. Communities of 60 or so people lived all year round on the coasts, combining seal hunting with fishing and the hunting of elk and beaver. At the Lundfors site, by the Skellefteå River estuary, burned bones and thousands of net sinkers indicate that ring seals were caught by means of extensive seal-netting systems. At a well-preserved settlement at Vuollerim, the remains of four semisubterranean (pit) houses, 11 meters (36 feet) long and 4 meters (13 feet) wide, have been excavated. These were winter houses, which provided shelter for three or more families each season.

OVE HOLST/UNIVERSITY MUSEUM OF NATIONAL ANTIQUITIES, OSLO, NORWAY

NATIONAL BOARD OF ANTIQUITIES, FINLAND

⚭ Much hunting and fishing equipment, including harpoons, points, and fishhooks, was made of wood or bone, but these materials are rarely preserved in archaeological sites. Such artifacts are best preserved in peat bogs, clay, or limestone-rich soils. Here, one of the points has been reconstructed as a harpoon head.

⬳ Sub-Neolithic net sinkers made of stone, juniper, and birch bark from Kangasala, in southern Finland. Nets were used to catch both fish and seals.

In the inland areas, dwellings were built partly of mounds of burned and cracked stones and clustered in groups of between two and five huts, each cluster inhabited by a single hunting band. The main winter food was elk, which were captured by means of hunting pits.

The cutting tools these people used were made of polished slate and flaked quartz. The same local materials were used in Finland, although unusually beautiful red and green slate tools from northern Sweden and Norway were widely circulated.

Coastal sites in northern Norway from about 4000 BC to the beginning of the first century AD are marked by rows of depressions that once formed the floors of pit houses—up to 80 at a single site. Permanent villages grew up in succession on the same sites. Later villages were built on beaches at lower elevations and closer to the changing shoreline. These differences in elevation have provided archaeologists with a means of dating prehistoric settlements throughout the north. Because northern shorelines were displaced at the end of the last Ice Age as the deglaciated land rebounded, we know that the higher the elevation of a coastal site, the older it must be.

Recently discovered rock carvings from Alta, in northern Norway, have been dated in this way. These carvings depict the animals the people of the time valued and the rituals associated with them. The subject matter of this rock art, which includes rock paintings in other areas, is remarkably similar to that of the Paleolithic cave artists of France and Spain, 32,000 to 12,000 years ago. Shamanism—human mediation with nature and animal spirits by special individuals, known as shamans—is the most characteristic belief system among northern peoples, from the Saami of Scandinavia to the Greenlanders.

☝ This polished black slate knife from the Lundfors site, in northern coastal Sweden, dates from about 3500 BC.
NOEL D. BROADBENT

☝ Stone sinkers and bark floats from a wicker fishing net dating from about 9000 BC that was preserved in clay at Antrea, in Finland.

☝ Flint arrowheads from Finland, dating from about 3000 BC.

Domestication of Reindeer

Farming cultures influenced the northern hunters and fishers in various ways. The Finnish groups, for instance, began to make pottery as early as 4200 BC, using large vessels to prepare and store food. But they did not farm or raise animals, and are therefore referred to as sub-Neolithic. By about 2500 BC, true farmers had moved up the Scandinavian coasts to above the Arctic Circle. Although probably only marginally successful at farming, they did introduce the concept and techniques of animal domestication. Similar contacts took place between herders and northern hunters in Siberia about the same time. This contact probably led to the domestication of reindeer, which was to become one of the most characteristic aspects of northern cultures in Eurasia. It is interesting to note that the oldest skis in the world, from Kalvträsk, in northern Sweden, also date from about 2500 BC. Without skis, reindeer herding would have been practically impossible.

These images of deer at the isolated rock art site of Vingen, in Sogn og Fjordane, western Norway, are usually thought to date from about 1000 BC, but could be much older. In these northerly areas, people continued to follow a hunting-based, Mesolithic way of life until well into the Bronze Age.

NOEL D. BROADBENT

The rock carvings found at Alta, in northern Norway, depict both the animals important to the people of the time and the rituals associated with them—subject matter remarkably similar to that of the Paleolithic cave art of France and Spain.

A Lapp herder tends a reindeer flock in Norway. Reindeer were probably tamed about 2500 BC, perhaps under the influence of Scandinavian herders who had migrated above the Arctic Circle by this time.

Reindeer can be tamed and bred like sheep and goats. Tame reindeer were primarily used, however, as decoys to attract wild reindeer, for pulling sleds, and for milking. Large herds of semidomesticated reindeer were not kept for their meat until late Medieval times. Until then, the indigenous people of Lappland, the Saami, were still hunters and fishers, not unlike their Stone Age forebears. Siberian people such as the Nenets, the Evenki, the Yakuts, and the Chukchi also combined traditional hunting and fishing with the benefits of domesticated reindeer.

To this day, reindeer are one of the Arctic's most productive land resources. Northern seas, likewise, are among the richest fishing waters on Earth. It is therefore not surprising that indigenous peoples living today throughout the circumpolar North are very protective of their right to continue to exploit these resources, which have under-pinned their way of life for thousands of years.

Noel D. Broadbent

BRYAN AND CHERRY ALEXANDER/NHPA

These Thule artifacts were among those recovered from a site on the east coast of Ellesmere Island, northwest of Greenland. In the center are two small female fetishes carved from ivory, and to the left is a harpoon head.

This ring of stones held down a skin tent at a Thule camp site at Cape Copeland, on Shannon Island, north-eastern Greenland. A sleeping platform can be seen at the back of the ring, on the right.

This small Thule pit house excavated on the south shore of Baffin Island has been partly reconstructed by retying the ten pairs of bowhead whale ribs that formed the roof rafters.

THE THULE CULTURE

The Arctic culture known as Thule emerged from the Birnirk culture of northern Alaska about AD 900. Centered on the hunting of huge bowhead whales, which weigh between 30 and 40 tonnes (about 30 to 40 tons), it appears to have spread rapidly eastwards, reaching the sea coasts of the Canadian Arctic, Greenland, and Labrador by the fifteenth century.

This migration took place during a warm period, when Norse settlers were also moving through ice-free waters into Iceland and on to settlements in southern Greenland. The warmer temperatures may have reduced the ice in Beaufort Sea and opened gulfs and channels to the east that allowed whales to migrate. Warmer winters would also have meant that fewer snow caves were available in the west as birthing dens for ring seals, on which the Birnirk people depended. No evidence of whale hunting has emerged from Birnirk sites, and whale-hunting technology may have come from the Punuk Islands, in the Bering Sea, where people had hunted whales for nearly a thousand years.

The earliest appearance of the Thule culture in the eastern coastal regions, during the middle to late eleventh century, may have overlapped with the occupation of the region by people of the indigenous Dorset culture. Because the latter disappeared suddenly, it was thought that the

Thule culture displaced it. More recent evidence, however, suggests that this culture may have collapsed, for unknown reasons, a century or two before the Thule arrived.

The most useful means of determining the relative ages of Thule sites has proved to be examining the progression in the style of harpoon heads. The distinctive decorated type known as Sicco, frequent in Punuk sites and rare in Birnirk sites, has been found in some eastern sites, suggesting a route for what may have been the earliest eastward migration. Whale hunters would have traveled across western waters to Barrow Strait and Lancaster Sound, and then north through Smith Sound to the east coast of Ellesmere Island and northwestern Greenland. Finds from sites in the middle of the eastern shore of Ellesmere Island, from the so-called Ruin Island Phase, tend to support this hypothesis. Named after a small island between northern Greenland and eastern Ellesmere Island, these predominantly Thule sites have yielded Sicco harpoon heads and a few other types of artifacts with Punuk characteristics, together with woolen cloth, boat rivets, and links of chain mail armor, the latter items suggesting the presence of Viking explorers. Radiocarbon dating places these finds in the late twelfth and early thirteenth centuries, a period consistent with Norse accounts of northern voyages from settlements in southern Greenland.

To the south, finds from earlier Thule sites seem more characteristic of the Birnirk-derived Thule culture. This suggests a migration from the Point Barrow region of northern Alaska about the late eleventh century, and a second wave a century later (characterized by the Ruin Island Phase) from regions of western Alaska strongly influenced by the Punuk culture.

A typical Thule dwelling—a pit house 3 meters by 3.5 meters (10 feet by 12 feet), dug 2 meters (about 6 feet) deep into the earth on the side of a hill—was lined with large boulders, whale skulls, and bones, rather than the driftwood so common in the west. Roof rafters of whale jaws would have been covered with walrus skins, sods of earth, and rocks. A sleeping platform of flat rock slabs was raised about 46 centimeters (18 inches) above the floor, for warmth. Since cold air flows downwards, a tunnel 3 to 6 meters (10 to 20 feet) long, sloping up the hill and ending in a deeper cold trap, gave access to the stone-paved living area through the floor. Large soapstone lamps, with cotton-grass wicks fueled by seal oil, provided light, as well as heat for cooking in soapstone bowls.

On the evidence of a few scenes engraved on ivory tools, whale-hunting teams probably consisted of three or four kayakers, plus a harpooner and paddlers traveling in a large, skin-covered umiak. Once a detachable harpoon head was sunk into a whale, lines attached to inflated sealskins were thrown out to prevent the whale from sounding, and the creature was then dispatched with lance thrusts to its vital organs.

But whales were probably seldom taken. Seals, walrus, caribou—and virtually all of the other animals, birds, and fish of the region—were more common prey. The Thule used a wide range of hunting equipment, including disarticulating harpoons, thrown by hand or by means of a throwing board, with the head and line attached to floats. Caribou were stalked with weak, sinew-backed bows, or driven between the converging sides of rock piles shaped like human figures (called inuksuit). Sleds drawn by four to six dogs extended the Thule hunting grounds onto snow-covered sea-ice. Familiar headlands and mountain peaks provided aids to navigation.

The Thule people made a vast range of tools and implements with specific functions. There were knives for butchering, carving, and cutting blocks of snow; the characteristic crescent-shaped woman's knife (ulu); and needles, thimbles, and needlecases. Most useful was the bow drill, a tool still in use well into historic times.

In the cooler thirteenth century, sea-ice reduced breathing space for the great whales. The Thule abandoned their deep, winter pit houses for snow houses built on the sea-ice, where seals could be hunted at their breathing holes. The homogeneous whale-hunting Thule culture was replaced by more specialized regional variants, from which emerged the traditional "tribes" of the Inuit (or Eskimos) of historic times.

Moreau Maxwell

Thule hunters drove caribou between drift fences called inuksuit, made from piles of rocks. The inuksuk (singular) shown here is on Kulusuk Island, in southeastern Greenland.

The bow drill was a bow-shaped piece of ivory or antler tied at each end by a thong wrapped around a wooden spindle tipped with a piece of stone. The opposite end of the spindle was set in a socket, held in the teeth. The sawing action rotated the spindle. Hard walrus ivory was drilled with a series of holes to allow segments to be broken off and made into harpoon heads and foreshafts.
MOREAU MAXWELL

A field crew from Calgary University, Alberta, Canada, excavating a Thule site on Ellesmere Island.

THE INUIT MUMMIES FROM QILAKITSOQ

C. ANDREASEN AND J.P. HART HANSEN

CLOSE TO THE OLD and abandoned settlement of Qilakitsoq, in northwest Greenland, a stunning discovery was made in 1972: two graves were found containing eight mummified Inuit clothed in animal skins. They were buried about AD 1475, making them the oldest and best-preserved find of people and garments from the Thule culture, the immediate ancestors of the present-day Inuit population in the eastern Arctic.

There were two children—a child of 6 months and a boy of about 4 years—and six women, ranging in age from about 18 to 50. All wore two layers of clothes of similar design and materials: the jacket, trousers, and boots are of sealskin, while the warm inner jacket is made of bird skin from five different bird species, and the stockings are of caribou skin. Inuit people's ability to survive in the harsh Arctic climate is primarily due to their skilful use of fur for clothing, a material that provides excellent insulation by preventing loss of body heat in the cold while allowing excess body heat generated during physical activity to be dispersed.

Most seemed to have been healthy, the adults having an average height of about 151 centimeters (4 feet, 10 inches). Some diseases were present, including an extensive cancer of the nasopharynx, a kidney stone, a few fractures, parasites, and a case of hip disorder and, probably, Down's syndrome. The cause of death could not be established in all cases, and it was impossible to determine with certainty whether the bodies had been interred at the same time. Tissue typing indicated that the group was probably closely related and consisted of three generations.

The adults' faces were finely tattooed with curved lines on the forehead, cheeks, and chin. These tattoos closely resemble those on 2,000-year-old figurines from northern Alaska—providing a tantalizing glimpse of a thousand-year-long spiritual tradition not evident from the Inuit material culture.

⊕ This 6-month-old baby and a boy of about 4 years were found lying on the belly of their presumed mother, who was about 25 years of age. The sealskin jacket and trousers are sewn together at the waist. The hood can be tied with the cord that ends at the top of the head, thus preventing the child from accidentally strangling itself.
JOHN LEE/NATIONAL MUSEUM OF DENMARK

THE GREENLAND NATIONAL MUSEUM AND ARCHIVES

THE GREENLAND NATIONAL MUSEUM AND ARCHIVES

⟵ Around the site, about 40 stone graves were built on bedrock. Only the two mummy graves were built on a slope of loose stones under an overhanging rock, thus providing protection from the sun, rain, and snow as well as good drainage. Combined with the arid and cold High Arctic climate, these factors kept the bodies dry and well preserved. One grave contained three adults and two children; the other contained three adults. The adults were wrapped in sealskins and were lying on top of each other. Apart from 26 pieces of skin and garments, no other grave goods were found.

↥ The sand beach in the sheltered bay provided excellent landing facilities for the fragile skin boats of the Thule culture. Several ruins of houses made of local turf and stone indicate that the site was primarily used in winter. At this time of year, ring seals were caught at their breathing holes in the ice. In the summertime, people hunted the seals, whales, and birds that were abundant in the area. The mountainous areas to the south of the settlement were caribou hunting grounds.

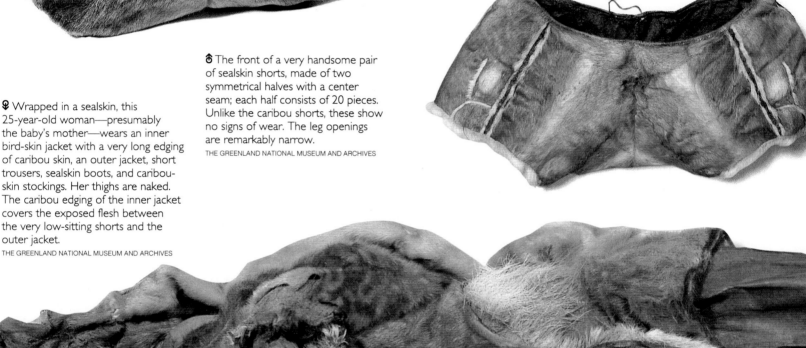

♀ The front of a pair of shorts elaborately made of 48 pieces of caribou skin joined together in a symmetrical pattern. This pair is very worn at the back, above the buttocks. Like other Inuit trousers, they are tied at the back by cord in a casing at the waist.

THE GREENLAND NATIONAL MUSEUM AND ARCHIVES

♂ The front of a very handsome pair of sealskin shorts, made of two symmetrical halves with a center seam; each half consists of 20 pieces. Unlike the caribou shorts, these show no signs of wear. The leg openings are remarkably narrow.

THE GREENLAND NATIONAL MUSEUM AND ARCHIVES

♀ Wrapped in a sealskin, this 25-year-old woman—presumably the baby's mother—wears an inner bird-skin jacket with a very long edging of caribou skin, an outer jacket, short trousers, sealskin boots, and caribou-skin stockings. Her thighs are naked. The caribou edging of the inner jacket covers the exposed flesh between the very low-sitting shorts and the outer jacket.

THE GREENLAND NATIONAL MUSEUM AND ARCHIVES

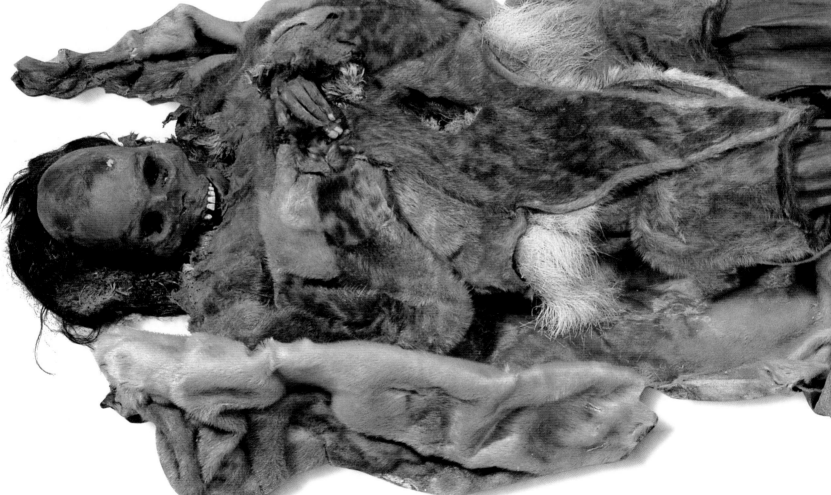

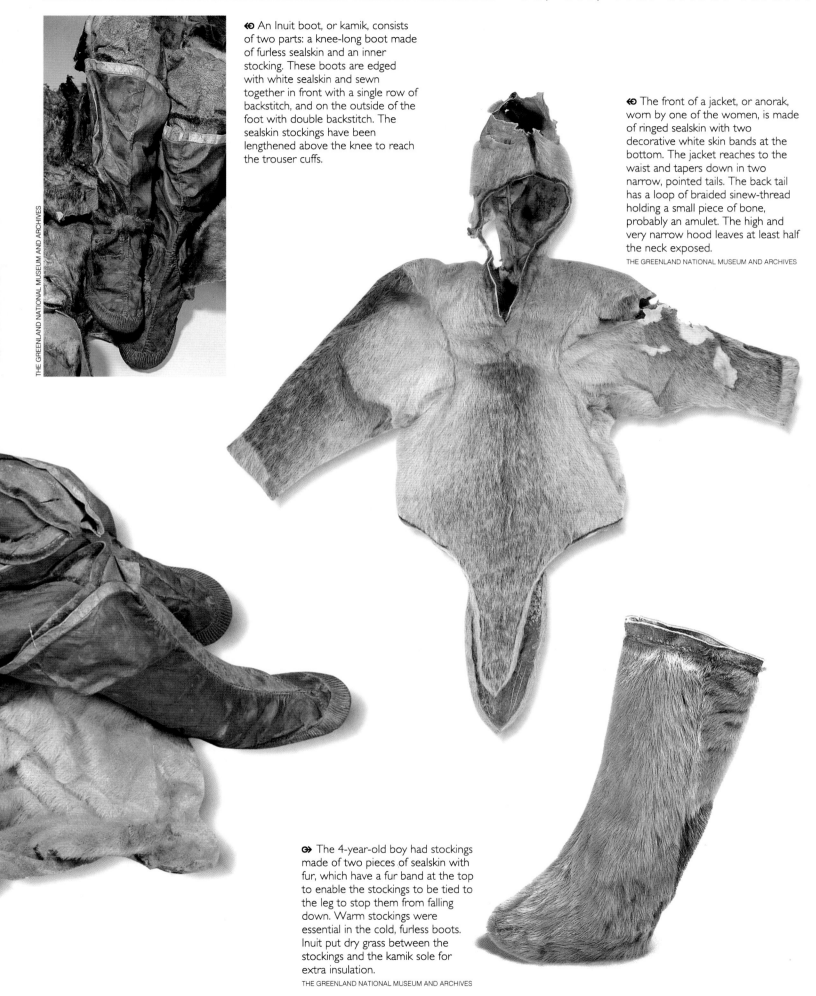

An Inuit boot, or kamik, consists of two parts: a knee-long boot made of furless sealskin and an inner stocking. These boots are edged with white sealskin and sewn together in front with a single row of backstitch, and on the outside of the foot with double backstitch. The sealskin stockings have been lengthened above the knee to reach the trouser cuffs.

The front of a jacket, or anorak, worn by one of the women, is made of ringed sealskin with two decorative white skin bands at the bottom. The jacket reaches to the waist and tapers down in two narrow, pointed tails. The back tail has a loop of braided sinew-thread holding a small piece of bone, probably an amulet. The high and very narrow hood leaves at least half the neck exposed.

The 4-year-old boy had stockings made of two pieces of sealskin with fur, which have a fur band at the top to enable the stockings to be tied to the leg to stop them from falling down. Warm stockings were essential in the cold, furless boots. Inuit put dry grass between the stockings and the kamik sole for extra insulation.

AUSTRALIA: THE DIFFERENT CONTINENT

1 0 , 0 0 0   B C   –   A D   1 8 0 0

An Aboriginal History

J. PETER WHITE

I N MANY PARTS of the world, it is useful to draw a sharp distinction between the Pleistocene and Holocene periods. In northern Europe, for instance, the last Ice Age ended rapidly about 10,000 to 12,000 years ago, and the major environmental changes that took place at this time had a significant impact on human life.

Throughout most of Australia, this boundary cannot be drawn as sharply, and the effects of environmental changes on human behavior can be seen only over longer time periods. Only in Tasmania and the highlands of New Guinea did extensive cold grasslands and shrublands give way to forests. The change that affected most people was the rise in sea level, but in most places the sea rose steadily over thousands of years—dramatic events like the formation of Bass and Torres straits, which separated first Tasmania and then New Guinea from Australia, were rare. It was not until about 4000 BC that the sea reached its present level, drowning much earlier evidence of coastal life. Even after the "end" of the Ice Age, about 8000 BC, climatic change continued. Some areas of southern Australia, for example, were a little warmer and wetter from 6000 BC to 3000 BC than they are today, allowing more people to occupy some inland lake areas.

◄○ Natural fire is endemic to much of Australia, and many plants depend on it for regeneration. Aborigines capitalized on this, using fire for thousands of years to "clean up the country", killing off dangerous animals and cooking edible ones in their burrows and nests.

⚬ Grindstones were used to convert the seeds of wild grasses into flour throughout many drier parts of the Australian continent.

A. FARR/AUSTRALIAN MUSEUM

MODERN AUSTRALIA
Australia has had its modern-day shape only since the sea reached its present level about 4000 BC. The majority of Aboriginal people lived around its well-watered eastern and northern margins, as Europeans do today.

CARTOGRAPHY: RAY SIM

⊕ *Opposite:* The shells in a midden usually reflect the immediate environment, since people nearly always eat shellfish close to where they are caught. The Lizard Island middens, in the Great Barrier Reef, are made up of the shells of shellfish that live on rocks and in coral crevices.

The area discussed in this chapter covers a range of environments, from subtropical to subtemperate (10 to 44 degrees South) and from rainforest to arid desert. We know that the societies that recently inhabited these 7.6 million square kilometers (almost 3 million square miles) spoke a variety of languages and lived their lives within a wide range of economic, political, and social structures. This suggests that Australian prehistory of the last 12,000 years should be looked at on a regional or even a local level in order to encompass this variety, but there is no space for that here. There is also a broad view to be obtained by focusing on particular aspects of the Australian past, and on some puzzles.

The Present and the Past
For the last 400 years, since the first European, Willem Jansz, landed on the western coast of Australia, white people have continually remarked on the fact that no Aboriginal people seemed to be farmers, gardeners, or pastoralists. Their apparent lack of defined fields, edible domestic animals, or settled villages allowed Europeans to see Aboriginal country as unproductive and unowned, available for whites to claim and colonize.

The European belief that Australia was a continent of wandering hunters and gatherers, inferior people who did not own or use their land, is still widespread. This is quite simply wrong. There is clear evidence that different territories had well-defined owners, who nurtured the plants

and animals within them in different ways and to varying degrees. European misconceptions arise because Aboriginal ways are not the same as those of Europeans. Many Aboriginal methods of using the land and its products are known only from relatively recent accounts—of early European visitors, anthropologists, and Aborigines themselves—since they are not of the kind that leave clear traces in the archaeological record.

The use of fire is a good example. In AD 1788 (the date of the first European settlement), Aborigines were observed to use fire in many parts of the country to "clean it up", to open pathways, to burn off dry vegetation to encourage new growth, to kill animals that were either food or vermin, and to prevent more destructive fires later. Their extensive knowledge of local environments allowed Aborigines to predict and control the extent, direction, and effect of these burn-offs. Thus, over time, these fires were used to create a mosaic of various vegetational environments that encouraged some plant and animal diversity. The Aborigines' use of fire was, and in some areas still is, widespread and frequent enough to constitute a land-management program—but a very different program from that of European Australians, most of whom view all fires as dangerous and a threat to life and landscape.

Aborigines had different ways of looking after useful plants, too, which in some areas occurred in such profusion that they resembled orchards or gardens. For example, it is hard to read explorer George Grey's statements about the western coast of Australia having, in 1841, "well marked roads, deeply sunk wells and extensive warran [yam] grounds" without concluding that Aborigines practiced organized gardening without fences. Other practices included the transplanting of useful trees, diverting small streams to irrigate areas of edible grasses, and digging to encourage roots to spread. It is such patterns of behavior that have led many scholars to argue that Aborigines in some parts of the country, at least, depended on agriculture for their livelihood.

How far back in time did these forms of behavior occur? This question is not easy to answer, because such things leave few traces in the archaeological record. It is difficult to trace the use of fire back very far—how are we to distinguish fires lit by Aborigines from those that occur naturally, often as a result of lightning strikes? There is at present no convincing evidence of the long-term or large-scale alteration of habitats as a result of firing. This does not mean it did not occur, especially in localities where Aboriginal firing would have enhanced naturally occurring trends towards the fire-dependent environments that are quite widespread in southern Australia. And, given that Aboriginal people knew how to make fire and that they had

GRAHAME L. WALSH

a very long-term relationship with particular areas of country, it seems very likely that they began to manage their environment many thousands of years ago, possibly from the time of their arrival, although the methods used probably became more sophisticated over the years.

Similar problems arise in trying to trace the history of plant use. Aboriginal methods of managing edible and useful plants do not substantially alter the local environment in the long term. As with the use of fire, a long history of refined techniques of management is to be expected, but is hard to prove.

The recognition of these problems is particularly important in relation to Australian prehistory, where the absence of large-scale changes in technology and the material culture encourages us to think of Aborigines as living off the land without owning or affecting it. Such beliefs are incorrect.

KATHIE ATKINSON/AUSCAPE

Harvesting the Sea

The continent of Australia gradually took on its present form as the sea rose towards today's level. As it did so, it flooded Bass Strait, separating the people of Tasmania from their close Australian relatives by many kilometers of stormy ocean. Tasmanians remained isolated from the rest of the world for more than 8,000 years. The rising sea had other effects as well. The most visible to us is that it drowned some of the commonly used resources in certain areas. In the far southwest, for instance, artifacts made from a distinctive fossil-bearing rock known as chert are widely found in sites dating to about 4000 BC, and only in a recycled form after that time. Cores drilled into the seabed off the western coast of Australia in the search for oil have revealed a chert seam that would have been exposed in the earlier Holocene period.

Since the sea level stabilized about 4000 BC, evidence of early coastal life has survived in the form of shell middens, which are found around much of the coast. People certainly ate shellfish in earlier periods, but most of the evidence of this has been destroyed by the rising seas. Several sites in both Australia and New Guinea show that people were gathering and eating marine shellfish during the Pleistocene period, as far back as 30,000 years ago. All these sites are close to the sea today and in locations where deep water is close to the present shore, so that changes in the sea level would not have greatly affected their distance from shellfish beds. (People rarely carry

⚬ Shell middens litter Australian coasts and are often the most visible signs of Aboriginal occupation. This one, at Princess Charlotte Bay, in northern Queensland, is on a large tidal mudflat.

GRAHAME L. WALSH

⚬ This midden at Princess Charlotte Bay is some 20 meters (63 feet) high, and is the relic of thousands of visits to a favored shellfishing area. Radiocarbon dates show that such mounds can be formed in less than a thousand years.

ARCHAEOLOGY IN THE SELWYN RANGES

IAIN DAVIDSON

As THE EXPLORERS Robert O'Hara Burke and William John Wills struggled through the summer heat to the south of the Selwyn Ranges in 1861, in their attempt to cross the Australian continent from south to north, Wills observed that "we found here numerous indications of blacks having been there, but saw nothing of them". This was the first recorded archaeological observation of the people who lived in the region. A few months later, the explorers themselves were dead of starvation, ignorant of how to survive there.

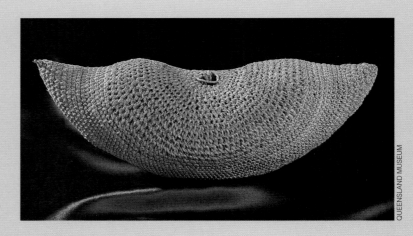

QUEENSLAND MUSEUM

Exploratory parties sent to search for the missing Burke and Wills brought back favorable reports of this area of northwestern Queensland, and pioneer pastoralists and gold prospectors lost little time in moving in. Twenty years after the event, so many Aborigines had been wiped out by the murderous attacks of the pioneer pastoralists that tribal structures had been all but destroyed, but in the late 1890s the Queensland Protector of Aborigines, Dr Walter Roth, was able to record some surviving information about the material and social life of the various tribes of the region, such as the Kalkadoons. Although they contain a wealth of detail, his studies are, inevitably, an impoverished account of the rich currency of life in northwestern Queensland before the coming of Europeans. They provide a valuable framework for understanding some of the archaeological discoveries in the Selwyn region.

Roth describes much of the equipment used in daily life: stone tools, along with the wooden tools they were used to make; string bags and nets; pearl shells and necklaces; and much more—items that rarely survive in the archaeological record. He also describes the network of trade and exchange that crisscrossed the region, still operating at that time but completely broken down within 20 years. Of the many items exchanged or traded, four stand out: axes (probably traded as axeheads), the nicotine-based drug pituri, ochers, and ceremonies. These

DISTRIBUTION OF TRADED GOODS IN NORTHWEST QUEENSLAND IN THE NINETEENTH CENTURY

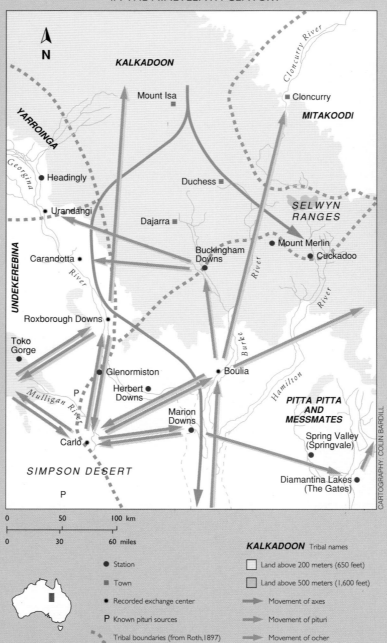

CARTOGRAPHY: COLIN BARDILL

KALKADOON	Tribal names
● Station	☐ Land above 200 meters (650 feet)
■ Town	☐ Land above 500 meters (1,600 feet)
● Recorded exchange center	→ Movement of axes
P Known pituri sources	→ Movement of pituri
Tribal boundaries (from Roth, 1897)	→ Movement of ocher

⚁ Finely woven bag used to carry pituri from the edge of the Simpson Desert to its trading destinations. Such bags were often decorated with ocher.

IAIN DAVIDSON

⚁ Pituri tree, *Duboisia hopwoodii*, on a dune on the northern margins of the Simpson Desert.

trading systems were essential to Aboriginal life in the region before that society was destroyed by the pastoralists. The challenge for archaeologists is to find out how trading systems emerged through the course of prehistory, and how the earlier inhabitants of the region managed without a trading system.

Axes made of stone mined from quarries near the present-day site of Mount Isa were traded to people all over a region extending from the Gulf of Carpentaria to the Great Australian Bight.

Pituri, made from the leaves and twigs of the shrub *Duboisia hopwoodii*, which grows in groves in sand dunes on the eastern

⚬ Men painted with feathers for the Molonga ceremony at Boulia, 1895.

margin of the Simpson Desert, particularly around the Mulligan River, was traded in all directions over an area of 500,000 square kilometers (188,000 square miles). The trade was carefully regulated, the precious narcotic drug packed and carried in special pituri bags, finely woven and often elaborately decorated with ocher.

Roth notes that the Kalkadoons obtained ochers at markets held along the Georgina River. We cannot tell from his account whether the reciprocal trade was because of different properties of ochers in different regions or because the social act of trade was more important than the items traded. Roth also describes how yellow ochers (goethite) were roasted to turn them red. As he records it, painting was mainly used for body decoration and to decorate portable items. He scarcely mentions the rock paintings and engravings that now are the most visible signs of Aborigines' presence in the region long before 1861.

Roth also records how a cermony, the Molonga, originating to the northwest of the Selwyn Ranges, was traded year by year, ultimately making its way as far south as Adelaide, in South Australia, and as far north as Alice Springs, in central Australia. Roth's account provides much more detail than archaeologists can ever expect to find

archaeologically, but it also points to the need for archaeologists to look beyond mere utility in seeking to understand the prehistory of trade and exchange.

The Archaeological Evidence

The Selwyn Ranges mark the watershed between the creeks and rivers that drain into the Gulf of Carpentaria and those that drain south towards Lake Eyre (although few of their waters reach the lake). People have long made use of the rock shelters and overhangs formed by these ancient, weathered cliffs. Aborigines lived in this region many thousands of years before the Kalkadoons of Roth's time, and archaeological investigations are gradually revealing the antiquity and nature of prehistoric Aboriginal trading systems and the nature and associations of Aboriginal rock paintings and engravings.

Cuckadoo 1 is a rock shelter in an isolated block of heavily weathered granite. Fourteen radiocarbon dates relate to various periods of human occupation. These suggest that the site was first used more than 15,000 years ago, close to the period of maximum aridity in this region; that the site was again used about 12,000 years ago; that it was then used intermittently between 4000 BC and 1000 BC; and that there has been a series of recent occupations in the past 2,000 years. The dates also indicate that the site was not used during four periods, each lasting more than a thousand years. This is what might

be expected in Australia's unpredictable climate, with its rapid oscillations between drought and flood.

There is no evidence of painting or engraving in Cuckadoo 1, but fragments of yellow ocher were found at the lowest levels, and a pit for the heat treatment of stone artifacts, dated to 2300 BC, also contained red ocher possibly resulting from roasting goethite. As well as changing the color of ochers, heating made them more suitable for use as paints by destroying the mineral structure of the clays in the raw ocher.

The only guide to ancient trading networks that usually survives in the archaeological record is the movement of axeheads. Because they are usually made of raw materials that are easy to identify geologically, they can be traced to particular sources. Axeheads made of Mount Isa metabasalt have been found 250 kilometers (155 miles) away, hidden on the floor of a cave near Cuckadoo 1, but there is no way of dating them. Fragments of Mount Isa axes were found at Cuckadoo 1 in layers less than 1,000 years old. We have shown, therefore, that Mount Isa axes were not only traded in the Selwyn Ranges, but also used there. The dating of these fragments is consistent with other evidence suggesting a recent development of the trading systems.

⚬ A typical "Kalkadoon" figure from south of the Selwyn Ranges.

Rock Paintings and Engravings

Few engravings in the Selwyn Ranges represent humans or other specific objects. Most motifs are geometric, often being based on circles and spirals, although some signs may represent animal tracks. The paintings, on the other hand, include more of what are called "figurative" signs, although it would be misleading to describe some of these signs as representational. At a few sites, engravings filled in with paint are found, and sometimes engravings and paintings are found together. There are also large numbers of hand stencils and non-figurative designs, including circles and meandering lines.

Several motifs are widely encountered throughout the region. Animal tracks, including those of macropods (kangaroos and wallabies) and birds (the latter in the form of tridents) are common in both paintings and engravings. It is clear that not all the bird tracks commonly called emu tracks should be interpreted in that way. Tom Sullivan, one of the Aboriginal men who is heir to traditional knowledge of the Selwyns, has identified some as nightjar tracks, others as brolga tracks.

The most distinctive motifs are called "Kalkadoon" figures. Some of these appear to represent ancestral beings, but others are unlikely to do so. Most have the appearance of a pair of broad "shoulders" and a rather featureless "head". The figures at some sites have no more features than this, while others are wearing headdresses.

Walter Roth photographed people, with feathering painted on their bodies and feathery headdresses, performing the Molonga ceremony at Boulia in 1895. These have some resemblance to these supposedly figurative rock paintings.

As Burke and Wills, conscious, perhaps, of their own place in history, observed the signs of the local inhabitants without seeing these inhabitants, they probably little realized that it was precisely those sorts of signs that would one day help to reveal the unwritten history of the land.

☙ Freshwater shellfish, especially the mussel *Velesunio ambiguus*, flourish in the lakes and rivers of southeastern Australia. People have collected them for at least the last 30,000 years.

☙ *Opposite:* The East Alligator floodplain, Kakadu National Park, in Arnhem Land, northern Australia. Plant foods were the staple diet of most Aboriginal communities, and in the freshwater lagoons formed in the wet season, there grew a variety of plants with edible roots.

⚘ A shell midden on the Wudbud floodplain, in Arnhem Land. The present-day floodplains of Arnhem Land have evolved during the last thousand years, and the middens on them are the results of shellfish collecting since then.

shellfish very far before eating them.) They are all also cave sites, where environmentally fragile shells have lain protected until excavated by archaeologists. Freshwater shellfish were also commonly gathered in earlier times, and their remains are found around old lake and stream shores.

Although shell middens become common from about 4000 BC, they are not found in all coastal areas: in some cases, they were never there, and in others, they have been destroyed. In some areas, notably around the southwest of Australia, Aboriginal people did not eat shellfish (which caused explorer Nicholas Baudin to write a surprised note in his journal in 1803). Probably, shellfish were of no interest to people living around King George Sound, since other resources, including fish, were more readily available.

In other parts of Australia, people collected shellfish at some times and not others. One of the clearest examples of this is to be found at Princess Charlotte Bay, in northern Queensland. This shallow bay has been slowly filling up with mud and sand since about 4000 BC. By about 2000 BC, there was sufficient mud to support relatively large populations of the bivalve *Anadara granosa*, and from time to time some of these were pushed by exceptional cyclonic waves into mounds

(known as cheniers) on the southern shore. The largest cheniers were created first, with later ones being longer, narrower, and not continuous. This process ceased about 500 years ago, not because there were fewer storms, but because there were fewer shellfish. Aboriginal people collected *Anadara* from at least 2500 BC until recently, but large middens perched on top of cheniers are only about 2,000 to 500 years old, with the biggest about 1,000 years old.

The largest middens were not created at the same time as the biggest cheniers, as we might expect, but later. The conditions in Princess Charlotte Bay that made Aboriginal shellfishing easiest were not precisely the same as those favoring the creation of cheniers. The Princess Charlotte Bay case demonstrates that resources are not permanent and that Aborigines made use of what was available from time to time.

In other areas, there is good reason to believe that middens that used to exist no longer do so. Discovery Bay, for example, on the southwest coast of Victoria, has 80 kilometers (50 miles) of sandy beach backed by an extensive swamp and dune system. The present coast, however, is well inland of the coastline of 4000 BC. Paleo-environmental evidence has shown that the dunes, with swamps between them, were built up from 4000 BC to 2000 BC. After that, erosion began, possibly as a result of drier conditions, with dunes moving inland and one chain of swamps being destroyed by the sea. Peat that formed in these former swamps is exposed on the present beach at low tide.

In terms of their dates, shell middens at Discovery Bay nearly all fall into two groups. The smaller group comprises middens found on soils that were formed before 4000 BC, and nearly all middens on those soils date to that time. The larger group consists of younger middens dating to within the last 2,000 years; they lie on the dunes and swamps closest to the sea. Nearly all those from the intervening period have obviously been destroyed. Because of this, it is clear that middens are not a reliable guide to the human population in these areas at different times.

In Arnhem Land, on the other hand, the shoreline is advancing rather than retreating. The middens here, including those around the mouth of the Blyth River, are not more than 1,500 years old; many hectares of land, including favored camping places of the Anbara people today, have been above sea level for only this period.

A similar, but more complex, story, which has major implications for the history of local Aboriginal groups, has been traced in the floodplains of western Arnhem Land, especially along the South Alligator River. Here, as at Princess Charlotte Bay, the story is one of a river valley first filled by the rising sea and then reclaimed by floodplain muds. Middens

composed of different varieties of shellfish occur throughout the period, but the major change in the area occurred since about 2000 BC, when extensive freshwater wetlands were first formed. The resources of these wetlands, including waterbirds and swampy plant roots, became the focus of many Aboriginal economies, with successive dry-season camps established along the edges of the wetlands and intensive production of stone tools for hunting and making numerous wooden artifacts. There is evidence that people transferred more and more of their activities from nearby rock shelters to the richer, open plains within the last thousand years.

Another example of how resources available to people could change has become apparent in the archaeological record of the last 2,000 years along the New South Wales coast. The common mussel, *Mytilus planulatus*, is found in shell middens in southern Australian and Tasmanian waters during the last 6,000 years, but represents only a very small percentage of middens north of 37 degrees South, except during the last 1,200 years or so. By the time of European settlement, it is found in quantity at some sites as far north as Sydney (34 degrees South).

Mussels are among the shellfish that have a free-floating stage in their life history; the chance distribution of young by the sea can play a major role in establishing new populations. Along the New South Wales coast, it seems likely that

mussels were established by chance over the last 2,000 years. Thickly clustered and easily gathered at low tide, they became a favored food of some Aboriginal people. The alternative explanation is that mussels were there all along, but were simply not collected, even though many other kinds of shellfish, some of them harder to gather, were collected. It is difficult to believe that this behavior would have been common to all the people living along this coast over a period of 1,200 years. There is, of course, a possible test: are mussels found in natural deposits, such as fossil beaches, in this area more than 2,000 years ago? We do not know, because this elaborate and expensive research has not yet been undertaken.

The final, and a most puzzling, situation involving the sea and its resources comes from Tasmania. Early Europeans there noted that the Tasmanians did not eat fish, although they did eat shellfish and crayfish. Several of the journals kept on Captain Cook's third voyage (AD 1777) record the Tasmanians reacting with "horror" or running away when fish that the Europeans had caught were offered to them. But Tasmanians had eaten fish until about 1500 BC: archaeological deposits dating from earlier times contain hundreds of fish bones. At least 31 types were caught then, including those that lived in both rocky reef and open-water (bay) habitats, although the former predominate. Most, perhaps all, could have been caught in traps in the form of a baited

box or a stone-walled basin filled by the tide.

This change in the Tasmanian diet occurred throughout the island over the span of a few hundred years or less, and suddenly at every site. It was clearly not caused by a shortage of fish, since colonies of fish-eating birds and seals continued to exist and be hunted by Tasmanians. No researchers have yet put forward a convincing environmental explanation, and it seems the answer must lie with the Tasmanians themselves. Whether the issue was one of simple dietary change (there was better food more easily obtainable elsewhere) or of religious belief is difficult to test. Many societies and religions have dietary restrictions, but both the suddenness of the change and the fact that it occurred throughout the island are surprising in the Tasmanian case.

How Many People?

Not all people lived along the sea coast, of course, although the richness and concentration of marine resources meant that population densities were high in these areas. Elsewhere, population density at the time of European contact, and probably in prehistoric times, was usually related to rainfall, with exceptions occurring along some major river systems such as the Murray. Like the Nile, this river flows in a fertile trench through very desolate surroundings for much of its length, and people living along it depended on rainfall in its headwaters rather than where they lived.

Determining population numbers of the past, especially among societies that do not settle in one location and do not build permanent houses, is difficult. Archaeological evidence is of limited use—while it can indicate the number of people who used a particular site over a certain period, it generally cannot reveal whether these people were all living at the same time. Nor are the number and distribution of stone and other artifacts much of a guide, since their presence in any area is related more to the availability of raw materials, the uses to which tools were put, and the chances of their survival than to the number of people. More useful are the remains of people themselves, although this evidence may be harder to interpret. For example, Steve Webb has recently shown that human bones from burials in the Murray River area have a much higher incidence of stress lines and other bone diseases related to a poor diet than do those from other sites. Elsewhere in the world, this is a feature associated with overcrowding in the early stages of communities settling in a particular area. This suggestion is lent some support by the fact that it is only along the Murray River that cemeteries are common, having been used, although not continuously, for the last 13,000 years. Groups of people often use cemeteries as a means of defining long-term ownership of an area, and such

KATHIE ATKINSON

overt markers of ownership become more important as population density increases.

On a different scale, we might ask what the Aboriginal population of Australia was at the time of European settlement and work back from there. The difficulty here is that during the early years of contact, Aboriginal societies were rapidly destroyed, both deliberately and through diseases, such as smallpox, to which people had no resistance. Estimates of the total Aboriginal population just before European settlement—about AD 1780—range from 300,000 to well over a million, with perhaps 600,000 being the best figure on current evidence. But should we think of this many people living in Australia for many thousands of years, or was this number reached only quite recently?

How we answer this question depends on our views as to how human populations grow and as to whether there have been any events in Australian prehistory that might have caused significant changes in population numbers.

☝ Hatchet head from Gunbalunya (formerly Oenpelli), in Arnhem Land, northern Australia. Hatchets with stone blades ground to a sharp edge were made over most of the continent, although not in Tasmania. Sometimes, the blade was made from a suitably shaped river pebble, but stone was also quarried, and hatchet heads were traded for hundreds of kilometers.
C. BENTO/AUSTRALIAN MUSEUM

Tools of the Past

Although they are not a guide to population density, the nature and distribution of stone tools can tell us several things about the prehistory of Australia. For example, they allow us to order sites chronologically, tell us something of the distribution of raw materials, indicate links between areas, and show how technology changed. Many researchers believe that they

☝ For a time, stone points were used as spearheads over a wide area of northern and central Australia. Many are made of silcrete, a rock that sparkles with tiny quartz crystals.
A. FARR/AUSTRALIAN MUSEUM

also hint at broader changes in Australian society from about 3000 BC on.

Throughout Australian prehistory, most tools consisted of flakes and pieces of stone with sharp edges appropriate to a variety of tasks. Tools were not formally shaped into regular patterns. An important exception to this was the manufacture of ground-edged hatchet heads, but these were found only in the tropical north, from at least 25,000 years ago.

At least three major changes in stone tools have occurred within the Holocene period. First, hatchets with ground stone heads came into use throughout continental Australia. The heads—all that survives—are found only in association with the two other changes described below, and their spread is thus dated from about 3000 BC. Why they spread at all, and only at this late date, is

◄ Backed blades, shaped like a penknife blade, were probably used as the points and barbs of spears. In a few sites, they have been found in their thousands, suggesting frequent retooling.
A. FARR/AUSTRALIAN MUSEUM

a puzzle. Hatchets seem to have been used for similar purposes throughout the country—wood-working, including making wooden artifacts; collecting honey and possums by enlarging holes in trees; and similar lightweight tasks. They were not suited to heavier work such as chopping down trees, even if this had been desirable. It is unlikely that people were not engaging in these activities earlier than 3000 BC, so there must be other reasons why hatchets spread. Since in the recent past they were frequently painted and exchanged with neighbors, and many were made of stone available from only a few quarries, elements of prestige, value, and power may have been attached to these artifacts.

The second change is that people in northern Arnhem Land started to make finely shaped spear-points from about 3000 BC. From the beginning, points were flaked on one or both sides, sometimes by pressure rather than percussion, which gives more control and produces a flatter flake. Stone points similar to these were used until the nineteenth century to tip spears, being replaced by metal in the twentieth century, when glass specimens were also made for sale to tourists and collectors. Once again, it is hard to find a simple functional explanation for the existence of these tools, since effective spears were certainly in existence before stone points were made. Whether the new points were more effective for hunting is hard to test, as is the idea that they developed as a component of more precisely balanced spears that could be thrown further and more accurately with the aid of a woomera (the Aboriginal name for a spear-thrower, a common weapon among hunter-gatherers that extends the power and length of the throwing arm). In some Arnhem Land sites, different raw materials, especially quartzite, became more common at about the same time as points start to appear. Some of this new stone came from specific quarries, which again suggests that exchange systems were developing, with associated concepts of prestige and exchange value playing an important part in the making and spread of these points.

Stone points have been found throughout northwestern Australia, being common for several

A. FARR/AUSTRALIAN MUSEUM

Comparable tools are found in many parts of the world, some as old as 30,000 years. Elsewhere, backed blades have been interpreted as points and barbs for arrows—a few have even been found mounted as such—but bows and arrows were not in use anywhere in Australia at the time of European settlement. People living in Cape York Peninsula were well aware of their cousins' use of these weapons in the Torres Strait islands and New Guinea, but they never adopted them. In Australia, backed blades were probably used as points and barbs on spears. This is confirmed to some extent by the resin found on the back or base of some tools, used to haft them in wood, as well as by the many discarded blades with broken tips found at some sites.

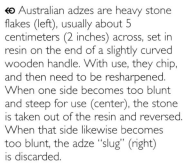

Australian adzes are heavy stone flakes (left), usually about 5 centimeters (2 inches) across, set in resin on the end of a slightly curved wooden handle. With use, they chip, and then need to be resharpened. When one side becomes too blunt and steep for use (center), the stone is taken out of the resin and reversed. When that side likewise becomes too blunt, the adze "slug" (right) is discarded.

hundred kilometers inland. They are also found in smaller numbers through the center of the continent almost as far as the south coast, but only from 2000 BC to 1000 BC. It looks very much as if they were initially popular, being distributed

P. G. FOX/THE QUALITY IMAGE

In much of interior Australia, stone tools, along with the debris that results from making them and local stones collected for hearths, comprise most of the archaeological record of Aboriginal societies. Little is preserved of bones and shells in such environments. This site is at Mootwingee, in western New South Wales.

Grinding stones used for seeds, sharp-edged flakes and the cores from which they were struck, adze slugs, and a few points constitute the range of stone artifacts found in central Australia. The items shown here are from the Amadeus basin, near Uluru (formerly Ayres Rock), in the Northern Territory.

and copied over a wide area, and subsequently became restricted to the original area. This makes it unlikely that they were designed specifically for use with spear-throwers, since spear-throwers were widespread.

The third major change was the development of backed blades—long thin flakes that are blunted (or backed) by chipping away one edge—which are today found over the southern two-thirds of Australia. They are small tools, less than 5 centimeters (2 inches) long, the oldest, dating to between 2000 BC and 2500 BC, having been found in south central Queensland. Like points, they are found right across the continent within a very short time, but unlike them, they are found in their thousands at some sites.

Backed blades come in a variety of shapes, from long, thin points to squat geometric forms.

REG MORRISON

ART OF THE ESCARPMENTS:
IMAGE-MAKING IN WESTERN ARNHEM LAND

PAUL TACON

ABORIGINAL PEOPLE believe that image-making has always been central to their way of life. Whether it be through rock painting, body painting, or the decoration of portable objects, the process of painting allowed these people to tap into the power of their ancestral past. As well, the painting process reaffirmed their links and affinity with the landscape and, through the use of specialized clan designs, with each other. The resulting "sense of being" helped them in making decisions and formulating plans of action. More importantly, images could be used to pass on complex cultural knowledge from one generation to the next.

PAUL TACON

⚑ In western Arnhem Land, hand stencils of important people were often filled in with clan designs after their death to honor them. This one is from Kakadu National Park.

The Antiquity of Image-making

The Aborigines of western Arnhem Land believe that their ancestors, the first people, were taught the skills and techniques of painting on rock by Mimi spirits. They believe that the Mimi also produced the earlier, monochrome styles of rock painting in the area, including the dynamic figures. These paintings differ from the more complex polychrome forms produced most recently, in the past few centuries. Archaeological research shows that the basic pigments used for image-making have been in use for possibly 50,000 years. Ground pieces of red ocher (hematite) have been found in every level of stratified deposits located in large rock shelters. This does not mean that the practice of rock painting dates from such early times or that paintings were executed at a constant rate. It does show, however, that ochers were consistently used and that some form of image-making or painting activity, the results of which have not survived, has taken place throughout the period this region has been occupied by humans.

The earliest rock paintings in western Arnhem Land are believed by many archaeologists to be at least 18,000 years old, but there is still considerable debate. Most of the art, however, can more confidently be placed in the Holocene period. Research is now being directed towards dating the art more precisely, and within a few years we will be able to assess its antiquity more

PAUL TACON

⚑ "X-ray" fish, such as this saratoga from Nourlangie Rock, are the most common subject in the recent rock art of western Arnhem Land, produced over the past 3,000 years.

PAUL TACON

☞ This dynamic figure from Deaf Adder Gorge, Kakadu National Park, is more than 10,000 years old. The figure is holding boomerangs, and the dashes near its mouth are possibly one of the earliest depictions of sound. Early forms and styles of painting such as this are believed by Aborigines to have been created by Mimi spirits in the ancient past.

accurately. The important point to note is that there have been many changes in rock painting over time—more so than in other forms of rock art found elsewhere in the world—in terms of form, style, and subject.

"X-ray" Paintings

The most widely known Holocene rock art has been called "X-ray" art, because it often depicts internal features of creatures. This form of art has been produced between a couple of thousand years ago and the present, much of it in this century. It has wide appeal for Europeans because of its detail and complexity, but it is also meaningful for various groups of Aboriginal people.

One should not really talk of an "X-ray" style, however, because the paintings with internal features are part of a much larger regional style as well as of a number of substyles associated with particular language groups. For instance, solid infill figures, various forms of stick figures, stencils, prints, and beeswax compositions were also made. The range of subject matter is large and varied, with new subjects continually being discovered. Although humans, animals, and mythical beings predominate, a variety of objects, activities, and abstract designs were also illustrated. Indeed, western Arnhem Land stands out from other rock art regions of the world because of this diversity.

Contemporary Practices

The last rock artist to paint prolifically in the region, Najombolmi, died in 1964. But rock paintings have also been done in the 1980s, and much of the tradition continues on bark or, more often, fabric and large sheets of paper. Rock paintings still hold considerable meaning for Aboriginal elders, and they are used in a variety of ways to pass on knowledge. "X-ray" paintings are particularly important in this regard, as their layered nature makes them especially suitable for conveying ideas about the different levels of meaning inherent in every aspect of existence. Western Arnhem Landers emphasize that theirs is a living tradition that changes with circumstance. Because of this, we should not be surprised or concerned that subjects and media derived from European traditions have been incorporated in Aboriginal images in recent years. What is most important is that the process continues.

☝ Beeswax compositions, such as this one in Kakadu National Park, western Arnhem Land, are often found in association with rock paintings produced in the past few hundred years.

⚲ Large polychrome "X-ray" paintings were commonly placed on shelter walls and ceilings in western Arnhem Land during the past 2,000 to 3,000 years. This one is in Kakadu National Park.

For many years, there have been suggestions that both points and backed blades were introduced to Australia from elsewhere, although from where has never been specified. Tools in Indonesia that are even generally similar are not old enough to be their ancestors, and such tools are rare in other areas of Southeast Asia. Two more likely explanations of these tools have been put forward. One is that they were more efficient hunting weapons, perhaps allowing different kinds of game to be hunted. The other—which would also apply to hatchets— is that they were invented and adopted as part of a growing exchange system, perhaps involving the use of selected, quarried stone, which also developed from about 3000 BC. The first is in theory able to be tested through the animal remains in archaeological sites, although it has proved difficult to find enough sites with sufficient remains for this purpose. The second explanation could be tested through more work on tracing the sources of raw materials used to make these artifacts. Interestingly, although Tasmanians were isolated from the mainland and made none of these new tools, raw materials are more widely distributed there, too, over the last 3,000 years or so. What this might indicate, we do not at present know.

Paintings and Engravings

The other prehistoric remains found throughout Australia are what can broadly be called art. A few paintings and engravings on rocks have been dated back to the Pleistocene period, but it is clear that nearly all are less than 5,000 years old. They range in style from the highly naturalistic X-ray paintings of Arnhem Land to the stylized figures found in western New South Wales and stencils of boomerangs, hands, and other objects found in the Carnarvon Ranges area, in Queensland, and, less commonly, in some other areas. Paintings made in the last 200 years are known to have had a wide range of social functions, from serving as elements of sacred and secret ceremonies to illustrating everyday events and common stories. While we cannot categorize prehistoric art in the same way, it seems very likely that some of it, at least, served similar functions.

In seeking to interpret Aboriginal art, it is important to note that regions in which similar art is found are often quite different in other important respects, such as technology (for example, types of weapons and dwellings), social organization (for example, marriage practices—which are usually governed by very complex rules in Aboriginal society— and whether or not circumcision is practiced), and

⚲ In western New South Wales, white paintings are often the most recent. This panel, at Gundabooka, may portray a dancing group, all of whom seem to be men, with the leader carrying significant objects.

KATHIE ATKINSON

COLIN KERR

language. In a few cases, a pattern of local variations can be identified. This is sometimes related to the environment—for example, among the engravings in the sandstone of the Sydney region, fish are more common in rock carvings nearer the sea—and sometimes to small-scale social or linguistic boundaries known from the recent past. For example, differently sized human figures or slight differences in the way kangaroos are painted can be linked to particular Aboriginal groups.

Research into Aboriginal art has largely centered on establishing the chronology of different styles. In the Arnhem Land area, it is clear that the X-ray style has been in use only during the last 2,000 years. Several other styles have been identified in the same area, and some are clearly older than others, since they are always found beneath them. In time, their exact age and relationships may be revealed by a new radiocarbon-dating technique known as the accelerator mass spectrometry (AMS) method. This uses a cyclotron to isolate the radioactive carbon atoms, which are then counted. It can be used on even the tiniest of organic samples, but it is an expensive process at present and therefore not widely used. Since many of the paintings contain organic material of some kind (such as saliva, blood, urine, or charcoal), many should be dateable by this method.

In the meantime, one of the best methods of establishing chronology is to examine the way in which images have been superimposed on each other. In an extensive study carried out in the Carnarvon Ranges, Mike Morwood was able to show a three-stage sequence consisting of designs made by pecking and rubbing, probably unpainted, followed by stenciled, painted, and drawn designs in a variety of colors, with white paint being used only within the last few centuries. The sequence may have started in Pleistocene times, but no definite dates have yet been established.

Some current research on dating is attempting to link paintings with coloring materials of various kinds found in archaeological deposits in the same site. This has been useful where a particular material is absent; for example, it has shown that the "Lightning Brothers" (large, paired, striped human figures) in a shelter near Delemere, in the Northern Territory, almost certainly date to within the last 200 years, because no older ochers occur in the deposit immediately below them. However, this method has been of less use where ocher is found throughout levels dating from both the Holocene and Pleistocene periods, as has often been the case.

Because of their exposed locations, it seems likely that the paintings in all these regions have been made in recent times, but this cannot readily be proved.

☝ The male and female human-like figures at Ubirr Rock (formerly Obiri), in Arnhem Land, represent beings who are involved with the continuous re-creation of the land, including its animals, plants, and people. Paintings such as these usually have many meanings, only some of which are known to any individual.

GRAHAME L. WALSH

☝ These "Lightning Brothers", at Yiwarlarlay, in northwestern Australia, were seen in a dream there by a Wardaman Elder in the 1940s and painted there soon afterwards, when European settlement prevented Wardaman people from visiting the shelter the Brothers originally inhabited.

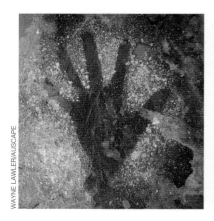

WAYNE LAWLER/AUSCAPE

☝ Hands mark many Australian rock shelters. This one, at Wuttagoona, near Cobar, in northwestern New South Wales, has been stenciled by paint being spat or blown around a left hand held against the wall. Women's and children's hands are sometimes featured.

☞ The rivers and swamps of Arnhem Land provide many significant food resources for Aboriginal people, among them the barramundi fish, here depicted at Nourlangie Rock, and painted and repainted in many other rock shelters.

GRAHAME L. WALSH

⚓ Fish traps, such as this one on Goold Island, in the Great Barrier Reef, Queensland, are commonly made in shallow tidal waters in Australia's tropics. Fish swim over the stone walls of piled-up rocks at high tide, to be trapped there when the tide falls.

⚓ Along the east coast, fishhooks without barbs were cut and ground from shiny shell. They were used as lures, without bait, and are usually regarded as women's tools.

A. FARR/AUSTRALIAN MUSEUM

Social and Economic Elaboration

In the 1980s, a number of researchers argued that the changes that can be observed in stone artifacts and rock art dating to after about 2000 BC, along with other changes, indicate that Aboriginal societies in many parts of Australia had become more "complex" in this period. The cases for and against this proposition are themselves too complex to be set out in detail here, but they are an interesting example of the ways in which archaeological data and how they are interpreted affect our understanding of prehistoric societies.

The idea that there had been significant increases both in levels of productivity and in production of goods and services was first suggested by Harry Lourandos some 15 years ago. Basing his work on one anthropological view of the way traditional societies were organized, he examined the archaeological record of southwestern Victoria and found most of the evidence there to be less than 5,000 years old. He considered that the demands of a changing society, including increased competition along with a growing population, would produce such changes. In particular, he pointed to three new features found in the archaeological record from this time: artifically constructed habitation mounds—up to 6 meters (20 feet) across and 1 meter (between 3 and 4 feet) high—large fish traps, and the extensive distribution of hatchet heads made of a greenstone available from only a few quarries. He also noted the dense populations and evidence of very large-scale social groups (which the early Europeans called

"nations") recorded at the time of European settlement. Lourandos rightly saw that if production and productivity could be shown to have intensified, then climatic, environmental, or technological changes were insufficient to account for this.

Similar, but less wide-ranging, evidence has been adduced subsequently by other researchers from different parts of Australia. In particular, sites containing backed blades, which date from about 3000 BC, are 10 times more common than earlier sites; and, per thousand years, the number of backed blades found greatly exceeds the number of other artifacts found in the older sites. This has been seen as evidence of population increase, although how this might have come about (whether through lowered death rates or higher birth rates or both), and why, has not been explained. An increasing complexity in social networks has been inferred on the basis of the exchange systems in operation over the last few thousand years, by means of which stone for hatchet heads, sandstone grindstones, pituri (a narcotic), seashells from the northern coasts, songs, ceremonies, and other social phenomena were carried over distances of hundreds of kilometers and sometimes right across the country— for example, shells from northern coasts have been found in sites close to the Southern Ocean. The development of regional art traditions throughout Australia has similarly been seen as evidence that societies were becoming more complex.

Taken together, such evidence does indeed seem to suggest that "something happened" in Australia about 2000 BC. But when each piece of evidence is examined individually, the apparent pattern becomes blurred. For example, in a detailed study of one area where many rock shelter sites have been found, Mangrove Creek, near Sydney, Val Attenbrow showed that, per thousand years over the last 11,000 years, there is no common pattern of increase between the number of rock shelter sites in use, the number of newly established rock shelter sites, and the numbers of stone artifacts found in all these sites—such as we would expect to find if the population were increasing and developing more elaborate forms of social organization involving, among other things, exchange systems.

Similarly, other researchers have pointed to evidence of social elaboration occurring in earlier periods—such as the establishment of cemeteries along the Murray River Valley (the present-day border between the states of Victoria and New South Wales) from 13,000 years ago—and to the fact that some apparent changes in production over the last 4,000 years—such as variations in the pattern of shellfishing, as reflected by the middens at Princess Charlotte Bay—may simply represent changes in the natural environment in certain periods.

There is no doubt that changes did occur in Australia in the Late Holocene period, but these do not point as clearly to the development of complex societies as has been suggested. It must be remembered that the mere fact that more archaeological evidence has come down to us from more recent times is not of itself evidence of social change. We would always expect to find more evidence from more recent times, since with every year all sites face another year's possibility of destruction.

Uncovering the Past

This chapter has touched on only a few aspects of recent Australian archaeology, but there are many others of interest. Returning boomerangs, for instance, are the most widely known Australian artifact but were made only in certain parts of eastern Australia. They were only one of many varieties of curved throwing sticks, many of which were not designed to return to the thrower. All kinds of boomerangs were used for hunting, but the returning ones were also for play. Fragments of boomerangs, probably of the returning form, have been found at Wyrie Swamp, in South Australia, dated to about 8000 BC, but this technology may be much older.

Contact with the outside world is another theme of interest. The native Australian dog, the dingo, has been on the continent for only about 4,000 years, and its closest relatives known so far are in India. The dingo is the only direct link yet

A boomerang stenciled onto a rock wall in the Carnarvon Ranges, Queensland. Returning boomerangs were used in this area, but the one shown here is a throwing stick that probably bounced end-over-end along the ground towards the prey.

shown between these two areas, but it surely did not migrate to Australia on its own. How did it get here, and what else came with it?

Fishhooks were made along the coast of New South Wales from about AD 800. Were these copied from New Guinean forms? If so, how did this come about, given that they are not found along much of the Queensland coast, which is closer to New Guinea? The best evidence of outside contact we have is that with Macassans, who collected trepang (sea slugs), pearl shell, and other valuables from the northern coast from about AD 1700, according to Macassan and Dutch records. Slim archaeological evidence in the form of shell copies of metal fishhooks suggests that outside contact extends back to at least AD 1000, but whether it occurred even earlier than this, in any form, is anyone's guess.

When Europeans arrived in Australia, they encountered societies as different from their own as any on Earth. Reconstructing the past through archaeology allows us to understand how these Aboriginal ways of life became uniquely suited to Australia's unique environment.

Dingoes belong to the same species as modern dogs and are found throughout Australia, except for Tasmania. Wild pups were often reared by Aboriginal people and kept as pets. They were occasionally used in hunting.

SALTWATER PEOPLE OF THE SOUTHWEST KIMBERLEY COAST

SUE O'CONNOR

THE PREHISTORY OF THE KIMBERLEY coast since 10,000 BC is as rich and diverse as the landscape in this far northwestern corner of Australia. The coastal region today supports vegetation ranging from lush rainforest thickets to open savanna. Dense mangroves fill the estuaries, whose tidal reaches stretch inland up to 70 kilometers (45 miles).

The people who traditionally lived in this area referred to themselves as "saltwater people", an apt description of their way of life. Along this part of the Australian coast, spring tides can be higher than 10 meters (33 feet), and fast currents and whirlpools are common. Despite this, the water-craft the southern Kimberley people used until early this century were simple double rafts made from two sections of lashed and pegged mangrove poles. While flimsy, these rafts did not easily overturn and sink in the precarious waters, and they could carry several people and their dingoes. They were not propeled, the people relying instead on their knowledge of the tides to travel between the offshore islands. Because of this, the Kimberley people are sometimes known as the "tide riders".

At the time of European contact, people were living permanently on some of the small islands offshore of the Kimberley coast. Most of these islands are too small to support land-dwelling vertebrates, and the inhabitants relied instead on the bountiful reefs for shellfish, fish, dugong, and turtle. They also collected the eggs of sea birds and a variety of fruits, seeds, and tubers. Such use of islands by coastal people in Australia seems to have been unique to the north.

Archaeologists have long wondered how far back this way of life goes. In many areas of Australia, shell middens date to between about 2000 BC and 1000 BC, whereas the sea reached its present level about 4000 BC. Because of this, some researchers have concluded that the Aborigines did not exploit marine resources intensively until well after the sea reached its present level.

Evidence from two Kimberley rock shelters, Widgingarri Shelter and Koolan Shelter, has made a unique contribution to this debate. These sites show that people were living in this region at least 28,000 years ago, when the sea was 20 to 50 kilometers (12 to 30 miles) distant. They then abandoned it during an arid phase that occurred between 25,000 and 13,000 years ago, when the sea had retreated to perhaps 200 kilometers (120 miles) from its present position and a vast coastal plain was exposed. As global climates warmed at the end

of the Ice Age, the sea level rose again, drowning this coastal plain.

At this time, Koolan Shelter sat high on a rocky mainland promontory, with a steeply sloping offshore contour. Rising seas therefore reached this site early, and radiocarbon dating of its upper shell midden layer shows that people returned here about 11,000 years ago. At Widgingarri Shelter, on the other hand, the offshore contour has a gentle declination, which means that the rising seas reached this shelter only shortly before the sea reached its present level, about 4000 BC. The earliest layers in the midden here date to about

5000 BC. The fact that the reoccupation of the shelters coincides with the rise in the sea level suggests that people had been pursuing a coastal economy in Pleistocene times, but any evidence is now drowned.

Sea and Land Resources

At both Koolan and Widgingarri, animal remains dating from the early Holocene period show that the people of the Kimberley drew on both sea and land resources for their diet, eating fish, dugong, turtle, shellfish, and a variety of land mammals, such as kangaroos, rock wallabies, and bandicoots. Outside the rock

☝ The Kimberley coast supports a range of vegetation, from high rainforest to open savanna. Spring tides can reach as high as 10 meters (33 feet), and estuarine tidal reaches stretch inland up to 70 kilometers (45 miles).

☝ The view from inside the Koolan Shelter, looking out towards the bay. People first lived in this shelter 28,000 years ago, and abandoned it when arid conditions set in between 25,000 and 13,000 years ago. They returned at the end of the Ice Age.

⚱ The Kimberley island people relied mainly on coastal resources for their food. Here, a man is butchering a turtle on High Cliffy Island.

⚱ Burning off spinifex on High Cliffy Island. Aboriginal people still carry out this traditional activity on offshore islands.

⚱ These women are using metal "wires", the modern equivalent of the traditional digging stick, to collect shellfish.

shelters, shell middens are rare in this region, probably because conditions do not favor their preservation.

Tools and Artifacts

A range of artifacts has been found in the rock shelter sites, including shell, bone, and stone tools. In the early midden levels, the stone tools are very similar to those found in the Pleistocene levels, the most common being simple retouched flakes. In the midden at Koolan Shelter, shell tools formed from large mud clam shells (*Geloina coaxans*) have been identified. The damage and residues evident on the edges of the tools indicate that they were used as handheld scrapers for working plant materials.

Between 3000 BC and 2000 BC, quite different types of artifacts are found. Points appear for the first time, the oldest dated to about 2500 BC. Most appear to have been mounted as tips at the end of wooden spears. Bone artifacts are also found, but only in the upper, more recent, layers of the middens. They may have been used as pressure-flaking tools to produce finely fluted stone points. Until recently, the people of this region used fire-hardened spears for fishing, and sometimes poisoned rock pools at low tide with certain plants. There is no evidence of the use of fish nets or fishhooks.

⚱ A stone house base on High Cliffy Island. The walls are up to a meter (more than 3 feet) high.

Coastal fishing here appears to have required only simple technology.

Early Use of Offshore Islands

The first evidence of the regular use of offshore islands in this region dates from about 4000 BC. Because the wet season is so severe, little surface evidence of prehistoric occupation is preserved on most of the islands, but there are several striking exceptions.

High Cliffy Island is one of these. Situated about 8 kilometers (15 miles) off the coast, it was cut off from the mainland by rising seas about 6000 BC. Many stone structures have been found here, some of which seem to have served ceremonial functions, while others were used as house bases. The walls of the house bases stand up to a meter (just over 3 feet) high and have a small entrance. According to the Aboriginal elders who use this region today, these structures were roofed with spinifex and paperbark, the latter brought by raft from the mainland. Although these stone structures have not yet been dated, evidence from a dated rock shelter on the island suggests that High Cliffy Island has been used most intensively since 1000 BC. It is possibly only from this time that people have occupied the island permanently, as they were observed to be doing at the time of early European contact.

adze

A heavy, wide-bladed cutting tool which is attached at right angles to a wooden handle. It was used for trimming and smoothing timber and for such tasks as hollowing out a dug-out canoe.

Anasazi

A culture found in southwestern North America in the late prehistoric era (about AD 200 to AD 1600). The Anasazi were agricultural people known for their pueblo-style architecture and finely painted ceramics. Although exact linkages are uncertain, it is clear that modern Pueblo Indian people are descended from Anasazi ancestors. The name Anasazi is derived from a Navajo word meaning "enemy ancestors".

anthropomorphic figure

A figure or object with a human shape or character.

Anthromorphic figure

Archaic adaptation

Throughout the Americas, archaeologists use the term Archaic to refer to post-Paleoindian people who subsist by hunting, gathering, and fishing. Initially, the term was used to designate a non-ceramic-using, nonagricultural, and nonsedentary way of life. Archaeologists now realize, however, that ceramics, agriculture, and sedentism are all found, in specific settings, within contexts that are clearly Archaic. In eastern North America, Archaic defines a specific period of time between the earlier Paleoindian cultures and the later Woodland cultures. Where such Woodland adaptations did not develop, Archaic refers to a more generalized, nonagricultural way of life, which in some places lasted for 10,000 years.

ard

A plow-like tool, drawn by animals, that scratched a groove in the ground but did not turn over the soil.

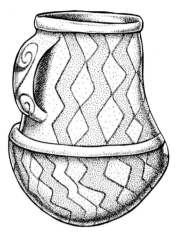

Anasazi pitcher

Atlantic period

In Europe, the climatic period immediately following the last Ice Age, beginning about 6000 BC, when the average temperature rose. Melting ice sheets ultimately submerged nearly half of western Europe, in the process creating the bays and inlets along the Atlantic coast that provided a new, rich ecosystem for human subsistence. The Atlantic period was followed by the subboreal period.

Austroasiatic language family

Austroasiatic is a major language family of northeastern India and the Southeast Asian mainland, comprising about 150 languages spoken by about 60 million people. It has two major groupings: the Munda laguages of northeastern peninsular India, and the Mon-Khmer languages of the Southeast Asian mainland. The Mon-Khmer languages include modern Vietnamese and Khmer (Cambodian), as well as many fairly isolated languages from southern China to as far south as Malaysia and the Nicobar Islands. The Austroasiatic language family appears to be the most ancient in its area, having been superseded in places by Indo-European, Tai, and Austronesian languages.

Austronesian language family

Austronesian is a major language family to which the languages of Taiwan, the islands of Southeast Asia, the Pacific (excluding much of New Guinea), Madagascar, and parts of the Southeast Asian mainland belong. Although all Austronesian languages are related, they are not necessarily mutually understandable.

backed blade

A small, blade-like flake, one side of which has been blunted by chipping, so that it can be fitted snugly into a haft or used while held in the hand without cutting the fingers.

barrow

A large mound built over a prehistoric burial place. Round barrows are known as tumulus; elongated mounds are known as long-barrows.

Battle-axe culture

A term applied to a number of Late Neolithic cultural groups in Europe that appeared between 2800 BC and 2300 BC. The Battle-axe culture is named after a characteristic type of polished stone axe.

Bell Beaker culture

A Late Neolithic culture from the third millennium BC in central and western Europe. The name is derived from the characteristic vessel form, which resembles a bell. The Bell Beaker culture belongs to the so-called Battle-axe cultures in Europe.

Beringia

The part of the continental shelf that connects Northeast Asia with present-day Alaska. When exposed at the time of the last glacial maximum, 18,000 years ago, it was a large, flat, vegetated landmass.

betel nut

The fruit of the betel palm, *Areca catechu*, which is chewed in New Guinea and in many parts of tropical Asia.

betyl

A sacred stone, often a standing stone, that has been fashioned into a conical shape.

bi disk

A flat jade disk with a small hole in the center, made in ancient China for ceremonial purposes. *Bi* disks were described in ancient Chinese texts as a symbol of rank, and were used as ritual objects in the Liangzhu culture of Neolithic China. They have been found in graves, arranged with *cong* tubes around the corpses of the elite. *Bi* disks are thought to have symbolized Heaven.

billabong

In Australia, a body of water, such as an anabranch or waterhole in a watercourse, that fills when flooded during the rainy season, and dries up in the dry season.

Bronze Age

A prehistoric period in the Old World, defined by the use of bronze as a new material for tools, weapons, and ornaments. In Europe, the Bronze Age proper spans the second and early first millennia BC.

buckler

A schematic motif that is found mainly in the megalithic tombs of Brittany, in France. It has been interpreted as a protective symbol.

Bubalus period

The earliest phase of rock art in northern Africa, represented by large-scale carvings of animals, which appeared between 12,000 BC and 8000 BC. The period is named after the now-extinct giant buffalo, *Bubalus antiquus*.

burin

A short, pointed blade tool with a chisel end, used to carve and engrave wood and bone (particularly antlers, which were made into spearheads and harpoon tips). The most common form has a sharp tip, formed by the intersection of two flake scars. The burin is associated with Upper Paleolithic cultures, especially the Magdalenian.

Chalcolithic period

Literally, the "Copper Stone Age". The Chalcolithic period is the transitional phase between Stone Age technology and the Bronze Age, when copper was used for tool-making and jewelry in cultures that otherwise were Neolithic in character.

chinampas

A system of cultivation on artificial islands built of vegetation and mud in shallow freshwater lakes. These remarkably fertile fields were created by massive Aztec reclamation projects in the Valley of Mexico.

coevolutionary perspective

A relatively recent theory in cultural evolution that contends that changes in social systems are best understood as resulting from mutual selection among components, rather than as a linear, cause-and-effect sequence. Accordingly, the multiple origins of agriculture can be best understood by exploring the evolutionary forces affecting the development of domestication systems. When viewed

Bronze Age helmet

in this way, domestication is not seen as an evolutionary stage, but as a process, and is the result of coevolutionary interactions between humans and plants.

cong tube
A tubular, jade object, square on the outside and circular on the inside, made in various sizes and used for ritual purposes in ancient China. *Cong* were described in ancient Chinese texts as symbols of rank and were used as ritual objects in the Liangzhu culture of Neolithic China. They have been found in graves, arranged with *bi* disks around the corpses of the elite. The *cong* is thought to have symbolized Earth.

corbeled roof
A simple form of roofing where successive courses of overlapping stones finally meet in the center and form a "false vault" when a capstone is placed at the top. The technique was used within the megalithic tradition in Europe.

Corded Beaker culture
A Late Neolithic culture in central Europe from the third millennium BC, named after a characteristic cord-marked decoration found on pottery. The Corded Beaker culture belongs to the so-called Battle-axe cultures in Europe.

cruciform chamber
A megalithic tomb, characteristic of the passage-tomb tradition in Ireland, in which a passage, a chamber, and three apses together form a cross-shaped structure.

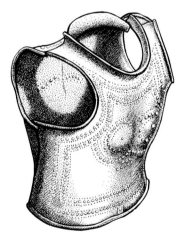

Cuirass

cuirass
A piece of armor to protect the torso, both front and back, and often molded to the contours of the body. Although the cuirasses that survive from the Bronze Age are of sheet bronze, this material can be easily pierced by an arrow or sword, and it is likely that the functional armor of the day was made of leather.

diaspora
The dispersion of people, either forced or voluntary, from a central area of origin to many distant regions.

dogu
A type of clay figurine, most often depicting a female, made in Japan during the Jomon period. The function of these figurines is unknown, but it is generally believed that they were some kind of fertility symbol.

dolmen
The French term for a megalithic tomb with a single capstone carried by orthostats, or standing stones.

Dyukhtai tradition
A Siberian cultural group of the Upper Paleolithic period. It existed along the Lena and Aldan rivers, between about 18,000 and 12,000 years ago. The people who first migrated into North America were probably from this cultural group.

einkorn
A variety of wheat with pale red kernels, *Triticum monococcum*, which was cultivated in Neolithic times. It probably originated in southeastern Europe and southwestern Asia, and is still grown in mountainous parts of southern Europe as grain for horses.

emmer wheat
A variety of wheat, *Triticum dicoccum*, which has been cultivated in the Mediterranean region since Neolithic times, and is still grown in mountainous parts of southern Europe as a cereal crop and livestock food. It is thought to be the ancestor of many other varieties of wheat.

faience
Bronze Age faience is a primitive form of glass. It is made by baking a mixture of sand and clay to a temperature at which the surface fuses into blue or green glass. Faience beads of Aegean and southwestern Asian origin were traded widely in eastern and central Europe, Italy, and the British Isles in the second millennium BC.

gorget
A piece of armor designed to protect the throat.

greave
A piece of armor designed to protect the lower part of the leg.

grinding stone
A stone used to grind to powder foodstuffs (such as grains), medicines, and pigments for decorating rock walls and bodies.

hand stencil
The impression of a hand produced by spraying thick paint (made from white clay or red or yellow ocher) through a blowpipe around the edges of a hand placed against a rock surface.

henge monument
A circular, prehistoric religious site constructed of wood or stones and enclosed by ditches and walls. Henge monuments are characteristic of the megalithic period in southern England in particular.

Lunula

Hohokam
A prehistoric cultural tradition of southwestern North America, dating from about AD 0 to AD 1450, generally correlated with the Sonoran Desert biotic province and centered on the well-watered river valleys of central and southern Arizona. Many Hohokam sites are characterized by extensive networks of irrigation canals.

hypogeum
A chamber tomb cut into rock.

iconography
The art of representing or illustrating by means of pictures, images, or figures.

intaglio
Incised carving (as opposed to relief carving), in which the design is sunk below the surface of hard stone or metal.

Iron Age
A late prehistoric period in the Old World, defined by the use of iron as the main material for tools and weapons.

kerbstone circle
A circle of stones bordering a burial mound.

kiva
A large underground or partly underground circular or rectangular room in a Peublo Indian village where religious and other ceremonies are conducted.

Lapita
A distinctive type of pottery with finely made bands of decoration in geometric patterns that appeared throughout much of the western Pacific about 3,000 years ago. In some sites, Lapita pottery is associated with elaborate shell tools and ornaments, the use of obsidian, and long-distance trade, so that it appears to represent a culture, although this is not yet clear.

loess
A loamy deposit consisting of fine particles of windblown soil, laid down during the Ice Age. Loess forms a fertile and easily worked soil.

long-barrow
An elongated mound covering a burial chamber, typical of the Early and Mid-Neolithic periods in Europe. In southern

England, the burial chamber consists of a megalithic tomb.

longhouse
An elongated wooden post house that appeared in central Europe with the first farming communities within the Early Neolithic Bandkeramik cultures, about 4500 BC.

lunula
A crescent-shaped neck ornament of sheet gold, characteristic of the Early Bronze Age in Europe.

macrofossils
Large-scale floral or faunal remains recovered from an archaeological excavation (as opposed to microfossils, which cannot be seen without magnification).

maguey
The fleshy-leafed agave plant of tropical America. American Indians ate both the flowerhead, which they harvested after it had bloomed, and the heart of the maguey, which they prepared by digging up the entire plant and roasting it in earth ovens for 24 to 72 hours.

mano
The Spanish term commonly used by American archaeologists for the smoothed, hand-held stone used to grind seeds, pigments, or other relatively soft material against the concave surface of a larger, usually immobile lower grindstone or metate. It is also known as the upper grindstone.

manioc
Also called cassava, manioc (*Manihot esculenta*) is a starchy root crop that can be processed into an important food. It was the staple diet throughout most of Amazonia and the Caribbean at the time of European contact. Manioc is the source of tapioca.

Megalithic tomb

megalithic tomb
A chambered tomb built of large stones. Its name comes from the Greek words *megas* (large) and *lithos* (stone).

menhir
A standing stone, most often referred to in a megalithic context.

Mesolithic
Literally, the "Middle Stone Age".
A transitional period between the
Paleolithic and the Neolithic, marked
by the retreat of the Pleistocene glaciers
and the appearance of modern forms
of plants and animals. Its peoples were
hunter-gatherers whose flint industries
were characterized by microliths. The
term Mesolithic is limited to Europe.

mesquite pod
The edible, bean-like seed vessel harvested from the mesquite tree (genus
Prosopis) of arid Central America. Native
Americans cooked the sugary pods into
a syrup; the seeds could also be roasted
and eaten.

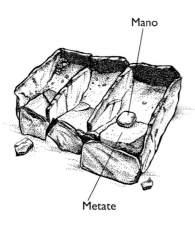
Mano

Metate

metate
The Spanish term commonly used by
American archaeologists for a smoothed,
usually immobile, stone with a concave
upper surface on which seeds, pigments,
or other relatively soft material can be
ground with the aid of a hand-held
upper grindstone, or mano. The metate
is also known as a lower grindstone,
or concave quern.

microlith
A very small arrowhead, barb, or other
implement, most commonly of flint,
made by removing a triangular, trape-
zoidal, or parallelogram-shaped section
from a microblade. Microliths were
mounted in wooden or bone shafts
as arrow tips, or along one or both sides
of a shaft to form a barbed spear or harpoon, or set in rows on sickles. Microliths
were characteristic of the Mesolithic
period in the Old World.

midden
An extensive deposit of settlement refuse,
which may include the remains of shells,
bones, ashes, and discarded implements.
Middens are commonly built up over
many years and mark the site of previous
human habitation.

mitochondrial DNA
A particular kind of DNA that is inherited
only through the mother, enabling the
tracing of accurate genetic links.

mobile
The settlement pattern of social groups
who move from place to place within a
given territory, building camps at each site.

Mogollon
A prehistoric culture of southwestern
North America. Unlike the Anasazi
culture, the Mogollon culture did not
survive as a recognizable group of
modern Native Americans. Remnants
of the Mogollon may have merged with
Anasazi peoples to become what is
known as the Western Pueblo people.

Near Oceania
Those islands of the Pacific that can be
reached by water-craft without going out
of sight of land. Basically, Near Oceania
comprises the Indonesian archipelago,
the Philippines, New Guinea, and the
Solomon Islands.

Neolithic
Literally, the "New Stone Age". The term
refers to the final phase of the Stone Age,
when farming became an essential part
of the economy.

nomadic
A term used by ethnographers to describe
the movement of whole social groups of
cattle breeders who utilize different parts
of a given territory in different seasons,
usually summer and winter pastures,
and build camps for those periods.

obsidian
A black, glassy volcanic rock often used
to make sharp-edged tools.

orthostat
A standing stone in a megalithic tomb,
supporting one or more capstones.

ossuary
A house containing depositions of
multiple human skeletons.

paleobotany
The study of ancient plants from fossil
remains and other evidence, such as vegetable materials, preserved by charring,
desiccation, or in waterlogged deposits.
Paleobotany provides information about
the climate and environment and about
materials available for food, fuel, tools,
and shelter.

Paleoindians
The big-game hunters of the Americas
from the earliest known, about 10,000 BC,
to about 6000 BC. Some investigators
regard the term as referring to all hunting
groups involved with now-extinct mammals, in which case the peoples who
hunted the species of bison that became
extinct about 4500 BC would also be
classified as Paleoindians.

Paleolithic
Literally, the "Old Stone Age". It began
some two million to three million years
ago with the emergence of humans and

the earliest forms of chipped stone tools,
and continued through the Pleistocene Ice
Age until the retreat of the glaciers some
12,000 years ago. The Paleolithic is equivalent to the Stone Age in sub-Saharan Africa.

passage tombs
A megalithic tomb in which access to the
chamber is obtained through a passage.

Pastoral Neolithic
A complex of cultures that appeared in
southern Kenya and northern Tanzania
about 3500 BC. The term pastoral refers
to abundant evidence that the people
herded domestic animals. It remains
unknown whether they also cultivated
plants. About 1,300 years ago, they were
absorbed or replaced by iron-using
pastoralists and mixed farmers.

phytolith
The tiny silica particles contained in
plants. Sometimes, these fragments can
be recovered from archaeological sites,
even after the plants themselves have
disappeared.

playa
The sandy, salty, or mud-caked floor
of a desert basin with interior drainage,
usually occupied by a shallow lake during
the rainy season or after prolonged, heavy
rains. The word also refers to the lake itself.

Pleistocene
The first epoch of the geological period
known as the Quaternary, preceding
the Holocene (or present) epoch and
beginning some two million years ago.
It was marked by the advance of ice
sheets across northern Europe and North
America. During this epoch, giant mammals existed, and in the Late Pleistocene,
modern humans appeared.

primary burial
The initial burial of a dead person.

pueblo
A Spanish term meaning town or village,
and applied by sixteenth-century explorers
to the village dwellings of the American
Southwest. When capitalized, Pueblo
generally refers to a specific Native
American group, culture, or site.

Stamp seal

Remote Oceania
The small islands of the Pacific that can
only be reached by sailing out of sight
of land. Remote Oceania includes all
the islands east of a line stretching from
the Philippines to the Solomons.

scraper
A core, flake, or blade with a steeply
retouched edge either at the side (side-
scraper) or end (endscraper). Scrapers
were used to dress hides and to shape
wood, bone, and ivory artifacts.

secondary burial
The practice of removing the remains
of a dead person from the site of the
initial burial to a grave or ossuary.

sedentism
A way of life in which people remain
settled in one place throughout the year.

shaman
A person believed to have supernatural
powers. In times of sickness, shortage
of game, or any other threat to a community's survival, the shaman is called upon to
mediate with the spirit world on the community's behalf. The shaman presides over
rituals, and may also be responsible for the
keeping of laws and the continuity of traditions. Shamanism is the dominant element
in the religion of most known arctic and
subarctic hunter-gatherers. Most shamans
are male.

Sherd

sherd
A small piece of broken pottery.

slash-and-burn agriculture
A method of agriculture in which
vegetation is felled, left to dry out, and
then burned. Seeds are later planted in
holes poked into the ashes.

stamp seal
A small, hard block that has a flat surface
engraved with a design that can be
transferred to soft clay or wax as a mark
of ownership or authenticity. Stamp seals
appear in Mesopotamia from the Halafian
period, in the fifth millennium BC, when
they were used to impress ownership
marks on lumps of clay; these were then
attached to goods.

steatite
A soft, gray stone, also known as soapstone. It was used particularly to make
stamp seals.

stele
An upright slab or column of stone,
often decorated with carvings or
bearing inscriptions.

subboreal period
A climatic period that occurred between about 3000 BC and AD 0. In northern Europe, it was characterized by a cooler and moister climate than that of the preceding Atlantic period.

taxonomy
The study of the general principles that regulate scientific classification. Biological taxonomists attempt to devise an orderly classification of plants and animals according to their presumed natural relationships.

tell mound
A mound formed by the repeated rebuilding of mudbrick houses on the same site. As older houses collapsed, their remains formed a raised base for later houses. Such mounds also incorporate other settlement refuse, graves, and many other materials, and sometimes reach considerable depth.

tournette
A turntable that was rotated manually to assist in the manufacture of a pot. It was a forerunner of the potter's wheel. In Mesopotamia, from about 5000 BC, some pots formed by hand were finished on tournettes. The fast-spinning potter's wheel was in use by about 3400 BC.

Urnfield period
A group of related Late Bronze Age cultures in Europe, characterized by the practice of placing the cremated remains of a dead person in a pottery funerary urn, which was then buried in a cemetery of urns. The practice dates from about 1300 BC, when urnfield graves became increasingly common in eastern central Europe; from there, this burial rite spread west, to Italy and Spain, north, across the Rhine to Germany, and east, to the steppes of Russia. Other features of the Urnfield period include copper-mining and sheet bronze metalworking. The Urnfield period continued until the start of the Iron Age, about 750 BC, when inhumation once again became the dominant form of burial in many areas.

umiak
A large, open boat used by Arctic peoples, made of skins stretched on a wooden frame.

wadi
An Arabic term denoting a channel of a watercourse that is dry except during periods of rainfall.

wet-rice technology
A type of farming in which rice is grown in specially prepared flooded fields known as paddies. Although rice can also be grown under dry conditions, wet-rice cultivation in paddy fields is much more productive, and has a considerable antiquity in Asia. The paddy fields are surrounded by low embankments, or evees, and must be continually leveled to maintain a constant depth of water, usually about 10 centimeters (4 inches). The fields can be flooded naturally or by irrigation channels, and are kept inundated during the growing season. About a

Yue axe

month before harvesting, the water is removed and the field left to dry.

yue axe
A broad-bladed axe used as a weapon in ancient China. Jade yue axes have been found in graves from the Liangzhu culture of Late Neolithic China.

Umiak

Emmanuel Anati

Emmanuel Anati is Professor of Paleoethnology at the University of Lecce, Italy, and Executive Director of the Centro Camuno di Studi Preistorici in Capo di Ponte, Italy. His principal areas of interest are the art and religion of prehistoric and tribal cultures, and he has conducted research in western Europe, southwestern Asia, India, Tanzania, Malawi, Mexico, and Australia. He founded the Centro Camuno di Studi Preistorici, and was founder and first Chairman of the International Committee on Rock Art. Since 1992 he has been Chairman of the Paris-based Institut des Arts Préhistoriques et Ethnologiques. He has edited several prestigious publications and is the author of more than 70 books and articles.

C. Andreasen

C. Andreasen is Associate Professor in the Department of Culture and Community Studies at the University of Greenland. His main areas of interest are the Paleoeskimo cultures and the Norse culture in Greenland, particularly the settlement patterns and cultural changes that resulted from trade and changing climatic conditions. His current project investigates humans and climate in northeastern Greenland over a period of 4,000 years.

Gina Barnes

Gina Barnes is Senior Researcher in the Department of Archaeology at the University of Cambridge, UK. Her main areas of interest are the formation of states and the rise of civilization in East Asia, and trade and political ties between early Korea and Japan. She is currently researching the early Korean stoneware and iron armor industries, and the application of Geographical Information Systems to settlement data from excavations at the Miwa site, at Nara, in Japan. Her publications include *Protohistoric Yamato* and *China, Korea and Japan: The Rise of Civilization in East Asia*, and she has translated several Japanese works into English.

Peter Bellwood

Peter Bellwood is Reader in Archaeology at the Australian National University, Canberra, Australia. He has a special interest in the prehistory and archaeology of India, China, Southeast Asia, and the Pacific islands, and has undertaken surveys and excavations throughout these areas, most recently at Halmahera, in the northern Moluccas, eastern Indonesia. He is currently researching the origins of the peoples of Indonesia and the Pacific islands, and the early expansions of agricultural populations and their languages. He is the Secretary-General of the Indo-Pacific Prehistory Association, and is the author of five books on the archaeology of the Pacific basin.

Anthony Bonanno

Anthony Bonanno is Professor of Archaeology at the University of Malta. He is a specialist in the archaeology of the Maltese islands, and is one of the five joint directors of the Gozo field project conducted by the National Museum of Archaeology in Malta and the universities of Bristol, Cambridge, and Malta.

Richard Bradley

Richard Bradley is Professor of Archaeology at Reading University, UK. His main areas of interest are European prehistory, landscape archaeology, social archaeology, and archaeological theory. He is the author of *The Passage of Arms* and joint author of *Landscape, Monuments and Society*.

Noel D. Broadbent

Noel D. Broadbent is Director of the Arctic Social Science Program in the Office of Polar Programs at the National Science Foundation, USA. From 1983 to 1988 he was Director of the Center for Arctic Cultural Research, and before that lectured in archaeology at the universities of Stockholm, Uppsala, and Umeå, in Sweden. He is the author and editor of five books, and has published numerous articles on various aspects of cultural history in northern regions.

Göran Burenhult

Göran Burenhult has been Associate Professor of Archaeology at the University of Stockholm, Sweden, since 1981 and is acknowledged internationally as a leading expert on prehistoric rock art and megalithic traditions. Between 1976 and 1981 he was director of the Swedish archaeological excavations at Carrowmore, County Sligo, Ireland, excavating one of the earliest known megalithic cemeteries, and he has undertaken field work on prehistoric rock art throughout the world, including the rock painting areas of the central Sahara Desert. Most recently he has conducted ethnoarchaeological expeditions to the islands of Sulawesi and Sumba, in Indonesia, to the Trobriand Islands of Papua New Guinea, and to the island of Malekula, in Vanuatu, to study megalithic traditions, social organization, and primitive exchange. He is the author of numerous scholarly and popular books on archaeology and ethnoarchaeology, and has contributed to journals, magazines, and encyclopedic works. Between 1987 and 1991 he produced a series of international television programs about aspects of archaeology.

Angela E. Close

Angela E. Close is Adjunct Associate Professor and Research Associate in the Department of Anthropology at the Southern Methodist University, USA. Her field work includes membership of the Combined Prehistoric Expedition, working mainly in Egypt on the Middle and Late Paleolithic and Neolithic periods. There, her main focus was the study of stone artifacts in terms of how they reflect social groupings, and of how their transport indicates the day-to-day movement of small groups of people. She is editor of the *Journal of World Prehistory*.

Kate da Costa

Kate da Costa is a postgraduate student in the School of Archaeology, Classics and Ancient History at the University of Sydney, Australia, where for two years she tutored in Near Eastern

Archaeology. She has worked on a number of excavations in Jordan, especially at Pella, in the Jordan Valley, where, among other remains, there is an important Natufian site. She is currently researching the day-to-day economics of local marketing systems in Byzantine Palestine. She also has a keen interest in computer applications in archaeology, a legacy of her first career as a computer programmer.

Iain Davidson

Iain Davidson is Associate Professor in the Department of Archaeology and Paleoanthropology at the University of New England, Armidale, Australia. He is currently working in the area of language origins, with William Noble, and on the archaeology of northwest Queensland. He has undertaken research in Australia into the colonization of the arid zone, and into trade, rock paintings, and engravings. He has also worked on the fauna and economy of Upper Paleolithic sites in Spain.

Marija Gimbutas

Marija Gimbutas is Professor Emerita of European Archaeology at the University of California, USA. For more than two decades, she excavated Neolithic sites in southeastern Europe (Bosnia, Macedonia, Greece, and Italy). She is well known for research on proto-Indo-European culture and its infiltration into Europe, and on the goddess culture and religion of Neolithic Europe. She has written more than 20 books, including *The Goddesses and Gods of Old Europe, 7000–3500 B.C.*, *The Language of the Goddess: Images and Symbols of Old Europe*, and *The Civilization of the Goddess: The World of Old Europe*.

Paul Gorecki

Paul Gorecki is Senior Lecturer in the Department of Anthropology and Archaeology at the James Cook University of North Queensland, Australia. His research interests lie in the initial colonization of Australia and Melanesia, Pleistocene developments in northern Queensland, the origins of horticulture in the island of New Guinea, the processes involved in the formation of archaeological sites, and hunter-gatherer behavior in tropical rainforest environments. He has conducted archaeological research in Australia, Papua New Guinea, the Solomon Islands, and New Caledonia. While in remote parts of these regions, he undertook ethnoarchaeological research, in particular into the contemporary use of rock shelters and caves by hunting parties.

Tancred Gouder

Tancred Gouder is Director of Museums for the Republic of Malta. He is a specialist in Phoenician archaeology and the archaeology of the Maltese islands, and for many years held the position of Curator of Archaeology for the Maltese islands, with responsibility for all archaeological research and excavation there. He is one of the five joint directors of the Gozo field project conducted by the National Museum of Archaeology in Malta and the universities of Bristol, Cambridge, and Malta.

Roger C. Green

Roger C. Green is Emeritus Professor (Personal Chair) in Prehistory in the Department of Anthropology at the University of Auckland, New Zealand, where he was Professor from 1973 to 1992. His main research interest is the cultural history (archaeology, paleobiology, and historical linguistics) of Oceania and, in particular, the Lapita cultural complex. He has published numerous articles on Oceanic prehistory and historical linguistics.

J.P. Hart Hansen

J.P. Hart Hansen is Director of the Department of Pathology and Associate Professor, Gentofte Hospital, at the University of Copenhagen, Denmark. He has worked in pathological anatomy, forensic pathology, arctic medicine, and paleopathology. He organized the multidisciplinary research program on the 500-year-old Inuit mummies from Qilakitsoq, in Greenland. He is Chairman of the Commission for Scientific Research in Greenland, President of the International Union for Circumpolar Health, and Past Chairman of the Nordic Council for Arctic Medical Research.

Anthony Harding

Anthony Harding is Professor of Archaeology at the University of Durham, UK. Since 1975 he has conducted excavation and field work in England on rock shelter sites, Neolithic ritual monuments, and prehistoric and medieval field systems; in Poland on Early Iron Age fortified settlement; and in Bohemia on Middle Bronze Age ritual settlement. He is currently working on Bronze Age settlement in northern England, and Bronze Age fortification in central Europe. He is author of *The Myceneans and Europe* and co-author of *The Bronze Age in Europe*.

Mark J. Hudson

Mark J. Hudson is a postgraduate student in the Department of Archaeology and Anthropology at the Australian National University, Canberra, Australia. His area of specialization is Japanese archaeology, particularly the Yayoi period. From 1991 to 1992 he was Visiting Research Associate of the Tokyo University Museum. He has published several articles on Japanese archaeology.

Tsui-mei Huang

Tsui-mei Huang is Associate Professor in the Graduate School of Fine Arts at the National Institute of the Arts, Taiwan. Her area of research is ancient Chinese art and, in particular, the political and social role and significance of jade in the Late Neolithic cultures of ancient China. She is also interested in Japanese painting of the seventeenth and eighteenth centuries.

Richard G. Klein

Richard G. Klein is Professor of Anthropology at the University of Chicago, USA, where he lectures on Paleolithic archaeology. His research interests are the ecology of early people and the evolution of human behavior, with particular reference to how this can be inferred from animal bones abandoned at archaeological sites. While most of his field work has been conducted in South Africa, he has also worked in Spain and eastern Europe.

Chao-mei Lien

Chao-mei Lien is Professor in the Department of Anthropology at the National Taiwan University, Taiwan. For more than 20 years she has conducted archaeological excavations and research in Taiwan, in particular at the important Neolithic site of Peinan. She is joint author of six volumes of site reports and oversaw the establishment of the National Museum of Prehistory located near the Peinan site.

Ronnie Liljegren

Ronnie Liljegren is Head of the Laboratory of Faunal History at Lund University, Sweden, and since 1986 has led the Swedish Late Quaternary vertebrate faunal history project. Before that he spent ten years studying the paleoecological effects of water level changes in the Baltic Sea.

Andreas Lippert

Andreas Lippert is Professor in the Department of Prehistoric Archaeology at Vienna University, Austria. He has excavated Neolithic, Bronze Age, and Iron Age settlements and cemeteries in Austria and Iran, and is particularly interested in the prehistoric archaeology of the European Alps. He is currently researching ancient routes over the Alps and Bronze Age and Iron Age copper-mining sites in the Pongau region of the eastern Alps. He was recently involved in post-excavation work at the "Similaun Man" site at Schnals, in South Tyrol.

Mats P. Malmer

Mats P. Malmer is Emeritus Professor of Prehistoric Archaeology at the University of Stockholm, Sweden. His area of specialization is the Stone Age and Bronze Age of Europe, and his current research interests include the Neolithic pile dwellings of Europe and rock art of the world. He has excavated archaeological sites of all periods from the Mesolithic to the Middle Ages, and is the author of a number of books and articles. He is a past president of the Swedish Archaeological Society.

Caroline Malone

Caroline Malone is Lecturer in Archaeology at the University of Bristol, UK. She is joint director of a project investigating the city and territory of Nepi, just to the north of Rome, and was joint director of the Gubbio project, a study of the long-term sociopolitical developments of an upland valley in the central Italian Apennines. She is one of the five joint directors of the Gozo field project conducted by the National Museum of Archaeology in Malta and the universities of Bristol, Cambridge, and Malta.

Moreau Maxwell

Moreau Maxwell is Emeritus Professor of Anthropology at the Michigan State University, USA. His area of specialization is Arctic archaeology. He has undertaken field work on several prehistoric and historic sites in the midwest of North America and for more than 30 years has conducted Arctic archaeological research on Ellesmere and Baffin islands. His books include *Eastern Arctic Prehistory*.

Sue O'Connor

Sue O'Connor is Lecturer in Prehistoric Archaeology in the Department of Archaeology at the University of Western Australia. Her current research interests include the Pleistocene prehistory of northern Australia, the prehistory of the semiarid zone of western Australia, and the nature of offshore island use in Australia. She has undertaken field work in many parts of Australia, including Tasmania, and has worked as a cultural resource manager for the National Parks and Wildlife Service of New South Wales.

Lennart Palmqvist

Lennart Palmqvist has been Head of the Department of Classical Archaeology and Ancient History at the University of Stockholm, Sweden, since 1988, and has lectured there in archaeology since 1976. His area of specialization is the archaeological landscape of Roman Italy, especially such features as Roman roads. He has conducted field work in Italy, Greece, and Turkey and is a Fellow of the Swedish Institute of Rome.

Gary O. Rollefson

Gary O. Rollefson is Research Associate at the Peabody Museum, Harvard University, USA. His area of specialization is the prehistoric archaeology of southwestern Asia, particularly prehistoric religion, lithics analysis, and arid lands adaptations. He is Principal Investigator and Co-director of the 'Ain Ghazal Archaeological Project, in Jordan. His teaching positions have included Yarmouk University, in Jordan, and San Diego University, in the USA, and he currently teaches at the University of Heidelberg, in Germany.

Peter Rowley-Conwy

Peter Rowley-Conwy is Lecturer in the Department of Archaeology at the University of Durham, UK. He obtained his PhD with research on the Late Mesolithic and Early Neolithic history of Denmark, and has subsequently researched the European Paleolithic, Mesolithic, and Neolithic periods and the origins of agriculture in Southwest Asia. He has also worked on the economic archaeology of the Nile Valley in the Late and post-Pharaonic periods.

Wulf Schiefenhövel

Wulf Schiefenhövel is Research Associate at the Unit for Human Ethology at the Max Planck Society, Andechs, Germany, and Professor of Medical Psychology and Ethnomedicine at the University of Munich. He has conducted field work in Papua New Guinea, Irian Jaya, Bali, East Java, and the Trobriand Islands. His main areas of interest are the evolutionary biology of human behavior, ethnomedicine, and anthropology, especially reproductive strategies, birth behavior, early socialization, nonverbal communication, aggression and aggression control, and cultural diversity and the evolution of culture. He serves on the boards of many publications.

Romuald Schild

Romuald Schild is Director of the Institute of Archaeology and Ethnology at the Polish Academy of Sciences in Warsaw, Poland, and Associate Director of the Combined Prehistoric Expedition, with which he is currently conducting research in North Africa. He has a particular interest in prehistoric flint mining and lithic technology. His work on the geoarchaeology of the ancient Nile is the basis of modern archaeological, geomorphological, and stratigraphical studies of the Pleistocene Nile and eastern Sahara.

Simon Stoddart

Simon Stoddart is Lecturer in Archaeology at the University of Bristol, UK. He is joint director of a project investigating the city and territory of Nepi, just to the north of Rome, and was joint director of the Gubbio project, a study of the long-term sociopolitical developments of an upland valley in the central Italian Apennines. He is one of the five joint directors of the Gozo field project conducted by the National Museum of Archaeology in Malta and the universities of Bristol, Cambridge, and Malta.

Paul Tacon

Paul Tacon is Scientific Officer in the Division of Anthropology at the Australian Museum, Sydney, Australia. His special area of interest is Aboriginal material culture and Aboriginal art forms. He has conducted archaeological and field research in northern Australia at Kakadu National Park, Arnhem Land, and Cape York Peninsula, in central and eastern Australia, and in Canada, the USA, and the UK. Much of his work has focused on rock art and contemporary indigenous art forms.

David Hurst Thomas

David Hurst Thomas is Curator of Anthropology at the American Museum of Natural History, New York, USA. He is a specialist in the archaeology of the American Indian. He discovered and excavated the Gatecliff Shelter, in Nevada, the deepest rock shelter known in the Americas, with tightly stratified deposits spanning the past 8,000 years. He is the author or editor of many distinguished publications, has written more than 60 monographs and scientific articles, is on the editorial board of several journals, and is a founding trustee of the National Museum of the American Indian. In 1989, in recognition of his services to American archaeology, he was elected to the National Academy of Science.

Robin Torrence

Robin Torrence is an Australian Research Council Fellow at the Australian Museum, Sydney, Australia. Her research interests are lithic studies and prehistoric exchange. She has conducted field work in North America, England, Greece (including a detailed study of quarries on the island of Melos, when working on prehistoric obsidian exchange in the Aegean region), and, most recently, on the island of West New Britain, in Papua New Guinea. She is currently investigating obsidian trade in the Pacific region, particularly in Papua New Guinea.

David Trump

David Trump is Staff Tutor in Archaeology at Madingly Hall at the University of Cambridge, UK. He has undertaken research at the British School in Rome and the British School in Jerusalem, and his specialist interest in the prehistory of the central Mediterranean is reflected in his major field projects at La Starza (southern Italy), Skorba (Malta), and Bonu Ighinu (Sardinia). He is one of the five joint directors of the Gozo field project conducted by the National Museum of Archaeology in Malta and the universities of Bristol, Cambridge, and Malta.

Fred Wendorf

Fred Wendorf is Professor of Prehistory at the Southern Methodist University, Texas. He is leader of the Combined Prehistoric Expedition, which is investigating the prehistory of northeastern Africa, the Nile Valley, the Sahara Desert, and central Ethiopia, and has carried out a long-term study of regional archaeology in the Sahara Desert. He was part of the international effort to save the archaeology of Nubia, threatened by the construction of the New High Dam at Aswan. He is a past president of the Society for American Archaeology, a member of the United States National Academy of Sciences, and co-editor of the *Journal of World Prehistory*.

J. Peter White

J. Peter White is Reader in Prehistoric Archaeology in the School of Archaeology, Classics and Ancient History at the University of Sydney, Australia. He has a special interest in the prehistory of Australia and the Pacific, especially Melanesia. He began research work in New Guinea in 1963, excavating for prehistory and studying the technology of Highlanders who grew up in the Stone Age. More recently, he has worked in New Ireland and undertaken taphonomic studies in the Flinders Ranges, Australia. He is co-author, with Professor J. O'Connell, of *A Prehistory of Australia, New Guinea and Sahul*, and has edited the journal *Archeology in Oceania* since 1981.

◄▶ Liangzhu jade ornament from a tomb at Yaoshan, in the Yangtze River basin, in China.
WENWU PUBLISHING